THE NEW RETIREMENT

THE NEW RETIREMENT

The Ultimate Guide to
THE REST OF YOUR LIFE

JAN CULLINANE AND CATHY FITZGERALD

Printed in the United States of America
Rodale Inc. makes every effort to use acid-free ∞,
recycled paper ♺.

Book design by Tara Long

Library of Congress Cataloging-in-Publication Data
Cullinane, Jan.
The new retirement: the ultimate guide to the rest of your life / Jan Cullinane and Cathy Fitzgerald.
p. cm.
Includes bibliographical references and index.
ISBN-13 978–1–57954–479–7 paperback
ISBN-10 1–57954–479–9 paperback
1. Retirement—United States—Planning. I. Fitzgerald, Cathy.
II. Title.
HQ1063.2.U6C85 2004
646.7`9—dc22   2004005600

Distributed to the trade by Holtzbrinck Publishers

2 4 6 8 10 9 7 5 3 1 paperback

We inspire and enable people to improve their lives and the world around them
For more of our products visit **rodalestore.com** or call 800-848-4735

CONTENTS

PART III: HOW DO YOU ENJOY YOUR RETIREMENT FOR YEARS TO COME?

PREFACE TO THE SECOND EDITION

When the first edition of *The New Retirement* reached the number two ranking on both Amazon.com and BarnesandNoble.com in 2005 (right behind *Harry Potter*!), we knew we had a book that was beneficial to the almost 80 million boomers approaching or beginning retirement. Our holistic approach to this transition—including the psychological, financial, geographical, and biological aspects of retirement—is one that makes *The New Retirement* unique.

We realized we would need a second edition—one with not only updated material, but a new edition that included the latest research, emerging locations and communities, up-to-date financial info, and new anecdotes from people who are "walking the walk." We also wanted our worksheets, questionnaires, quizzes, niche retirement lifestyles, suggestions for second careers, and references including the best books, magazines, Web

sites, and specific contact information to be the latest and greatest out there.

With the second edition of *The New Retirement*, we've added a hot new country to consider for relocation outside of the United States (Panama), new states to think about for relocation, and more than fifty new specific communities/areas/lifestyles. Of course, all the information having to do with money matters, health, the emotional issues of retirement, work-related issues, relocation, and references has been revised and reworked to ensure the most up-to-date and comprehensive guide possible.

The new edition was created, in part, because of the rapid, ever-changing landscape shaped by the boomers. And we have to be honest—doing all this research, visiting all these places, reading all the latest research, and listening to literally hundreds of retirees and prospective retirees (and in some cases having them write anecdotes for us) is just plain fun! Again, as in the first book, we did receive help from CPAs, certified financial planners, and other experts in the areas of finances to flesh out our chapters on "How Do You Make Your Money Last as Long as You Do?" and "What Are the Tax Issues Affecting Retirement?"

We think you'll agree that the title of book is still aptly named: *The New Retirement: The Ultimate Guide to the Rest of Your Life.*

ACKNOWLEDGMENTS

We are grateful for the help and assistance we received writing this second edition. Thanks to our spouses, Roger and Dennis; our editors, Nancy Hancock and Mariska van Aalst; our publicist, Meghan Phillips; and our agent, Rosalie Siegel.

And to the CPAs, certified financial planners, and other experts who generously shared their technical knowledge, we are indebted. Finally, we'd like to express our appreciation to those who have retired or are planning to retire for sharing their stories, concerns, and experiences with us.

INTRODUCTION

The average American spends more than 90,000 hours working toward retirement but fewer than 10 hours actually planning for it. *The New Retirement: The Ultimate Guide to the Rest of Your Life* provides a one-stop resource for the almost 80 million baby boomers approaching this important transition. While most retirement books deal only with the financial issues or the location aspect of retirement, *The New Retirement* offers a comprehensive, balanced view of the subject for people who are planning to relocate or those who plan to age in place. This book is easy-to-read, concrete, practical, full of illustrative anecdotes, and hands-on. The end of the book provides additional references.

The New Retirement serves as a guide for individuals such as:

✳ Jayne K.—53 years old, CPA, single. She retired as chief financial officer of a biotech company in Gaithersburg, Maryland, as a multimillionaire after exercising her stock options. She's financially savvy, and she'd like to live in a city that's both amenable to singles and has a warmer climate, yet with four distinct seasons.

✳ Carl and Betty A.—late 50s. Carl retired from an assembly plant at Ford Motor Company, and he and Betty want to sell their home, buy an RV, and travel around the country during their retirement years.

✳ Mike and Carol T.—60 and 56 years old, respectively. He was a self-confessed workaholic partner in a prestigious law firm. She's a golf fanatic, regular exerciser, and does a lot of volunteer work. Retired for 2 years, and financially stable, they are having some difficulties with their roles in retirement. Carol is used to her routine; Mike feels he doesn't have any hobbies or interests because of his all-consuming career and misses his status and the structure of work. They'd like to keep their primary home in St. Louis, near most of their four grown children, yet they love the ocean and warm weather.

✳ Ed L.—56 years old, a high school Spanish teacher, planning to retire in 4 years with his partner, Kevin, who works in retail. They are interested in moving to a gay-friendly community and are concerned about whether they will have enough money to retire.

✳ Rosalyn and Phil S.—53 and 62 years old, respectively, a two-career couple with a major manufacturing company. Rosalyn is a marketing manager; Phil works in human resources. They have been transferred six times and, as a result, feel they have no real "home." Rosalyn is several years younger than Phil and would like to continue working, although they are concerned about the impact this might have on the personal dynamics of their relationship. They would like a low-cost, safe retirement area, have no children, and would like to live in an adult community.

How can *The New Retirement* assist this diverse group of people? It is the first book to approach retirement from the following multiple perspectives.

✳ The "who" of retirement: examines the scientific research concerning people who have or are planning to retire, then analyzes and summarizes the studies to see what can be learned from them.

✳ The "what" of retirement: explains how to reprogram your time, explores work issues, describes lifelong learning opportunities, and suggests leisure and volunteer activities.

✳ The "where" of retirement: explores whether readers should move at all. It describes specific places to retire, including recommended communities. In addition, it covers the process of choosing a place, housing possibilities, and issues such as universal design.

✳ The "how" of retirement: clearly lays out a blueprint for planning your retirement. Additional simple, clear worksheets help to ensure a secure financial future.

The authors, Jan Cullinane and Cathy Fitzgerald, give seminars about retirement and have researched and traveled extensively, investigating places to retire, interviewing people planning to retire and those who have already taken the leap. They have also consulted experts in various fields, using their skills and knowledge, to bring together the most current, the most sound, and the most accurate advice available. *The New Retirement: The Ultimate Guide to the Rest of Your Life* is the only book you'll ever need on this subject.

PART I

WHAT SHALL YOU DO
WITH YOUR RETIREMENT?

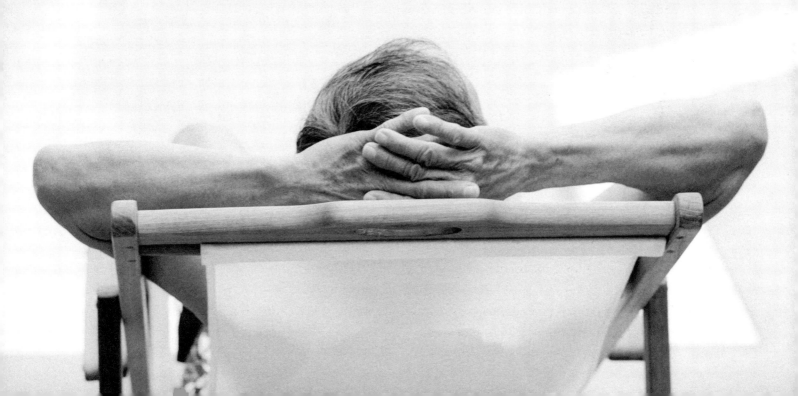

1

WHAT MAKES RETIREMENT SUCCESSFUL?

"Don't simply retire from something; have something to retire to."
—Harry Emerson Fosdick

To paraphrase the Temptations, "Get ready, 'cause here we come!" With longer life spans, better health, more education, and greater geographical mobility and affluence, those of us approaching retirement or recently retired are reshaping the meaning of retirement itself.

Retirement is a fairly recent phenomenon; at the beginning of the 19th century, few people retired, because they simply could not afford to do so. As white-collar jobs replaced a predominantly agricultural economy, however, incomes rose, and people had more money with which to retire. They lived longer and had more leisure activities from which to choose. The advent of Social Security and pensions also contributed to the ability to retire.

Today, however, the conventional definition of retirement itself needs to be retired! Before the baby boomers, retirement was seen primarily as a male's onetime passage from the workforce, and research concerning retirement dealt almost exclusively with men. Retirement was viewed more in isolation, as a solitary passage, though the reality is that most retirees are married. Retirement is now recognized as a process, involving perhaps several forays into and out of alternative projects, pastimes, and jobs. And now that almost half the workforce is female, retirement is no longer a male phenomenon; it's also recognized as more of a couples' issue.

We frequently hear predictions by pundits and the

press about how the future of retirement will resemble the past of retirement. That is, in the future as in the past, we will work until we die. The news contains innumerable anecdotes about middle-aged workers losing their nest eggs (or having a "cracked" nest egg or not having one at all). Surely each of us could add tales from our own acquaintances, if not ourselves, to the list. The stories make interesting news, but the facts point in a different direction: We are spending more of our lives in retirement than at any time in history, which is a trend that's projected to continue into the foreseeable future.

REAL RETIREMENT

Let's take a look at three couples to see how the concept of retirement has changed.

Mike and Mary (born 1900; retired 1965): Lucky to be alive! The very idea of retirement must have seemed peculiar to Mike and Mary. Certainly none of their forebears were likely to have lived long enough to provide an example of retirement. With a life expectancy of about 47 years, neither Mike nor Mary should have anticipated living long enough to retire, but they defied the odds and lived well past their working years. In fact, Mike and Mary would live through our collective awakening to the idea of "life after work."

Retiring in 1965, Mike and Mary would have felt lucky to be alive. Moreover, their admittedly modest (possibly nonexistent) expectations about retirement surely would have been exceeded. During their working years, it would have been unfathomable to them that, at age 65, they would be able to stop working, yet continue to receive a check and have something enjoyable to do in their leisure years.

Ken and Doris (born 1920; retired 1982): A well-deserved respite. Ken and Doris came of age during the Great Depression, when a quarter of all workers were unemployed. Their defining life experience was undoubtedly World War II, when Ken was shipped overseas to fight the Nazis as an officer in the venerable Eighth Air Force, while Doris stayed at home to work as a typist at the local aircraft assembly plant. After the war, Ken began his civilian career as a mechanical engineer at

FDR signed the Social Security Act into law on August 14, 1935. In January 1940, Ida May Fuller became the first recipient of Social Security benefits. And did she ever benefit! Ida lived 35 more years, and she collected more than $22,000 before finally giving out at the age of 100.

the Company, and Doris left the formal workforce to pursue the business of raising her children and keeping house. Ken toiled loyally for the Company over the next 38 years, earning his steady pay raises and sharing in the economic success of both the Company and the country during the expansionary years of the 1950s and 1960s.

Ken and Doris no doubt possessed a strong work ethic born of their experiences both in weathering the Great Depression and in fighting the war. But Ken and Doris were also human, and they wanted to retire at a reasonable age in order to pursue the life of leisure. Gladly for them, retirement was swiftly becoming an institution in the United States, and when the couple retired in 1982, they could have reasonably expected to live in leisure for 18 or so years. Moreover, they would be able to afford a comfortable retirement. During the 1950s, Social Security benefits increased by nearly 80 percent, truly helping to make retirement an entitlement. Additionally, in the sixties, the Company introduced a pension plan to provide postretirement income to its employees. Medicare became a reality in the sixties as well, providing health-care benefits to older people. Ken and Doris had cause to feel financially secure about retirement, as did many of their contemporaries. In fact, during the 1960s, about 50 percent of all Americans were covered by private pen-

sion plans in addition to Social Security. That must have been nice, but then again, their respite was hard earned and well deserved.

Bob and Cindy (born 1950; retiring circa 2010): The retirement "boom." The baby boomers are only now beginning to retire, and yet we are reminded of this demographic phenomenon at every turn. No single topic, save perhaps the dying sport of shuffleboard, is more commonly identified with retirement than is the demographic fact of the baby boom. Most commonly we hear the dire predictions of a bankrupt Social Security system or of intergenerational strife caused by the increased financial burden on future workers required to subsidize the retirement of the boomers.

Though these concerns are real, Bob and Cindy are likely to enjoy a long and prosperous retirement, relative to that of prior generations. Because of the steady increase in life expectancy, Bob and Cindy could enjoy 30-plus retirement years, longer than any group of retirees in history.

Though the terms *leisure* and *retirement* call to mind images of relaxation, Bob and Cindy are not likely to spend the second half of their lives idle. The most important questions about their retirement relate to how and where they will spend their time. Whereas previous generations were lucky to see retirement at all, the current generation of retirees can safely expect to spend a significant portion of their lives retired, but probably not merely relaxing—perhaps working, and certainly not bored.

Because both the duration and nature of retirement have changed, Bob and Cindy need the resources to plan adequately for an active, emotionally satisfying, and financially secure retirement.

Imagine you have reached this milestone called retirement. Envision your typical day. Is it spent walking on the beach, playing tennis, or golfing? Are you volunteering? Pursuing an advanced degree? Working, like 80 percent of boomers ages 45 and older expect to do (based on a survey by AARP)? Doing absolutely nothing?

The good news is that 92 percent of US retirees report being very happy or quite happy, according a 2005 survey conducted by AXA Financial. So is there a perfect time to retire? Are there secrets to a successful retirement? Recent scientific studies involving the psychology of retirement address our current realities of this important time and can provide practical suggestions for achieving a successful and satisfying retirement.

TIMING IS EVERYTHING

To work, or not to work? Ignoring financial considerations for the moment (we'll address them in Chapter 9), the psychological research is a bit inconclusive about work after retirement and its effect on well-being. In a nutshell, it just depends!

There are two competing outlooks. The first, continuity theory, is the perspective that our levels of self-esteem and life satisfaction stay the same, independent of work. Under this theory, it wouldn't matter whether a person worked; he or she would maintain the same feelings of well-being. The second perspective, role theory, has two sides. Although role theory considers working to be paramount to a person's identity, retirement can improve feelings of well-being if the career being left was considered very difficult or stressful; or, retirement can cause distress if people feel they have lost a valuable role by not being employed. It turns out that the effect of leaving the primary career is more a function of how you perceived that career—that is, whether working played a crucial role in your life, was something to give up with relief, or was immaterial to how you thought about yourself. Consider the following studies.

Reasons to Retire

In a survey of more than 700 soon-to-retire, newly retired, and retired men and women, participants in the Cornell Retirement and Well-Being Study were asked their reasons for retiring. Their responses:

Women

* To do other things (69%)
* Financial incentives (40%)
* Have enough income (38%)
* Spouse retired (33%)
* Older worker policy (24%)
* Poor health (24%)
* Didn't like work (24%)
* Didn't get along with boss (22%)
* Family health (21%)
* Not appreciated (19%)
* Job ended (7%)

Men

* To do other things (70%)
* Financial incentives (62%)
* Have enough income (45%)
* Didn't like work (33%)
* Older worker policy (22%)
* Poor health (21%)
* Didn't get along with boss (19%)
* Not appreciated (17%)

* Family health (16%)
* Job ended (13%)
* Spouse retired (9%)

This ranking gives some insight into the when of retirement. The desire to do something else and the perception among both the men and the women that they were financially able to retire were paramount. Note that for women, however, the fact that their spouses retired was a much more motivating force to retire than it was for men. While virtually all those surveyed had done some planning for their retirement, more than half felt they had not planned enough. So here's a word to the wise: Plan ahead.

Working can provide rewards and satisfaction such as status, intellectual engagement, social interaction, purpose, feelings of pride and accomplishment, structure, and, of course, a paycheck and health coverage. Regardless of your reason for retiring, whether you stop working entirely, cut back on hours, or pursue other endeavors such as volunteering, enjoying a hobby, or cultivating a skill, you will still want to experience these rewards in your everyday life.

In another study, 17 employed and 54 retired professors, ages 70 to 74, were interviewed to determine the

---

According to the Life Events Scale, which ranks 42 life events from most stressful (death of a spouse) to least stressful (minor law violations, such as a parking ticket), retirement ranks 10th!

reasons some retired and some continued working. Whether deciding to retire or remain employed, both groups reported high levels of satisfaction with life, although the employed faculty ratings were higher (97 versus 90 on a scale of 100).

For those who remained employed, the primary reason was because they enjoyed their work (77 percent). Other factors included work being important to them (35 percent), financial issues (12 percent), and inertia (6 percent). For those who retired, the primary reasons were a desire to do other things (35 percent) and because it was time (35 percent). Additional factors included changes in the work environment (24 percent), tired of work (20 percent), health issues (17 percent), and could afford to retire (13 percent).

Interestingly, there were more married couples among the retired group than the working group, and the retired group also had more children and grandchildren than those who were employed.

This study is noteworthy because it removes the entire issue of having to leave the workplace (there was no mandatory retirement age). There's no one right answer to the question "When should I retire?" The answer can partially be determined by the role work plays in a person's life, as well as the satisfaction that working provides. The reasons to work or not work were primarily psychological, and unlike in the Cornell survey mentioned earlier, financial aspects played a minor role in deciding whether to retire.

Are you ready to launch your retirement? Take the quiz of the same name on page 440 and see.

Gender and Retirement

Research has shown some common threads about the effects of retirement and working (or not working) on couples. One study looked at transitions in retirement involving 534 married couples in their fifties, sixties, or seventies who were retired or about to retire from several large businesses in upstate New York.

Husbands and wives reported greater marital satisfaction if they retired at the same time. While men with nonworking spouses had greater marital satisfaction than those with working wives, regardless of whether the men themselves worked, those men who didn't work

---

Suicide rates for women decline after retirement but increase for men. One hypothesis is that women have or develop more outside interests, so they don't need to depend on employment in order to feel fulfilled.

but had working spouses reported the most marital conflict. Women experienced the highest marital satisfaction if they entered new jobs after retiring and their husbands were also working, but men who worked after retiring from their primary job experienced more marital discord than those men who didn't work.

You may have heard the saying "Twice the husband but half the money." According to Ronald J. Manheimer, executive director of the North Carolina Center for Creative Retirement at the University of North Carolina, women's fears in retirement include losing one's identity (becoming more prevalent with the increase in the number of retiring professional women), being responsible for their spouses'/significant others' social lives and entertainment, experiencing a disruption of their established patterns, needing to take care of everyone, financial and health issues, and outliving their spouses. Men's concerns include lack of status, lack of social support, lack of purpose, declining physical abilities, poor communication with significant others, and boomerang kids.

On the flip side, women's fantasies include returning to school, becoming an entrepreneur, beginning meaningful volunteer activities, renewing relationships, and enjoying life. Men's dreams include an active lifestyle, getting in shape, reviving romance with their spouses, increasing involvement with their grandchildren, and developing new skills. Both men and women include travel on their wish lists.

The first 2 years of retirement are comparable to the first 2 years of marriage or parenthood; it's a time to negotiate (or renegotiate) roles and share ideas and dreams. As when getting married or having a child, it's important to discuss and plan for the future before retiring, from an emotional as well as a financial standpoint. Realize that the transition to retirement is a period of marital challenge for both sexes. Take heart—although there are lots of adjustments to be made, 60 percent of couples report that there is (ultimately) an improvement in their marriages after retirement.

If the role of work is important to you but is causing stress in the relationship, take a look at alternative forms of work. Work doesn't necessarily mean only paid and full-time work. It could include volunteering, community service, working fewer hours, doing projects, or starting a new, scaled-down career. All of these could fit

Should you retire? Ask yourself these three questions: Do I have enough? Have I had enough? Do I have enough to do?

the definition of productive work. In the United States, success tends to be defined in monetary terms, but separating success and productivity from paid employment will create many more options for making retirement a time of new and meaningful roles.

EASE THE TRANSITION TO RETIREMENT

Obviously, retirement brings about a shift in roles and activity. People who can adjust and adapt to these changes will have a more successful transition to retirement. But what personality traits facilitate the easiest transition? Research indicates there are two chief ways of looking at the world that increase the chances for smooth sailing through this choppy time: an internal locus of control (the belief that outcomes are under one's control) and retirement self-efficacy (the belief or self-confidence that one can cope with the changes retirement brings). Here are some tips to help ease the transition, no matter which outlook on life you adopt.

Consider moving to neutral ground. Shortly before retiring, Brian and Joanne K. sold their home and moved to an active-adult community in their same town. This had the unintended but positive effect of creating a new environment that was free of their previous territorial patterns (her kitchen, his garage).

Take action. Demonstrate that you believe outcomes are under your control (even if you don't) and that you are confident you can cope with retirement changes (even if you aren't). For example, if you're married, be willing to go beyond conventional gender-based roles. Renegotiate! Consider housework or yard work. Take, for example, Shelley and Marty L. Marty is a recently retired CPA, and Shelley recently sold her college-prep test business. While they were both working, they employed a cleaning service for their home. Now that they are retired and decided they could do this themselves, Marty cleans the house every Wednesday while Shelley golfs in a women's nine-hole group. After 2 years, so far so good. Or look at Joanne and Craig C. Craig has a demanding career in IT, and Joanne has the demanding role of running their household, which consists of four (three of whom are now grown) children, two dogs, and a cat. However, the one thing Joanne detests is cooking. In their retirement planning, they have decided on what they call the "twice a day" rule—and no, we're not talking about sex. Joanne and Craig have agreed that when Craig is retired 2 years from now, Joanne will make two out of three meals a day, but that's it. A third meal will be eaten out, ordered in, or cooked by Craig. Joanne wants to retire too!

Develop resilience. Resilience, the ability to bounce back after adversity, is an important ingredient in the recipe for successful retirement. It is possible to cultivate this quality. Accept that change is part of life; concentrate on changing adverse circumstances that can be altered; act decisively rather than wishing problems would just disappear; maintain perspective; take big problems and break them into smaller, manageable challenges; foster positive relationships; and take good care of yourself.

Consult others. Discuss how your friends and relatives in the same situation adjusted (and compromised and renegotiated) during this transition period. Consulting with a counselor or couples' therapist, a life coach, or a trusted religious leader, and/or attending seminars on retirement (if they include more than just financial issues) may help if there is difficulty transitioning.

Saddle up! Right after retirement, retirees report an increased energy level. Use this "honeymoon period" to your advantage and plan, plan, plan.

On Being Single

You may have been single all your life or ended up single as a result of divorce or death. According to Elizabeth Holtzman, MSW, MA, at the University of Massachu-

setts in Amherst, there are some psychological aspects that relate specifically to being a single retiree.

"Being single both simplifies and complicates the problems of retirement," she says. "It simplifies them because you have only yourself to look after; you can make your own choices. On the other hand, you don't have a partner to share things with or lean on emotionally or financially. Being a single retiree may lead to isolation and loneliness."

Luckily, there are tangible ways to combat these psychological considerations. For one, you can choose to live in a location that is single friendly. Some specific places include Sarasota and Naples, Florida; Las Vegas; and Asheville, North Carolina, and there are other suggestions discussed in Chapters 5 and 6. And consider taking your friends with you! We have met a number of singles in the same socioeconomic group who look at possible places for relocation together. They'll already have a social nucleus in their new home.

Another way to combat loneliness is to join a social-support group, which is equally as important for couples as it is for singles. If you've stopped working, or you relocate to a new area, isolation could become an issue. Consider moving into an active-adult community that

---

Consider this Zen saying: "The barn burned down. Now I can see the moon."

has built-in social activities or a master-planned community with a clubhouse or center that offers planned get-togethers and outings. Other options include returning to paid employment, volunteering, checking out the local senior center, starting or working on a hobby that involves people—in other words, joining in! One easy, free way to share your interests with others is Meetup (www.meetup.com). This is a free Internet site that allows you to get together with others (perhaps at a library, Starbucks, or park) who share similar passions. Simply put in your zip code and see what groups are out there, or start your own Meetup group. See Chapters 2 and 6 for more specific suggestions.

As a single, since there is no financial backup, it's especially important to begin your retirement planning early. If you're a woman, this is particularly true, since women generally are paid less than men, may have been out of the workforce for years to raise children, and may or may not have the funds to support the retirement lifestyle they would like. It's a good idea to seek professional advice now from a certified financial planner or a CPA to begin the planning process.

Believe That You Have Enough Money

The perception that you have enough money to retire has a bearing on your feelings of satisfaction concerning retirement. In one study, more than 1,000 people age 55 and over were surveyed about their satisfaction in retirement. The study found that satisfaction increased with the number of years a person saved for retirement. Of those who saved for 25 years or more, 60 percent said they were "extremely satisfied" with retirement, as did half of those who saved for 15 to 24 years. Less than half of those who saved for fewer than 15 years could report the same feeling.

Note that the correlation is between feeling financially prepared and feeling satisfied in retirement, regardless of actual net worth or wealth. So save, save, save!

Research at Penn State University determined that it's not the absolute amount of money a person has that contributes to feelings of happiness; rather, it's the comparison of income level with one's peer group. The researchers call this a hedonic treadmill, since incomes tend to rise over time, and people have to spend more energy to "keep up with the Joneses." The study also

---

"Walking is inexpensive, familiar, and safe. That's why many have argued that the most effective piece of exercise equipment is a dog."
—Dr. Penteleimon Ekkekakis

found that physical health was the largest predictor of happiness, followed by income, level of education, and marital status.

Studies also show people who place a high priority on the pursuit of money and the accumulation of material things are more depressed and suffer from lower self-esteem than those who make relationships their top priority. Trite but true: Money really can't buy happiness!

Have a Support System

How important is it to be connected to others? According to the research, very! Two studies illustrate how vital social support really is.

The 22-percent effect: Lynn Giles, PhD, and three other researchers followed 1,500 older people for 10 years and found that those with extensive social networks outlived those lacking social support by 22 percent. Interestingly, it was friends and not relatives who had this effect. (This is not to say relatives aren't important; they just weren't a factor in increasing longevity in this study.) The effect of friends increasing life span persisted, even when those in the study experienced huge changes such as the death of family members or a spouse.

The 2½-year effect: One 13-year study, involving 2,812 men and women in New Haven, Connecticut, 65 years of age and older, investigated the relationship between social activity and longevity. It found that men and women who were socially active lived an average of 2½ years longer than those who were not socially active.

This study is important because it links a longer life span to activities such as playing cards, eating out, or going to movies with others, without regard to physical exercise. It had been widely thought that activity prolonged life because of the physical aspect; now we know that social engagement alone can increase the life span. That doesn't mean you can retire to the couch though!

Why do friends increase longevity? Although the research doesn't answer this question, perhaps friends encourage their friends to take care of themselves, seek medical help when necessary, model coping mechanisms, or lift their moods.

Women might have an easier time reaping the benefits of social support because they tend to cast their nets wider than men when choosing friends. Men tend to find their friends at work. So what's a guy to do? Give

---

To determine your strengths, overall happiness level, and satisfaction with life, and to take several other assessments, go to www.authentichappiness.com and complete the free questionnaires.

these ideas a whirl: group activities such as watching or participating in sporting events, attending spiritual retreats, joining organizations such as model railroad clubs, eating out with others, and volunteering.

DON'T WORRY, BE HAPPY!

Recently, psychologists have taken to identifying people who consider themselves happy and examining what traits they share. This focus on a wellness model, rather than a disease model, has resulted in some interesting findings.

One recent study investigated the relationship between positive thinking and the risk of frailty. The researchers followed 1,558 older adults for 7 years and compared frailty (determined by speed of walking, strength of grip, weight loss, and fatigue) and measured positive thinking by asking participants how many particular positive thoughts they had over the course of the study (such as "I felt hopeful about the future"). As a group, frailty increased among the aging adults, but those with positive emotions and thinking were less likely to become frail.

Previous research has shown that positive thinking can decrease the time required to recover from serious illness, and it lowers the risk of strokes and heart attacks. A study that followed 545 men for 15 years found that the most optimistic men in the group were half as likely to die from cardiovascular disease than those men who were least optimistic. Talk about the power of positive thinking! Why does it work? A few possibilities have been proposed. Positive emotions may directly influence body chemicals in a way that affects health. Positive people tend to have increased social interactions, which may result in more access to resources. And positive people may be better at coping with and addressing problems.

University of Pennsylvania psychologist Martin Seligman, PhD, has been studying happiness and optimism for more than 25 years and suggests we go beyond seeking pleasure and instead look for gratification. What's the difference?

Pleasure is not necessarily meaningful and does not always result in a greater good. (For example, eating a piece of cheesecake may feed your stomach, but not your soul.) Gratification involves cultivating and nurturing your strengths and putting them to positive use. Consider Darla and Jim W., whose first child died just prior to childbirth. Although devastated by the loss, they set up a foundation at a local hospital to provide indigent women with the financial resources to bury children who died under similar circumstances. Darla and Jim took their strengths of compassion, generosity, and financial savvy and parlayed them into a gratifying experience in

HOW TO HAVE A SUCCESSFUL RETIREMENT

✳ Have something to wake up for

✳ Have a willingness to renegotiate roles

✳ Have a social-support system

✳ Have a high level of activity (both physical and mental)

✳ Have a strong financial plan

✳ Have a healthy spouse

✳ Have a healthy attitude

✳ Have a sense of humor

the midst of their sorrow. Likewise, we can cultivate happiness by incorporating strengths such as kindness, humor, optimism, and courage into everyday life.

To become a happier person, Dr. Seligman suggests you find your calling. A job provides a paycheck; a career provides power, prestige, a paycheck, and a personal commitment; but a calling is a passion where the activity itself is its own reward regardless of any status or income it may provide. A calling can be any line of "work," be it caregiver, artist, spouse, or engineer. It's a matter of finding an activity that provides challenges that mesh with your unique strengths.

Another way to become happy is by learning to see the glass as half full. "Pessimists tend to have hopeless thoughts, or worse, they stamp themselves with a nega-

tive label, such as 'jerk,'" says Dr. Seligman. If this sounds like you, he suggests speaking to yourself as a close friend would. Tell yourself that you learned from the experience and will do better the next time. And rather than name-calling, try something like, "Sometimes I'm not as considerate as I'd like to be, but overall, I'm a kind person." Dr. Seligman coined the term "learned helplessness"—giving up because you feel you can't change outcomes—and says we can escape this belief with "learned optimism."

He advises "not to ruminate about bad events that happen to you. . . . I recommend fun distractions, because studies show that if you think about problems in a negative frame of mind, you come up with fewer solutions." Plus, you're more likely to become depressed.

"Happiness makes up in height for what it lacks in length."
—Robert Frost

Pessimists can overcome this cycle though and train themselves to think more optimistically—once they boost their moods. "It takes most people a few weeks to get the knack, but once the technique is learned, the less likely they are to relapse," says Dr. Seligman.

So put a stop to distorted ways of thinking. When you think something negative, note it, evaluate it, and replace the thought with something more realistic. It takes practice, but it's an effective tool for increasing happiness.

Accentuate the Positive

Here are some specific suggestions for boosting your mood.

* Accept yourself as you are, and accept that you deserve to be happy.

* Live joyfully in the moment. Do today what you would do if you found out you had only months left to live. As comedienne Grace Hansen noted, "Don't be afraid that your life will end; be afraid that it will never begin."

* Help others, and ask for help when you need it. Be able to answer the question: "What did I do for someone else and for myself today?"

* Plan pleasurable activities in advance. Looking forward to something is a mood-brightener.

* Just do it! Though most of us believe that we must change our attitudes before we change our behaviors, the reverse is also true. Behaving in a desirable way can actually change your brain's chemistry and thus affect your way of thinking.

* Be aware of stereotypes. Negative attitudes about aging are believed to begin in childhood; many people grow up with erroneous beliefs about getting older. If you have a jaundiced view of aging, knowing the origin of your feelings may help to change them.

* View the world optimistically.

* Foster an internal locus of control for your successes and an external locus of control for your failures. Locus of control, a concept developed by Julian Rotter in 1966, refers to how you perceive the outcomes of certain events. People with an internal locus of control generally believe that personal actions are responsible for outcomes, while those with an external locus of control attribute outcomes to forces beyond their control (fate, luck, society, etc.). We have to be realistic, however, and recognize when failure is due to lack of effort or our own limitations. And of course, sometimes things may truly be beyond our control!

* Laugh often, smile frequently, and look for the

humor in daily life. Work at being curious, realistic, and flexible. Remember, you cannot always control what happens to you, but you can control your response.

✳ Cultivate a sense of wonder about the world.

✳ Think of five things each day for which you are grateful—and write them down.

Healthiness Equals Happiness

Sure, you feel better when you're well, but it's the physical act of exercise that brings about a shift in mood. A psychological bonanza of more pleasurable feelings results from just a short investment of time. In one study, men and women, average age 53, completed surveys before, during, and after a 15-minute walk. Everyone reported a more positive affect (feelings or emotions) and greater energy, both during and after the walk, and felt greater calmness and relaxation 15 minutes after completing the walk.

Healthwise, marriage really is for better or for worse! If one spouse has high blood pressure, high cholesterol, depression, asthma, ulcers, or arthritis, the other spouse is much more likely to suffer from the same disease. Couples tend to share many lifestyle choices, such as nutrition, exercise, smoking, drinking, and work habits. They also tend to share such factors as emotional stressors (financial problems or dealing with children), aller-

gens, and other environmental risk factors. People tend to marry people like themselves—similar backgrounds, education levels, and economic status. It turns out that this holds true for health status as well. One study of more than 4,700 married men and women between the ages of 51 and 61 investigated the relationship between spouses and health status. The researchers found that men ages 51 to 55 who are in excellent health have barely a 5 percent chance of being married to women in fair health and just a 2 percent chance of being married to women in poor health. Bottom line: We choose spouses whom we can not only grow old with, but whom we can grow old well with.

Health is not just an individual matter. As Sven Wilson, the study's author, points out, "household matters!" Taking stock of your present health situation as a couple may provide a window to your future health. Since each of you shares the same environmental conditions, psychological stresses, and behavioral patterns, the concept of spouses tending to mirror one another's health level is something to consider as you plan your retirement. For example, knowing that your spouse is in poor health in his or her fifties could be the impetus to purchase long-term care insurance or perhaps help determine where you live—staying near family or choosing a location near excellent medical facilities.

(true **LIFE**) **John K. retired early. Here is his story.**

I started working for my company at the age of 20. It was my first and last full-time job for more than 35 years. I realize it is not typical anymore, but nonetheless, it afforded me the opportunity to experience retirement at a relatively young age.

The day I retired, I was happily living in Atlanta, Georgia, and didn't particularly want to change the lifestyle I had grown accustomed to. While working, I was responsible for the retirement of thousands of individuals at a major corporation. We would inform employees who were retiring or simply planning for a future retirement of benefits they had earned while employed. During the course of retirement planning, I would hear individuals' concerns as they approached their ultimate decision at the end of their working careers: Should I retire now, can I afford to retire now, what would happen if I stayed just a little longer? At my company, and I suspect at most major corporations, you might be putting yourself in a precarious situation if you even hint at retiring. What does it mean to your position? Am I putting my job and livelihood in jeopardy? This particular decision is totally individual and no amount of discussion with others can totally alleviate the fear of the unknown. I can think of only a few situations and a few lucky people who can be rather calloused toward retirement. They are generally the ones with exceptional skills or knowledge who would have no difficulty in re-entering the working world; but for the rest of us, when the door closes, entry back through the same door at the same compensation level is virtually unheard of.

I'm now 57, and along with my wife, Janet, I am now retired and living in a little slice of paradise in Florida. Surprisingly, for someone as heavily involved in the retirement process for as many years, I spent relatively little time planning for my own pending retirement. Like the proverbial auto mechanic who drives a vehicle in need of repair, my wife and I seemed to put others first, and at the end of the day, found our own plan lacking.

Nonetheless, here we are, having relocated to what we believe is our dream location in a small city within an hour's commute from a major city, just far enough away not to be a bedroom community to the busy working world. We live near the ocean, near our golf club, and near the fitness center that we use, surprisingly, several times a week.

I was blessed to work for a company that offered its employees the opportunity to take an early retirement, and I was fortunate enough that it afforded me the opportunity to leave at age 55. But, I wondered, should I retire?

Up until the summer I was to retire, I was still having trouble with the question of whether I should leave at the earliest opportunity or stay a little longer. Isn't 55 a little early to retire? I knew I would like more time for myself, but did I really need to leave my job to get a little additional time? What was I going to do, where was I going to live, was I really ready to make such a big change in my life? When these are theoretical questions, they are fun and somewhat easy to answer, particularly when you are years away from retirement or the idea of living the rest of your life free to do whatever you desire. But always remember the degree of difficulty ratchets up as one approaches his own retirement.

I was a retirement manager; I should have had the definitive answer. After much deliberation, I started wondering if maybe there is no such definitive answer. Maybe the selection as to when one retires is a little bit like horseshoes. It doesn't have to be right on the stake; it has to be only close enough. I have never met the person who has been able to answer the question: How much is enough?

As in life or work, a little luck is essential. I was lucky that Janet was motivated several years before my retirement and encouraged me to at least think about and shop for possible locations to consider for retirement. Vacations would turn into real-estate explorations. We would enjoy shopping, the treat of the rich and famous, yet free, providing you don't buy anything! She encouraged me to look for properties somewhere in the South, somewhere not too far from our children, who were living and working in Atlanta, and not so far away as to make us feel isolated. We started our search within the state of Georgia, but we quickly moved south to Florida. We did however, have one advantage. After living 30 miles from the Canadian border during our early years, we had experienced enough ice and snow to realize we were more heat tolerant than cold tolerant.

We struck gold one sunny afternoon. We ran into a gregarious real-estate agent named Howie Molloy. After hellos were exchanged, we said, "Howie, we have only 20 minutes to look. We're on our way back to Atlanta, and it's a work day tomorrow." Howie said, "Twenty minutes is more than enough." It had to be a combination of things—the end of a vacation, the warm sunshine, the sound of the ocean, or the voice of a true believer and his story of the pending dream soon to be developed. Janet was sold immediately; I consented a little later, and I justified the transaction in my own mind by telling myself that she was only asking me to purchase a vacant lot. It was to be in a newly formed subdivision with the promise of sunny weather, beautiful aesthetics, and unlimited activities. For me, the big plus was buying undeveloped property with the worse-case scenario that it would become investment property with the potential of appreciation. Another upside was the procrastination factor. The longer it took us to decide whether we would ultimately build and relocate to Florida, the more it would continue to work in our favor. It was a little like a savings account, accruing interest as time passed.

I did retire at my earliest opportunity, which in hindsight turned out to be the best decision I could have made, and a new lifestyle started. Our new lifestyle started in the same house, in the same neighborhood, and with the same friends and activities we had throughout our active working life. I didn't envision a need for change because my friends who I had played golf with were still in the neighborhood, my friends who I rode motorcycles with were still in my neighborhood, and the circle of friends we relied on for all our activities were still in place just a few miles away. Plus, we had lived in Atlanta for more than 15 years. We knew

we were living in a great city, and why should we make a change because everything was going wonderfully. Yet, our vacant lot in Florida was still there, appreciating in value and serving as an outlet if we ever desired it to become one.

Our new retirement lifestyle started affecting me right away. After 35 years of working at a large company, being surrounded by numerous people every day, and being fully engaged 10 to 12 hours daily, it had gotten into my blood. I didn't miss working 10 to 12 hours a day. What I missed was the interaction of people and life's pace in general. I would wake up in the morning wanting to spend a 10- to 12-hour, fast-paced, exhilarating day, the same as I had been accustomed to. Schedules weren't meshing. I was available; where was everyone else? Just because you retire doesn't mean everyone else is retired. Wouldn't it be nice if all of our friends were the same age and were retiring at the same time? It would be a little bit like high school, when we all had the same schedule and everyone in the class was the same age.

One phrase I kept hearing over and over was: "I would like to, but I am so busy, I just can't." Whether it was golf, biking, or grabbing a bite to eat, I kept hearing "It's so crazy over here, I just can't get away." I felt like the person who steps off a fast-moving commuter train: I found myself on the platform with a little extra time on my hands before my next appointment, but everyone else was still on the train, moving as fast as ever, and getting further away every minute. In reflection, had I not stayed in Atlanta immediately following my retirement, I would have never fully realized that my old working environment, my wonderful Atlanta, wasn't going to coincide with my retiree expectations.

So we decided to build a house on our Florida property. That Florida lot, our savings account, was about to be cashed in. Our backup plan was being executed. We were relocating within a reasonable

---

Life's a Test—And You're Graded on a Curve

At age 4, success is . . . tying your shoes.

At age 12, success is . . . having friends.

At age 16, success is . . . having a driver's license.

At age 20, success is . . . having sex.

At age 35, success is . . . having money.

At age 50, success is . . . having money.

At age 60, success is . . . having sex.

At age 70, success is . . . having a driver's license.

At age 75, success is . . . having friends.

At age 80, success is . . . tying your shoes.

drive of friends and family, improving on our weather, increasing the numbers of activities available to us, and placing ourselves in a community with like-minded individuals who were living at a high rate of speed; all I had to do was join the crowd and try to keep up. People here were enjoying similar activities, including golf, exercise, swimming, and tennis.

We have lived here only a short time, but the number of guests and family members who have visited has been a pleasure. I remember once seeing a movie in which the underlying theme was: "If you build it, they will come." Well, we built it, and they are coming. Our daughter's family loves our new location, the grandchildren look forward to visits, our sons think it is wonderful, and our daughter-in-law has plans to visit for the summer already. Our lives have been enriched with the new relationships and friends we have made since our move, and more important, we still carry with us the friendships that we have established over the years and cherish so much. ⓛ

HOW DO YOU REPROGRAM YOUR TIME?

"Do one thing every day that scares you."
—*Eleanor Roosevelt*

Now is the time to think about the next phase of your life. A 2006 Pew Research Center survey found that expectations and reality differ when predicting the age of retirement. While workers think they'll retire when they are 61, the average age of retirement is actually 57.8 years of age. Today's retirees are generally more affluent, younger, and healthier and can expect to live as many as three decades in their "golden years." In fact, terms such as *zoomers* (coined by Tim Smart, *U.S. News & World Report*), and the concepts of redirecting, refiring, or reinventing your life after leaving your primary career, have all appeared in the media, reflecting the reality that retirement doesn't mean sitting on the sidelines of life.

As noted in Chapter 1, activities that are challenging and provide a sense of self-worth are one of the keys to a happy retirement. Yes, you can play golf and watch television, but what other options exist? What types of volunteer and lifelong learning opportunities are there? What are some interesting hobbies? Should you start a second (or third or fourth) career?

If you were to do the math, you'd realize there are 168 hours a week to fill which you can do mindlessly or mindfully. Complete the "Time on Your Hands" worksheet on page 445, to see how you will/do spend your time. Assuming you have the financial wherewithal, ask yourself if there are things you'd like to try or if you want more time to pursue certain interests. (To give you some insight on this, do the worksheet, "Should You Stop Working?" on page 446.) If the answer to this question is no, and your spouse or significant other is amenable, keep working. It may be the best thing for you. If the answer is yes, however, the big question then is, how do you reprogram your time?

PERSONALITY AND GOAL-SETTING

Are you a planner? One of the authors (Jan) has her next 4 years of vacations planned out, knows the next 5 books she is going to read, and looks at *TV Guide* for the coming week to see if there are any programs she'll need to tape because of conflicting commitments. Cathy, on the other hand, lives mainly in the moment, picks up and goes on trips (without hotel reservations) at the drop of a hat, signs up for a cooking class or tennis round-robin at the last minute, and jumps in to volunteer for a worthy cause without any hesitation. Although they have different personalities and vastly different methods, Jan and Cathy have one thing in common: They both have goals they want to accomplish.

In order to have a successful retirement, you'll want to set goals. Otherwise, rather than enjoying leisure activities, you'll really just be experiencing idleness, and the research shows that people who aren't engaged in purposeful activities are generally not as happy as those who are. Whether you're talking about starting a new business, taking up birding, becoming a mentor, or trying out for a community theater production, it's best to be flexible, try out new things, have a natural curiosity about life, and have some kind of plan for your future. So regardless of your individual personality traits, how do you go about setting goals?

First, take the time to decide what you'd like to accomplish, and make lists. If you are part of a couple, set down both individual and joint ideas relating to work, leisure activities, health, lifelong learning, relationships, or any other area. Recognize that each person in the relationship has valid needs and wants. Decide which are interests you share, and realize having time apart for separate interests is also important. Brainstorm all possibilities, then evaluate and prune the unworkable ones.

SMART. This easy-to-remember acronym describes the characteristics of goal-setting: Specific, Measurable, Attainable, Realistic, and Time sensitive.

Now comes the fun part. Take your list, pick three items on it, and turn them into goals. Here's how:

* Turn each item into a specific, positive statement. For example, "I don't want to be intellectually stagnant" doesn't cut it. "I want to take a European history course at the local community college during the fall semester" does.

* Make your goals achievable within a defined time period. If you know you're scheduled for hernia surgery on October 1, you may want to rethink whether you can complete a fall semester history course. You want to dream, yet still be realistic.

* Remind yourself of your goals. Writing them out and placing them in a visible spot will help reinforce them.

Some people already know the goals they wish to attain, while others may want to consider some possibilities in the areas of education, hobbies, volunteering, the world of work, and travel (which is such a big area, we've given it a chapter by itself). And still others, well, they could use a little help deciding. If this sounds like you, keep reading.

LIFELONG LEARNING

Remember the three Rs? There are more opportunities than ever for the mature learner to complete a degree, go back to school for professional reasons, or pursue classes for enrichment, to increase social contacts, or just for the fun of it. In some cases, you don't even have to "go back." If you have a computer and a modem, you can curl up with a cup of coffee in your favorite robe and slippers and take a course online! About a third of all adults are enrolled in some type of formal education, according to the Department of Education. (If you're interested in *moving* to a college town, see Chapter 6.)

Degree Programs

The majority of adult students (about 70 percent) enroll in higher education to attain a degree. Most are seeking bachelor's degrees, some are working on master's degrees or doctorate degrees, and others are after associate's degrees. The reasons vary: finishing a degree that was interrupted years ago by family or work constraints, working on professional development, achieving a goal for which they now have the time and financial resources, or training for a new career.

If pursuing a degree is a path you want to consider, keep in mind that many colleges and universities will exempt you from entrance exams such as the SAT and ACT if you're over a certain age. If you're thinking of advanced degrees in medicine or law, however, you will need to take the MCAT or LSAT. When applying to a college, you'll probably have to provide any previous transcripts you have, which will be assessed by the college counselor to determine which credits you already possess may be applied toward your degree. You may also be able to receive credit by taking the CLEP (College-Level Examination Program) test, a credit-by-exam program that tests your knowledge of undergraduate subjects (www.collegeboard.com/clep). There are almost 3,000 colleges in the country that give credit and/or advanced standing for successful completion of CLEP exams.

If finances are a concern, there are several avenues to explore. Many colleges and universities offer classes at free or reduced tuition rates to mature learners. Community colleges often offer particularly attractive incentives. For example, at Kankakee Community College in Illinois, students 60 and older can enroll in credit courses without any tuition charges, provided there are enough paying students to cover the cost of the course. Check out the deals at the college or university near you. You may also be eligible for tax breaks, such as the Hope Tax Credit or a Lifetime Learning Credit (call the IRS Help Desk at 800-876-1715 or visit www.irs.gov and read Tax Topic 605: Education Credits or IRS Publication 970:

Tax Benefits for Higher Education). Consider tapping into your IRA (without a tax penalty) for approved educational needs. College, federal, and state loans and grants are available, as well as scholarships. Meet with a financial-aid officer at the colleges you are considering, and check out the Free Application for Federal Student Aid (FAFSA) at www.fafsa.ed.gov, Sallie Mae (www.salliemae.com), Free Scholarship Search (www.freschinfo.com), and Fast Web (www.fastweb.com). If you're female, the Business and Professional Women's Foundation offers scholarships if you meet certain criteria (www.bpwusa.org or 202-293-1100), and the American Association of University Women Education Foundation offers fellowships, grants, and awards (www.aauw.org or 800-785-7700).

The term *college senior* can have a whole new meaning.

Distance Learning

If you've always wanted to conquer calculus, but fear you'll be in a class of young adults desperately competing to get into medical school—or if taking a class while sipping coffee in your robe and slippers appeals to you—distance learning is the way to go.

Almost 60 percent of students are past "traditional" college age, according to Eduventures, an educational research and consulting service.

Distance learning, also called distance education, is found in a variety of formats. There are classes offered in "real time," classes that you can take on your own schedule, classes where you never meet in person, and classes in which some actual face-to-face interactions are required. Entire degrees (from a bachelor's to a doctorate), certificate courses, credit and noncredit classes, continuing education courses, and courses for professional development are all possibilities with distance learning. Delivery of class materials can be via the Internet, videoconferencing, satellite, cable TV, and so on.

If you're looking to take classes toward a degree, or transfer credit classes to another institution, it's imperative that you choose your distance-learning classes from an accredited institution, and if you want your credits to transfer, check to see whether the receiving college will accept your distance-education credits. To be honest, the perception of diploma mills dies hard. Surveys show about one out of three employers looks somewhat askance at a distance-education degree. So before signing up for credit courses, do your homework. Visit www.distancelearn.about.com for a wealth of information on distance learning, accredited institutions, free online courses, financial information, and the like. Another site, www.classesusa.com, also contains information related to distance education.

People who do best with this type of instruction are self-starters who like to work independently, have good time-management skills, are goal oriented, and feel comfortable using technology as a teaching tool. If you know you'd miss the interaction of spirited discussions and immediate feedback from professors and fellow students, distance learning wouldn't be the right choice for you. In fact, distance-learning courses have a dropout rate about 20 percent higher than do brick and mortar courses.

Cost varies widely. For example, at the University of Phoenix, a major accredited player in distance education, about 100,000 students "attend" online undergraduate, graduate, and doctoral programs. The cost per credit for an undergraduate course is about $500; for a graduate course, about $600; and for a doctoral course, about $700. You can register for unlimited 30-day access to one course for $9.95 or for a year's unlimited access to personal and business classes for $99.99 through QuickKnowledge (www.quickknowledge.com or 888-606-0004). If you don't want to pay at all,

---

More than 2.3 million students take distance-learning courses in the United States, according the to Distance Learning Link Program.

ThirdAge (www.thirdage.com) offers free online workshops, such as Get Ready to Invest or Master Your Sex Life. SeniorNet (www.seniornet.org) offers free tutorials, guides, and discussion-based courses as well.

The world of education is literally at your fingertips.

Adult Education

Although adult education courses can be taken in the distance format, let's turn our attention to taking courses in an actual classroom setting but without worrying about credits, degrees, or transferability.

As mentioned before, many institutions of higher learning give breaks to mature learners. At Florida's state universities, for example, tuition is waived for adults age 60 and older if there is space available, they meet Florida residency requirements, and classes are not taken for credit. State colleges and universities in Texas allow seniors (65 and older) to take up to 6 free hours of credit or noncredit courses per semester or summer term, if space allows. Of course, credit-free also means exam-free, homework-free, and term paper–free! Great deals are out there. Contact the local colleges to see about their individual tuition policies.

If you're more interested in a residential program (but not a dorm!), look into Senior Summer School (www.seniorsummerschool.com or 800-847-2466). You can take a 2-week current events class offered by San Diego State University for an all-inclusive (sans transportation) price of $1,600. Elderhostel (www.elderhostel.org) combines education and travel. How about the 12-day "Birding: The Hot Spots of Costa Rica" offering for about $1,900? Sign us up!

If you'd rather stay closer to home and are interested in learning for its own sake, many noncredit adult-education classes, community classes, and enrichment classes exist. One member-driven organization of adult learners, the Osher Lifelong Learning Institute (www.osherfoundation.org), is represented on campuses in about 40 states and in Canada. For example, the University of South Carolina (Beaufort) charges a $25 annual membership fee and registration fees ranging from $4 to $60 per term. You may then take as many courses during each term as you'd like. You can take peer-taught courses in areas such as language, political issues, science, and literature.

With all the options available, lifelong learning can easily become a reality.

Grandma Moses (Anna Mary Robertson Moses) began painting in her late seventies and continued painting for more than 20 years.

HOBBIES

Winston Churchill once said, "Broadly speaking, human beings can be divided into three classes: those who are toiled to death, those who are worried to death, and those who are bored to death." To be sure you don't fall into the third category, consider some hobbies as you reprogram your time. A hobby enriches your life by increasing your knowledge, sharpening your skills, and/or bringing you inner peace.

You may already be an avid golfer, tennis player, reader, oenophile (wine lover), or philatelist (stamp collector). There are an endless variety of hobbies out there; the second stage of your life is a perfect opportunity to hone old hobbies and explore new ones. Here are some examples.

Genealogy. If you want to find out more about your ancestors, there are dozens of books written on the subject, courses you can take, and the treasure trove that is the Internet. (Check out the resources listing for this chapter for a few suggestions.)

Dance. Exotic, salsa, line, ballroom, square, swing . . . you get the idea. Some of these don't even require a partner—just show up.

Photography. With digital cameras, you can now zip your creations to far-flung relatives with the press of a button.

Reading. After relocating to Bellingham, Washington, Melanie F. began a book club that meets every 6 weeks. Members alternate picking books and hosting the meetings in their homes. She not only met more people and expanded her social-support group, but she's reading a heck of a lot of good literature. Many books now contain discussion guides because of the booming popularity of reading clubs. Your local library or bookstore can give you information about setting up book clubs as well as recommend lists. (The bookstore where Melanie's club members purchase their books gives them a 10 percent discount.) Or you can access a site such as www.bookbrowse.com. If you don't want to leave your home, you can join an online book club; for a few possibilities, browse www.book-clubs-resource.com.

Exercise/sports. Improving your body as well as your mind is certainly a noble endeavor. Your local health club, YMCA/YWCA or Jewish community center, and many medical centers offer fitness programs or facilities, from aerobics and swimming to weights and yoga. Sign up with a personal trainer for a few classes to get started on the right track, or lace up those sneakers and start walking. Consider taking up a new sport. So many baby boomers have taken up snowboarding that they've been called "grays on trays." What about bowling? Nancy and Jeff S. recently moved to northeast Florida and invited some new friends and acquaintances to bowl once a week. Sixteen people now meet at Coquina Lanes every Thursday at 4:00. They've named themselves the "Alley Oops."

Acting. If you've been longing to perform under the bright lights, consider joining an acting troupe. Helene G. lives in Leisure World in Silver Spring, Maryland, and snagged a role as Anna in *The King and I* through Leisure World's Fun and Fancy Theatre Group. If you don't want to be onstage, consider a behind-the-scenes role such as helping with makeup, lighting, costumes, scenery, or publicity. If you are uncertain where to look, call the theater department of your local college or university and ask for suggestions, or look under "theaters" in the Yellow Pages. In 1999, there were 79 senior performing groups in the United States. This number has mushroomed to about 600 today.

Birding. The U.S. Forest Service reports that the quickest growing outdoor activity in the United States is birding. With 10,000 bird species, enjoyment of nature, and the social aspect of being in a group, this is a great hobby. A few good sites include: www.birding.com, www.birder.com, www.audubon.org, and www.birdwatching.com. As this last Web site states, enjoy "your lifetime ticket to the theater of nature."

Games. "Use it or lose it" is an adage frequently invoked in relation to keeping our brains energized. Research has shown people who stay cerebrally challenged tend to lead richer, fuller lives and may even stave off diseases such as Alzheimer's. Jason R. and his wife, Beverly, arrange a monthly game night with four other couples. They usually alternate among Pictionary, Trivial Pursuit, Outburst, Charades, and card games and enjoy the social interaction as much as the intellectual stimulation. On a more solitary note, you can enjoy crossword puzzles, sudoku, acrostics, and jigsaw puzzles. Try www.upuzzles.com or www.queendom.com (click on "mind stretchers") for a good selection, or the hot Nintendo game Brain Age, which was designed by a neuroscientist.

VOLUNTEERING

If you find that classes, working, hobbies, and/or travel aren't enough to give you a feeling of satisfaction and fulfillment, consider Winston Churchill's words: "We make a living by what we get; we make a life by what we give."

More than one in three American adults volunteered in 2005, averaging about 50 hours per year, according to the federal government. The study found that women donate their time more than men. Utah has the most volunteers (50 percent of its residents) and Nevada the fewest (19 percent). Although by no means all-inclusive, here's an A-to-Z list of volunteer opportunities.

Adult literacy. One in four adults in America struggles with literacy issues. To address this crisis, Proliteracy Worldwide (www.proliteracy.org or 888-528-2224) is attempting to recruit 100,000 volunteers.

Big Brothers/Big Sisters. According to the organization, the only requirements are a willingness to make a new friend and a desire to share some fun with a young person. Contact www.bbbs.org or check the Yellow Pages for a local agency.

Community policing/patrols. Contact your local police department or the Office of Community Oriented Policing Services (COPS) at www.cops.usdoj.gov

Disaster response. The workforce of the American Red Cross is 97 percent volunteers! This organization provides training, if necessary. Go online to www.red cross.org (click "volunteer") or call your local Red Cross unit or the National Headquarters at 800-733-2767.

Elimination of substandard housing. Habitat for Humanity is working in more than 80 countries to build affordable housing for people in need. Visit www.habitat.org, call the affiliate nearest you, or contact their Partner Service Center at 229-924-6935.

Food for the homebound. Bring food to people who are disabled or homebound through Meals on Wheels. More than one million nutritious meals are served every day through churches, charities, and citizen and community groups. Find a provider in your area, or contact the Meals on Wheels Association of America at www.mowaa.org or 703-548-5558.

Guardian ad litem or court-appointed special advocate work. Represent neglected and abused children during judicial proceedings. Contact CASA (Court Appointed Special Advocates for Children) at www.nationalcasa.org or 800-628-3233.

Hospice care. Bring dignity and comfort to the terminally ill and their families. "Hospice is not a place but a concept of care." Contact the Hospice Foundation of America (www.hospicefoundation.org or 800-854-3402).

Income-tax preparation. Be one of more than 32,000 volunteer tax aides through the AARP Foundation. Contact www.aarp.org/taxaide or call 888-227-7669.

Job assistance. Dress for Success helps low-income women enter the workforce through the donation of work and interview-appropriate clothing. Or donate your time as a personal shopper, office helper, or clothes sorter for this global organization. Contact www.dress forsuccess.org and click on "locations" for the closest affiliate, or call 212-532-1922.

K.E.E N. (Kids Enjoy Exercise Now). Pair up with a mentally or physically challenged child or young adult and participate in recreational activities. Check out www.keenusa.org or call 866-903-5336.

Library work. Be a greeter, give tours, assist in clerical work, help introduce patrons to electronic resources, shelve books, prepare children's programs, index newspapers, and so on. Call your local library for available positions.

Mentoring. Help a young person improve his or her life by being there and providing a good example. Many companies, churches, and civic groups sponsor mentoring programs. Or contact the National Mentoring Partnership at www.mentoring.org, where you can enter your zip code and find a list of local organizations that provide mentoring or call 703-224-2200.

Nurturing. Join the Foster Grandparent Program and help children and teens with special or exceptional needs. There are several requirements to be a foster grandparent relating to your age, time commitment, and training. Foster Grandparents receive a modest stipend if income-eligible. For more information, contact www.seniorcorps.org or call 800-424-8867.

Offering assistance to the elderly and homebound. Join the Senior Companion Program and help those in need with transportation to appointments, shopping, and other helpful chores. Senior companions receive reimbursement for some costs and service-related accident and liability insurance. The Senior Companion Program can be accessed through www.seniorcorps.org or 800-424-8867.

Providing help for the homeless. On any given night, almost a million people will be homeless. Churches, companies, and many civic organizations aid the homeless, or you can contact the National Law Center on Homelessness and Poverty, whose goal is to help prevent and end homelessness. They can be reached at www.nlchp.org or 202-638-2535.

Quilting. If you like to sew, you can provide new, homemade blankets or quilts to ill or traumatized children from birth to 18 years of age through the 100 percent volunteer Linus Project (www.projectlinus.org or 309-664-7814), or make a quilt/sleeping bag for a homeless person (www.reese.org/sharon/uglyqult.htm or 717-289-4335).

Reading. Read to children in clinic waiting rooms through Reach Out and Read (www.reachoutandread.org or 617-629-8042) or Recording for the Blind and Dyslexic (www.rfbd.org or 866-732-3585).

Special Olympics work. Join more than 700,000 Special Olympics volunteers at the local, state, national, or international level. Contact www.specialolympics.org or call 202-628-3630.

Tutoring. Go through a community or faith-based organization to tutor children or adults, or contact VolunteerMatch at www.volunteermatch.org or 415-241-6868 for opportunities near you.

Ushering. If you want to enjoy operas or plays as well

as contribute to the art world, consider volunteering to be an usher. Generally, theaters prefer a commitment on a regular basis, and of course you'll need to arrive early, be helpful and courteous, dress the part, and be able to assist those who need it. Contact your local performing-arts center.

Voter registration. The voter turnout since 1972 has remained virtually unchanged. Help get the vote out! Contact your Board of Elections to become a voter registration volunteer.

Walking a shelter dog. Contact your local Humane Society, Animal Shelter League, or ASPCA. Get exercise while you do a good deed!

Xenophon Therapeutic Riding Center. Sign up to help with therapeutic riding lessons for disabled children and adults. You may groom the horses, provide lessons, or work on landscaping or repairs. For a list of additional therapeutic riding centers, go to www.narha.org and click on "Find a Center."

Your chance to make a difference. Here's the catchall category. Think of what you can do to give back. For example, the fourth Saturday of every October has been designated "Make a Difference Day" by *USA Weekend* magazine. To get involved with this initiative, go to www.usaweekend.com and click on "Make a Difference Day." The site has an idea generator to help you formulate a project as well as register a project. Or, think locally. Which of your friends, neighbors, or relatives could use a hand with his or her household or yard chores, grocery shopping, or babysitting? Offer your services; people often feel uncomfortable asking for help.

Zoo work. What's doing at the zoo for volunteers? Interpret exhibits, help maintain the grounds, care for baby animals, assist with promotional events, be a docent, help the keepers feed the animals, or clean and maintain animal exhibits.

If that list isn't enough, here are some additional organizations that list numerous opportunities to volunteer.

More than 35 million Americans over 50 belong to AARP, an organization that "is dedicated to enhancing quality of life for all as we age." Put "volunteer" in the search bar at www.aarp.org or call 888-687-2277.

Network for Good (www.networkforgood.org) was founded by the AOL, Cisco Systems, and Yahoo!. This site allows you to volunteer and/or donate money.

Points of Light Foundation, founded by President

A winning combination: Researchers at Johns Hopkins University found that previously sedentary volunteers in Baltimore elementary schools burned twice the number of calories over a period of a year.

George H. W. Bush in 1990, works with the Volunteer Center National Network to help bring solutions to community problems. Contact the foundation at www.pointsoflight.org or 800-750-7653.

VolunteerMatch helps you to search for volunteer opportunities (almost 40,000 of them!) by zip code or type of organization. Contact them at www.volunteermatch.org or 415-241-6868.

Volunteers of America has faith-based programs that work to rehabilitate people, not just treat their symptoms. Their outreach includes correction facilities, schools, churches, and social-service and law-enforcement agencies. Offices are community based, so find one near you, go to www.volunteersofamerica.org, or call the national office at 202-729-8000.

STAYING IN THE GAME

Will you learn, then earn, and then return? According to the 2006 "Retirement Confidence Survey," sponsored by the Employee Benefit Research Institute (EBRI), 77 percent of boomers plan to work full or part time after leaving their primary careers, or alternate work and leisure time before retiring completely. Finances are the biggest reason for working, but enjoyment of work and being enticed by the idea of doing something different career-wise are also factors.

Let's take a look at the financial aspects of work first. The EBRI found that 68 percent of current workers (including their spouses) had less than $50,000 socked away for retirement, and almost 60 percent reported that they didn't expect to receive any health insurance from their employers.

Assume that you don't have to work for financial reasons. Should you still work? The nonfinancial rewards of work can be just as compelling. As described in Chapter 1, these include a sense of identity, status, intellectual engagement, social interaction, structure, and feelings of pride and accomplishment. Recall that in the Cornell Retirement and Well-Being Study, referred to in Chapter 1, the major reason for retiring for both men and women was "to do other things." If there aren't other things you'd rather be doing, by all means, keep working as long as you can (if you have a significant other who's okay with it).

Ironically, it's the more affluent retirees, affected by the recent stock market decline and now unable to survive on their investments, who are returning to work in the greatest numbers. People at the lowest income levels don't have as many investments and tend to live primarily off Social Security.

Of course, work options don't have to be all or nothing—full time or no time. You can work part time or part of the year, consult on a freelance basis, transition to a new career, or start your own business.

Let's say you want to work, for whatever reason, but also wish to change gears. What are some of the realities and options of staying in the workforce or reentering it after leaving a primary career?

Ageism

Does age discrimination exist? Not legally. The federal Age Discrimination in Employment Act (ADEA), passed in 1967, states, "It shall be unlawful for an employer to fail or refuse to hire or to discharge any individual or otherwise discriminate against any individual with respect to his compensation, terms, conditions, or privileges of employment, because of such individual's age."

There can be a gap between legality and reality, however. During 2005, the Equal Employment Opportunity Commission (EEOC) received 5,088 age-discrimination complaints, the average job search was 17.8 weeks for people under 55 years old, but 24.1 weeks for those over 50, and Texas A&M Economics professor Joanna Lahey found that companies were more than 40 percent more likely to interview a younger job seeker rather than an older job seeker.

Unfortunately, some employers feel that older workers are more set in their ways, have less energy and more health problems, aren't as technologically savvy, require higher salaries, and won't work as hard or long as younger workers. Historically, the implicit agreement was that an employee would stay with one company throughout his or her work career, starting out at lower wages, but progressing to higher wages as he or she became older. This paradigm is no longer true. With people routinely changing jobs every several years, and younger workers wanting higher wages when they come on board, the old way is no longer the model.

Most experts are upbeat about the future of older workers, however. With baby boomers retiring from primary careers (more than 76 million), and fewer younger workers to replace them (48 million Gen X employees), labor shortages will force companies to retain, retrain (if necessary), and value the older employee. For many employers, the bottom line will be

(continued on page 37)

The distinction of oldest employee goes to F. Waldo McBurney, 104, a Kansas beekeeper and author of *My First 100 Years!*

BEST EMPLOYERS FOR PEOPLE OVER 50

Here's a look at AARP's 2006 top 25 rankings of the best employers for workers over 50. If you live in one of these areas, check these companies out.

✳ Mercy Health System (Janesville, Wisconsin)

✳ Lee Memorial Health System (Ft. Myers, Florida)

✳ Bon Secours Richmond Health System (Richmond, Virginia)

✳ Leesburg Regional Medical Center and the Villages Regional Hospital (Leesburg, Florida)

✳ Yale-New Haven Hospital (New Haven, Connecticut)

✳ VW of America, Inc. (Auburn Hill, Michigan)

✳ MIT (Cambridge, Massachusetts)

✳ Oakwood Healthcare System Inc. (Dearborn, Michigan)

✳ First Horizon National Corp. (Memphis, Tennessee)

✳ Hoffman-La Roche Inc. (Nutley, New Jersey)

✳ Centegra Health System (Woodstock, Illinois)

✳ Stanley Consultants (Muscatine, Iowa)

✳ Scripps Health (San Diego, California)

✳ Brevard Public Schools (Viera, Florida)

✳ Beaumont Hospitals (Southwood, Michigan)

✳ Principal Financial Group (Des Moines, Iowa)

✳ The Aerospace Corporation (El Segundo, California)

✳ Inova Health System (Falls Church, Virginia)

✳ The YMCA of Greater Rochester (Rochester, New York)

✳ St. Barnabas Health Care Organization (West Orange, New Jersey)

✳ SC Johnson (Racine Wisconsin)

✳ Atlantic Health System (Florham Park, New Jersey)

✳ St. Mary's Medical Center (Huntington, West Virginia)

✳ Virginia Commonwealth University (Richmond, Virginia)

✳ Carondelet Health Network (Tucson, Arizona)

whether the employee meets their company's needs; the experience, work ethic, and maturity of boomers will become valuable commodities.

Job-Hunting Suggestions

First, consider what's important to you. Is the amount of money crucial, or is flexibility, novelty, helping others, or using your strengths just as high a priority? Will you need additional formal education? Are you willing to make trade-offs? A career counselor or career coach can help crystallize and focus your priorities and narrow your job search. For assistance from one, contact the National Board for Certified Counselors and Affiliates (www.nbcc.org or 336-547-0607) or the Coach Connection (www.findyourcoach.com or 800-887-7214), or join a group such as the Five O'Clock Club (www.fiveoclockclub.com or 800-538-6645), which assists in job searches.

You can also take self-tests to help you determine where your interests lie. Free self-assessments are available at www.careergames.com. This site also gives tips on interviewing, negotiating, and answering difficult interview questions. For additional free career quizzes, see the Web sites for this chapter in the back of the book.

Let friends, former colleagues, members of groups or professional associations you belong to, and acquaintances know you are looking for work—and what type of work you desire (about 35 percent of people are hired through networking). Volunteer in an area you are interested in, or work at a temporary staffing service to "try out" different work paths. (Adecco, www.usadecco.com, is one such company.) Not only will you find out if you're interested in the field, but you'll be ready and willing if the company decides to hire. Use newspapers or online search engines such as Monster.com and Hot Jobs.com (although only about 7 percent of jobs are filled through Internet sites, according to the *Wall Street Journal* Executive Career Site). You can also go online to sites geared toward workers 50 and older, such as Seniors4Hire (www.seniors4hire.org or 714-848-0996) or Senior Job Bank (www.seniorjobbank.org or 888-501-0804).

If you have a particular area of expertise, look for Web sites that reflect your background and have job postings. For example, Mary S. relocated to New Jersey after a divorce and wanted to continue in her profession as a media specialist in an elementary school. She went

---

To file an age-discrimination complaint with the EEOC at either the state or federal level, call 800-669-4000.

FROM CPA TO AP-ECON

Stephen L. worked for many years as a CPA, first in an international accounting firm, then as a controller of a telecommunications firm. After almost 30 years, Stephen decided to change gears and become a high school teacher, something he had always wanted to do but felt he couldn't afford with a non-working spouse and three young children. He knew his credentials, including salary and years of service, would be intimidating to a private high school, so he fashioned his résumé to illustrate the strengths that pertained to his teaching business classes, including his instructing continuing-education classes for his colleagues, his computer proficiency, and his organizational abilities. He downplayed the elements of his jobs that were not as relevant, such as familiarity with depreciation methods for financial reporting. Today, Stephen is happily teaching AP economics, personal finance, marketing, and accounting (of course!) in a Catholic coeducational school in Virginia.

to Rutger's University Web site and found media specialist positions that required her specific credentials, as well as openings in the area where she was relocating. Also, don't overlook small companies!

To find out where the jobs are (and hence, where the demand is), check out the U.S. Department of Labor's Occupational Outlook Handbook, which is revised every other year; it contains a treasure trove of information about growth projections, wages, education, and working conditions for specific careers. Predicted areas of highest employment growth until 2014 include healthcare (no big surprise as we boomers advance in age), employment services, technical (think computer) services, the leisure and hospitality industry (all the boomers are ready to spend their money!), and the financial-services industries. If these areas appeal to you, you're in luck! Click on www.bls.gov/oco to access the newest edition of the handbook online.

The Bureau of Labor Statistics estimates that by 2010 approximately 33 percent of the labor force will be comprised of "mature" workers (those over 45).

You'll also have to update (or dust off) your résumé. Don't feel obligated to list every job you've ever had; concentrate on those positions that are pertinent to the employment you are seeking. If you're looking to change careers, or if you're reentering the workforce after a hiatus, concentrate on the transferable skills applicable to the new position, and downplay job titles if necessary.

Emphasize your accomplishments, results, and outstanding qualifications in a succinct paragraph at the top of your résumé. Include any computer expertise, coursework, or professional development to accentuate your openness to learning, as well as your e-mail address. When e-mailing a résumé, don't send it as an attachment in case it can't (or won't) be opened, and e-mail a copy to yourself prior to sending it to a potential employer to make sure it looks like you want it to look. In your cover letter, emphasize that you are a proven entity (don't say you've worked for 30 years) and that you are flexible, adaptable, and willing to learn, and that you have transferable skills.

There is some disagreement as to what type of résumé older workers should use. A functional résumé highlights accomplishments and talents and downplays *when* the work was done. But many employers and recruiters know this type of résumé can be hiding work gaps and age, and dislike them. Chronological résumés are the preferred choice among most of those in hiring positions, but they can be a disadvantage if your latest experience doesn't match the new position, or if age matters. Combining both types into a "chrono-functional" résumé could be the best bet. An excellent site for résumé types, sample résumés, and tips on negotiating and networking can be found at www.careerjournal.com. Click on "Job-Hunting Advice."

Once your foot is in the door—you have the interview—again emphasize your flexibility, motivation, interpersonal skills, and willingness to learn. Let them know you want to contribute to the company and that you're not looking for a job because you're broke! Use your age to your advantage, stressing your experience with problem solving, a proven track record, and strong work ethic. If you're happy to work part-time, let the prospective employer know you are a bargain. You have tons of experience, but you don't have to be paid what they might pay a younger, full-time employee. Slip in (assuming it's true) how you're still playing tennis or love

For more suggestions on answering difficult interview questions, go to www.aarp.org and type "tough interview questions" into the search bar.

to downhill ski, hike, or swim to convey that you are a vital, energetic person. Address any questions (insidious or obvious) about your age forthrightly by reassuring the interviewer you can handle the job as well as bring experience, enthusiasm, and wisdom to the position. If asked how you feel about working for someone younger than you, AARP suggests you respond, "When I get to the point where I can't learn from someone younger or older than I, I will stop working." Be sure you're knowledgeable about the company, and follow up with a handwritten thank-you note.

New Careers

Don't sell yourself short! There are jobs to consider besides the usual greeter, retailer, cashier, food preparer, and server positions. Here are just a few possibilities to ponder if you'd like to embark on a new direction.

Health-care worker. For careers in demand, look to the health-care industry and consider diploma courses to become a home-health aide, medical assistant, pharmacy technologist, nurse aide, EKG technologist, or physical-therapy aide. These are relatively short courses (weeks or months), relatively low cost (usually under $1,000), and many employers will reimburse your tuition costs if you work for them. There are 2-year associate of arts or associate of science degrees in such areas as medical transcription or respiratory therapy. Look to your local community college or technical school for more information. If you have the time, energy, and money, look into pharmacy school. There is a huge demand for pharmacists, and the pay is excellent.

Captioner. A captioner converts the spoken word to text. Hearing-impaired students, television broadcasts, conventions, stockholder meetings, and court proceedings may all use the services of a captioner. There is an increased need for captioners due to mandatory closed captioning for 95 percent of all new television programs. Captioning can be done on-site or off-site, in real time or not. If you are working as an independent contractor, there are costs for the necessary equipment (around $15,000). Salaries average about $50,000, but can get into the six figures. For a list of programs and career paths, contact the National Court Reporters Association at www.ncraonline.org or call 800-272-6272.

Seasonal work. If you love the great outdoors, consider working at a national park, ski resort, ranch, theme park, tour company, on a ship, etc. For a seasonal commitment, you can receive lodging, meals, and a paycheck. It won't be the Ritz, and you won't make a fortune, but it may be the right thing if you're open to new experiences and like to work hard. For more information, contact www.coolworks.com—there is even a link for the "older and bolder"—or call 406-848-2380. Check out Xanterra Parks and Resorts (www.xanterra.com or

303-600-3400) if you're interested in managing the concessions (lodging, food, gift shops, etc.) at national or state parks or resorts.

Bank teller. If you like detail, you may want to pursue this position, which handles the routine operations of a bank. About 25 percent of bank tellers work part-time.

Customer-service representative. These employees serve as the liaison between the public and their companies. Most are employed by financial, communication, and insurance institutions. The U.S. Department of Labor predicts that employment of customer-service representatives will increase faster than the average through 2010. Maybe by then we won't always get a recording when we call a company! Or consider working from home. Although it seems that scams abound in this category (stuffing envelopes, anyone?), there is a definite legitimate side to this industry. "Homeshoring" allows customer-service agents to work out of their homes, primarily in phone work and data entry. Some people hired for this type of work are independent contractors; others are employees of the company. Examples of firms that hire stay-at-home customer-service reps include: Working Solutions (www.workingsolutions.com), West Corporation (www.workathomeagent.com), LiveOps (www.liveops.com), and Alpine Access (www.alpineaccess.com). Pay ranges from $6 to $20 an hour, and there are certain home setup requirements.

Nursing-home feeding assistant. A new federal regulation allows people to be feeding assistants in nursing homes after an 8-hour training course. Previously, you had to be a nursing assistant, with at least 75 hours of training. The rule pertains to nursing homes that accept Medicare or Medicaid. Contact nursing homes near you for more information.

Tour guide. Escort groups or individuals through museums, important buildings, parks, and the like. For example, Tourmobile Sightseeing in Washington, DC, provides narrated shuttle tours to the historic sites in Washington and Virginia. Contact the attractions you are interested in and see if they hire and train tour guides.

Mystery shopper. According to Service Intelligence, a mystery shopping company, secret shoppers "anonymously observe and document the quality of service at a

---

Try out a new career. Vocation Vacations (www.vocationvacations.com or 866-888-6329) allows you to "test drive your dream job." Actor, alpaca farmer, wine-bar owner, jewelry designer . . . the list is exhaustive, and you pay a fee to be mentored by a pro in your area of interest.

store or business on a given day. Clients can then evaluate a sample of service delivery, product knowledge, and facility maintenance at corporate stores or franchises." Retail, health care, banking, finance, and fast-food restaurants are examples of where you could be a mystery shopper. Pay is about $10 to $25 per hour. Contact Service Intelligence (www.experienceexchange.com or 678-513-4776) or Mystery Shoppers (www.mystery-shoppers.com or 800-424-0871).

Focus-group member or survey subject. Who doesn't like to give their opinion? And what's better than giving it and being paid for it? Participating in surveys or focus groups can result in gifts or extra cash and is a fun way to spend a few hours. One of the authors served in a focus group after being approached by an employee of a consumer-research group in a fast-food restaurant. Two weeks later, for about 2 hours, 10 of us met in a conference room in an office building and were questioned on our eating habits, amounts we spent on meals, how often we ate out, and our favorite kinds of food, while researchers behind one-way mirrors were taking notes (they informed us of this). When the pleasant discussion,

accompanied by snacks, was over, we were each handed $60 in cash. To find a research company near you, access the New York American Marketing Association Greenbook (www.greenbook.org) and search their national directory by desired location, or look for ads in local or college newspapers. Earn cash or prizes over the Internet at www.buzzback.com. Whether you are asked to participate in a survey is a function of the demographics a company needs.

Bed-and-breakfast owner. What about using your home or purchasing a place for a B and B? Some retirees go this route, but be sure to consider some of the issues involved: The location must be desirable, the place you plan to use must be zoned for a B and B, and you'll need to obtain insurance. Gross annual income for an average-size bed and breakfast is around $60,000. If interested, visit some B and Bs and take a seminar about owning and operating one. You can take online courses at www.seminars-on-line.com, which run from $60 to $200 depending on content and length, of course.

Job-sharer. Consider taking a full-time position and sharing it with a coworker. Robert T., for example, taught

---

Wonder what kind of a reference a former employer is giving you? You can hire a reference company to check for between $50 and $65. An example of a company that performs such a service is www.jobreference.com.

HOW MUCH DOES IT *REALLY* COST TO START A BUSINESS?

New York Magazine (February 2006) provides the start-up costs for eight businesses started by real people:

Bakery: $38,005

Bar: $110,000

Bike shop: $ 90,000

Furniture store: $238,000

Handbag shop $ 72,500

Kids' store: $ 77,500

Restaurant: $341,500

Wine store: $156,913

high school biology for many years but wanted to scale back and have his afternoons free for golf and volunteer work. He was able to work out a deal with a new mother, Cay S., who also wanted to return to teaching science, but on a part-time basis. So they shared the full-time science position, prorating their benefits (sometimes one person is covered by a spouse or has other arrangements and may be able to forgo all or some of the benefits). If you're interested in this type of position, and you have a willing coworker, submit a proposal to your employer outlining the concept of job-sharing, how the position would be structured, and what the benefits are to the employer.

Teacher of English as a second or foreign language (ESL/EFL). If you'd like to combine work and travel, consider teaching English in a foreign country or at one of many locations within the United States. Many positions require a college degree; some require a TEFL

(Teaching English as a Foreign Language) certificate, which can be obtained in the United States. TESOL (Teachers of English to Speakers of Other Languages (www.tesol.org or 888-547-3369) gives locations of courses and answers many questions about pursuing this career). ESL Teacher's Board (www.eslteachersboard.com) lists positions and descriptions for ESL teachers. For example, a 1-year contract teaching in China (Guangzhou) with a TESOL or equivalent certification is advertised with a salary of about $2,500 per month.

Club Med staffer. No, you don't have to be a hard-body to apply for a position with Club Med, and about 90 positions are available, from accountant to wind-surfing instructor. See www.clubmedjobs.com for more specifics.

Work on a cruise ship. Contact each cruise line separately for a listing of available positions. Some Web sites charge a fee for this service. For a list of cruise lines, go to www.raynorshyn.com, and click on "Official Cruise Line Links." For men only (who like to dance): You can be a gentleman host on a cruise ship www.theworking vacation.com).

Realtor. Real estate attracts those who are people oriented, flexible, realize that there won't be a steady paycheck, and don't wish to have a nine-to-five job. You'll need to take the appropriate real-estate course, pass the licensing exam, and be sponsored by a broker or real-estate company in the state in which you wish to be licensed. Contact the Board of Realtors in the location where you wish to be licensed to find out the specifics.

Trucker. "Get your motor running. . . ." The American Trucking Association estimates that there is a need for 540,000 truckers a year, particularly long-haul heavy-duty truck drivers. Average weekly pay in 2004 was $682, and this is expected to rise with a shortage of truckers. Background checks, an English language requirement, a commercial driver's license (CDL), and training if you're an entry-level CDL driver are usually necessary for employment.

Starting Your Own Business

The dream of some retirees is to take a passion or hobby and turn it into a money-making venture, whether it's painting, writing, opening a restaurant or boutique, or having a consulting business. Although 16 percent of workers over 50 are self-employed, the reality is that about half of businesses fail within the first 4 years. Here are a few things to think about if you're contemplating starting your own business.

Money. Cash-flow problems are the biggest contributor to small-business failures. Look into sources of outside money, rather than funding your business with personal savings. A business plan that includes all the financial information should be reviewed by an accountant or financial planner and should also define your niche market.

Personality. You need perseverance, since the time to plan and turn a profit can take a few years; the ability to cope with rejection, since you are likely to experience some; the stamina to start a new venture; and the desire and energy to solicit business. Think about why you are pursuing the goal of having your own business: Are you bored? Looking for a new life experience? Using it as an escape from dealing with other issues? Do you want to make money? Or is it a combination of factors?

Sole proprietorship, joint enterprise, or franchise. Consider whether you'd like a partner to share the work as well as the profits, or decide if a franchise is a possibility for you. Investments in franchises can range from under $15,000 to $400,000 or more. Check out www.franchisedirect.com, or www.franchise.com for more information.

Will it be "everyone back in the (labor) pool"? Some will be pushed in, some will tentatively test the water, some will jump in wholeheartedly, and some will avoid the (labor) pool like hydrophobes.

In summary, instead of retirement being about what you're not doing (working, raising a family, rushing from one commitment to another), make it about what you are doing (letting your creative juices flow, learning new things, rediscovering yourself and those you love, giving back, and "smelling the roses"). As George Lorimer, editor of the *Saturday Evening Post*, said, "You've got to get up every morning with determination if you're going to go to bed with satisfaction." It's really never too late to start something new. Golda Meir was first elected prime minister of Israel at 71!

WHAT ARE THE OPPORTUNITIES FOR TRAVEL?

"Twenty years from now you will be more disappointed by the things that you didn't do than the ones you did do. So throw off the bowlines. Sail away from the safe harbor. Catch the trade winds in your sails. Explore. Dream. Discover. . . ."
—*Mark Twain*

Dreaming about that once-in-a-lifetime South Seas vacation? Considering comforting children in an orphanage in Yaroslavl, Russia? Single and interested in travel? Disabled but wish to take a trip? Longing to meet emperor penguins in Antarctica nose to beak? Want an educational vacation, or looking for a place to take the grandkids?

Where can you find the best options for a last-minute getaway? How can you feel confident you're getting a bargain? Let's take a look at some specific aspects of travel. It can be an exciting and rewarding way to spend some of those 168 hours per week as you reprogram your time in the second half of your life.

WHERE TO START

Travel is often at the top of the list of activities that retirees say they look forward to during the less stressful years after their primary career is "history." One of the big decisions people who are not seasoned travelers face is whether to travel with a group or to plan the trip yourself and travel alone or with a small group of friends.

Visiting Italy on a 2-week group trip planned by a large travel agency, for example, will not be the same trip that four friends might plan with a map and a rental car. With an agency, most of every day will be planned: transportation, sightseeing, meals, lodging, and for the most part, the cost is up front. You might also have the opportunity to make some new friends. If you make your own plans, you have the opportunity to change those plans on a whim and explore new places you stumble across.

What kind of traveler are you? Do you want a knowledgeable guide to lead you through unknown places and help you understand the new culture or are you more likely to strike out on your own, meet the local people, and create your own itinerary?

true LIFE **Frequent travelers Lesley and Fred K. share a few thoughts and tips on do-it-yourself travel.**

Fred and I discovered a love for travel when we were still just dating and our college team went to the Rose Bowl. We traveled with friends on the charter trip to California, and instead of just lounging by the pool during the days leading up to the game, we bought a guidebook and rented a car.

Over the years we enjoyed many family vacations with our four children, but once the youngest was in junior high we realized our dream of taking a "just us" vacation and traveled to Europe. Since then we have gone to Europe at least 20 times and have planned each trip ourselves. Sometimes the vacations are months in planning, and others are much more spontaneous. A new destination requires more preparation, but stumbling across a great airfare to London may inspire us to book tickets for the next weekend! Here are some things that work well for us.

1. If you're traveling to a new country and you'll be visiting several cities, try going to a smaller city first. For example, arriving in Paris after an overnight flight can be overwhelming and even discouraging. Try taking a train or driving to the Normandy coast or the Barbizon Forest area and settling in for a few days. You'll be much more comfortable with the language, the pace, and the culture and ready to get the most out of your time in Paris.

2. Do your homework. We usually read multiple guidebooks to get a good overview. After our basic plan is in place, we select hotels for at least the first and last

destinations. Many hotels can be booked online, or you can call the hotel directly. Don't hesitate to ask for special offers. We once traveled to London at the last minute and called our favorite hotel, and I discovered that dinner and two tickets to a play of our choice was included if we stayed three nights. We prefer smaller independent hotels, inns, or guesthouses instead of chain hotels. Often, the hotel owner was the person to welcome us and ask us to sign the guest register. Experiences like this often set the tone for our overall European experience. Karen Brown's books are an excellent reference for charming places to stay, and they offer good sample itineraries.

3. We have found Rick Steves's books to be our favorite resources in planning what to see and do. Trip after trip, his recommendations have been right on target.

4. Whenever possible, take guided walking tours. There is no better way to really understand and appreciate what you are seeing. We usually feel very smart and informed after going on a walking tour, and the guides are excellent resources for restaurant recommendations.

5. If we miss a sight, or wish we had more time to spend in a particular locale, we always promise ourselves we will come back . . . and we do. The second time around (or third or fourth!), we are much more confident in our

TRAVEL INSURANCE

Taking a trip can be a substantial financial investment. Is travel insurance a good idea? In some cases, yes. Travel insurance can provide emergency medical evacuation or medical/dental referrals; reimburse you for lost or stolen luggage, a missed connection, or for trip cancellation due to your illness or that of a family member; pay for damage to rental cars; and assist with other travel needs. Keep in mind that terrorism or acts of war are rarely covered; read the policies very carefully prior to purchase! To compare travel-insurance quotes from more than 10 companies, contact www.insuremytrip.com or call 800-487-4722. Based on information you provide (cost of trip, age of travelers, medical limitations, etc.), you will be able to easily compare and contrast benefits.

choices and find the return trips especially enjoyable.

6.   Our experience has shown that it is easier and cheaper to reserve our rental car before we leave the states. Also, rates can be significantly less for a car with standard transmission.

7.   Forget about traveler's checks; cash machines are everywhere. Don't spend a lot of time figuring out how to save pennies here or there in exchanging money.

Be brave, plan your own trip if you wish, and enjoy learning about the culture when you spend time with the locals. Remember, spending the first few days in a small town will make you more comfortable in the big city. Don't be afraid to return to the same location. As they say, the third time's the charm! ⓣ

true LIFE **Linda and Frank B. take the attitude of "leave the planning to them" (the tour groups) when traveling to a foreign locale.**

When we plan trips to any remote or exotic location such as Africa, China, Machu Pichu, or the Galápagos Islands, we choose to go by guided tour. Safety and health are our primary concerns, but language barriers, difficult climates, political changes, and cultural differences also present challenges for most travelers that are best dealt with by competent tour companies. For example, while in Kenya, a member of our group was hurt in an accident while we were tenting on the Masai Mara. Our group leader contacted Nairobi, had a plane dispatched to our grass landing strip to collect the injured woman and her spouse, flew them back to the city, and had a representative meet them planeside and whisk them to a private hospital where she received excellent care (her MRI cost was $12.00!). She was then taken by the representative (who waited with the spouse at the hospital) to a hotel and checked into their room. The same representative returned the next morning to escort them to the doctor's office for a checkup and then returned them to the hotel. All this was part of the tour's service for its clients. I cannot imagine doing all that on one's own while trying to speak and understand Swahili!

When most of us think of taking guided tours,

Check your e-mail for free at a public library while you're vacationing.

the image of the old movie, *If It's Tuesday, This Must Be Belgium*, pops into our heads. However, the idea of spending an entire trip on a bus, trying to cover as much ground as possible in a 10-day period, is not the type of tour we're discussing. The groups we travel with are limited in size and focus on an in-depth immersion so that at the end of the trip, we will not only have seen fabulous sights, but with the help of our guides, we will have an understanding of the importance of the places we have visited as well as the history and culture of the people who live there. Using our trip to Africa as an example once again, we had one guide who traveled with us day and night. Drivers and guides in each country we visited supported her. All were well-versed in history and anthropology, and the drivers were fully trained mechanics (a good idea when driving in the bush! Did you know that "safari" literally means driving in circles?), which, combined, gave us a wonderful education while allowing us to be totally at ease in our surroundings.

From our point of view, one of the best things about traveling with a group is the people we meet.

Though we all arrive at our destination as strangers, we already have several things in common, such as an interest in that particular part of the world, a sense of adventure, and a love of travel. We have met fascinating people from all over the world and have become life-long friends with some. On the other side of the coin, it is a given that in every group there will be someone who is perpetually late, or complains about the food, or should have simply stayed home. However, the guides are trained to contain the negativity, and, overall, it is a minor hiccup!

Finally, if you are thinking of taking an exotic trip, research tour groups that specialize in the part of the world you wish to experience. There are many excellent companies to choose from, such as Lindblad if you have a hankering for taking an ice breaker to the North Pole (they have their own ships and oceanographers), or Abercrombie and Kent if you're heading to Africa (they have been there for decades and own their own jeeps, which is important because they control the maintenance of the vehicles, train their drivers and guides, and are well connected with the various governments).

According to the Travel Industry Association of America, adults 55 and over account for one-third of all trips taken within the United States.

NATIONAL GEOGRAPHIC ADVENTURE MAGAZINE'S TOP 10 OUTDOOR ADVENTURES

Grand Canyon	Boundary Waters, Minnesota
Appalachian Trail	Wind River Range, Wyoming
El Capitan	Hiking the Narrows in Zion National Park, Utah
Mendenhall Glacier, Alaska	Tree climbing in Atlanta
North Woods, Ossipee River, Maine	Hiking the Tahoe Rim Trail, California

Pesky details such as check-ins at airports and hotels are done behind the scenes, luggage is handled for you, and your guides truly educate you and want you to have a great experience. It's a win-win way to travel!ⓉⓁ

Okay, let's think about your destination. If you have the desire to travel, are not in the mood for a repeat trip to your favorite spot, and are feeling adventurous, these Web sites will be the encouragement you need to branch out and take a leap.

www.about.com/travel will make you feel more confident in choosing a novel location. Here you'll find information about what visitors need to know when traveling in Europe, the United States, or Asia. Find out about the latest budget-travel tips, the best B and Bs, or maybe the latest scuba diving information.

www.ricksteves.com/tours has been conducting all-inclusive budget tours since the 1970s. Rick Steves also publishes a series of guidebooks that concentrate on Europe, and he has had a travel show on PBS since 1991.

www.officialtravelinfo.com helps with destination information, vacation planning, and tourism information and provides virtual tours. Click on a map to choose your desired location. It can be fun to take a virtual tour in Africa, even if you have no plans to travel there.

www.go-today.com offers city and country packages, cruises, and unique tours at budget prices.

www.towd.com As the Web site states, "The Tourism Offices Worldwide Directory is your guide to official tourist information sources: government tourism offices, convention and visitors bureaus, chambers of commerce, and similar organizations that provide free, accurate, and unbiased travel information to the public.

Businesses such as travel agents, tour operators, and hotels are not included."

www.atlasnavigator.com links to virtually every airline, airport, hotel chain, and car-rental agency in the world. Everything is in one location! Check out all travel options at once.

www.infohub.com lists guided or self-guided vacation options. Some categories to consider include: trips geared to active or soft adventure, families, hobbies, romance, spirituality, culture and history, sports, and nature and wildlife. You can also read travel stories and learn about these trips and the guides who lead them. How about taking a gourmet vacation and visiting various cooking schools?

www.shawguides.com *Forbes* and the *Wall Street Journal* pick this as a top site to give you literally thousands of choices for learning and creative career programs worldwide. Here are just a few: cultural travel, cooking schools, golf and tennis schools, photography workshops, language vacations, and writers' conferences and workshops.

www.resortquest.com has more than 20,000 vacation rental condominiums, villas, and homes in 16 states as well as in Canada.

www.tntvacations.com, www.funjet.com, and www.vacationexpress.com allow you to peruse different packages, then either book online or through a travel agent.

true LIFE **Planning can be vital.**

Debbie, a retired community college professor, and Steve W., a retired executive from AT&T, wanted to hike, along with their three grown children, to the bottom of the Grand Canyon and spend the night there at Phantom Ranch, then hike up the next morning.

Since Phantom Ranch has such limited space, they called exactly 2 years prior to their trip, the longest advance reservations that the national park will allow. They were lucky and reserved five spots; within minutes, everything at the bottom was booked. ⓽

BE AN AIR COURIER

With overtones of Mata Hari or Agent 007, air couriers might seem to exist in a murky area of semilegitimate travel. Nothing could be further from the truth. Air couriers transport packages on overseas flights in exchange for reduced airfare—or sometimes even for free. Courier travel is overseen by the Federal Aviation Administration and has been around for 30 years. The concept behind courier travel is this: If time is of the essence in getting such things as legal or financial documents or computer-related parts from point A to point B, having a courier accompany them will get parcels through customs more quickly than if they are sent as cargo.

As an air courier, one needs to be flexible. Since you usually are not allowed to touch what you are ferrying, the package(s) go as part of your checked baggage, often permitting only one carry-on bag for yourself. You can generally make arrangements 1 to 3 months ahead of time. Last-minute opportunities with even larger savings over the usual 20 to 85 percent savings on airfare are also possible. You need a passport, and you are responsible for obtaining any necessary visas.

Of course, where you go will be dictated by the company's need. Popular destinations include Europe, the Far East, Mexico, and South America. Departures tend to be from major cities (New York, Miami, Chicago), and it's the courier's responsibility to get to these cities. You arrive at the airport, and someone from the company meets you there to assist you while you check in. When you deplane, you are met by another agent from the company, to whom you hand over your baggage claim and shipping papers, and you're done. Unless you're also functioning as a courier on your return flight, you can go back according to your prearrangement with the company (usually from a few days to several months later). Note that being a courier is most often a one-person deal. If you have a travel companion, that person would be on his or her own for airfare. Keep in mind that being a courier is a function of supply and demand. Courier companies charge the couriers higher airfares when there are more people willing to travel. During the "off" traveling times (winter and fall), your round-trip air prices will be much more attractive than during prime tourist season.

Okay, but how do you actually do it? Courier associations act as the intermediary between you and the courier companies. There is an annual membership fee ranging from $25 to $50 for access to the information. Contact these companies, which have been in existence for several years: Air Courier Association (www.aircourier.org or 877-303-4258), International Association of Air Travel Couriers (www.courier.org), or Courier Travel (www.couriertravel.org.). Another route is to approach courier companies directly, but there is a lot of turnover among these organizations. One to try is: Global Delivery Systems (www.globaldelsys.com or 800-995-2210).

true LIFE **James D. of Wood Ridge, New Jersey, became interested in serving as a courier after sitting next to men and women who were working as couriers on several vacation flights.**

"I realized it was so very easy, I would save a great deal of money, and I really had to do very little. I

PLANES, TRAINS, AND AUTOMOBILES

Some of these sites are specific to transportation; others allow searches for hotels or vacation packages as well.

* www.expedia.com (allows you to preview some destinations through a slide show)

* www.johnnyjet.com (deals in all categories)

* www.travelocity.com (deals in all categories)

* www.southwest.com (If Southwest flies from an airport near you, it's worth checking out their travel center.)

* http://cityguide.aol.com (lets you check out visitor information for the chosen city)

* www.airtreks.com ("We make around-the-world travel easy and affordable.")

* www.ryanair.com (low-cost European airline)

* www.orbitz.com (offers flexible stays, weekends, and bonus days options that you can use to search for cheaper travel times)

* www.raileurope.com (offers special savings if you're over 60)

* www.amtrak.com (Click on "Hot Deals" for some attractive deals.)

* www.sidestep.com (allows you to check out dozens of sites at the same time)

always wanted to go to Hong Kong, and after joining and checking out listings on International Association of Air Travel Couriers, www.courier.org, I was given a choice of three different flights from JFK to Narita, Japan, and then on to Hong Kong through a company called Jupiter (www.jupiterair.com). It would cost only $350 for the round trip. I quickly sent in a deposit to hold my flight, which was only 3 weeks away.

I had to be at the airport 3 hours before the flight. I met with a representative from Jupiter. My "cargo" was 67 cases of a popular weekly magazine. They were being shipped to Tokyo in my name for a swift and easy transfer through customs as my "personal baggage." I was given a little sticker to wear on my jacket, the airline ticket, and the receipts for the 67 cases of magazines. Then I was off to Tokyo. After the long flight, I was warmly welcomed by several staff members from Jupiter and waited for a few minutes for the cases of magazines. The staff put the magazines on the baggage movers and then we stood in front of the customs agent. He asked what was mine and what belonged to Jupiter. The customs agent opened three of the boxes and made sure they contained what they were supposed to contain. Then I was free to leave.

I was given the next airline ticket (to Hong Kong), and off I went for the next leg of my trip. I went to Kowloon and enjoyed the area for 10 wonderful days. Being a courier is great. An inexpensive flight to Asia, and nothing to carry but a few baggage tickets. I was determined to do it all again . . . and I have." Ⓛ

DISCOUNT TRAVEL

Chances are, the person sitting next to you on the airplane did not pay the same price for his or her ticket that you did. Two staterooms on a cruise liner boasting the same amenities can also have very different price tags.

What kind of shopper are you? Are you a full-price purchaser, ready to buy what you want when you want it? Are you willing to put up with the hassle of bargain shopping? Does price matter to you? If it does, and you look at getting a good deal as a challenge, keep reading and you'll find no end to the bargains available for

travel. These budget tips work especially well for retirees, since many are last-minute opportunities, and retirees tend to be more spontaneous because time is not the ruling factor in their lives.

The best tool to use in bargain shopping for travel is the Internet; it will become your best travel agent. When choosing a Web site, find one that is easy for you to navigate since the market is flooded with sites, and you have many from which to choose. Check multiple sites carefully before trusting that one's rates are indeed the lowest. Use your own experiences from past travel as a comparison, and make a few phone calls directly to a hotel or airline, the old-fashioned way, just to be sure. Some Web sites post comments from fellow travelers revealing the positive and the negative aspects of their budget-travel experience. One way to look at bargain shopping for travel is that your savings can fund your next trip! So if words like *discount*, *budget*, *bargain*, *good deal*, and *cut-rate* are music to your ears, let your fingers do the walking through the Internet, and start packing!

Where to Stay

Where to rest your weary head? Many budget options exist, including renting a villa, condo, or home for short-term or lengthy stays, or finding the ideal bed and breakfast or hotel. There are some outstanding places to stay that do not fit into the usual categories. Many active-adult communities offer inexpensive packages for a 2- to 4-day visit in exchange for a few hours of your time, universities offer rooms at reasonable prices in vibrant locations during their summer sessions, and even four- or five-star hotels offer lower prices if you know when to go. As with any agreement you enter into, however, caveat emptor (let the buyer beware). There can be restrictions, fees, penalties, etc., when booking travel, so read everything carefully!

www.globalfreeloaders.com is a free service that has more than 6,000 people in 100 countries willing to let you stay at their homes for free. (You need to be willing to do the same.)

www.evergreenclub.com (815-456-3111) is the "champion of the cost-conscious vacationer," according to *Frommer's Budget Travel* magazine. Joining the Evergreen Club ($30 for one person, $37.50 for two), allows people over 50 to access private homes and stay for rates of $15 per day for two people. Hosts provide clean, comfortable accommodations, hearty breakfasts, and acquaint you with their area.

www.lasvegas.com (866-678-2582) is a guide to bargains in Las Vegas (including shows, tours, and golf), as well as an opportunity to browse all the available hotels using a rating system that allows you to compare amenities and prices.

www.vacationrentals.com is a service for rental owners and renters. If you wish to rent, just click on the desired vacation location (both U.S. and international) and contact the property owner directly. You may also list, for free, a property you would like to rent.

www.ase.net searches more than 150,000 accommodations throughout the world and permits you to select the type of lodging, amenities, and price range you desire. This search engine can also show the results in different languages and display prices in various currencies.

www.hotels.com (800-246-8357 in the United States and Canada) claims to "have the best prices at the best places. Guaranteed." With more than 70,000 properties worldwide, this Web site has an extensive list of offerings.

www.quikbook.com (800-789-9887) has received kudos from *Condé Nast Traveler* magazine, *Forbes* "Best of the Web," and Frommers.com. Quikbook promises no ads or pop-ups, just great values on upscale hotels without charging for cancellations or changes to your reservation. Choose from premier collections, seaside favorites, hip hotels, historic hotels, spa retreats, and many more.

www.bbonline.com (800-215-7365) allows you to choose from 5,200 bed and breakfasts in the United States, Canada, Mexico, and the Caribbean with the help of 20,000 color pictures.

www.innsite.com provides information, by location or activity, on bed and breakfasts, country inns, and small luxury hotels in more than 50 countries.

www.hiayh.org proves that hostels aren't just for young people! This Web site will lead you to affordable accommodations in more than 4,000 locations in 60 countries.

Timeshares/Fractional Ownership/ Interval Ownership

You can create a mini-vacation by signing up for a promotional stay offered by the timeshare/fractional ownershp/interval ownership industry. Even if you have no intention of buying, you can enjoy these resort areas and learn what they have to offer. If you spend a few hours listening to their pitch (warning: they can be high-pressure), you can take advantage of a short stay in a nice area at a greatly reduced price. Or check to see if a time-share resort is close to where you are planning to vacation and stay a few extra days, or perhaps receive a gift certificate to an area restaurant for your time. Only about 10 percent of the visitors are persuaded to purchase a timeshare, but Cay S. visited one for fun and now is the happy owner of a week's stay in Duck, North Carolina. Look into offers from the Marriott Vacation Club International (www.vacationclub.com or 800-845-4226),

---

SAIL THE SEVEN SEAS

A staggering 80 percent of people who take a cruise do so again, and, according to the Cruise Information Service, there are 40 new cruise ships under construction. These two facts indicate there must be something to this type of travel! Check out the following cruise-related Web sites.

✳ www.vacationstogo.com (Check "90-Day Ticker" for cruise discounts.)

✳ www.cruise411.com ("Every cruise line, every ship, every cabin at the lowest price . . . guaranteed.")

✳ www.cruisevalue.com (Compare options among cruise lines.)

✳ www.cruisecompete.com (Enter the desired cruise, and agents will e-mail you a price.)

✳ www.cruisecritic.com (allows you to see ratings and reviews of the major cruise lines, as well as the best current bargains in the cruise industry.)

the Hyatt Vacation Club (www.hyatt.com), or the Ritz-Carlton Club (www.ritzcarltonclub.com or 800-221-5780).

Developing Communities

Along the lines of a timeshare vacation, you might enjoy staying in or near a developing community, with an orientation and a tour of the neighborhood as part of the package. Rates vary but usually include use of the facilities, breakfast and/or dinner, and perhaps a round of golf. Check out Del Webb's "Experience the Lifestyle" at www.delwebb.com (under FAQ) or 888-717-9777 or "Be a Preferred Guest" at Robson Communities in Arizona or Texas (www.robson.com or 800-732-9949). This is also a strategy for choosing a place to relocate, since you have an opportunity to interact with residents and really get a feel for the community.

Universities

Do you remember dormitory life way back when? Many universities, both stateside and international, will give you the chance to relive that experience when the students are away for the summer. For more than 100 sites in Britain and Ireland, explore www.venuemasters.com. In the States, contact the college or university directly for availability and rates. As an example, Catholic University of America in Washington, DC, charges $30 per night (pretax, double occupancy) with a minimum 3-week stay for an air-conditioned room with a kitchen, living room, and shared bath (no linens). Call 202-319-5291.

Bid Your Price

If you're one who enjoys leaving it up to chance, you might like to try "blindfold bookers." These Web sites ask you to bid on lodging, flights, rental cars, or vacation packages. You usually have a short time to decide and sometimes do not know exactly which hotel or airline you're getting, but once you bid (and it's accepted), it's yours! The hotels are rated, the airlines usually guarantee no more than one stop, and the prices are great.

The downside? Your credit card is immediately charged, and you may not be able to make any changes once your offer is accepted. If plans change, you're

How about staying in a monastery? Just off the Chicago Loop, the Benedictines are rolling out the red carpet for $145 a night, www.chicagomonk.org, or if you are visiting Rome, check out www.santasusanna.org for recommendations in the Eternal City and other cities in Italy.

stuck. In addition, some sites add a processing fee to each transaction. Better think about trip insurance if you go this route and if there's any chance you'd have to change plans (although keep in mind trip insurance doesn't cover everything either!). Two to look into are: www.priceline.com (pick a specific flight, hotel, or car, name your price, and find out the details after you pay); and www.ebay.com/travel (where you can sell as well as buy all things travel related).

Last-Minute Deals

These Web sites are great for the spontaneous traveler who is looking for adventure and is ready to go at the drop of a hat. These opportunities can come and go very quickly, so if you see something perfect, grab it, but keep in mind that you probably won't be able to make changes or cancel your trip after you book it.

* www.site59.com (one-stop, real-time, last-minute [59th minute] weekend packages)

* www.11thhourvacations.com (cruises, flights, hotels, and vacation packages)

* www.lastminutetravel.com (cruises, cars, hotels, and flights)

* www.moments-notice.com (cars, cruises, hotels, and flights)

* www.hotwire.com (more last-minute deals)

HOME/HOSPITALITY EXCHANGE

Want to live like the locals? Stay in a neighborhood, shop where they shop, maybe drive their cars, almost literally walk a mile in their shoes? If this type of travel appeals to you, consider a home exchange or hospitality exchange. Home exchanges allow you to use someone else's home while they are using yours. Or, you could go the route of a hospitality exchange. In this type of arrangement, you alternate hosting one another in your homes. If you're considering a particular location for retirement, a home exchange might be the perfect way to "try out" a place.

There are obvious financial benefits to home or hospitality exchanges. The cost of hotel rooms is inching upward, and depending on the size of your group, you may need more than one hotel room. With a home exchange you have access to a full kitchen and all the comforts of home (or apartment, yacht, condo, RV, etc.). In addition, you can be immersed in the area and live where "real" people live. If you go the hospitality-exchange route, you'll also have built-in tour guides for your visit and may end up making lifelong friends.

The downside? Well, of course, it's all a matter of trust. Several months prior to your trip, it's a good idea to engage in conversations via e-mail, phone, or letters to get a sense of your swappers and the particulars about

HOME/HOSPITALITY EXCHANGE INFORMATION

A sizable number of organizations are in the business of home/hospitality exchanges.

✳ HomeExchange.com (www.homeexchange.com or 800-877-8723). You can access the available homes for free, but in order to list your home, you pay a $99.95 annual membership fee. This site also provides a guide called "Trading Places," which includes sample contact letters and agreements.

✳ Intervac Home Exchange (www.intervacus.com or 800-756-4663) has been around the longest (50 years) and boasts the largest percentage of international listings, about 80 percent.

Depending on type of membership (Web or Web and printed material), fees range from $80 to $170 per year.

✳ Global Home Exchange (www.4homex.com or 250-740-1740) is a Canadian company that charges approximately $50.00 per year (US) for membership.

✳ Accessible Vacation Home Exchange (www. independentliving.org, then click on "Vacation Home Swap") is an exchange organization that specializes in homes that are accessible to the physically disabled.

---

the residence. Also, there could be a question of parity. Switching a 1,000-square-foot apartment in Washington, DC, for a veritable chateau in France may not seem equal, but this should not be the point in home exchanges. Housekeeping standards can be an issue as well if your cleanliness habits differ appreciably. The abilities to be flexible in your scheduling, to compromise, and to plan in advance are important qualities for this type of travel.

When choosing a company to list or search properties, there are several things worth noting. When listing your home, provide a photo and be honest about its amenities.

Seventy percent of Americans do not have a passport.

If you are exchanging cars, it's probably a good idea to get a contract. (Global Home Exchange offers a sample on their Web site—www.4homex.com.) Obtain insurance in case the trip is cancelled by either party. Make room in your closets for your visitors. Secure or remove any items you don't want used. Inform your neighbors there will be visitors so they can welcome them (and not call the police!). Come to a prior agreement on such things as phone and electric bills. Leave a guide containing information about your home's appliances, your area's attractions, contacts for repairs, etc. In general, being upfront and taking time to plan go a long way.

CRUISIN' THE USA

Since 9/11, more people have elected to vacation closer to home, traveling to places they can drive to themselves. So, although piling the kids in the van or station wagon every summer may be a thing of the past for you, this mode of travel is now at an all-time high.

And it's not just travel by car. Purchases of motorcycles and recreation vehicles have increased, notably among baby boomers. People who have never bought a motorcycle in their lives are now "easy riders." About 33 percent of Harley customers are first-time purchasers, and the surge in buyers over 40 has increased the average age of new Harley owners to 45 years old. Recreational-vehicle acquisition has also seen a significant increase. In a 2006 survey conducted by the National Association of RV Parks and Campgrounds (ARVC), the demographic profile of an RV owner in the United States comes as no surprise. Almost 9 million adults own RVs, with the greatest number being boomers. Grandparents make up about 63 percent of all RV owners!

If you go the route of driving yourself when you travel, there are several options to ease your journey on the long and winding road. Almost everyone is familiar with the American Automobile Association (AAA). This organization has been in existence for more than a century. Perks of membership include road service, maps, towing, TripTiks (which can be printed from your computer), tour books, books listing RV sites and campgrounds, recommended driving trips, insurance, discounts, and other services. Membership fees are approximately $58 annually but can vary if you add additional members of the family to your plan or wish to extend your coverage

"If you drop your camera in water, let it sit overnight in a bag of rice. The rice will draw out the condensation." (Source: *Budget Travel*)

options. With various AAA discounts, the membership fee can more than pay for itself.

There are also several clubs specifically for RVers, such as the Good Sam Club (www.goodsams.net), Coast to Coast (access through www.rv.net or 800-368-5721), and Escapees RV Club (www.escapees.com). If you're single, that doesn't mean you have to go it alone. Several clubs include Loners on Wheels (www.lonersonwheels.com), Retired Singles (www.retiredsingles.com), and RVing Women (www.rvingwomen.org or 888-557-8464), which, as the name implies, is for females who either own a RVs or would like to become part of the RV lifestyle.

You can also become part of a pack if you choose to travel by cycle. The American Motorcyclist Association (www.amadirectlink.com) was founded in 1924 and has more than 260,000 members. It provides services similar to those of AAA. Great American Motorcycle Touring (www.greatamericantouring.com or 800-727-3390) offers tours, self-guided tours, and custom tours. No bike? No problem! You can rent one through GAMT if you don't own one or don't wish to ship or drive yours to the departure city. Retreads Motorcycle Club International (www.retreads.org) has two requirements to join: a love of biking and an age of at least 40.

SOLO TRAVEL

The single traveler is anything but alone! The Travel Industry Association notes that this segment of the travel business accounted for about 30 percent of all U.S. travel in 2004; a staggering 38 million middle-aged singles (average age 45) took a solo trip. Although some of these were business trips, leisure travel accounted for almost 70 percent. The increase in the number of single people, coupled with the affluence of these age groups, has contributed to this fast-growing trend.

Many people feel comfortable traveling alone, responsible only for themselves in choosing an itinerary, selecting restaurants, arranging their schedule, etc. The once-upon-a-time perceived stigma of a woman traveling

---

You can purchase CDs or cassettes that discuss the history, stories, side trips, and landmarks of an area through a company called Ride with Me (www.rwmaudio.com or 800-752-3195). These audio companions are synchronized with the milepost markers. Selections can be by route number, state, national park, or favorite place.

alone has largely disappeared, although common sense should be exercised whether you are male or female.

If you're contemplating traveling solo, but are a little uncomfortable with the concept, travel guru Arthur Frommer recommends considering volunteer or learning vacations. A trip that has an outer-directed goal with like-minded participants often works well. Earthwatch, the Sierra Club, Elderhostel, the Omega Institute, and Habitat for Humanity all sponsor these types of trips. For more specifics on this kind of travel, see the section on "Volunteer Vacations" on page 71 and the suggested reading.

If you're looking for trips that cater to mature singles, several companies fit the bill. Windjammer Barefoot Cruises (www.windjammerbarefoot.com) has sailings designated specifically for singles. Celebrity, Cunard, Crystal, Seabourn, Silversea, Radisson, and Holland America are other cruise lines to investigate and often provide gentleman hosts for dancing and dining. Of course, if you're a man looking to socialize, choosing one of these cruise lines would be good planning as well. Adventure travel also attracts large numbers of mature singles—try Overseas Adventure Travel (www.oattravel.com or 800-493-6824) or Backroads (www.backroads.com or 800-462-2848).

If you are happy traveling alone but don't want to underwrite the cost of a room or cabin by yourself, you also have several options. Often, the cruise line or company (such as Club Med) will arrange a roommate to avoid the single-supplement charge for singles staying in a double room. Occasionally, single-supplement charges will be waived; it never hurts to ask! Several organizations will set you up with a roommate as well. O Solo Mio (www.osolomio.com or 800-959-8568) has been around for more than 10 years and arranges singles' tours both nationally and internationally. O Solo Mio will match you with a same-sex person of similar age, smoking preferences, and sleeping habits (i.e., night owl or early bird). All Singles Travel (www.allsinglestravel.com or 800-717-3231) will also match you with a roommate to avoid the single supplement.

Got kids? Single Parent Tours (www.singleparent tours.com or 877-464-6778) is a great place to look for a trip for a single parent and the children!

More daring is the free classified-ad service you can access through Aim-Higher Travel (www.aim-higher.com or 877-752-1858). This organization has been in business since 1998 and also deals in singles' cruises and tours. Another possibility for finding traveling companions includes the free message board on www.travelchums.com, where you can fill out a questionnaire online.

If you're female, there are travel groups designed specifically for you, such as Gutsy Women Travel (www.gutsywomentravel.com or 866-464-8879).

A little off the beaten path is Sacred Sites Tours (www.sacredsitestours.com or 612-823-2442). This group leads small groups (12 or fewer) of women and girls on tours of mythical, historical, and other enchanted spots in England and Scotland.

How about Shop Around Tours (www.shoparoundtours.com or 212-684-3763)? Go in search of a good deal on an insider's bargain-hunting trip to Italy.

Women Welcome Women World Wide (5W)—www.womenwelcomewomen.org.uk—is an international-travel group that enables women of different countries to visit one another and helps to foster friendship, connections, and cross-cultural understanding. This company has been around for more than 20 years and currently has 3,000 members in 70 countries. There is a membership fee.

GROUP TRAVEL

More than a quarter of the U.S. population is over 50, and by 2020 this number is expected to increase by one-third. This may be news to you, but it's not news to tour companies! Travel companies are cropping up to cater exclusively to the mature traveler (50 to 55 and older), and companies that have been in existence for many years recognize the power of the baby-boomer market. Senior travelers are more often than not interested in the ease and comfort that a tour affords. Travel companies that court seniors offer soft adventure, luxury cruises, educational opportunities, and tours that combine all three.

Making the decision to travel with a group instead of traveling on your own seems to be a path many boomers are taking. Tour companies eliminate the planning details, and for the budget conscious, tours are often the better bargain. When airfares, hotels, and food are purchased in great quantities, the price goes down (of course, you do sacrifice spontaneity). Tours that are designed for the mature traveler give more attention to health and mobility issues, with slower-paced days and comfortable nights. Some even promise

---

If you're a single man between the ages of 45 and 72 and would like to be a gentleman host, apply to the cruise lines directly or to a site such as the Working Vacation, www.theworkingvacation.com or 708-301-7535. In most cases, gentlemen guests pay the cruise line between $28 and $38 a day. Their hosting services are considered voluntary. In exchange, they receive cabin accommodations, dining privileges, and complimentary shore excursions.

that you won't need to have your suitcase ready by 6 a.m. every day!

A good place to start looking if you are interested in booking a tour would be the companies that have been in existence for many years. These companies specialize in tours that vary greatly in cost, from budget to luxury. Most travel companies will customize a tour for you if you provide your own group consisting of 15 people or more. Dozens of good companies exist.

Grand Circle Tours (www.gct.com or 800-959-0405). In existence since 1958, GCT agrees with John Steinbeck that "people don't take trips, trips take people." Prices vary greatly, as do the locations.

Globus and Cosmos Tours (www.globusandcosmos. com. The Globus family offers great group travel.

Tauck Tours (www.tauck.com or 800-788-7885). A family business since 1925, and more than half of its travelers repeat customers, Tauck has won more than 50 awards and is known for its all-inclusive, upscale travel.

Trafalgar Tours (www.trafalgar-tours.net) has been in existence for around 60 years. Take escorted motorcoach tours to a variety of destinations worldwide. One of the authors accompanied her elderly mother, along with two sisters, on a 9-day Trafalgar tour of Italy. Although some excursions were extra, and the hotels were mediocre, prices were reasonable, and they enjoyed the services of a terrific tour guide.

"Soft" Adventure Travel

If the same old trip to the beach doesn't sound like enough this year, give some thought to learning new skills and trying them out in a fresh place. Many mature travelers are ready and willing to try a new venture, especially with a group of their peers and the promise of creature comforts at the end of the day. There is no end to the opportunities if you are ready to take the plunge. An adventure cruise with Elderhostel will take you sailing on the Dingle Peninsula of Ireland, or maybe you would like to explore the Galápagos Islands. Perhaps you'd like to start out easy and ride a bike from Cumberland, Maryland, to the nation's capital and stay at upscale bed and breakfasts along the way. Whatever you choose to do, and wherever you choose to take your adventure, there is a trip for you.

Keep in mind that there is no guarantee of compatibility or safety when joining a pay service or accessing free match-up sites. In general, organizations where you pay a fee for services tend to attract fewer "undesirables."

Abercrombie & Kent. This tour company has been in business for 45 years and offers upscale adventure tours on all seven continents. Expect the very best in accommodations. Contact www.abercrombiekent.com or 800-554-7016.

Country Walkers. Explore new environs on foot with an experienced guide, choosing from a number of worldwide tours. Stroll through a village in Greece or kayak down a river in New Zealand. Country Walkers has more than 25 years of experience, and they promise to deliver an exhilarating adventure. Contact www.countrywalkers.com or 800-464-9255.

New England Hiking Holidays. "Footpaths by day! and Country inns by night!" Enjoy the expertise of more than two decades of successful trips and the comfort of knowing that two guides accompany each trip—one for the fast walkers and one for the slightly slower group! Take a walking trip within the United States, Canada, or Europe, or sign up for a multiadventure, which combines walking with kayaking, snorkeling, or biking. Contact www.nehikingholidays.com or 800-869-0949.

Elder Treks. With a 20-year history, Elder Treks offer adventures in 80 countries for the 50-plus age group. Plow your way through the ice pack to the North Pole on an icebreaker, or explore Mongolia by camel. Contact www.eldertreks.com or 800-741-7956.

Senior Cycling. No one is concerned with how far or how fast you go; you can choose your own level of difficulty. These "old folks on spokes" offer bicycle trips throughout the United States. Contact www.seniorcycling.com or 540-668-6307.

Walking the World. Experience the world as an active participant. "You'll get to know an area not by how it looks through the window of a bus, but by its true flavor!" Since 1978, Walking the World's trips "for people 50 and better" include such places as Costa Rica, Switzerland, Italy, and Germany. Contact www.walkingtheworld.com or 877-340-9255.

Elderhostel. With thousands of participants enjoying thousands of varied trips in many different countries, choosing an adventure will be your greatest problem! Contact www.elderhostel.org or 800-454-5768

Travel Quest International. Things are looking up! Travel Quest International offers astronomy-related tours to such places as China, Costa Rica, Russia, and

---

No shirt, no pants, no problem! Bare Necessities Tour and Travel (www.bare-necessities.com or 800-743-0405) offer clothing-optional cruises for more—naturally!

on the seas (through Princess Cruise Lines). Contact www.tq-international.com or 800-830-1998.

Travel Without Temptation. Sober Travel Adventures (www.sobertraveladventures.com or 770-432-8225), Meetings en Route (www.sobersailors.org or 866-678-8785), or Sober Vacations International (www.sobervacations.com or 800-762-3738). Enjoy meetings and speakers as well as snorkeling, scuba, golf, and other great holiday activities. "Alcohol-free vacations for people who crave adventure . . . one day at a time!"

World Wildlife Fund. Travel the world and see spectacular wildlife in its natural habitat. WWF trips are geared for young adults through active seniors. Contact www.worldwildlife.org/travel or 888-993-8687.

50plus Expeditions. Exotic travel for the 50-and-up group. Trips are rated easy, moderate, or demanding, and locations include the Arctic, Antarctica, Asia, East Africa, Latin America, and North America. Contact www.50plusexpeditions.com or 866-318-5050.

Adventure Network International. This group specializes in Antarctica. You can choose a trip from luxury level to extreme-endurance level. Prepare to bundle up! Contact www.adventure-network.com or 801-266-4876.

Learning Vacations

Budget traveler Gary Langer once wrote, "Travelers and tourists, the distinction is simple: Tourists are those who bring their homes with them wherever they go, and apply them to whatever they see. They are closed to experiences outside of the superficial. Travelers, however, leave home at home, bringing only themselves and a desire to learn." If you feel as Mr. Langer does and want more out of your next vacation, you may be ready for a learning vacation, or the most fabulous field trip you have ever taken! Check out the following.

www.closeup.org/lifelong.htm (800-256-7387). Would you like to spend a week in our nation's capital and learn what makes it work? In cooperation with Elderhostel, the Close Up Foundation offers a week-long program combining a vacation with firsthand knowledge of our nation's capital.

www.travelearn.com (800-235-9114). With 25 years of experience, TraveLearn provides learning vacations for "people who take their minds with them on vacation." As an example, you can experience the archaeology, ecology, and culture of Peru during a 16-day excursion that includes lectures and seminars.

www.smithsonianjourneys.org (877-338-8687). Smithsonian Journeys has been a leader in educational travel for more than 3 decades. Thousands of travelers have enjoyed the network of resources available to the Smithsonian that make this a unique travel and learning experience. The itineraries range from a guided tour of the Metropolitan Opera to 17 days in Burma.

CYBERSPACE AWAITS!

Ready for more? Take a stab at these additional Internet sites and explore the many options you have. There is a lot of overlap among sites, so get comfortable, and start exploring from the coziness of your computer chair.

✳ SmarTours (www.smartours.net or 800-337-7773) has one goal: "Top-quality, exciting tours at the lowest possible price." Highlights include airfare on major scheduled airlines, deluxe and first-class hotels, and professional English-speaking tour guides.

✳ If you're traveling on a budget or looking for that luxurious, once-in-a-lifetime trip or something in between, www.tourvacations togo.com (800-680-2858) will provide itineraries from the world's leading tour companies, giving you options and prices in an instant. To choose a vacation, search this site by region, tour company, or specialty, or pick from specially priced tour packages.

✳ For escorted, independent, group, and custom-designed tours to international and exotic destinations, try www.gate1travel.com (800-682-3333).

✳ If you are interested in tours to Hawaii, Mexico, the Azores, or Costa Rica, check out Sun Trips (www.suntrips.com or 800-248-7471), in business for more than a quarter of a century.

✳ Find cruises, bargain packages, and seasonal specials at www.vacmart.com (800-288-1435).

✳ Love to fly Southwest Airlines? Customize your vacation, beginning with round-trip airfare on Southwest (www.swavacations.com or 800-243-8372), including great prices on hotels (budget to luxury), car rental, area attractions, and more.

✳ If you practice a vegetarian lifestyle, you can travel without concern about food via www. vegetarianusa.com.

www.unex.berkeley.edu/travel (510-642-3824). London theater, China's ancient cities, Sicilian mosaics! "We invite you to take more than just a trip. Please join us for a challenging intellectual adventure." The average age of participants is 50 to 60 years old in this "Travel with Scholars" extension of UC-Berkeley. Two years of college is a prerequisite for the Oxford program.

www.amnh.org—click on "AMNH Expeditions" (800-462-8687). The American Museum of Natural History has been offering educational travel for more than 50 years. More than 20,000 travelers have explored the world on AMNH Expeditions—from pole to pole and everywhere in between—in the company of AMNH scientists.

www.metmuseum.org (212-650-2110). Click on "Events and Programs," then "Travel Programs." And what programs they have! You will enjoy reading about these trips even if you never go; check out "Temples, Gods, and Gardens: The Greek Isles."

www.elderhostel.org Elderhostel and Specialty Travel also offers a wide variety of educational travel, including biblical tours, cooking tours, and tours that focus on birding, antiquing, creative workshops, and adventures afloat. Plan to spend some time on these Web sites; the opportunities are endless.

www.princess.com (800-774-6237). The educational program on Princess Cruise Lines is cleverly titled ScholarShip@Sea. Classes in computer technology, culinary/creative/visual arts, and other special topics (such as spelling bees!) are offered.

www.soulplanettravel.com and **www.soulofamerica. com** are two travel organizations responding to the needs and desires of African-Americans to patronize African-American-owned bed and breakfasts and hotels and to participate in African-American culture tours, cruises, etc.

Gay Travel

www.gaytravel.com, **www.gay.com/travel**, and **www. gayres.com** provide travel opportunities for gays.

The latter lists gay-friendly hotels around the world.

Volunteer Vacations

Vacation: "A time of respite; a scheduled period during which activity is suspended; a period of exemption from work granted to an employee for rest and relaxation." If Merriam-Webster's definition of "vacation" is accurate, then what does volunteering have to do with vacationing? Most people look upon public service as a punishment issued by a judge in lieu of jail time. It may be difficult to believe, but tens of thousands of people the world over are scheduling time away to be of service to others. The idea is to help yourself while helping others. If retirement seems to be lacking in purpose and fulfillment, take a look at the voluntourism opportunities that might provide adventure for you and help for those who really need it.

Cross-Cultural Solutions (www.crossculturalsolutions.org or 800-380-4777) is a not-for-profit international volunteer organization that operates in Africa, Asia, Eastern Europe, and Latin America. The *New York Times* refers to Cross-Cultural Solutions as "akin to a mini-stint with the Peace Corps." Work may include caring for infants, teaching teenagers, helping set up a small business for working adults, as well as providing the local people the opportunity to learn about your culture.

Farm Sanctuary (www.farmsanctuary.org or 607-583-2225) in New York cares for injured, abused, or abandoned farm animals and promotes a vegan lifestyle. You can help out with farm chores or office work. If your interest leans more toward pets than farm animals, contact Best Friends Animal Sanctuary (www.bestfriends.org or 435-644-2001). This is the largest pet sanctuary in the United States, is located near Kanab, Utah, and cares for an astounding 1,500 cats, dogs, and other pets.

Global Volunteers (www.globalvolunteers.org or 800-487-1074) offers more than 150 1-, 2-, or 3-week projects year-round. Volunteers are involved in painting and constructing homes, tutoring schoolchildren, improving public health, and teaching English. Global Volunteers are at work in more than "100 host communities in 20 countries on 6 continents."

The Flying Doctors (www.flyingdocs.org or 800-585-4568) enables volunteers to provide nonskilled assistance in setting up a clinic and providing medical and dental services in Mexico, Central America, and the Coachella Valley of California in the United States.

Habitat for Humanity (www.habitat.org or 800-422-4828) volunteers work in foreign countries as well as throughout the United States. "Habitat has built more than 200,000 houses around the world, providing more than 1,000,000 people in more than 3,000 communities with safe, decent, affordable shelter." The opportunities are extensive.

If you have an RV or have always wanted to rent one, try RV Care-A-Vanners. This group works with Habitat affiliates. A Care-A-Van usually lasts 2 weeks and includes 8 to 20 volunteers. Participants travel together and work together at the Habitat sites. Bring tools,

---

In most cases, your driver's license is all that is necessary to rent or drive a vehicle in another country, but some countries require an international driver's license or special insurance. Contact an organization such as AAA or a rental agency in the country you are planning to visit for details.

WOMEN-ONLY ADVENTURE TRAVEL

These trips combine the best of adventure with single-sex travel.

✳ www.mariahwomen.com (800-462-7424). "Mariah's women-only trips combine river wilderness adventures with exploring the natural and cultural environments of unique international destinations in the safe and secure company of other women!"

✳ www.adventurewomen.com (800-804-8686). You'll want to be an adventure woman! Founded in 1982, Adventure Women is the oldest women-only adventure travel company for women 30 and older. "Our groups are small and nonsmoking, and trips are rated easy, moderate, or high energy—an activity level for every ability," they state. Choose from 23 different vacations, including hiking, sea kayaking, and cultural and ecological journeys, or maybe follow Marco Polo's footsteps.

✳ www.callwild.com (888-378-1978). For more than 25 years, this women-only tour group has been providing adventure travel for women from every walk of life: "Our customers find that a hike through a beautiful stretch of wilderness, followed by a gourmet meal, with good companionship, is a memorable experience."

energy, enthusiasm, and flexibility! You can contact RV Care-A-Vanners at rvinfodesk@habitat.org.

Earthwatch Institute (www.earthwatch.org or 800-776-0188) is involved in ongoing research run by members of the scientific community. In 2006, Earthwatch sponsored more than 155 research projects in 48 countries and 16 U.S. states. Topics include ecology, zoology, archaeology, world health, and more. Earthwatch provides short-term volunteer opportunities lasting about 10 to 14 days. Some weekend opportunities exist.

American Hiking Society (www.americanhiking.org or 301-565-6704) provides a rewarding experience while visiting picturesque backcountry locations. Meet new people while constructing footpaths or rebuilding existing trails, cabins, and shelters. Enjoy evenings around the campfire and rest up for another great day outdoors.

Similar Web sites to check are www.wildernessvolunteers. org and www.sierraclub.org (click on "get outdoors").

In general, when researching volunteer vacations, you'll need to find out the specifics from the organization in which you're interested, such as age requirements, your expenses (which can vary tremendously depending on the trip), time frames, any special abilities or physical level required, what to wear, what to bring, and how you apply to the program. As far as tax deductions go, you will need to find out what's eligible from the IRS and your tax advisor. At a minimum, the organization must be nonprofit and tax exempt, which many of these organizations are. Items that may be deductible (assuming you itemize on your tax return) include auto mileage, tolls, parking, food, and lodging. Of course, this applies only if the purpose of the travel is volunteering. Keep careful records! You can call the IRS for help at 800-829-1040; if hearing-impaired, call 800-829-4059.

A volunteer vacation is not an oxymoron. There are hundreds of volunteer organizations around the world just waiting to hear from you.

TRAVELING WITH GRANDCHILDREN

Traveling with your grandchildren can deepen relationships and create lifelong memories. This type of travel ranks high on the trips mature travelers would like to take. In fact, in a survey of group travelers by the National Tour Association and Group Leaders of America, travel involving grandparents and grandchildren ranked ninth out of the top 50 tours and destinations available.

The leader in grandparent/grandchild travel is Grandtravel (www.grandtrvl.com or 800-247-7651). This organization has been around for about 20 years. Grandtravel offers national and international itineraries designed to be enjoyed by both generations; teachers or leisure counselors escort the trips. Tours, scheduled primarily in the summer months, include Greece, Alaska, Kenya, Australia, and France.

The Sagamore Foundation (www.sagamore.org or 315-354-5311) offers a grandparent/grandchild summer camp in New York's Adirondack Mountains that includes hikes, indoor and outdoor activities, and campfires.

Want to test-drive an RV or motorcycle to see if this type of travel appeals to you? Try Cruise America (www.cruiseamerica.com or 480-464-7300), which has 150 rental centers in the United States and Canada.

Register through Elderhostel. Elderhostel also offers a large number of intergenerational trips of varying lengths and destinations (www.elderhostel.org or 800-454-5768).

true LIFE **Phil and Carol W. are experienced travelers, authors of *Live Your Road Trip Dream*, and most of all, grandparents who love to create travel memories with their ever-expanding tribe of grandchildren. At last count they lay claim to 11, ranging in age from 6 months to 17 years old, including some "steps" along the way.**

Phil and Carol are young retirees who believe that creating memories *with* their grandchildren is much more important than what they *give* their grandchildren. "We could never compete with the outpouring of 'things' from the parents and other more distant grandparents, so we decided early on to make our presence known by being present with the kids as they grew," comments Phil. "It has really developed in us a sense of who each of them is as people, and they will surely look back on growing up, feeling that they really *knew* Grammie and Wookies," adds Carol. (Grandpa Phil used to have a beard and became known as "Whiskers" to the first grandchild. Later, another grandchild couldn't yet say "Whiskers" so it came out "Wookies," and the name has stuck ever since.)

The 48-Inch Trip

When the first two of the grandchildren reached the size to go on the big rides at Disneyland, we decided that would make a fun excursion for all of us. Who doesn't love Disneyland, especially with a wide-eyed 8- and 9-year-old in tow?

In the years that have followed, each grandchild anxiously anticipates their turn for their "48-inch trip." The most recent two had already been to Disneyland many times, so it seemed a lot less special as the time drew near to plan the trip. We looked for alternatives, discussed choices with them, and decided on San Diego, California, instead. We all had a great adventure.

We take them two at a time (always cousins—much better than siblings from both an economic and companionship viewpoint) and find that it has worked well. Now that the Disneyland requirement has been broken, we're sure that each set of "48 inchers" will want to put their own marks on their special trips with us.

Lessons Along the Way

Kids are such great sponges. They absorb everything that they see and hear, especially when on their best behavior traveling with us. We take the time alone with them to really learn about them and to impart bits of wisdom that we learned over the years. We know they find some of what we say "quaint" (or worse!), but we also know that they do absorb life lessons from us too.

Each summer we team up with another set of grandparents and take all those who are ages 5 and above and who want to go on an outing. It started out as just a day trip, but each year gets more elaborate. One thing that has been consistent from the beginning has been the "teaching moments."

One year it was learning about the Lewis and Clark expedition as we traveled via train to Fort Clatsop in Oregon, where the party stayed the winter. A large book with lots of pictures (borrowed from the library) formed the basis for talking about the adventure. Last year, we went to Wildlife Safari (a drive-through wild-animal park in Oregon). Before we left, each child was assigned an animal we would see in the park and had to do an oral report in front of the others. Such moaning you have never heard! They tried everything to get out of it. But once they all got into it over pizza at the motel, they really learned a lot. They asked questions of each other, the older ones helped the little ones, and it turned out to be an overall great experience that they still talk about. This year the trip was river rafting. We got creative and had each child decorate their own "River Rat Hat," which was then judged by the guides. Their creations definitely reflected their own personalities!

No matter what we do, we always try to find a way to expand their knowledge and have fun in the process. We think it is a formula that they will remember long after last year's toys are gone. ⓣⓛ

If planning a trip on your own, consider a cruise. The more family-oriented cruise lines include Disney, Carnival, Princess, Norwegian (especially the Norwegian Dawn), and Royal Caribbean. Destinations such as dude ranches (for example, the Triangle C Dude Ranch in Wyoming, www.trianglec.com, click on "Dude Ranch Vacations," or call 800-661-4928), resorts that cater to families, spas that allow adult indulgence yet provide activities for kids, and fascinating cities are other possibilities.

The financial costs of traveling with grandchildren can vary, but the emotional rewards can be priceless!

Want to try out a new career? Check out www.vocationvacations.com or 866-888-6329.
This site is discussed more fully in Chapter 2.

TRAVELING WITH PHYSICAL DISABILITIES

It's estimated that between 50 million and 65 million Americans have some type of disability. The travel industry is responding to this huge market. Don't let the fact that you need a scooter or wheelchair to get around slow you down. If you are hearing or vision impaired, need dialysis, require oxygen, or have other disabilities, you can still enjoy travel. You may need to do more homework than others, but accessible travel is out there.

Various travel organizations specialize in meeting access needs. Accessible Journeys (www.disabilitytravel. com or 800-846-4537) organizes group trips and cruises, helps with independent travel, and can provide a healthcare professional as a travel companion. Nautilus Tours and Cruises (www.nautilustours.com or 818-591-3159) and Flying Wheels Travel (www.flyingwheelstravel.com or 507-451-5005) also assist with disabled travelers, both nationally and internationally. Access-Able Travel Source (www.access-able.com or disseminates information on travel agents, cruises, accommodations, equipment rental, etc. Wilderness Inquiry (www.wildernessinquiry. org or 800-728-0719) has been in business since 1978 and promotes inclusion of all ability levels and ages in the exploration of wild areas. One example is hiking and kayaking in Misty Fjords National Monument, Alaska.

If you have physical challenges, taking a cruise can be one of the better ways to vacation. New ships are being built with accessibility in mind, and older ships are being retrofitted to ensure smooth sailing with staterooms and hallways that accommodate wheelchairs and scooters; pools with lifts; newsletters, elevator buttons, and menus in Braille; amplified telephones; close-captioned TVs; roll-in showers; and lower closet bars and sinks. Ports of call and shore excursions are becoming more accessible as well. Contact the access desk at the appropriate cruise line to discuss your needs. Now you don't have to miss the boat!

On a broader note, resource organizations for the disabled include Mobility International USA (www.miusa. org or 541-343-1284) and the Society for Accessible Travel and Hospitality (SATH), which can be contacted at www.sath.org or 212-447-7284. One of the goals of Mobility International is to promote "the inclusion of disabled people in all types of exchange, community, and volunteer-service programs." SATH works to provide barrier-free travel both nationally and internationally, provides tips on travel (such as how to travel with a

---

The U.S. National Park Service offers a Golden Access Passport that gives free lifetime entrance to U.S. national parks for persons who are permanently disabled, regardless of age.

speech impairment), and provides a good resource list for the disabled traveler.

So now you're ready, willing, and able. Take the attitude of Pastor Charles Swindoll, who said, "The longer I live, the more convinced I become that life is 10 percent what happens to us and 90 percent how we respond to it." Bon voyage!

TRAVEL THOUGHTS AND TIPS

If we still haven't exhausted you with all there is to do during your 168 hours each week, here are some further ideas and suggestions about travel that don't fit neatly into one of the categories we've already discussed.

Lodging

Check out Hideaways International (www.hideaways. com or 800-843-4433). For $185 per year, you are given access to information on villas, yachts, condos, castles, etc., all over the world. Hideaway International has been in business for more than 20 years.

A number of sites allow potential renters to contact owners directly. EscapeHomes (www.escapehomes.com or 415-252-9500) targets vacation properties and second homes; Beachouse.com (www.beachhouse.com or 949-863-0050) is for those who believe life is better at the beach. Try Unusual Villas (www.unusualvillarentals. com or 800-846-7280) for more than 2,000 villas (and islands) worldwide. Of course, if you own a place in a desirable location, you may also list your own property on these sites.

"Cuchi-cuchi!" Maybe you want to stay in a celebrity villa. You can rent homes owned by Charo, Merv Griffin, and others through Overseas Connection (www. villasoftheworld.com and click on "Celebrity Villas," or 888-728-4552). Gulp! Prices are all over the place, with a 74-acre Caribbean island with one home on it going for $210,000 a week during high season, but hey, it sleeps 28, so just prorate it among your friends. Of course, more reasonable rates exist for other celebrity villas.

If you've already stayed at the Ritz or Four Seasons and are looking for something more over the top, consider these far-out places (your grandkids will thank you!).

Treehouses: Out 'n' About Treesort (www.treehouses. com or 541-592-2208) in Takilma, Oregon, offers 14 different tree houses that range in cost from $120 to $220 per night, depending on tree house style and number of people. In Australia, check out the wallabies and tree frogs from your rainforest tree house located 90 minutes from Cairns (www.rainforesttreehouses. com.au). Prices start about $180 per night, depending on the time of year.

Ice hotels: The Ice Hotel Quebec and the Ice Hotel in Sweden have similar amenities, including art galleries, an Absolut Ice Bar, spa, wedding chapel, and movie theater. The Ice Hotel in Canada (www.icehotel-canada.com or 877-505-0423), for example, takes 5 weeks to build, opens around the first of January, and is open for about 3 months. Temperatures range between 23 and 28 degrees Fahrenheit, and you'll snuggle in a sleeping bag on top of deer pelts. One night's lodging, including breakfast, starts at around $300 per person, double occupancy.

Caves: Kokopelli's Cave Bed & Breakfast is located north of Farmington, New Mexico. Carved out of sandstone that is 65 million years old, this 70-foot-below-the-surface cave apartment has one bedroom, hot and cold running water, a hot tub, washer and dryer, and kitchen. Located near Mesa Verde National Monument, there are mountainous vistas of Arizona, Colorado, New Mexico, and Utah from the cliff face where you enter to descend to the dwelling. Rates are $240 for one or two persons per night. Contact www.bbonline.com/nm/kokopelli or 505-326-2461 for pictures and more details. The Desert Cave Hotel (www.desertcave.com.au) is located in the opal-mining town of Coober Pedy in the northern outback of South Australia. Built into a sandstone hill, the hotel opened in 1988 and has 50 suites, 19 of which are under-ground. With the cool, constant underground temperatures, lodgers experience a delightfully cool sleep in the middle of the desert. The cost is about $200 per night.

Under the sea: The Jules' Undersea Lodge in Key Largo, Florida (www.jul.com or 305-451-2353), is the world's first underwater hotel. You'll need to scuba dive to access this unique lodge 21 feet below the surface, but once there, you'll enjoy hot showers, comfy beds, and a kitchen. Your view out the windows, however, will be quite different from a regular hotel! The lodge was originally a research lab, but it has operated as an underwater hotel since 1986. Different packages are available, beginning at $445 per person including dinner and breakfast. If you're not certified in scuba, no problem. You can take a 3-hour course at Jules' that will allow you to enjoy this memory-making experience.

Scary: Double your fun. Stay on the HMS *Queen Mary* (www.queenmary.com or 562-435-3511), and you'll be sleeping on a ship as well as an allegedly haunted floating hotel. Now permanently docked in Long Beach, California, the ship has several "hot spots" where apparitions and strange smells, noises, and temperature variations have been reported. One of the cabins (B340) is no

---

"Travel and change of place impart new vigor to the mind."
—Seneca

longer used for passengers because of inexplicable oddities. A ghost tour by a paranormal researcher is even available. The liner has 365 staterooms that range from $179 to $660 per night.

Various other hotels are allegedly visited by ghosts, including the Hilton Hotel in Honolulu, Hawaii (808-949-4321), the Lizzie Borden Bed and Breakfast in Fall River, Massachusetts (508-675-7333), and Cloudcroft the Lodge in Cloudcroft, New Mexico (800-395-6343). Restaurants aren't immune either; check out the spectral beings that supposedly haunt Portland White Eagle Café and Saloon in Portland, Oregon (503-282-6810), Pirate's House Restaurant in Savannah, Georgia (912-233-5757), or Ashley's Restaurant in Rockledge, Florida (407-636-6430).

Lighthouses: There are quite a few lighthouses, many privately owned, that allow overnight stays. Several examples include: Big Bay Point Lighthouse Bed and Breakfast (www.bigbaylighthouse.com or 906-345-9957) in Big Bay, Michigan, which hugs a cliff on Lake Superior. More than a century old, its rates range from $105 to $190, depending on room and time of year.

With the Selkirk Light House (315-298-6688) in Pulaski, New York, you rent the entire lighthouse, consisting of two floors and four bedrooms. Rates begin at $135 for two people, with additional charges for extra people and certain days of the week. Part of the rental income goes toward the lighthouse's renovation. For additional lighthouse lodging, type "lighthouse directory" into your search engine.

Vineyards: Want to see the birthplace of that Chardonnay or Merlot? Chateau Darmagnac (www.france-plus.com and click on "Holiday") is in France's Bordeaux country. Experience wine making and tasting right on the premises, as well as golf, tennis, fishing, proximity to other vineyards, and visits to the nearby Atlantic coast. Prices range from 300 to 400 euros per week (to convert euros to dollars, go to a currency converter site such as www.xe.com). Or consider a stay at Carriage Vineyards (www.carriagevineyards.com or 805-227-6807) on California's central coast, midway between San Francisco and Los Angeles. Prices begin around $200 per night during high season.

Air, Sea, and Auto Travel

For the best seats on a plane, try to get an exit row since these seats offer more legroom. If there are two rows of exit seats, choose the second row because the first row

---

When business travelers leave the big city after their meetings, you can often negotiate a good price for a first-class hotel room.

doesn't recline. If there are two of you traveling and there are three seats across, reserve the aisle and window seats. The middle seats will be the last to be assigned, so the two of you may have the row to yourself. Conversely, if only middle seats are available when you book, ask to be put in a middle seat between two people with the same last name. Obviously, they are banking on the former tip! If they really want to sit together, one may switch with you, and you can end up with a window or aisle seat. If you want to try to get a different seat than the one assigned, call your airline after midnight on the day of departure. Seats may open up because of cancellations. Of course, you can also ask about changing your seat when you check in. For seating arrangements on various airlines and comments about seating, look at www.seatguru.com. It's a very helpful site.

For better seats, you can also try getting bumped on purpose. If time is not of the essence in arriving at your destination, ask at the gate to be put on the list of people volunteering to be bumped. Obviously, the earlier you're at the airport, the better your priority on the list. Airlines routinely overbook to ensure as full a plane as possible. Joyce L. and her daughter, Jessica, were ready to return to Chicago from a vacation in France when American Airlines announced it was looking for volunteers to be bumped. Not needing to get back immediately, Joyce and Jessica volunteered. They were put up at Euro Disney for the night (sent by cab), about 40 minutes from the airport, and were given a generous voucher for dinner and breakfast, as well as airline vouchers for $2,000. The only snag to the plan was that their luggage had been checked through to Chicago, and Joyce's carry-on luggage, which held toiletries, was now replaced by a gargoyle that she had bought on their travels! Moral: Having a carry-on bag containing toiletries (be aware of the carry-on rules though!) and a change of clothes is a good move if you're hoping to be bumped. (The flight they took out the next day was also overbooked, but they passed on that opportunity.) Different airlines have different deals; make sure you understand what you're being offered before accepting! For more information, check out www.bumptracker.com.

And here's a tip regarding bargain fares: Discount fares are released on the Internet on Wednesdays at 12:01 a.m. Sign up for automatic notifications through your preferred airline. Since airlines have become more stringent about extra luggage (right now Delta charges $25 for bags over 50 pounds and $100 if they weigh

---

Most automobile rental agencies start their weekend rates at noon on Thursday and end at midnight on Sunday. You can often obtain better rates during this time frame.

between 71 and 100 pounds), it may be cost effective to send that extra luggage ahead. This is also an option if you just don't want to lug your luggage. If you want pickup service at your residence or business and quick delivery to your journey's end, you'll pay for the convenience of this door-to-destination service. Two to consider are: Virtual Bellhop (www.virtualbellhop.com or 877-235-5467) and SkyCap International (www.skycap-international.com or 877-775-9227), which is associated with FedEx. Less costly alternatives, but more work for you since you must pack and deliver your luggage, are the U.S. Postal Service, Federal Express, or Amtrak. Or compare shipping rates from multiple carriers at www.iship.com.

You could also look into repositioning cruises. When cruise ships move from one region to another to reposition for a new itinerary, they often offer steep discounts as well as longer times at sea since they are on "one-way" cruises and frequently have fewer ports of call than do regular cruises. If you want to stretch your travel dollars, it's worth considering.

Entertainment

You can do a myriad of things on your getaway, some of which you can enjoy again and again.

Discount tickets. Join (for free) the Playbill Club at www.playbill.com, and become eligible for reduced Broadway, off-Broadway, and regional theater tickets, as well as restaurant, hotel, and merchandise discounts.

Golf, anyone? The John Jacobs' Golf School (www.jacobsgolf.com or 800-472-5007) provides accommodations, meals, and golf lessons in dozens of locations. Prices begin around $500.

At amusement parks and casinos, Tuesdays, Wednesdays, and Thursdays are usually the least crowded days to visit, with Wednesdays being the best of the three.

Other Assorted Points

There may come a time when you need to find a doctor when you're traveling. The International Association for Medical Assistance to Travelers (IAMAT) at www.iamat.org or 716-754-4883 provides free membership (although they would appreciate a donation) that

---

Freedom Paradise Resort (www.freedomparadise.com or 866-548-3995), near Cancun, Mexico, caters to the plus-size customer. Reinforced furniture, extra-large towels, broader chairs, wider walkways, king-size beds, boutiques with plus-size clothing, and easily accessed swimming pools make this a welcoming vacation spot for people who aren't comfortable around the bikini set.

includes a directory of physicians in 125 countries. The doctors speak English and have been trained in North America or Europe. A set schedule of fees has been established. In existence since 1960, the organization also provides information about disease outbreaks, sanitary conditions, and required immunizations.

For the upscale traveler who wants all the fun without the hassles of planning a trip (and is willing to pay for the service), consider using a personal tour guide. Hiring a personal escort—someone who is an expert in the area you plan to visit—is becoming a more common option for a small group or family. This type of travel can be expensive; indeed, the cost is about what it takes for an additional person to go on the vacation. But having a guide who is familiar with the customs, history, food, and culture of an area (and who may also serve as a driver) can be a great boon to a trip. To hire a travel escort, try Abercrombie & Kent (www.abercrombiekent.com or 800-554-7016). A&K can make any of their general escorted tours into a personal tour, or you can create your own itinerary. You could also contact colleges or tour companies to see if they can provide an expert in the area you wish to visit. The guide may go with you, meet you there, or be with you for all or part of each day.

How much do we love to travel? A study by the National Tour Association found that almost 90 percent of us would choose an experience that enriches us over material goods. So let's go!

HOW TO DECODE A TRAVEL BROCHURE

Brochure Term	Translation
Tropical	Rainy
Secluded hideaway	Impossible to find or get to
Explore on your own	Pay for it yourself
Standard	Substandard
Deluxe	Standard
Light and airy	No air-conditioning

4

WHAT AND WHERE IS HOME?

"Home is where the heart can laugh without shyness."
—Vernon Baker

Fill in the blank: "Home is where the _____ is." For many, the old adage is true; it is where the "heart" is. But some of us would like to fill in the blank with different words—golf, ocean, hiking, nature preserve, social contact, culture, etc. The word *home* conjures up many images. Defined as "the place in which one's domestic affections are centered," it has been celebrated by artists, poets, writers, and philosophers. With the number of multiple corporate relocations in our mobile society, "Where is home?" can become a difficult question to answer. Is it your current residence? Where you were born and grew up? Where most of your family lives? It's an important concept and a vital one to think about if you're contemplating moving upon retirement. Will there be a "Dinosaur Age," with retirees roaming the Earth in search of nirvana?

A 2005 survey by the National Association of Realtors found that 42 percent of boomers say they want to live in the South when they retire, 32 percent in the West, 15 percent would like to retire in the Midwest, and 12 percent in the Northeast. When you're talking about 76 million boomers, that's a lot of (potential) moving vans! Although many people stay put to be near family and friends, an interesting and surprising national survey by Clyde and Shari Steiner, authors of *Steiner's Complete How-to-Move Handbook*, found that the third most frequently cited reason for a move is to escape from family members and friends!

Whatever your reasons, will you pack up your things like a nomad and join the more than 50 percent of Americans who live in coastal cities? Will you ponder a second home? Which factors should you consider before relocating? How can you "try out" new places to live, and what housing possibilities exist? Should you consider renting? What if your adult kids decide to move back in with you? What is universal design, and how can it help you? And if you do decide to pull up roots, how do you increase your chances for a successful move? Enough questions—let's start answering them!

Historically, the majority of people did not move when they retired, but predictions about today's boomers paint a different picture. A 2004 survey by Del Webb, builder of active-adult communities, found that 55 percent of boomers plan to pull up stakes when they retire. If you've thought about the possibility of moving after retiring, take our survey, "To Relocate or Not to Relocate: That Is the Question" on page 440. .

In addition to quality-of-life factors, Harry Dent, author and futurist, suggests you consider quantitative factors such as job opportunities, income growth, population growth, how much land and water is available for development, real-estate appreciation, and office building vacancy rates. Dent also recommends using psychographics, or lifestyle analyses, in helping to choose a retirement location. One of these lifestyle analysis systems, called PRIZM, from Claritas, a marketing info research firm, "classifies neighborhoods into one of 62 categories based on census data, leading consumer surveys and media measurement data, and other public and private sources of demographic and consumer information."

For example, on the Claritas Web site (www.claritas. com), we clicked on "Free Resources," then "You Are Where You Live." We then entered 33480, the zip code for Palm Beach, Florida, which we know is an expensive area. Three lifestyle segments that surfaced were "Upper Crust" (median household income over $110,000) (affluent retirees), "Middleburg Managers" (middle class, over 55, and comfortable retirement incomes), and "Movers

---

Splitters is a fairly recent term used to describe people who can spend equal amounts of time in multiple homes, due to technological advances, the nature of their professions (sales, consulting, self-employment), and/or less-expensive travel options such as Jet Blue or Southwest. As Southwest's tagline states, "You're now free to move about the country."

and Shakers" (highly educated, business-class, dual-income couples). This is a thumbnail sketch of the type of information that PRIZM provides. Try putting in the zip code of your present locale or one you're considering, and see the demographics of people who live there!

Perhaps all these factors are not burning issues for everyone. Some people love snow and cold weather, some are unconcerned with job opportunities or the quantity of available land, and for the very wealthy, a low cost of living may not be paramount. (When we prioritized our own criteria with our spouses, climate and proximity to the beach were paramount.) Each person has to rank what is most important as he or she (including a significant other, if there is one) goes through the decision-making process. You may realize you have the qualities that are most important to you in your current location and decide you're already in the best possible place.

A HOME AWAY FROM HOME

One home or two? According to the Research Institute for Housing America, 15 percent of boomers over 50 own a second home. If you have the financial wherewithal and the desire for a second home, this is a path to consider. Perhaps you're very satisfied with your social group, you love your doctors, you know the maître d's of the best restaurants by name—the only things you're missing are dramatic mountains to ski, a sandy beach to stroll, or a secluded cabin from which to enjoy Mother Nature. Or maybe you'd like to be a snowbird (flee the cold winter weather for warmer destinations) or a sunbird (avoid the swelter of summer by going to a cooler location). A second home is also a way to sample an area as a future permanent retirement spot.

If you think you might want a second home, check out Chapter 5, where we recommend some specific locations and communities. Or take a look at places the editors of RealEstateJournal.com identified as attractive locations for a second home. Criteria included lower-than-average home costs, higher-than-average employment opportunities, and access to recreation and culture. Their 2006 list of a dozen recommended locations: Bath/Beaufort County, North Carolina; Blairsville, Georgia; Clarksville, Virginia; Cloudcroft, New Mexico; Dadeville, Alabama; Driggs,

---

If you need some suggestions, try the free, easy survey at www.findyourspot.com, which asks you to choose from a number of lifestyle options and then generates a list of potential places to consider for relocation. Or, try www.bestplaces.net and click on "Take the 'Find Your Best Place' quiz."

THE IDEAL SPOT TO LIVE

What are your requirements for the good life? What is nonnegotiable if you're choosing a place to live? In general, various authorities point to certain characteristics for an ideal retirement location. These factors mirror the results of a 2003 *Where to Retire* magazine subscriber survey. Features to consider in choosing a retirement community are:

1. Low crime rate
2. Active, clean, safe downtown
3. Good hospitals nearby
4. Low overall tax rate
5. Mild climate
6. Friendly, like-minded neighbors
7. Scenic beauty nearby
8. Low cost of living
9. Good recreational facilities
10. Low housing cost
11. Active social/cultural environment
12. Nearby airport with commercial service
13. Major city nearby
14. No state income tax
15. Continuing-care retirement communities available
16. Friends and/or relatives in area
17. Full- or part-time employment opportunities
18. College town with adult education available

Perhaps you have one or two other criteria to add to the list (e.g., beach or lakefront property available, place of worship within walking distance, etc.).

Idaho; Eureka Springs, Arkansas; Heber City, Utah; Helen, Georgia; Jemez Springs, New Mexico; South Padre Island, Texas; and Steamboat Springs, Colorado.

Pros of a Second Home

Historically, real estate does tend to appreciate over time—helping to reduce the cost of combining the best of both worlds (main home in a city full of cultural amenities with a second home in a laid-back beach area, for example). You may get away more often knowing there's a place waiting for you. You may be able to rent your place when you're not there to help defray costs. It may be a magnet for family and friends to visit (hmm . . . could this also be a con for some?). If you're not a planner, you'll

---

THE HURRICANE EFFECT

Will the dozen hurricanes in Florida since 1995 affect this state's ranking as a top retirement mecca? David Lereah, chief economist for the National Association of Realtors, predicts that the number of hurricanes, coupled with huge increases in homeowner insurance, could cause people to choose other areas for retirement and result in increased migration away from affected coastal areas.

---

always have a reservation at your seasonal destination. And you can double your social contacts by having two residences.

Cons of a Second Home

There are the issues of cost and maintenance—and of dealing with both from a distance. And if you have a finite amount of money (and who doesn't?), would owning a second home tie up so much money that it would preclude travel or other expensive, enjoyable activities? Some people have found it harder to make friends when shuttling between homes. Victoria and Bruce F., for example, own homes in Chicago, Illinois, and Beaufort, South Carolina. Although friendly with both sets of neighbors, they found there was a readjustment period when they returned to either home. Plans had been made, groups had been formed, and it took a while to reintegrate back into the social scene. Finding someone to keep an eye on each home in their absence was also critical.

A Few More Specifics

Consider distance. If getting to your second home becomes a major hassle in terms of time or cost, buying it may become a decision you'll regret. If you're looking for a weekend-type retreat, you may want to limit the driving distance to 3 hours or less (not more than a tank of gas away). If you're planning on living there for weeks or months at a time, however, this is less of an issue.

If you're thinking about a resort area for your second home (or even your primary home), find out the percentages of full-time and part-time residents, as well as rental restrictions. You may find your neighbors change from week to week.

Water damage can be a nightmare if you're not home.

When you're leaving your house for an extended period, turn off the main water shut-off valve and, if the pipes could freeze, drain the water lines at the lowest point. Don't forget exterior hose bibs and pipes. Claudia A. had a disaster while just picking up her dry cleaning. The rubber supply hose from the washing machine (located on the main floor) burst, causing water to ruin the hardwood floors in the kitchen, powder room, and hallway, and to pour into the basement. If the interior temperature where you live could go below the freezing point, add ethylene glycol (antifreeze or windshield washer fluid) to other drains with water-filled plumbing traps (tubs, showers, toilet bowls, floor drains, etc.) after you've removed as much water from them as possible.

Appliances can cause an electrical fire even if they are turned off. Switch off circuit breakers to everything but the lighting and heating you want to utilize while you're absent. Dishwashers have a little bit of water in the bottom to keep the seals pliable and protect the motor. To prevent that water from evaporating, add ½ cup of liquid bleach and 3 tablespoons of mineral oil. The bleach will kill bacteria, and the oil will float on top of the water, preventing evaporation.

Dispose of perishable foods, or take them with you. Safely store any valuable and/or sentimental items.

If your house is in a northern climate, when leaving for an extended period it's helpful to leave the windows cracked to allow the humidity to equalize inside and outside the house, preventing condensation and the growth of mold and mildew within your home. Ask someone you trust to close and lock the windows after a few weeks. Also, installing a low-heat thermostat (set around 40 degrees Fahrenheit) will prevent pipes from freezing while saving money over conventional thermostats, which typically have their lowest setting around 55 or 60 degrees. If you leave a southern home vacant during the summer, Pacific Gas and Electric Company recommends you set your air conditioner above 85 degrees and close the drapes.

You'll need a mechanism for receiving bills as you alternate between residences. Many companies send bills over the Internet, a trend that's accelerating. It has the added plus of eliminating the paperwork that traditional snail mail entails. So if you're comfortable with the computer, your bills are often only a click away, no matter where you are. Or you can have the post office forward your mail.

The median price of a single-family detached home was $225,700 in 2006, according to the National Association of Realtors.

There's nothing like the human touch. If you know someone who can periodically check on the house and get in touch with you if there's an issue, you'll feel much more relaxed about your second home. If you notify them, the police will also drive by to check things out.

FINDING A PLACE

So you've decided to consider moving or maybe buying a second residence after retirement. How do you go about it?

First, reflect on why you're considering moving. Do you want to escape from something unpleasant in your current location (shoveling snow, meddling in-laws, high cost of living, a house that won't suit your needs as you get older)? Are you attracted to a place because of the lifestyle it offers (easy access to water, proximity to your children, low maintenance, etc.)? Usually, there is more than just one reason for contemplating relocation. Let's face it; most of us are living in a particular place because of job considerations. With this fact removed from the equation, it opens up a world of possibilities; you can now focus on lifestyle rather than livelihood!

Once you've completed the first step of thinking about why you'd like to move, reexamine the issues shown in "The Ideal Spot to Live" on page 87. Go ahead and prioritize them.

Now, the research part begins. You need to find communities that include your most important criteria, within the confines of what you can afford. Some of these, like proximity to friends and family (keep in mind that they could move too!) or climate, are easy to determine. Others, such as safety issues, transportation, or property taxes, require more digging. The Internet is a fabulous resource to ferret out this information. A site such as www.money.cnn.com (click on "Real Estate," and then "Best Places to Live") allows you to search by various criteria, such as small cities, most singles, best educated, most job growth, etc. Or, let's say you want a place with tons of amenities (such as golf) or a gated community. Check out sites such as www.private communities.com, www.coastalresortcommunities.net, or www.golfcoursehome.net. Will an active-adult community fit your lifestyle? Try www.activeadultliving. com, which details around 2,000 developments. Or you can take a look at Chapters 5, 6, and 7, where we do the

---

A cost-of-living calculator can help determine how far your money will go in a new location. Try the one at www.bankrate.com (click on "Cost of Living Comparison" calculator).

analysis for you, summarize the positives and negatives of specific places, and suggest communities for relocation. (For books and magazines that rate places to live, see the resources for this chapter.) Solicit recommendations from neighbors, friends, and family who share a similar outlook to help devise a list of potential places.

If you like the idea of one-stop shopping, and the ability to meet with approximately 50 representatives of master-planned communities in a number of different states, check out the LiveSouth Real Estate Shows (www.livesouth.com or 800-713-4263) and Ideal Destinations (www.idealdestinations.com or 888-248-3252). You'll have the opportunity to ask questions, attend seminars, and sign up for discovery visits. (In the interest of disclosure, Cathy and Jan present seminars at these shows.)

Another thought is to look where you have frequently traveled or vacationed. If you continue to return to the same place year after year, it's a sign that it could be the location for you. Linda and Michael D., for example, were drawn to the small-town beauty and sparkling summers of Charlevoix, Michigan, every summer from their primary home in Houston, Texas. When they decided they wanted to purchase a second home, it was a no-brainer.

As you investigate each area, it's helpful to take notes that reflect how each proposed community meets your most important needs. You can use a worksheet, such as "Compare Your Housing Costs" on page 449, to see how the costs of buying a home compare to your present home's costs. Most chambers of commerce are happy to send you information for free. A site such as www.touristinformationdirectory.com allows you to access the state's chambers of commerce with a click; you can then narrow it down to specific cities and towns within each state and request relocation information from them. Although you may also get mail from real-estate agents, banks, and other businesses, we think it's a small price to pay for the valuable information you'll accumulate.

As you gather research on areas you're considering for relocation, it's important to document how they overlap with your lifestyle wishes. Again, taking notes as you go will save lots of time later!

Of course, you need to know what you'll have to spend on your next home. For a quick estimate of how much money you can expect to realize from the sale of your current home, or ask a local Realtor to do an analysis or check Zillow (www.zillow.com).

TRYING A PLACE FOR FIT

Now that you've constructed a list that fits your lifestyle, at least in theory, it's time to visit! There's no way of getting around this part, unless you're choosing a place you already know. But hey, this is the fun part! Many communities (especially the larger new ones with a long build-out time frame) offer discovery tours at reduced rates that allow you to take a tour, talk with residents, and sample such amenities as a round of golf or a meal at the clubhouse. Take advantage of these offers! You can get a real sense of the area and people and see if there's a good fit between you and the location. Perhaps you can either arrange a sabbatical from work to start your investigation or volunteer in the areas you're considering.

After you've completed this vital step, you'll have a much better feel for what you want, and you'll be able to narrow your list to a few contenders. (If nothing grabbed you, maybe you need to either go back to the research stage or decide that for you, "there's no place like home"—your current home, that is.)

Here are a few more specific ideas.

Sample all seasons. If you find you're crawling along in traffic for hours with the thousands of snowbirds who have flocked to your potential new home, you might think twice about relocating there. Likewise, if you visit a place only in the winter, you could be in for a shock when the summer humidity sets in. The mountain community that is so beautiful in the late summer may strike you differently as you slide on black ice during the winter.

Get the local newspaper. You can access many newspapers online or at the library or have a subscription sent to your home. Being in touch with the everyday events of your potential retirement haven clues you in on the events, issues, real-estate prices, and flavor of a community.

Talk to the locals. Visit a community center or strike up a conversation at a park or casual restaurant. You can find out invaluable information that the chambers of commerce or Realtors may not offer. The existence of paper factories or rendering plants is worth finding out about beforehand! What will happen to that big field behind your potential home? If you live inland, but close to the ocean, how will you ensure you have access to the beach?

Let your fingers do the walking. Get a copy of the

"When you're 17, you dream of a summer romance. When you're 47, you dream of a summer house."
—Marjorie Garber, *Sex and Real Estate*

area's Yellow Pages. You'll get a sense of the scope of restaurants, physicians, churches and temples, theaters, hospitals, parks, etc. Preview housing and rental costs from home on www.realtor.com (put in the zip code of the area you're considering). Rent or try a home exchange. It's a good idea to try out a prospective location for an extended period to ensure it's really for you. A site such as HomeAway, Inc. (www.home away.com) allows you to search more than 85,000 vacation rentals worldwide. Companies such as Homelink (www.homelink-usa.com or 800-638-3841) or Intervac (www.intervac-online.com or 800-756-4663) allow you to arrange a temporary swap of your home for one in a different location. (You will pay a fee for the service.) Try out homesharing. If you have the right personality, you could try out an area by sharing a residence with another (unrelated) adult. This could allow you to sample an area while saving financially. If you're single, you might find the safety and companionship aspects attractive as well. Contact the National Shared Housing Resource Center (www. nationalsharedhousing.org).

Be a freeloader. Global Freeloaders (www.globalfree loaders.com) is a free online service that allows you to stay at someone's home for free (though you need to be willing to reciprocate). The price is right!

Make sure there's a place for your "toys." Some developments include RV and boat storage on the premises. For example, the Villages of Westminster in Williamsburg, Virginia, provides on-site (hidden, fenced, and secured) storage for about 30 RVs and/or boats for a nominal yearly fee. This can be an attractive incentive for some buyers.

Practice retirement! Try living on your projected retirement income for a while, and try out those activities you're planning on doing when you actually do retire. It can be very instructive!

We realize people have many personality types. The methodical may go through all of these steps; others may stumble onto a place, fall in love, snap up the first home they visit, and live happily ever after (or not). We simply want to suggest ways to increase the chances of finding your ideal place.

 Laurie S. talks about relocating as a single woman.

In 1999, I retired from a 32-year teaching career and decided to look at retirement options. As a single woman, I felt that it was important to explore the following criteria.

1. Affordability
2. Friendly like-minded people in a community
3. Medical services nearby

4. Safety

5. Close to cultural events and other amenities

As I developed my retirement budget, I looked at various communities and asked many questions. Living on a fixed income, I needed to look for any hidden costs. After considering the cost of a new home, I took a look at:

1. Neighborhood association fees

2. Club and social dues

3. Property tax and state and federal taxes

4. Utility fees

5. Lawn maintenance

6. Insurance—homeowners, wind damage, hurricane damage, and fire

7. Pest control

8. Ongoing maintenance

Community and amenities were very important to me. My chosen community is a mix of ages from about 30 to 80, but there are not many other singles. Exercise and physical activities are of the utmost importance to me, and I picked a community with a state-of-the-art fitness center and spa, with highly qualified personal trainers. For people who love golf, swimming, and boating, it is all here at the Club at Hammock Beach in Palm Coast. Cultural events, concerts, and ballet are close by in Jacksonville. Safety is important if you are living alone, and I liked that this gated neighborhood has 24-hour security.

My last thought is about health care. Make sure your insurance is accepted easily and doctors are accessible. Unfortunately, as we age, this becomes more important. ⓣⓁ

TRENDS IN HOME BUYING

You've zeroed in on the perfect town. It's safe, close to a major airport, and has great weather and terrific medical facilities—the top things on your personal-priority list. You're ready to choose your residence. What are some recent home-buying trends of which you should be aware?

As you outfit yourself and your dream house, try these Web sites to see whether you're getting the best prices: www.pricegrabber.com, www.shopping.com, www.nextag.com, or www.bizrate.com. Comparison shopping is only keystrokes away!

Given that there are almost 80 million baby boomers, builders need to know what customers want so they can "build it, and they will come." Studies by the National Association of Home Builders and Countrywide Home Loans surveyed home buyers 50 and older and found that they are looking for:

✳ Energy-efficient and low-maintenance homes. And they want services to care for their yards and the exterior portions of their homes.

✳ Building "green" for environmental and health reasons.

✳ Secure homes and communities. Security systems, lighting, and limited access were important. There are more than 8 million people living in gated communities in the United States.

✳ High-speed Internet connections. Homeowners want to be wired with broadband Internet service.

✳ "Smart" houses. Buyers want to turn on some calming music, turn off a few extraneous lights, and make the house a bit warmer—all from one control panel! Or close their garage door—from their office; lower their oven temperature—with their cell phone; or see who's ringing their doorbell—on their television. That's the magic of "smart" homes, or home automation. If you like high-tech gadgets, explore a site such as www.smarthome.com or call 800-762-7846.

✳ Proximity to shopping, restaurants, physicians, and places of worship.

✳ Quality workmanship.

Another survey of boomers, by Del Webb, found these additional wants on boomers' wish lists:

✳ New construction. More than 40 percent of boomers said they plan on moving into a new home after they retire.

✳ Great rooms, home offices, gourmet kitchens, and exercise rooms.

✳ Amenities such as computer labs, tennis courts, fitness centers, and pools.

Almost 80 percent of potential home buyers surf the Internet to collect information. Sites such as www.realtor.com or www.rent.com are quite useful for doing preliminary research. You can plug in many different parameters to narrow a search to your specifications.

❋ Intergenerational communities where children and grandchildren are welcome.

Another trend in new homes is the "his and her" house with two master closets, two sinks at different heights, two home offices, two retreat areas . . . you get the idea. Outdoor fireplaces, summer kitchens, more outside living areas, fountains, meditation rooms, and in-home theaters are also attractive to people who can foot the bill.

Additionally, a substantial number of boomers would like to move into active-adult, resort-style living environments without moving to another state or even far from their existing communities. They'd like to stay close to their families and friends but still have all the bells and whistles. In response, many developers are building country club–style developments in what are not normally thought of as retirement havens. For example, there are active-adult communities in New Jersey, Massachusetts, and the Chicago area.

In a nutshell, boomers are choosing lifestyle, and it's pretty obvious they aren't planning on downsizing that!

RENT OR BUY?

The prevailing mantra has generally been that it's better to own than to rent your residence. Is this an ironclad rule?

Not always. If you're trying out a place for retirement, renting could make sense. That way, if you find out it's not really the place for you and you decide to move within a few years, you won't risk losing some of your investment in a new home. Or, if you're not sure your future retirement income will support the cost of a house, renting could be an attractive option because you're not responsible for property taxes, upkeep, and possibly some utilities. If you're able to invest the money you save by renting, you could end up with a greater monthly retirement income. Buying, on the other hand, allows you to build equity, provides some tax breaks, and conveys the emotional pleasure of being a homeowner. Rents can increase annually, but you usually know your mortgage payment from year to year (unless you get a variable interest rate mortgage). As a homeowner, you are in control of changes to your

---

If you're building your own home, you may want to consider the "New Home Construction Bidsheet" from nationally syndicated columnist Tim Carter at www.askthebuilder.com. It covers all aspects of construction and can be e-mailed to you as an Adobe PDF file for $37.

home and not subject to the vagaries of a landlord or a lease.

To do the math on renting versus buying, use an online calculator such as www.smartmoney.com/home/buying/ (go to "To Rent or to Buy?" under "Worksheets"). After you input the data, the calculator will help determine the right direction for you.

New or Resale?

Assuming you decide you want to own, not rent, is it better to buy new or purchase a resale? Again, it depends.

The pros of a new home include more choices, options, and upgrades; more energy efficiency; home-builder warranties; more modern layouts and use of space; lower costs associated with repairs; and, in a new community, greater ease making friends since your neighbors are often new to the area as well.

The pros of a resale include more bang for your buck. On a square-footage basis, resales are usually less expensive; may already have amenities such as mature landscaping, watering systems, and window treatments; have no surprises in terms of the neighborhood because what you see is what you get; are often closer to stores and restaurants; and often have larger lots.

Tanya and Bruce F. were transferred several times during their careers with General Electric. When moving to an area, they always bought new. The main reason? They felt it was easier for their children (and them) to make new friends. Dorothy and Thomas S., on the other hand, like the traditional layouts and established landscaping of an older home. In addition, they are very handy at repairs and like to be within walking distance of town. The moral: There is no right or wrong. There is only what works for you.

CUSTOM BUILDING

We've discussed purchasing a residence, but what if you've found the perfect piece of land and decide to build your retirement retreat while you finish up your last year(s) on the job?

The land under your prefab housing may be purchased or rented. Be careful about renting: There have been cases where people owned their homes but rented the land, and the land was sold for redevelopment. This has happened in a number of older trailer parks. The homes often cannot be moved, or it's prohibitively expensive, and the owners end up having to abandon them.

PREFAB HOUSING TERMS DEFINED

According to the Clayton Homes Web site, a *manufactured home* has been "built entirely in the factory under federal code administered by the Department of Housing and Urban Development (HUD)," while a *mobile home* is "the term used for homes built prior to June 15, 1976, when HUD code went into effect. Voluntary standards were previously in effect." A *modular home* is "built to state, local, or regional code where home will be located. Multisection units are transported to sites and installed." A *panelized home* is "built in factory, where panels that include windows, doors, wiring, and siding, are transported to site and assembled. Codes are set by state or locality where sited." Lastly, a *precut home* involves "materials that are factory cut to design specifications and then transported to the site and assembled. Examples are: kit, log, and dome homes. Standards are set by state and locality."

First, take stock of your existing home and write down any "must-haves" for your new one. For example, Celia and Jim M.'s previous home had a garage with access directly into their kitchen. In their next home, they made it a point to have the entrance into the laundry room. Angela and Michael R. put a high premium on having a first-floor master bedroom and bathroom. Bob and Paula F. looked for a flat driveway so they could install a basketball hoop for their four grandchildren. Rob L. wanted his kitchen sink to have a window above it so he could look outside while performing the unpleasant task of washing dishes, and wanted granite rather than Formica for his countertops. Caroline B. is not happy with the scarcity of outlets in her existing home; she vows to address this in her next one.

Be aware of any restrictions or covenants governing your new home. Jasmine and Charles K. ended up having to move their driveway 18 inches because it was not installed the required distance from their lot line, and Patricia and Pete P. didn't realize their teenage children were prohibited from parking their cars on their community's street.

Contact the local homebuilders' association and obtain a list of local builders. Look through the real-estate sections of the newspaper and see who is building homes in your price range. Check out any models or projects of potential builders. Get recommendations from your soon-to-be neighbors and from Realtors, and contact references provided by the builders after you meet with them. Visit the referenced homes if possible; if not, at least check out the outside. Be aware of warranties and service after the completion of your home, find out how long the builder has been in business, and be sure you feel that your personalities click. Check out builders with the Better Business Bureau. Consider hiring an architect and interior designer, as well. Input from these professionals can be invaluable to this big investment. They should be willing and able to work as partners as your residence is planned. If you obtain a loan, be sure the term of the construction loan is sufficient so that you don't end up paying penalties, as did Carla and Fred T. whose Florida home took almost 8 months longer than estimated to complete.

Use technology. E-mail and digital photographs will go a long way toward keeping everyone apprised of issues and progress. Of course, you'll need to visit the site in person periodically to see how things are going. In addition, it would be helpful to hire someone to check things out on a regular basis; in some cases, the architectural firm may do this, or perhaps a trusted friend or neighbor can keep an eye on things.

HOUSING OPTIONS

Condos, modular homes, manufactured homes, zero-lot-line homes, apartments, carriage homes, single-family homes, townhomes—the list of housing choices is extensive. (If you're looking for a less typical arrangement, such as living in an RV, in a hotel, or on a ship, check out Chapter 6.) Consider: What lifestyle are you seeking? Do you love gardening, or would you rather leave yard work to someone else? Does the thought of having someone sharing adjoining walls bother you? Do you want your community to be age restricted, or do you relish interacting with all age groups? Does the security of a gated community appeal to you, or do you feel you'd be living "behind bars"?

If you hope to avoid a Realtor's commission and want to try to sell your own home, think about using one of these online assists (remember, about 80 percent of us use the Internet for home shopping): www.sellyourhomeyourself.com, www.privateforsale.com, or www.forsalebyowner.com. Only about nine percent of home sales are by owner, and, of course, you'll pay for the ad.

If you're contemplating a change (say, from a single-family home to a condo), it's a good idea to rent in your potential new spot to see if that style of living is for you. It will also provide you the opportunity to become better acquainted with the area. Here are some things to keep in mind as you decide on housing.

Full-time versus part-time residents. If you are a full-time resident living in an area of many part-time residents (or the other way around), there may be friction. The full-timers may want strict noise ordinances; the part-timers may not care if people are having parties in their absence. Part-timers may want liberal rental arrangements; full-timers may want renters who will be there a minimum of 3 months for more continuity. Mary Lou and Bill S. live full time in a condo in Myrtle Beach, South Carolina. They find that during high season they can sometimes go for days without seeing a familiar face. Also, the sounds of people pushing carts full of luggage while moving in and out can be quite loud. Although this doesn't bother them, for others it would be anathema. If there are covenants governing these issues, you need to be comfortable with them before committing to a purchase.

Fees. The cost of a home is just one factor in choosing your residence. Keep in mind all those amenities in a planned community (golf courses, spas, pools, tennis courts) have to be paid for by someone, and that someone is probably you and your neighbors! Association dues can be quite steep, depending on the community. Frank D. found that when he tried to sell his three-bedroom townhome in a good school district in Maryland, people were attracted by the listing price of $260,000 but were turned off by the high monthly-association fees for repairs and maintenance. So you'll need to be sure to account for these; keep in mind that associations can raise dues as well.

Restrictions. Besides such understandable issues as whether rentals are allowed, neighborhood covenants can include all kinds of things, such as what time your garbage cans can be put out for trash pickup, what color you can choose for the exterior of your home, what type of basketball hoop (if any) you can install, and what changes you can make to your landscaping. Of course, the idea is to protect the value of your property, but make sure you can live with the rules and regulations.

A Clemson University study that found "good" landscaping increased the selling price of a home by 4 to 5 percent over that of a home with "average" landscaping, and "excellent" landscaping increased the selling price by an additional 6 to 7 percent (or more).

Low-dough options. If you're looking for a single-family home but cost is a limiting factor, consider pre-fabricated housing. About 10 million American households call their manufactured houses "home." Modular homes, kit homes, and manufactured homes have come a long way, baby! Materials and looks have improved, they are better and more quickly built and they can cost about 10 to 20 percent less than a "stick-built home." Keep in mind, though, that manufactured home values usually decrease over time. Take a look at some examples: Champion Enterprises (www.champion homes.net or 248-340-9090), Clayton Homes (www. clayton.net or 800-822-0633), or Fleetwood Enterprises (www.fleetwoodhomes.com).

Universal Design

Whether you stay put, buy new, buy a resale, rent, or remodel, you need to know about a concept called "universal design." According to the Center for Universal Design, the intent of this type of design "is to simplify life for everyone by making products, communications, and the built environment more usable by as many peo-ple as possible at little or no extra cost. Universal design benefits people of all ages and abilities." Translated into specifics (we love specifics!), it means 27-inch-high electrical outlets to minimize bending, rocker switches to make turning lights on and off easier, nonslip flooring, wider hallways to accommodate a wheelchair (if necessary), etc. In other words, universal design makes a home more accessible, no matter what your age or condition. For a terrific list of exterior and interior universal design ideas, see the "Smart Ideas Checklists" on page 431.

SELLING YOUR HOME

Let's say you decide to move and put your home up for sale. What are some tried-and-true methods for ensuring you get top dollar for it?

Choose your real-estate agent wisely. It goes without saying that he or she should be in good standing, belong to the Multiple Listing Service, and have a current real-estate license. It's preferable if real estate is the agent's full-time profession and if he or she is a local resident and really knows the area. Choose someone who will be

---

Thinking of hiring a contractor and building a home yourself? Go to www.beconstructive.com and click on "Consumers," then "Homebuilder's Checklist" to access a detailed chart of products and services you should consider.

honest in his or her comments about your home and know how to show it off to its best advantage. Ask friends, neighbors, and relatives for recommendations, interview several agents, check their references, and be sure you feel comfortable working with your pick. Although your agent will market and advertise your home, the National Association of Realtors reports that more than 80 percent of sales are due to agent contacts, not advertising or open houses. (In one of the author's former neighborhoods, for-sale signs go up infrequently. One agent knows the area so well and has so many contacts that a call to her usually results in a sale without a sign ever going up.)

Curb Appeal

A potential buyer's first impression is very important. Here's how to improve your home's curb appeal.

First impressions count! If prospective buyers aren't enticed or excited about your home when they pull up to the curb and get their first look, you're already fighting an uphill battle. In fact, they may never even set foot inside. The idea is that the potential purchasers should become emotionally involved with your house, envisioning it as their own and relating to the lifestyle it projects.

Take stock of the yard. Trim your trees, shrubs, and bushes and remove dead flowers, leaves, weeds, and other debris. Be sure landscaping hasn't overwhelmed the house and that windows aren't blocked by plants. Lay down a fresh layer of mulch. Keep the lawn (which should be healthy and weed-free) mowed at an attractive height (no scalping), and edge along driveways or sidewalks. Kill grass growing through sidewalks. Think color! If you're selling at the right time of year, plant flowers (yellow is particularly effective) or use hanging baskets, such as blooming flowers from a nursery.

Paint, repair, and replace. Windows or outside trim that is peeling or a front door that is bleached out from the sun are turnoffs. Replace or polish doorknobs or knockers that have become dull or damaged from the elements. Repair any fences, shutters, roofing, porches, screens, cracks, etc. Make sure your mailbox or mailbox slot is in good shape. Replace your welcome mat.

Clean. Wash windows and any outside light fixtures and make sure all light bulbs are working, while you're at it. Sweep walkways, decks, and porches. Hose off the driveway, and try to remove any oil stains. If you have or can borrow a power washer, it's great for sprucing up outdoor furniture, decks, siding, and the driveway. If not, use your hose and extra elbow grease. Tidy up the grill and surrounding area, and clean out gutters.

Downplay pets. Not everyone will be as fond of your pets as you are! Remove any "presents" your dog may have left on your property. It might be a good idea to leave the dog with a neighbor or relative during showings.

Straighten up the garage. This is one of the author's own litmus tests when considering a home. Unclutter the garage. Remove cars during a showing so the buyers can see how spacious and well-maintained it is. Remove oil spots from the floor; painting the garage floor with an epoxy paint can make the floor gleam. Consider painting the walls as well. Neatly arrange mowers and tools. Buy new trash cans.

Interior Fixes

You'll need to spruce up the inside of your home as well. Here's how.

Clean. The proverb "cleanliness is next to godliness" is so very true when it comes to selling your home. Cleanliness includes odor removal, so if you have pets or there's a smoker in the house, get out the Febreze or have carpets, window treatments, and furniture professionally cleaned. Sometimes you don't notice the odors in your home; ask the Realtor or a friend for an honest opinion. Windows, mirrors, and glass doors should sparkle, and floors should shine.

Minimize. Go through closets, basements, the garage, and other storage areas. Give away things you no longer use (you probably won't fit into those size-2 jeans again) to a worthy cause, such as Goodwill, the Salvation Army, or St. Vincent de Paul (of course, document this for tax purposes), or have a garage or yard sale prior to putting the house up for sale. Or put things outside with a sign that they are free for the taking. We've done this a number of times, with great success (because of our homeowners' association rules, we only do it the evening before and the day of trash pickup). Make your drawers, closets, bookshelves, cabinets, and countertops look spacious. Store excess personal items in another location. Remove furniture that makes a room look crowded, and arrange what's left to make the room appear larger.

Repair and replace. Again, go through your home and replace faded or ripped cushions, window treatments, and carpeting. Buy new towels, throw rugs, and shower curtains for bathrooms. Fix any nail holes showing in the drywall and replace missing screws, handles, and light bulbs. Be sure all windows open and close

---

Warning: A number of problems have been associated with Exterior Installation Finish System (EIFS), or synthetic stucco. There are lawsuits against manufacturers, installers, and builders using this product. Water can get in, but not out, which may result in decay of the underlying wood and perhaps mold growth and termite infestation. If purchasing a home of this type, be extremely cautious.

easily and that faucets and appliances, including your air conditioner and furnace, are in good working order.

Make it cozy. Have the smell of freshly baked cookies or pie wafting through the house when people come to look. Put fresh flowers around the house, and have some soft music playing in the background. Leave lights on, even during the day. Keep shades open so the light comes in, and so that your home doesn't look foreboding from outside. Remove personal mementos (such as photographs or diplomas); it's easier for a potential buyer to imagine the house is his or hers without them.

Consider hiring a professional home stager. Ever go into a model home and notice how the lamps never have cords, the desks never have bulky computers, and the bedrooms often have no dressers? Tricks like these are hallmarks of home stagers. Stagers can make a home look spacious and attractive, but, of course, you'll have to pay for it. They may charge by the hour or the job; some bring in rented furniture to show your home to its best advantage. Ask neighbors or Realtors (especially the larger realty companies) for referrals. Or find an accredited staging professional in your area at www.stagedhomes.com or 800-392-7161. While this can be a pricey way to go, it may increase the amount you'll get for your home. Surveys comparing staged versus non-staged homes reflect a sales price of up to 7 percent more for a staged home, and 50 percent less time on the market.

Leave. Don't be in the house while it is shown. This makes it easier for everyone involved.

BUYING A HOME

We've already mentioned the factors to consider when choosing a new community. Once you've been sold on the area, here are a few tips for buying your home.

Construct a wish list. Know what you want in a new home (hopefully you made this list while living in your previous residence) so you can approach the process

---

Century 21 offers a "Mature Moves" service. Targeted to people between 55 and 70 years of age, the service helps to clarify a client's psychological needs (such as proximity to relatives) and physical needs (such as universal design issues) and assists in purchasing a home that meets those goals. Find a "Mature Moves" professional at www.century21.com (click on Century 21 "Mature Moves" under "Real Estate Services and Resources" on the site map) or 800-446-8737.

from a methodical, logical perspective rather than an emotional or seat-of-the-pants approach.

Consider using a buyer's agent. A buyer's agent represents the buyer, not the seller. Buyer's agents exclusively represent your interests. Some agents represent both seller and buyer. This certainly seems like a conflict of interest, but one of the authors had this type of agent and was extremely pleased with the outcome when she sold her home. Ask friends for recommendations, call the larger real-estate firms, or look under "Real Estate" in the Yellow Pages; companies will often advertise that they have buyer's agents.

Have the home professionally inspected. The American Society of Home Inspectors is the largest and oldest professional association of home inspectors in the United States. Locate an inspector on their Web site (www.ashi.com) or call them at 800-743-2744. If it's a new home, with many warranties, you may not need to do this, but you never know. Pat and Phil D. had an inspection on their new home and found that their chimney flue had been improperly installed. The builder rectified it prior to their closing.

Know these things. Is your home under a flight path, or can you hear the sounds of the highway? If there is vacant land nearby, find out how it's zoned, as well as any developments in the pipeline. Be sure there are no paper plants, landfills, or businesses nearby that would be unpleasant neighbors. (One of our neighbors downsized and unwittingly moved close enough to a rendering plant to "enjoy" the smell.) Orientation of the house is important: Is the main living area on display to the neighbors if you have your shades up? Will cars shine their headlights into your home as they make a turn into your neighborhood? Is it impossible to make a left turn out of your neighborhood in the morning because of traffic? Is the home situated on an embankment that could be subject to erosion? Even if you're an empty nester, is the home in a good school district? Are you buying the most expensive home in the neighborhood (not so good) or the least expensive home in a good neighborhood (better)? Has the house been professionally staged? You may be falling in love with an unrealistic picture of how it will be lived in. Are there many renters in the development, which can depress property values? Is the area safe?

Have your loan preapproved. You'll be in a much stronger negotiating position if you've been preapproved by the mortgage company. Check out several mortgage companies before committing, and get written specifics,

---

If you need storage or assistance loading or unloading, check out www.emove.com to find help.

including your interest rate and for how long it's locked in.

Consider the future. Eventually, you or your heirs will most likely sell your home. Even as you're buying, think in terms of what will sell later, such as a minimum of 2.5 bathrooms, at least three bedrooms, a garage (preferably two or three-car), and a kitchen that opens into a family room or at least has a view of the family room. Amenities such as parks, walking trails, and open spaces are also high on buyers' lists.

See what happens in the rain. One author had a home in a previous neighborhood that backed up to a retention pond. Although the pond works as it should, the level of water becomes frighteningly high in a heavy rain. It's a good idea to visit the home you're considering purchasing during a downpour to check out the effects on the inside and outside of the house.

THE BUY-SELL CONUNDRUM

In most cases, you'll need the money from the sale of your existing home to buy your new home. You may have to put things in storage for a while or find temporary housing, but it's better than having two mortgages, unless you know you can carry two homes. Perhaps you can have a contingency on the sale of your house, but many potential buyers won't go for that; or maybe you can state in your contract that you'll remain in the house for a specified time after the sale, paying the new owners a daily agreed-upon "rent" while you find a new home. Maybe your buyers will agree to a far-off closing date. In actuality, you may just have to move out and make the best of it while you search for your new place! If you have grown children, perhaps you can temporarily move in with them. (This could be payback if they've boomeranged back to your home in the past!)

Walk around. Talk to people living in the neighborhood. You'll get a good sense of the issues affecting the development and see whether you'd feel comfortable living there. Return at least three times over a 24-hour period to get a feel for the community at different times of the day. Finding out, if possible, why the seller is listing the home can be important in negotiating the best price. Loss of a job may be a big incentive for a quick sale, for example.

To get a rough idea of the cost of a proposed move, go to the North American Van Lines Web site, www.navl.com, and click on "Request a Free Estimate" then on "Household Move," then on "Get a Ballpark Price."

Ask a few questions. What did the seller pay for the house? This is a matter of public record and can help you estimate how much equity the sellers have in the house. You can find out through the local tax assessor's office, and the information is usually available online for free. For example, if the sellers bought their home for $300,000 2 years ago and they're now asking $500,000, you might well question the inflated asking price. Other questions: How old is the roof? Air conditioner? Hot-water heater? Other appliances? Sellers fill out a disclosure form, but if they have lived there a relatively short time, they may not know those answers. Ask about the previous owners, and see if you can contact them.

Read everything carefully before signing!

Best advice? Caveat emptor (let the buyer beware).

MOVING DAY

Now you need to get from here to there. Will you move yourself, like more than half the population does (according to U-Haul), or use a professional mover for some or all of the work? Regardless, planning is imperative. To help plan your move, see the "Moving Planner Checklist" from North American Van Lines on page 435. They provide a handy list of things to do from 2 or more months ahead of time through moving day.

If you go the do-it-yourself route by renting a moving truck, you will save money, but check into getting additional coverage on your homeowner's policy. Most rental companies exclude many items (such as jewelry and furs and damages due to improper packing).

How much will movers cost? Price is affected by the weight of your belongings, distance, location (moving to a rural area may be less expensive than moving to the middle of a city), access issues for the moving van, time of the move (nonsummer months can be less expensive), amount of packing involved, and any other services you require, such as storage. Friends and relatives can be a good source of recommendations for moving companies, and it's a good idea to consult the Better Business Bureau to see if there are any complaints against the companies you're considering.

Experts recommend that you obtain estimates from at least three moving companies. Estimates can take several forms; most often, they are binding or nonbinding. A binding estimate is just that; you are bound to pay the price in the estimate whether the final cost of the move is more or less. A nonbinding estimate approximates the cost of your move; you are then limited to paying no more than 110 percent of the amount of the nonbinding estimate at delivery and must pay any additional charges within 30 days; your final cost is determined by actually weighing the shipment. There is a third type of estimate called a not-to-exceed estimate; it may go by other names (such as a price-protection estimate). In this type of estimate, you pay the lower of the actual cost of the move or the binding estimate cost. Of course, if you tack on additional services (such as storage), or ship additional pieces of furniture, you will be charged extra,

Clarify with the mover how payment will be made. Some do not accept major credit cards; others do. Many do not accept personal checks. You may need a certified check, money order, or cash. Get everything in writing.

What if you have problems with the move? Is there any recourse? Short-circuit any problems by signing up with a reputable company, but if issues arise, you do have some rights. Federal law requires your mover to provide a pamphlet, "Your Rights and Responsibilities When You Move." If you have a complaint about your mover you'd like to file with the Federal Motor Carrier Safety Administration, log on to their site at www.fmcsa.dot.gov and click on "Safety Violation and Household Goods Consumer Complaints" or call them at 800-832-5660.

THEY'RE BAAAAAAAACK! (BOOMERANG KIDS)

What if your kids fly back to the nest? This phenomenon is referred to as "boomerang kids," and we didn't feel we could wrap up the chapter without discussing this not-so-uncommon event.

About 30 percent of boomers have had children move back home. Several explanations have been advanced for this increasing trend: the not-so-great job market, the need to pay back college loans, sky-high rents, boomer parents not wanting their children to grow up, kids having been overindulged and spoiled, marriages occurring later in life, divorce among young adults, changing parent-child dynamics (parents acting more like friends than parents), and a drawing out of the period before kids become fully functioning adults. (*Newsweek* termed this *adultolescence*.)

What's a no-longer-empty nester to do? Some parents love the idea that their children are returning. It makes them feel younger, and they are gratified that their children feel comfortable using them as a safety net. Katie H., for example, moved back into her parents' home after college graduation during her first year of teaching. It enabled Katie to buy a car and save enough money to move into an apartment (with a roommate) during her second year of teaching. Katie's parents were delighted to have her living at home.

Others aren't quite so delighted. Cecilia and Kyle P.'s son also moved home after graduation. He's sleeping in until noon every day, barely contributes to the housework, and makes only a token effort to look for a job. In short, they are losing their minds!

Expert Advice

Here are some thoughts on living with a boomerang kid.

Discuss a time line. Adult children should understand this is a temporary arrangement. A specific move-out date should be determined (for example, 2 years would be pretty generous).

Develop house rules. We're talking adult children here, so the idea is to foster independence. Consider charging rent and/or having your children cook, contribute to the upkeep of the home, and wash their own clothes. Determine guidelines for such things as smoking in the house, having friends or significant others over, and/or people spending the night.

Be a cheerleader. In some cases, you may need to give a little nudge to get your bird out of the nest. Let your children know that you know they can do it. Encourage them to work toward independence, whether it's by sending out résumés, looking for roommates, or getting counseling if they need it. You and your spouse or significant other should be in sync on the time line and house rules.

Examine your own agenda. If you're an empty nester, does having a child back in the home satisfy a need to be needed? Do you lack confidence in your child's ability to fend for himself or herself? Do you want your children to stay dependent forever? If that's the case, counseling may be helpful for you as well. *Psychology Today* termed this inability of parents to let go *permaparenting*. (For info on caring for your aging parents, rather than your adult children, see Chapter 8.)

What is home? Where is home? It may be a no-brainer if you're not going anywhere, or finding your potential utopia may open up almost limitless possibilities that you'll need to whittle down. Keep in mind, though, that there could be many correct decisions; it's doubtful that only one place would fit your personal lifestyle requirements.

If you are one of those people who have a yen for the unusual, though, Chapter 6, "What Are Some Niche Retirement Lifestyles?" is for you!

 "Chance favors the prepared mind." A wise man, that Louis Pasteur!

In researching retirement areas for our seminars and the first edition of this book, we discovered a place in the southeastern United States that looked great on paper. We (along with our spouses) flew from Cincinnati to Florida in the morning, looked at oceanfront lots in a brand-new golf community, made and had our offers accepted, and flew home that evening.

All our previous homework and legwork made a "snap" decision possible, and as a result we are now building homes on the ocean—a lifelong dream for the authors and their spouses.

PART II

WHERE SHOULD YOU SPEND YOUR RETIREMENT YEARS?

WHERE SHOULD YOU MOVE?

Recommended Locations within the United States

"If you have built castles in the air, your work need not be lost; that is where they should be. Now put the foundations under them."
—Henry David Thoreau

Where are the beautiful beaches? The gorgeous golf courses? The best boating spots? The places with the lowest cost of living? The best opportunities for outdoor pursuits? In other words, if you're thinking about relocating, where should you move?

Of course, we recognize that many people will remain where they are when they retire. But for those who do want to move, this is the chapter for you. The legwork to determine some of the most desirable places to live in the United States has already been done!

To accomplish this monumental task, we first examined current books, periodicals, Internet resources, and articles that rate the best places to retire. Cross-referencing these sources, we generated an extensive list of potential places to relocate, supplemented by additional locations garnered from our own and others' experiences. We then visited these areas, exploring neighborhoods and the towns' amenities, speaking to residents, and investigating trends. We interviewed retirees, people who were close to retiring, and well-traveled baby boomers to get additional information and insights. Our retirement seminars, "Retirement Living from A to Z," gave us the opportunity—via discussions, Q and A segments, and just plain chit-chatting—to tap into the

<hr/>

BEST BEACHES 2006

Dr. Stephen Leatherman of Florida International University, aka "Dr. Beach," does an annual ranking of beaches based on 50 criteria (previous number one winners aren't included in the newest list). Here is his latest top 10:

❋ Fleming Beach Park (Maui, Hawaii)

❋ Caladesi Island State Park (Dunedin, Florida)

❋ Okracoke Island (Outer Banks, North Carolina)

❋ Coopers Beach (Southampton, New York)

❋ Hanalei Bay (Kauai, Hawaii)

❋ Main Beach (East Hampton, New York)

❋ Coast Guard Beach (Cape Cod, Massachusetts)

❋ Coronado Beach (San Diego, California)

❋ Hamoa Beach (Maui, Hawaii)

❋ Barefoot Beach Park (Bonita Springs, Florida)

<hr/>

concerns and interests of those about to retire or recently retired. Finally, we narrowed down our list to those communities we simply liked the best, based on activities such as riding bikes on the beach on Hilton Head Island, playing tennis in Chapel Hill, patronizing restaurants in Santa Fe, golfing in Scottsdale, visiting the Friday farmers' market in Flagler Beach, and walking on the college campus in Tucson. (As you might guess, these visits were the toughest part of our job, but it had to be done!)

Is the list comprehensive? Of course not. New communities develop, revitalization occurs, and unforeseen circumstances, such as the moving or bankruptcy of a large employer or a major natural or man-made disaster, can change the complexion of a town. In addition, it would be impossible to visit every single community in the United States. What is desirable for one person (warm winters, for example) could be a negative for someone else. So using the surveys of what people want in a retirement area as the basis for selection, and coupling them with other research and our own biases, we produced our final list. We know you may feel you're already living in the perfect location, and if it isn't included here, we're always open to suggestions and new locales to check out!

Again, our recommended locations are not all-inclusive,

nor is there any such thing as the perfect retirement location. For example, you may have to balance fantastic weather with lots of traffic, or a wonderful beach area with mediocre medical facilities. We also realize some people want a second home in a place that wouldn't have to meet the same criteria as their permanent home. So near the end of the chapter we provide a list of suggestions for second-home locations. We also present our honor roll of what we feel are the best of the best primary-home locations.

For each city we recommend, we provide assessments of the major features a person should consider before deciding to relocate. We'd like to point out a few things about some of our sources for each location.

Population figures are from the most recent figures available. We've based the cost of living partly on the ACCRA (former acronym of the American Chamber of Commerce Researchers Association), which produces the Cost of Living Index. This is a measure of goods and services (transportation, medical costs, groceries, housing, utilities, and other miscellaneous items) for cities with populations of at least 50,000. The U.S. average

Cost of Living Index is pegged at 100. For example, New York City had an ACCRA cost of living index of 201, while Charlotte, North Carolina, was 101 for the same time period in 2006. Thus, it would cost twice as much to live in New York City as in the Charlotte area. If a city did not meet the size criterion (or did not elect to participate, since membership in ACCRA is voluntary), another cost of living index is provided, if available. For example, Florida has the Florida Price Level Index. This index compares cost of living within counties in Florida, with 100 as the Florida state average. Finally, in some cases, cost of living is described more vaguely, such as "about average," "lower than average," or "above average." Hard numbers are provided, if available, and most data is from 2006.

As for safety, we generally included only locations with average or lower-than-average crime rates. If a recommended area has an unusually high (or extraordinarily low) crime rate, we comment on it; otherwise, you can assume the safety data is around the average.

Most of our safety statistics were published by the FBI in its Uniform Crime Report, which computes a

---

Which states have the highest percentage of residents age 65 and older?
July 2004 census estimates list the following: California, Florida, New York, Texas,
Pennsylvania, Ohio, and Illinois.

crime index for cities with a population of more than 100,000. In 2005 the average U.S. crime index was 469 crimes per 100,000 inhabitants. Keep in mind, however, that reporting is voluntary, and you won't find FBI statistics on towns with populations under 100,000. Another source of our safety statistics was the Florida Department of Law Enforcement Uniform Crime Reports for 2005, which provides a crime index rate for each county in Florida.

We've attempted to provide the most recent unemployment data available in 2006, and we have listed the largest employers for an area. Although not everyone plans to work after retirement, we believe that a good place to relocate is one where there is a reasonable amount of economic vitality. And people do change their minds and decide to go back to work.

When suggesting notable neighborhoods, we often, but not always, chose newer and larger communities with a long build-out time frame. In fact, some of the larger gated communities may have completion dates that extend a decade or more. Although we realize this type of neighborhood is not everyone's preference, investigating newer and larger communities provided

more opportunities to interact with people who have relocated than did older, smaller neighborhoods. It also gave us insight into new building trends and demographic patterns, and if you're moving to a new location, it is often easier to begin new relationships if everyone is relatively new to an area. As far as prices on homes and lots within communities, we know these can change by the day. So use the pricing as a good guide, but check the Web sites or contact the community directly for the latest prices. Contact information is included for each development.

At the end of each city discussion is a summary of what we think are the strengths and weaknesses. We also offer a "report card" that summarizes our overall assessment of each city. This is, of course, ultimately a subjective grade, but one that's grounded in fact, research, firsthand experience, and first-person consultations. Since we only included places we thought were worth considering for relocation, the report cards tend to have higher-than-average marks (not unlike all the above-average children in Garrison Keillor's *Prairie Home Companion*).

Let's take a look at some places you may want to consider sinking new roots into.

Median prices for a single-family home by region in 2006: Midwest ($173,900), South ($184,800), Northeast ($277,100), and West ($352,700).

ARIZONA

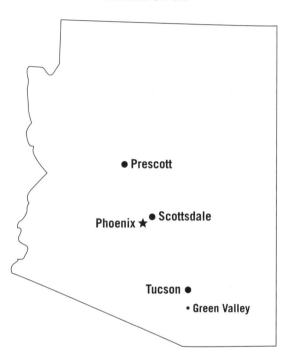

Capital: Phoenix
Nickname: The Grand Canyon State
Motto: "God enriches"
Flower: Saguaro cactus blossom

Bird: Cactus wren
Population: 6,000,000
Fascinating Fact: Lake Havasu City is now home to the original London Bridge.

Prescott

REPORT CARD

Overall rating:	A-
Climate:	A
Cost of living:	A-
Health care:	B
Transportation:	B
What's to do:	A

Prescott's rich history dates back to the gold rush days of 1838 and is reflected by the fact that it has more than 500 buildings on the National Register of Historic Places. This western town is located in Arizona's central mountains, about 100 miles northwest of Phoenix and 90 miles southwest of Flagstaff. There's a small-town feel, the people are friendly, and the residents think their

---

You may have heard about the guy who had his head in an oven and his feet in a bucket of ice. When asked how he felt, he answered, "On average, I feel great!" Consider the statistical averages in this book in the same light.

city has almost perfect weather. With an ideal four-season climate and summer temperatures that rarely top 85 degrees, they may be right!

In the hot summer months, sunbirds (including residents from the Phoenix/Scottsdale area) flock to Prescott to cool off. The airport, Ernest A. Love Field, provides commuter service to Phoenix Sky Harbor International Airport.

Arizona's natural beauty can be enjoyed with day trips to some pretty exciting places. Prescott National Forest, with 450 miles of scenic trails for hiking, backpacking, horseback riding, and mountain biking, provides the outdoor enthusiast with a great playground. The Grand Canyon is a 265-mile round-trip excursion. Or take the Soldier's Trail to Flagstaff and visit Montezuma's Castle and Montezuma's Well, ancient Indian cliff dwellings from the twelfth and thirteenth centuries. Alpine skiing in the Arizona Snowbowl, outside Flagstaff, is easily accessible and only about 90 miles away. And gorgeous Sedona is about an hour's drive away.

Prescott's elevation is 5,347 feet. The altitude, coupled with mountain breezes, abundant sunshine, and moderate year-round humidity of 45 percent, make the climate in this small Arizona town something to brag about. July and August tend to be the rainiest months, with cooling afternoon thunderstorms.

Who Lives in Prescott?

You will find a diverse population among Prescott's 40,400 residents. Caucasians comprise about 88 percent of the total, Hispanics about 8 percent, and Native Americans and Asians also have a presence. The median age is 45 years.

What's the Cost?

In 2006, the Prescott-Prescott Valley area had an ACCRA index of 107, based on a national index of 100. A typical three-bedroom home costs about $400,000.

What's to Do?

Much of the activity in the city of Prescott is centered in the downtown Courthouse Plaza. The white granite courthouse sets the stage for many a Prescott festival—Bluegrass Festival, Territorial Days, Fair on the Square,

What's It Like Outside?	Jan.	Apr.	Jul.	Oct.	Rain (in.)	Snow (in.)
Average high (°F)	50	67	88	72	12	17
Average low (°F)	21	34	56	37	–	–

and Fall Fest, to name just a few. When you are downtown, it's hard to miss the friendly small-town atmosphere and easy to understand why Prescott has the nickname "everybody's hometown."

Community theater draws on local talent to provide a full season of drama, musicals, and slapstick. The 1,200-seat performing-arts facility at Yavapai College hosts a variety of entertainment throughout the year and houses an art gallery and sculpture garden. Three museums—the Phippen, Smoki, and Sharlot Hall—will take you back to the days of the Old West in Prescott while you enjoy a fascinating history lesson through the eyes of the Anglos and the Native Americans.

The Prescott National Forest—home to the world's largest contiguous stand of Ponderosa pine—provides visitors with 20 recreational facilities, including an equestrian facility for campers with horses. At over 7,000 feet, the Granite Mountain Wilderness Area will challenge even the most experienced rock climber. Hiking, hunting, fishing, backpacking, horseback riding—it's all here if you're up for adventure.

Speaking of adventure, why not ride an authentic 1901 steam train to the Grand Canyon? Travel through Arizona's Old West on this 2½-hour trip from the town of Williams, which is about an hour's drive from Prescott, to the Canyon.

Where Are the Jobs?

The town, the school district, retail establishments, Prescott newspapers, and the Arizona Department of Transportation are among the biggest employers. Companies such as Better-Bilt Home Products, Printpak Inc., and Ace Retail Support Center also provide a significant number of jobs. The unemployment rate is about 3 percent. Prescott was ranked third in "Best Metros for Job Creation" by Milken Institute's *2005 Best Performing Cities Index.*

Where Are the Doctors?

The Yavapai Regional Medical Center serves the Prescott area. It's an acute-care, comprehensive hospital. The Northern Arizona Veterans Administration Medical Center also has its main facility in Prescott.

Where Are Some Notable Neighborhoods?

Location, location, location. Just about 7 miles from downtown and very close to the new Prescott Community

---

Money magazine rated Prescott third among its "2006 Top Five Towns for Retirement."

Center you will find new townhomes, condos, and cottages in the Falcon Point neighborhoods, located within the master-planned community of Prescott Lakes. Prices start from the mid $400,000s. This is a golf-course community (join or not, your choice) with swimming and an athletic club. Contact www.canavest.com or 928-717-0742 for more info.

Check out Stone Ridge (www.stoneridgeaz.com or 888-765-3320). This community offers 18 holes of golf and lots of hiking and biking trails. Prices range from the $200,000s to about $450,000.

Ruger Ranch (www.rugerranch.com or 888-845-5263) boasts "untouched frontiers" where you can hike, ride, and hunt. Thirty-six acres are priced from $260,000, and the development is not far from the town of Prescott.

The Ridge at Iron Springs, www.theridgeprescott.com, has Craftsman architecture with careful preservation of native trees in its wooded environment. Lot and home packages start in the $600,000s.

Talking Rock (www.talkingrockranch.com or 866-433-4220) is a private, gated golf community 20 minutes from downtown Prescott that features more than 1,000 acres of open space and an 18-hole golf course. The Ranch Compound offers a fitness center, swimming, and tennis. Cottages start in the mid $500,000s, and lots are priced from the $200,000s to the mid $400,000s.

How Do I Pursue Lifelong Learning?

In addition to its degree and certificate programs, Yavapai College offers noncredit courses through its Osher Lifelong Learning Institute. Prescott College is a small, private liberal-arts college of about 1,000 students with an adult-degree program; Northern Arizona University offers programs in conjunction with Yavapai College; and Embry-Riddle Aeronautical University (ERAU) specializes in aerospace and aviation.

Strengths

"Everybody's hometown" has the allure of the Old West and the scenic beauty of the Granite Dells, freshwater lakes, and the surrounding mountains. This town is away from it all, yet close enough to big-city life—Phoenix is 100 miles away, and Las Vegas fewer than 300. The climate is hard to beat.

Where do people in the United States live? More than 50 percent of us live on only 20 percent of the land, and that land is within 50 miles of the oceans, Great Lakes, and the Gulf of Mexico.

Weaknesses

Except for commuter service to Phoenix and Kingman, air travel requires a drive or flight to the Phoenix Sky Harbor Airport. It does snow, and the temperatures on winter nights are often below freezing.

FYI

Check out these sources for additional information: Prescott Chamber of Commerce (www.prescott.org or 928-445-2000), *The Daily Courier* (www.prescottdaily courier.com or 928-445-3333), and the Arizona Republic (www.azcentral.com or 800-332-6733).

 Shawn and Brian W. recently moved to Prescott. Here are their thoughts.

Prescott not only provides some of the most amazing natural beauty to be found in the Southwest, but it's also a center for Arizona state history, tradition, and culture. This small town offers something for everyone—golf courses, rodeos, theaters, art galleries, museums, and shops and boutiques as well as lakes, rock walls perfect for climbing, and hiking. No matter which type of event you attend, it is sure to both entertain and educate at a reasonable price, making living in and visiting Prescott affordable for everyone.

There is never a shortage of places to visit should you decide to venture out on a beautiful day. For the nature lovers, a good day trip might be a visit to the Grand Canyon, Camp Verde, or a self-guided tour of Yavapai County Forests and Grasslands. If you are more of an off-road adventurer, a scenic driving tour of ranches and abandoned mines in the neighboring towns of Jerome, Sedona, or Williams will not disappoint.

However, should you decide to stay within the Prescott city limits, you will be welcomed into this small town with open arms. The old-time charm of the historic district removes you from the hustle and bustle of city life and provides a relaxing retreat as you visit any one of its locally-owned and operated restaurants or boutiques. You will immediately feel the embrace of this close-knit community as you attend events such as Tent City (a fair displaying

Four beautiful lakes surround Prescott. Willow Lake and Watson Lake are minutes from downtown, Goldwater Lake is 8 miles south of the courthouse, and Lynx Lake is a 55-acre man-made lake 15 minutes away.

local artists and musicians) or the Parade of Lights (a festive holiday tradition for all ages). But if the atmosphere is not enough, its four seasons of incredible weather are sure to impress any person looking for that perfect place to relocate. ⓛ

Scottsdale

REPORT CARD

Overall rating:	A-
Climate:	B+
Cost of living:	B-
Health care:	A
Transportation:	A
What's to do?	A

Are you ready for a move to the "Valley of the Sun"? Located in central Arizona in the Sonoran Desert, Scottsdale, "the West's most Western town," offers you quick access to the big-city life of Phoenix and the benefits of a college town in Tempe. Scottsdale is upscale and dynamic, with a mix of Southwestern and contemporary art galleries, great dining and nightlife, and shopping that—well, you need to see it to believe it! Approximately 8 million visitors come to Scottsdale

each year, and golf is just one of the attractions. Scottsdale is one of the foremost golf destinations in the nation. *Money* magazine ranked Scottsdale number seven on their list of 100 "Best Places to Live" in 2006. *Money* reports that Scottsdale has more than 134 public golf courses within a 30-mile radius that can be played year round. Or eat at any one of 3,822 restaurants within a 15-mile radius. If you choose the restaurants, you may need to ride all 58 miles of bike paths in Scottsdale! Think relaxation and rejuvenation—words used to describe Scottsdale's spa experience. Currently, more than a dozen resort spas find their home in Scottsdale. There is no ocean, but there are mountains to climb and rivers to raft.

The Phoenix Sky Harbor Airport is a short 20-minute drive from Old Town Scottsdale. About 20 major airlines fly in and out of Sky Harbor. If you're looking for a diversion, the Grand Canyon is a 4½-hour drive, and Las Vegas is about 3 hours away.

Who Lives in Scottsdale?

This vibrant city continues to grow beyond its 226,000 official residents. About 40 percent of the population is over the age of 55, with a median age of 40 years. There is a sharp seasonal increase in population when it's cold in other areas of the country.

Only 17 percent of land in Arizona is available for private ownership.

With 330 days of sunshine each year, outdoor activities are a way of life, although sometimes it's necessary to enjoy the outdoors before dawn to avoid that searing sunshine in July and August!

What's the Cost?

When cost of living is calculated, Scottsdale is blended into the Phoenix-Mesa metropolitan area. Accordingly, the ACCRA index is 100. (Scottsdale, however, is a fashionable resort town with expensive housing, dining, and shopping. Thus, the combined ACCRA is not a true reflection of the cost of living here.) Depending on the zip code, median home-sale prices range from $300,000 to $650,000.

What's to Do?

Scottsdale offers an extensive list of action-packed outdoor activities. Off-road Jeep and Hummer tours, rafting, tubing, and water sports, ecological outings, and hot-air ballooning are activities that keep residents (and tourists) in love with the Valley of the Sun. If you start out hiking in one of many city or state parks, you may be ready to tackle 2,700-foot Camelback Mountain before you know it.

Folks in Scottsdale are not always horseback riding and hiking though. They take tremendous pleasure in the arts as well. ArtWalk, a Thursday night tradition, finds the art galleries open late with special exhibits and artist receptions. One- to three-hour tours and desert walks are available at Frank Lloyd Wright's Taliesin West. Arizona State University's Kerr Cultural Center offers musical and theatrical events, as well as visual-arts exhibits.

Into sports? Scottsdale Stadium is home to the San Francisco Giants' spring training, and the Chicago Cubs train in Mesa, Arizona, just a short drive away.

Living in Scottsdale means all of Arizona is yours to explore. Short drives take you to Sedona, the Grand Canyon, Monument Valley, the Petrified Forest, and Lake Havasu with its 23 miles of shoreline and that refreshing, cool blue water for swimming and waterskiing.

But save some energy for shopping! Fashion Mall's hundreds of boutiques, galleries, and department stores are a good place to start. It's the Southwest's largest shopping destination. Other unique shopping experiences await you at Borgata of Scottsdale and El Pedregal Festival Marketplace.

What's It Like Outside?	Jan.	Apr.	Jul.	Oct.	Rain (in.)	Snow (in.)
Average high (°F)	65	84	106	88	7	0
Average low (°F)	41	55	81	60	–	–

If this list of things to do has you exhausted, plan a visit to one of the many resort spas in the area.

Where Are the Jobs?

The tourism, retail, health-care, and hospitality industries are the major employers. Prestigious companies such as Motorola, the Mayo Clinic, PCS, and Vanguard have a presence here as well. Scottsdale's average unemployment rate is about 3 percent.

Where Are the Doctors?

The big name in Scottsdale is the Mayo Clinic. Need we say more? There is a hotel right on the campus grounds of this comprehensive facility. Healthsouth Scottsdale Rehabilitation Hospital and Scottsdale Memorial Hospital also contribute to health care, and there are a number of other facilities in the area.

Where Are Some Notable Neighborhoods?

Several of the suggested notable neighborhoods have a city address other than Scottsdale but are within a 30- or 40-minute drive of the amenities of the Scottsdale/Phoenix area.

Toll Brothers builds beautiful estate homes in the gated community of Windgate Ranch (www.windgate ranchscottsdale.com or 480-596-7300). Amenities include three pools, a 10,000 square-foot clubhouse, hiking and walking trails, and gorgeous sunsets! Three hundred and fifty new homes are planned for 2008 in addition to the three neighborhoods under construction at this time. Prices begin in the high $700,000s. The Mayo Clinic and the airport are both about a 20-minute drive.

Sun City Anthem at Merrill Ranch is an active-adult community that is part of the 32,000-acre, multigenerational, master-planned Anthem at Merrill Ranch (www.suncityanthem.com) community—both communities were developed by Del Webb. Sun City Anthem community opened in 2006, and when completed will have more than 4,000 residences. There is a 48,000-square-foot activity center that hosts the Arizona State University Lifelong Learning Academy, 18 holes of Championship golf, shopping, walking trails, and so

Scottsdale has the highest concentration of spas in the United States, according to *Luxury Spa Finder* magazine.

much more. Priced from $200,000, this looks like a great opportunity in the Scottsdale area.

Desert Mountain (www.desertmountain.com or 800-255-5519) is a gated golf community with 90 holes of Jack Nicklaus Signature Golf as well as tennis, spa, fitness, and swim facilities. Desert Mountain is very exclusive, very expensive, and very beautiful. Available lots in this 8,000-acre enclave begin around $400,000. There will be about 2,600 residences when complete, and a new parcel is opening soon. You'll need millions to live in this fabulous community of custom homes.

How Do I Pursue Lifelong Learning?

Arizona State University serves 63,000 students on three nearby campuses: Tempe, Phoenix, and Mesa. Scottsdale Community College offers 2-year associate degrees, and the Frank Lloyd Wright School of Architecture offers master's and bachelor's degrees.

Strengths

The warm, dry, sunny climate will encourage an active lifestyle. The beauty of the desert surroundings with the mountains as a backdrop is hard to beat. New communities are springing up in all the neighboring areas, providing ample housing choices and adding to the growth of the city. The populace is highly educated, with almost half the residents having at least one college degree. And

the Dodgers are moving their spring training to Glendale, Arizona in 2009.

Weaknesses

One hundred and six degrees is hot, no matter what they say about the comfort index! The millions of tourists visiting the golf courses, spas, and restaurants create lots of traffic. Depending on where you're from, you could get homesick for green grass and trees with falling leaves.

FYI

Check out these sources for additional information: City of Scottsdale (www.scottsdaleaz.gov or 480-312-6500), Business Chamber of Commerce (www.scottsdalechamber.com or 480-355-2700), the *Arizona Republic* (www.azcentral.com or 800-332-6733), and the *Scottsdale Tribune* (www.eastvalleytribune.com or 480-946-5000).

Tucson

REPORT CARD

Overall rating:	A-
Climate:	A-
Cost of living:	A-
Health care:	A
Transportation:	B+
What's to do:	A

Located less than an hour from the Mexican border, Tucson is a diverse city that reflects its Native American, Hispanic, and Asian heritage. Surrounded by 9,000-foot mountains, this desert valley city is about 2,500 feet above sea level. The name Tucson is derived from a Native American word meaning "water at the foot of black mountain." Southern Arizona enjoys more than 300 days of sunshine a year, and the convenient location of the University of Arizona contributes to the city's vitality. If you're into outdoor activities, affordable housing, warm days and cool evenings, ample cultural opportunities, and a city that's very accessible through its International Airport, consider Tucson.

Who Lives in Tucson?

The population of Tucson is about 515,000, although this increases seasonally with the influx of snowbirds. The median age of a Tucson resident is 36, with about 10 percent of residents between 50 and 60 years old. Tucson has an educated workforce; more than half have attended college, compared to the national average of only 38 percent.

What's the Cost?

Tucson's 2006 cost of living index is 99, based on a national index of 100. The average sale price of a single-family home is $275,000.

What's to Do?

Baseball fan? The Arizona Diamondbacks, Chicago White Sox, and Colorado Rockies all have their spring training in Tucson. There are several lakes near Tucson for water sports, as well as Biosphere 2, in nearby Oracle, Arizona. Tucson's offerings also include Colossal Cave Mountain Park; several museums; three observatories; snow skiing from December to April only 30 miles away at Mount Lemmon; 50 nearby golf courses; greyhound, horse, and NASCAR racing; excellent shopping; and a sizable number of major destination resorts such as Canyon Ranch and Miraval Resort and Spa. Ballet, live theater, a symphony, and opera are some of the cultural opportunities. If you're hankering for a taste of the Wild West, visit Tombstone, "the town too tough to die," a preserved Old West town that is a "real" town as well.

Tucson is a popular place for cyclists in the winter. Visit in November and take part in the Tour de Tucson!

Where Are the Jobs?

The largest employers in Tucson include the University of Arizona, Davis-Monthan Air Force Base, and Raytheon System (space vehicles and missiles). Unemployment in Pima County (where Tucson is located) is about 4 percent.

Where Are the Doctors?

There are 17 hospitals in Tucson, with more than 1,700 physicians and 400 dentists. The University of Arizona in Tucson has the only medical school in the state and also has a transplant program.

Where Are Some Notable Neighborhoods?

Dove Mountain (www.dovemountain.com or 888-603-7600) is a master-planned residential golfing community 25 miles northwest of Tucson. Encompassing 5,600 acres, with close to 2,000 acres reserved as open space, it features homes from several builders and a wide swing in housing prices—from the $300,000s to several million dollars. Toll Brothers is building homes within this community from the $700,000s.

SaddleBrooke (www.robson.com or 800-732-9949) is an active-adult community developed by Robson Communities. Surrounded by the Santa Catalina Mountains, it offers several different housing options, with prices ranging from the mid $300,000s to over $1 million. Its country-club amenities include golf, a fitness center, restaurants, and tennis. The Preserve at SaddleBrooke is another active-adult community tucked into the northeastern section of SaddleBrooke, with homes starting in the high $600,000s. In addition, SaddleBrooke has a host of conveniences on-site, including a post office, market, doctor's office, bank, and beauty salon. SaddleBrooke is about a 25-minute drive northeast of downtown Tucson.

Starr Pass Country Club and Spa (www.starrpass.com or 800-503-2898) is a golf community that's home to 27 holes of Arnold Palmer golf as well as the JW Marriott Resort. It is located just 5 minutes from downtown and 15 minutes from the airport and sits 300 feet above the city lights. Homes are priced from $250,000, and luxury estate homes are priced as high as a million. Available home sites start in the $200,000s.

What's It Like Outside?	Jan.	Apr.	Jul.	Oct.	Rain (in.)	Snow (in.)
Average high (°F)	65	82	100	84	12	0
Average low (°F)	39	66	73	57	–	–

FYI

Check out these sources for additional information: Tucson Chamber of Commerce (www.tucsonchamber.org or 520-792-1212), the *Arizona Daily Star* (www.azstarnet.com or 520-573-4511), and the Tucson Citizen (www.tucsoncitizen.com or 520-573-4561).

How Do I Pursue Lifelong Learning?

Tucson boasts the University of Arizona, a large university with its own medical school. Pima Community College serves around 73,000 students at multiple campuses and is one of the largest community-college systems in the nation. University of Phoenix, Inc., is a private, online, accredited institution that caters to working adults and has a campus in Tucson.

Strengths

During the winter, the ability to bask in the sun in the morning and ski in the afternoon is pretty impressive. The Sonoran Desert beauty, lush compared to the other three deserts of the West, the lower cost of living, and the revitalization of the downtown are all plusses.

Weaknesses

Summers are hot, although the humidity is low. The intense rain during monsoon season can also temporarily disrupt travel on some low-lying roads due to flooding.

CALIFORNIA

Tucson receives at least half of its annual rainfall during "monsoon season," which is July through August. This is a time of heavy rains and thunderstorms, during which the average rainfall is 6 inches in what is normally a dry region.

Capital: Sacramento
Nickname: Golden State
Motto: "I have found it"
Flower: California poppy
Bird: California Valley quail
Population: 37,800,000
Fascinating Fact: California raises the most turkeys of any state.

San Luis Obispo

REPORT CARD

Overall rating:	B+
Climate:	A
Cost of living:	C
Health care:	A
Transportation:	B
What's to do:	A

San Luis Obispo (SLO), in the heart of California's central coast, is located roughly halfway between Los Angeles and San Francisco. The city is 8 miles from the Pacific Ocean and is situated between the peaks of the Santa Lucia Mountains.

If you've dreamed of the perfect California climate and the West Coast's scenic beauty but have been overwhelmed with images of L.A. and other major cities, consider this city. San Luis Obispo is the county seat of San Luis Obispo County and is the commercial and cultural hub of California's central coast. The town was established with the construction of the Mission de Tolosa in 1772, the fifth in California's chain of 21 missions. Many special events are held at Mission Plaza, with its charming creek-side setting, including the Mozart Festival in the summer and a Wine Festival in the fall. California Polytechnic State University is located in the community and is an integral part of everyday life. The university sponsors cultural and sporting events, often free to retirees. The San Luis Obispo Regional Airport offers service from three regional carriers—United Express (SkyWest), American Eagle, and America West (Mesa)—with about 40 flights offered daily.

The people in San Luis Obispo are "in love with downtown"! There has been much discussion among town leaders and residents about the height restrictions on businesses and condominium buildings, because people want to live and work downtown. How tall should taller buildings be?

A short drive north from SLO is the small town of Paso Robles, known to most locals as wine country. It boasts 170 wineries and more than 100 tasting rooms!

How many cities have the enviable problem of too many people wanting to move downtown?

Who Lives in San Luis Obispo?

The population of SLO is about 44,000, with approximately 261,000 residents in San Luis Obispo County. About one-fourth of the city residents are 55 or older, and the median age in the county is 37. In terms of demographics, the population is about 76 percent Caucasian and 16 percent Hispanic, with the balance a combination of African-Americans, Asians, and Native Americans.

If the temperatures don't impress you, does 315 days of sunshine a year? Or consider a growing season of 339 days; gardening could be a full-time job! Most of the rain falls between November and March.

What's the Cost?

The cost of living would be considered well above average—with an index of around 175. The median single-family home selling price is $440,000, a number that is rising in spite of a general cool-down in the housing market.

What's to Do?

With the Pacific Ocean about 10 minutes away, the pleasures of the sea are within your reach every day. You can swim, boat, kayak, fish, and surf, not to mention such land pursuits as biking, golf, tennis, hiking, and visiting vineyards.

The mild climate will encourage outdoor activities in town as well. Every Thursday night an average of 15,000 residents enjoy the farmers' market. Listen to live music and entertainment and chow down on BBQ and other foods at restaurant booths while shopping for fresh-picked produce and flowers. The Mozart Festival, over 2 weeks long in late July and early August, celebrates all kinds of music with more than 30 concerts in various locations, including the Performing Arts Center and many outdoor venues.

San Luis Obispo County is home to five state parks and the Los Padres National Forest. The city has 21 parks, and there are five regulation-length golf courses within 15 minutes of SLO. With a world-class performing-arts center, theater, shopping and fine dining, as well as cultural and sporting events offered through the

What's It Like Outside?	Jan.	Apr.	Jul.	Oct.	Rain (in.)	Snow (in.)
Average high (°F)	66	73	84	76	23	0
Average low (°F)	43	47	56	50	–	–

university, you would not find it difficult to be active in this community.

Where Are the Jobs?

The largest employers include the county government, as well as the university, Pacific Gas and Electric, health services, the school system, tourism, and retail. The unemployment rate is about 4 percent. SLO was ranked among *Forbes'* 2006 top cities for business.

Where Are the Doctors?

San Luis Obispo is served by two major hospitals: Sierra Vista Regional Medical Center and French Hospital Medical Center. Catholic Healthcare West acquired the French Hospital Medical Center in 2004.

Where Are Some Notable Neighborhoods?

For starters, especially if you want to live downtown, check out the city's new communities. (Enter "city of San Luis Obispo new housing developments" into the "Google" search bar and click on the first entry under "Web results.") Lots of new apartments, condos, and single-family homes are being built downtown, often over the shopping and businesses as SLO is building up to new heights.

Centex Homes (www.centex.com) is developing two new communities in SLO. 3592 Broad is a development of duplex, triplex, and single-family homes in a creek-side setting. The opportunity to walk to shopping, with homes priced from the $500,000s, makes this a desirable neighborhood.

The Cottages at River Oaks (www.riveroakspaso robles.com or 805-238-1031) is located in Paso Robles, just north of SLO. Choose from three floor plans in this master-planned, gated community near Cuesta College's North County Campus. This is a new urbanism community, with schools, professional offices, and a marketplace. Prices start at $350,000.

A short 20-minute drive north toward Atascadero,

Forty-five minutes to the north of SLO is the Hearst Castle San Simeon State Historical Museum. This estate, built by William Randolph Hearst and architect Julia Morgan, is well worth the trip. The estate contains 165 rooms with 127 acres of pools, gardens, and terraces. The main house has 38 bedrooms and 41 bathrooms, for a total of 60,000 square feet.

you will find el Jardin de Las Lomas (www.las lomashomes.com or 805-462-9557) amidst acres of dedicated open space. Homes are priced from the $600,000s.

How Do I Pursue Lifelong Learning?

California Polytechnic State University, one of the largest schools of engineering and architecture in the West, is located in SLO. With 20,000 full-time students, Cal Poly is a real presence in this town. It also houses the Osher Lifelong Learning Institute, which allows members five classes within the institute for a membership fee of $60 per term, which allows one to take up to five courses. Another 20,000 students are enrolled in Cuesta Community College.

Strengths

If you have been dreaming of the West Coast, and California in particular, San Luis Obispo might be the spot for you. The reality is that this university town appears to have endless sunshine, mild temperatures, beautiful topography, and a strong sense of community. The Pacific Ocean is only 8 miles away, and a long weekend in San Francisco or L.A. is a beautiful 4- or 5-hour drive away. The California Crime Index ranks SLO as one of the safest communities in the state.

Weaknesses

A regional commuter airline will get you where you need to go, but not always as quickly as you would like. SLO, like all of California, is expensive. There are not a wide variety of job opportunities here, and it's a hike to a major city. Some find the presence of the nearby Diablo Nuclear Power Plant unsettling.

FYI

Check out these sources for additional information: Chamber of Commerce (www.visitslo.com or 805-781-2670), SLO Downtown Association (www.downtownslo.com or 805-541-0286), County Visitor and Conference Bureau (www.sanluisobispocounty.com), the *Tribune* (www.sanluisobispo.com or 800-288-4128),

---

The abbreviation for San Luis Obispo (SLO) is well-suited to its laid-back pace. For a change of pace in the "land of the car," try Amtrak. Amtrak has reasonably priced service on the West Coast, and its California car has special bicycle racks, so bring your bike and explore SLO.

and the *New Times* (www.newtimeslo.com or 800-215-0300).

Temecula

REPORT CARD

Overall rating:	A
Climate:	A
Cost of living:	B
Health care:	A
Transportation:	A
What's to do:	A

All great places in California are not on the coastline. Temecula is located in a lush valley about 20 miles inland from the Pacific Ocean communities of San Juan Capistrano and Oceanside. Its location just 85 miles south of Los Angles and 60 miles north of San Diego makes visiting these great cities very accessible when the traffic permits! With more than 3,000 acres of picturesque wine country, Temecula is reminiscent of the Napa Valley. The geography, climate, and soil combine to produce award-winning wines. Stop by and visit any of the 20 or so wineries and enjoy a tasting, or visit a charming inn and restaurant. With an elevation of 1,500 feet above sea level, Temecula prides itself on clean air and more than 300 days of sunshine. The best news is that you will find less traffic and more affordable housing than in most southern California towns.

Who Lives in Temecula?

The population of Temecula is 91,000, with a median age of 31, and 14 percent of the residents are over the age of 55. Demographically, approximately 70 percent are Caucasian, 19 percent Hispanic, 3 percent African-American, and 5 percent Asian.

What's the Cost?

One of the attractive aspects of living inland in California is the lower cost of housing—lower at least than the cost of housing in San Diego or Orange County. Now for the bad news: The median price of a home in Temecula is $465,000.

What's It Like Outside?	Jan.	Apr.	Jul.	Oct.	Rain (in.)	Snow (in.)
Average high (°F)	72	72	90	84	19	0
Average low (°F)	40	47	60	53	–	–

The Chamber of Commerce in Temecula reports that the overall cost of living index is 150, based on a national average of 100.

What's to Do?

Temecula's mild, dry climate provides great weather for a healthy lifestyle. Outdoor activities include golf (55 public and private courses within an hour's drive), tennis, hiking, and spending time in one of the 36 city parks.

Lake Skinner, 10 miles east of Temecula, offers great camping, including equestrian campsites. Diamond Valley Lake is the largest body of freshwater in southern California. Both lakes offer similar recreational activities, including swimming, fishing, and boating. Known as California's "other wine country," Temecula's 20 wineries and many wine festivals round out the list of outdoor fun.

Old Town boasts approximately 650 antiques dealers, unique shopping, and fine dining. Be sure to visit the farmers' market on Saturday mornings or on Wednesdays at the Promenade Mall. The Arts Council of Temecula Valley helps the approximately 30 arts and cultural organizations support the visual and performing arts in the area.

Where Are the Jobs?

Between 2000 and 2005, the job growth in Temecula increased by 50 percent. In addition to the school system and health care, major employers include Guidant, International Rectifer/Hexfet, and Albertson's. Unemployment is about 5 percent.

Where Are the Doctors?

Temecula Valley is located between the medical teaching institutions of Loma Linda University and the University of California, San Diego. The Inland Valley Regional Medical Center, an acute-care facility and trauma center, provides the residents of Temecula with very good medical care.

Where Are Some Notable Neighborhoods?

Twenty-five miles north of Temecula is K. Hovnanian's Four Seasons at Hemet (www.khov.com or 866-694-4293), an active-adult community, offering a total of 1,100 single-family homes upon completion. Homes are priced from the high $200,000s. This is a gated community situated along a public golf course and featuring a clubhouse, The Lodge, with swimming, billiards, a

---

Although separated from the Pacific Ocean by the Santa Rosa Mountains, the Rainbow Gap allows mild beach breezes to flow into the Temecula Valley and helps moderate temperatures.

theater, and areas for cookouts and dancing. A 2005 "Best of Seniors' Housing" award winner, Four Seasons at Hemet is an age-restricted community that suggests that if you aren't 55, you'll wish you were!

DR Horton (www.drhorton.com or 951-694-0908), one of the largest home builders in the United States, is offering the Bungalows at Temecula Lane. Plans are for single-family attached and detached homes from the upper $300,000s.

Check out all the homes at Morgan Hill (www. mcmillin.com) where McMillan Homes is building a small community of 59 single-family homes, Blackstone at Morgan Hill, priced from the $600,000s (951-302-8829). Ruffino at Morgan Hill has 131 single-family homes priced from the $520,000s (951-302-3353), and Montevina at Morgan Hill has 146 single-family homes priced from the $500,000s (951-302-9268).

How Do I Pursue Lifelong Learning?

Residents of Temecula can attend Mt. San Jacinto Community College, and the University of California has a site in Temecula. California State-San Marcos is about half an hour away.

Strengths

The beauty of the green valley and snowcapped mountains all wrapped up in the southern California climate make this town of 91,000 people a great place to retire. There are jobs to be had and tennis and golf to be played. The Pacific Ocean is only 20 minutes away. Homes are not cheap, but affordable (especially for southern California).

Weaknesses

I-15, a main artery between San Diego County and Riverside County, coupled with Temecula's affordable housing (for California), has created an increase in population and an increase in traffic. If you're considering relocating from a less expensive area, the cost of living is high.

FYI

Check out these sources for additional information: Temecula Valley Chamber of Commerce (www.temecula.org or 866-676-5090); and the *Press-Enterprise* (www.pe.com or 951-375-3701), and the *Temecula Valley News* (www. temeculavalleynews.com or 951-676-1839).

Drive south from Temecula and you will find the Pechanga Resort and Casino, operated by the Indians of the Pechanga Band. If you enjoy gaming and great entertainment, this is the place to go.

COLORADO

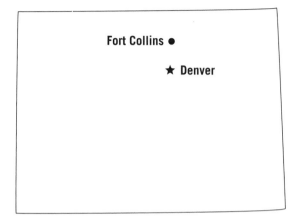

Fort Collins ●

★ Denver

Capital: Denver
Nickname: Centennial State/Colorful Colorado
Motto: "Nothing without providence"
Flower: Rocky Mountain columbine
Bird: Lark bunting
Population: 4,670,000
Fascinating Fact: The longest continuous street in the United States is Colfax Avenue in Denver.

Fort Collins

REPORT CARD

Overall rating:	A
Climate:	B
Cost of living:	A
Health care:	A
Transportation:	B
What's to do:	A

Fort Collins is located at the foothills of the Rocky Mountains in northeastern Colorado, about 65 miles north of Denver, on the Cache La Poudre River. It offers a small-town feeling but with the big-city amenities that many people desire. It also fits the bill if you are looking for a college town. Colorado State University is located in Fort Collins, and its more than 20,000 students bring vitality to this community that's located 5,000 feet above sea level.

Fort Collins has been recognized in many publications as a great place to live. Arts and Entertainment (A&E) television rated Fort Collins one of the "10 Best Cities to Have It All," Business Opportunity Index ranked it "Fourth Best for Business Opportunity," *Money* maga-

---

The Cache La Poudre River allegedly gets its name from a stash of gunpowder hidden along the river's banks by French trappers in the 1800s.

zine ranked it "One of the Top Ten Best Places to Retire," MSN.com rated Fort Collins as one of the "Top Five Places to Retire," and Loveland/Fort Collins is the number one "Best Place to Reinvent Your Life," according to *AARP* magazine. The newest accolade is being ranked number one in *Money* magazine's "2006 Best Places to Live." With tributes like this, how can you go wrong?

Residents describe Fort Collins as "Fort Fun" as they brag about the long list of things to do in their city. With 300 days of sunshine (coupled with low humidity) and outdoor activities that include hiking and biking on 20 miles of trails and resort skiing (a 2- to 4-hour drive away), this Colorado town is enticing. If sports are your passion, take a short drive to Denver and cheer on the Denver Broncos, Colorado Avalanche, Colorado Rockies, and Denver Nuggets.

The Denver International Airport is about 1½ hours from Fort Collins, and the Airport Express operates hourly bus service to the airport. It's also possible to take a commuter plane between Denver and the Fort Collins-Loveland Airport.

Fifty inches of annual snow seems like a lot, but the brilliant sunshine and mild temperatures melt a great deal of that snowfall early in the day.

Who Lives in Fort Collins?

About 128,000 people live in the 50 square miles of Fort Collins, the county seat for Larimer County. The median age is 28, and about 16 percent of the population is over the age of 55. About 85 percent are Caucasian and another 13 percent Hispanic. You will find a large number of Californians fleeing the crowded lifestyle of their home state for the sunshine and beauty of this small Colorado town.

What's the Cost?

The cost of living index in Fort Collins is slightly higher (103) than the ACCRA national average of 100. The median price for an average, three-bedroom home is $230,000.

What's to Do?

While you can't see the ocean from Fort Collins, there is the Cache La Poudre River, which is a National Wild

What's It Like Outside?	Jan.	Apr.	Jul.	Oct.	Rain (in.)	Snow (in.)
Average high (°F)	41	59	86	64	15	50
Average low (°F)	12	31	54	34	–	–

and Scenic River. Poudre Canyon is a great spot for whitewater rafting, kayaking, camping, fishing, and hiking. Visit Rocky Mountain National Park and view elk, mule deer, black bear, and more, or enjoy mountain hiking. If you're into skiing, the popular ski resorts of Beaver Creek, Breckenridge, Copper Mountain, and Keystone, with their own picture-perfect towns, are just a few hours away. Or enjoy the New West Fest in Fort Collins's Historic Old Town every August. This event showcases more than 300 arts and crafts and food booths, as well as concerts throughout the afternoon and evening.

Moving indoors, there are scores of local groups to inspire your more artistic side. Canyon Concert Ballet offers dance training and performances, and the Fort Collins Children's Theater stages live plays using local actors and actresses. There are several art galleries, and the Lincoln Center has programs that include professional theater, dance, and children's programs. And don't neglect the shopping. There is a pedestrian mall in the historic downtown that includes fine restaurants, bars, and lots of shops.

Where Are the Jobs?

Fort Collins is considered the regional employment and retail hub for northern Colorado, southern Wyoming, and western Nebraska. Major employers include such prestigious names as Hewlett-Packard, Agilent Technologies, Anheuser Bush, and Waterpik Technologies. Colorado State University, the Poudre school district, and Poudre Valley Health Systems are big employers as well. The unemployment rate is about 4 percent.

Where Are the Doctors?

The Poudre Valley Hospital (around 280 beds) provides medical care and serves as the regional trauma center. With close to 40 specialties, this hospital provides excellent health care.

Where Are Some Notable Neighborhoods?

Maintenance-free townhouses and patio homes, as well as estate-size residences and single-family homes, are available at Water Valley (www.watervalley.com or 970-686-5828). This community is situated on a golf course (27

Looking to hoist a cold one? In December 2006, *USA Today* included the New Belgium Brewing Co. of Fort Collins on its list of "10 Great Places to See What's Brewing in Beer." Check it out at www.newbelgium.com or 888-622-4044.

holes), surrounded by five scenic lakes (with sandy beaches) and 7.5 miles of recreational trails. Condominiums are priced starting in the mid $100,000s, and estate homes on the shore of the lakes are often in the millions. There is a price point for almost everyone in this community that is a 15-minute drive from Fort Collins.

Morningside Village (www.chateaudevelopment.com or 970-223-2200) is located 12 minutes from downtown Fort Collins and has a community pool with expansive parks and walking paths. The Cottage Series is priced from the $200,000s. The Verandas is the newest phase, priced from the $190,000s.

Centex (www.centex.com or 970-484-8182) offers Brightwater Landing in Fort Collins, with low-maintenance homes priced from $165,000 to $220,000. Amenities include a playground, lots of open space, and access to close-by outdoor activities.

If you are willing to drive a little, check out Fox Acres in Red Feather Lakes, a small mountain town with this beautiful private, gated, golf club community about an hour's drive northwest from Fort Collins. The *Denver Post* named the golf course on their list of "Top Ten Colorado Private Courses." Fifteen pristine lakes, beautiful mountain views, and friendly people make this 460-acre development a must see (www.foxacres.com or 970-881-2191). Homes priced from the $400,000s; lots from the $100,000s.

How Do I Pursue Lifelong Learning?

This is an easy question to answer! Colorado State University is a land-grant institution with more than 20,000 full-time students, and it's waiting for you to enroll. To encourage lifelong learning, mature students pay reduced tuition. Another institution, Front Range Community College, with about 10,000 students, offers classes in more than 100 subjects, as well as a host of continuing education classes.

Strengths

Panoramic views of the snowcapped Rocky Mountains, the proximity of some of the country's best ski resorts, sunny days, a beautiful river, and the benefits of living in a town where learning is a high priority make Fort Collins hard to beat.

Weaknesses

Snow. If it doesn't melt early in the day, you are stuck with it! The Denver airport, your best means of air travel, is 1½ hours away. Traffic delays and lack of public transportation are issues in Fort Collins.

FYI

Check out these sources for additional information: Chamber of Commerce (www.fcchamber.org or 970-482-3746), City of Fort Collins Web site (www.ci.fort

-collins.co.us or 970-221-6500), the Fort Collins *Coloradoan* (www.coloradoan.com or 970-493-6397), and the Northern Colorado Business Report (www.ncbr.com or 970-221-5400).

FLORIDA

Capital: Tallahassee
Nickname: Sunshine State
Motto: "In God we trust"
Flower: Orange blossom
Bird: Mockingbird
Population: 18,000,000

Fascinating Fact: Clearwater has the highest number of lightning strikes per capita of any city in the country.

Because so much of Florida is so popular for people thinking about relocating, we have divided the state into "coasts" and Central Florida: the *First Coast* (Jacksonville, Ponte Vedra, Palm Coast, and St. Augustine), the *Treasure Coast* (Vero Beach), the *Paradise Coast* (Naples, Bonita, and Sarasota), the *Emerald Coast* (the Panhandle), and Central Florida (Ocala, Gainesville, and a town and community unto itself, The Villages).

THE FIRST COAST: Jacksonville, Ponte Vedra, St. Augustine, and Palm Coast

Jacksonville is the first major city located on the Northeastern border of the state (just below Georgia) and is known to the people here as "the First Coast" or "where Florida begins." North of Jacksonville, on I-95, are the resort communities of Amelia Island and Fernandina Beach. Fernandina Beach is listed on the National Register of Historic Places, and Amelia Island offers beautiful oceanfront properties and fabulous golf courses, as well as a Ritz-Carlton resort.

Named for our seventh president, Andrew Jackson, Jacksonville is a metropolitan center of more than 1.2 million people. Jacksonville is the fourteenth largest city in the United States, and it is actually the largest city in land area in the contiguous United States. With 68 miles of Atlantic coastline and the beautiful St. Johns River, this is truly a city on the water! The Jacksonville Landing, with its shops, restaurants, and entertainment, comes with a water taxi to transport visitors across the St. Johns River.

Riverside and Avondale, located on the west side of the St. Johns River, are traditional neighborhoods that have been part of the Jacksonville landscape for many years. Housing options include waterfront estates, restored historic homes, and renovated loft condominiums and apartments. Add more than a dozen parks with tennis and paths for jogging and biking as well as great restaurants, galleries, and boutique shopping, and you have small-town charm close to the big city.

The cost of living in Jacksonville is very close to the national average, coming in with an index of 99, compared to the national average of 100. The median price of a new three-bedroom home is about $285,000, and the average rent for a new three-bedroom apartment is slightly less than $1,000 a month. The renowned Mayo Clinic is in Jacksonville, and a new Mayo Hospital (one of two Mayo Hospitals in the world) plans to open in 2008.

The city has a lot to offer in the way of sports. It has the NFL Jaguars and a minor-league baseball team, the Suns. In January of 2005, Jacksonville played host to Super Bowl XXXIX. Carnival Cruise Line is using Jacksonville as a new port destination, and the airport (just 15 minutes from downtown) offers 250 daily flights from 15 major and regional airlines.

The St. Johns River will be the location of a new urban master-planned community, Shipyards, developed by the Land Mar Group. The plan is to construct four towers that will include condominiums with all the amenities people are looking for (but not expecting!) in city living—swimming, tennis, fitness, green space, and restaurants. Prices begin in the $300,000s. (Explore at www.shipyardsjax.com or 904-562-7447.)

Located minutes from Amelia Island and Fernandina Beach and 25 minutes north of the Jacksonville airport is the community of North Hampton (www.north-hampton.com or 866-998-8300). This 700-acre gated community, also developed by the Land Mar Group, has an Arnold Palmer Signature Golf Course, swimming pools, and many other resort amenities. Prices range from the mid $200,000s to more than $1 million for homes; lots begin in the $100,000s.

true LIFE — An "Aha" Moment

By the time we reach retirement or we are at least thinking about it, do we find ourselves so set in our ways about where we will live or the way it's going to be when we live there, that we shut ourselves off to any new alternatives? Consider this couple's "aha" moment that came to them in their late fifties.

Due to his numerous insurance-management relocations during their 36 years of marriage, Mike and his teacher/Realtor wife, Colleen S., found themselves enjoying living all along sunny Florida's Atlantic coastline—in the cities of Miami, Hollywood, Ponte Vedra Beach/Jacksonville, Melbourne, and most recently, Jupiter/West Palm Beach. Except for a wonderful 7-year sidebar in their early thirties to work and live in the glorious mountain resort of Highlands, North Carolina, Florida has always been their home.

This couple bought nine homes over the years. A few were oceanfront condos, some were in sleepy beach town developments, one was a golf-course home, one a woodsy mountain retreat, another a grand, 50-year-old mini-estate across the street from the ocean. All but the mountain home were in the suburbs of some big city, and from each, a 30- to 45-minute commute to their jobs was a given.

When they recently received another great business opportunity that necessitated a return to the Jacksonville area, it was a dream come true for Mike and Colleen, since the Ponte Vedra Beach/Jacksonville area, with all it has to offer, had been the hardest place for them to leave in the past.

While looking for another home at the beach and hoping to save travel time every day, Mike and Colleen rented a spacious, brand new three-bedroom/three-bath riverfront condo. Replete with all of the finest amenities and spectacular river views, it sits amazingly right in the heart of downtown Jacksonville, an easy three-block walk to Mike's new office. All of a sudden, commuting became a thing of the past! Aha!

In addition to this, shocking as it seemed, from day one, they found they were completely enchanted by everything else that inner-city, riverfront living had to offer! They bought the condo right away and will keep it through their last years of work and most definitely for retirement.

During their first 6 months there, Mike and Colleen found themselves inundated with weekend visits from curious family and friends, wondering if this couple had truly lost their minds. The last place expected that these two would *ever* move would be in the downtown area of *any* city! But then they saw through new eyes what got this couple's attention.

They discovered that downtown Jacksonville is going through the most incredibly pleasing and well-designed riverfront renovation. The skyline looks as if the architects, both past and present, somehow collaborated at the outset to produce an artistically beautiful cityscape masterpiece. Little parks, dancing fountains, tree-laden boulevards, and a magnificent 3-mile-long river walk with shops, entertainment, and restaurants also enhance this southern city's charm.

They marveled at the city's great bridges spanning the mighty St. Johns River, seeming to extend a welcome mat to all. Handsome luxury riverfront condos nearing completion beckon weary commuters or evening and weekend event-goers to rethink their driving times and bedroom-community lifestyles.

Most of these luxury condos will have boat slips, a real plus for riverfront living. They see how the city planners and developers are preparing Jacksonville for what seems to be a nationwide trend in new housing; these urban visionaries realized that this quiet little gem of a city with an astoundingly picturesque river has been overlooked for far too long.

Mike and Colleen found it exciting that as the city renovates, just a few miles away in all directions from the booming downtown area, the revitalization has been contagious. Older city homes are being grabbed up by the dozens and are being renovated by young doctors, attorneys, and corporate execs who want to live where they work and play, as well as retirees seeking the vibrancy of life in the city. New grocery stores, restaurants, and other suburban facilities are popping up in these little enclaves as well. Three major shopping malls are only 10 minutes away in any direction, and the beach, excellent golf courses, and the airport are only a 20-minute drive from the city's center.

This couple has seen the already thriving venues right in the heart of the city—the many theaters, the Jacksonville Jaguars Alltel Stadium, the fabulous new Baseball Grounds of Jacksonville, huge convention centers, art and science museums, a performing-arts center, a new sports and concert arena, and first-class restaurants. There are numerous houses of worship, renowned hospitals and health centers, and a magnificent new library.

Architecturally beautiful skyscrapers that house major insurance, transportation, banking, and other corporate headquarters are interspersed among lovingly renovated historic buildings. Water taxis and free trolleys carry people back and forth to big-name hotels, corner cafés, wine bars, bistros, and even to Paris Hilton's new nightclub.

Everything is within walking distance for Mike and Colleen, and walk they do, from their wonderful riverfront condo, every day, enjoying all this city has to offer every step of the way. They have been to baseball games, concerts, football games, and live performances; dined in most of the restaurants and little cafés; attended services at the cathedral; paid weekly visits to the library; played tennis at the condo; danced at the Landing; rode on the river taxi and on the trolleys; went to the museums; and look forward to doing the 3-mile river walk almost every day. This couple has literally walked into the best, most carefree and exciting lifestyle that they've ever known.

When you're lucky enough to have an "aha" moment, that means you finally "get it," and for Mike and Colleen, finally "getting it" couldn't have come at a better time in their lives! ⓣ

Ponte Vedra

REPORT CARD

Overall rating:	A
Climate:	B+
Cost of living:	A-
Health care:	A
Transportation:	A
What's to do:	A

About 20 miles east of Jacksonville, Florida, nestled between the intracoastal waterway and the Atlantic Ocean, lies a lovely little enclave called Ponte Vedra Beach. It is relatively unknown, yet visitors are surprised by its manicured golf courses, five-diamond resorts and restaurants, beautiful white beaches, and trendy little boutiques. It is home to the National

What's It Like Outside?	Jan.	Apr.	Jul.	Oct.	Rain (in.)	Snow (in.)
Average high (°F)	64	82	91	79	52	0
Average low (°F)	41	57	74	62	–	–

Headquarters of the Professional Golf Association (PGA) and the International Headquarters of the Association of Tennis Professionals (ATF), where grass, red clay, and hard courts are open to all, but on a Sunday evening, visitors often can find top tour players preparing for tournaments.

The Tournament Players Championship (TPC), which boasts not only the largest purse in golf but also the deepest field of players, is played at Sawgrass Country Club. Here at Sawgrass you will find the most photographed hole in all of golf, the island green on the 17th hole. The TPC course at Sawgrass is open to all players during the year, and they come from all over the world to face the challenge of the dreaded 17th-island green. Several top tour players, Jacksonville Jaguars, and tennis players call Ponte Vedra Beach home and mix with the locals at many of the colorful little pubs, restaurants, and piano bars sprinkled throughout the town.

Real estate here includes everything: lovely condos along the beach, tennis or golf rentals, five spectacular gated golf communities, Old Ponte Vedra (where homes look across the canals and lagoons that snake along the two golf courses that are part of the five-diamond Ponte Vedra Inn and Club), magnificent ocean compounds, and homes along the intracoastal waterway. Real estate has seen a healthy appreciation over the years as northerners have discovered the beauty of the area. The mood here is relaxed, the look is understated elegance, the locals are friendly, and many are transplants, so the community complexion is diverse.

Ponte Vedra Beach is a 25-minute drive from downtown Jacksonville, the cultural center of the area, and there you will find many concert and theater venues and Alltel Stadium, home of the Jacksonville Jaguars. Jacksonville hosted the Super Bowl in 2005, and the world witnessed the beauty of the downtown area, which spans both shores of the St. Johns River. Several colleges and universities are located in Jacksonville, which, because of its 355 urban parks and large undeveloped green spaces, is the largest land mass city in the United States. The Mayo Clinic is also located here, just minutes from Ponte Vedra Beach.

The climate here is mild. Since it is located in northern Florida, above the frost line, temperatures in January

In 2006, *Money* magazine named Ponte Vedra among the 50 "Best Places to Live in the U.S.," and the number one place in Florida. It's no wonder that St. Johns is the second fastest growing county in Florida.

are typically in the 60s or 70s, but the summers are not as intense as they are further south. Because of its location, the area has not taken a direct hit from a hurricane since 1964. Ponte Vedra Beach is not a resort destination and so the population does not change during the year. People often come upon this lovely little city while traveling south along A1A, and they are so charmed by its beauty that they stay!

Who Lives in Ponte Vedra?

The population of Ponte Vedra is about 30,000, and the median age of the residents is about 40. Over the next 20 years, the Town of Nocatee (www.nocatee.com) will be under construction and will ultimately add 15,000 households to the area and increase the population of Ponte Vedra considerably.

What's the Cost?

Ponte Vedra is a residential community with varied housing options. The average price of a new home (excluding land) is about $330,000. The ACCRA cost of living index for Ponte Vedra is 150, and for northeast Florida in general it's 96, compared to a national average of 100. It's possible to rent an apartment, buy a condominium, or purchase a million-dollar estate home or even an oceanfront estate in Ponte Vedra.

What's to Do?

Boating enthusiasts are at home in Ponte Vedra, and some lucky residents have found a home for their boats as well! Many neighborhoods have deep-water canals with boat docks behind the homes and access to the Intracoastal Waterway. Beautiful marinas that offer boat storage and access to the Waterway are also a part of many neighborhoods.

Did someone mention shopping? The new St. Johns Center will please even the most seasoned shoppers. Tennis, golf, and biking should round out the day, after you return from the beach, that is. Remember Jacksonville with its museums, ballet, theater, and sports attractions is only 30 minutes away.

Where Are the Jobs?

The U.S. Naval Air Station, Blue Cross/Blue Shield of Florida, Winn-Dixie Stores Inc., Citibank, and Mayo Clinic are just a few of the top 20 employers in the Jacksonville area. The unemployment rate in the Jacksonville area is about 3 percent.

Where Are the Doctors?

In addition to the Mayo Clinic and the new Mayo Hospital expected to be completed in early 2008, Ponte Vedra is home to several other outstanding medical facilities, including Baptist Medical Center South, Shands Jacksonville, and St. Luke's. Great medical care is readily available in northeast Florida.

Where Are Some Notable Neighborhoods?

If you want to build a beautiful estate home on the Intracoastal Waterway or on a golf course, check out the Plantation at Ponte Vedra (www.theplantationpv.com or 904-543-7532). The area and the homes are beyond beautiful and include an Arnold Palmer Golf Course and a private beach club. Prices begin in the $600,000s and escalate to $2 million. Marsh Landing and Sawgrass are similar neighborhoods that offer some new construction but mostly resales.

If you are looking for something less costly and smaller, check out Summer House (www.summerhousepv.com or 904-543-0904). These condominiums are located less than 1 mile from the beach and offer beach shuttle service, as well as many other services. One-bedroom bungalows are priced below $200,000.

Sweetwater is an age-restricted community built by Del Web (www.delweb.com or 866-308-9322) with price ranges from the mid $200,000s to the upper $400,000s. You can choose a condominium, a single-family home, or a carriage home and enjoy every imaginable amenity including the 22,000-square-foot Summerland Hall Amenity Center. Sweetwater is located just 10 minutes from the beach, 15 minutes from downtown Jacksonville, and 7 minutes from the Mayo Clinic. The community opened in 2005.

The Town of Nocatee (www.nocatee.com) is being developed by the PARC Group and will have a build-out estimated at 20 years. This 15,000-acre master-planned community will include schools, a new YMCA, shopping, parks, entertainment, and homes at almost every price point. Construction has begun; it's in the first years of many! The following builders have made commitments to build in the Town of Nocatee: Del Webb, Toll Brothers, Cornerstone Homes, Centex, and Pulte.

How Do I Pursue Lifelong Learning?

Twenty-one colleges, universities, community colleges, and technical schools are within a 1-hour drive of Ponte Vedra. The University of North Florida and Jacksonville University offer 4–year degrees in many areas.

Strengths

Ponte Vedra is a spectacular bedroom community located just south of Jacksonville. It offers easy access to downtown Jacksonville and all that city has to offer, and don't overlook the other Florida attractions close by. St.

Augustine, the nation's oldest city, is a 30-minute drive. Orlando and the Walt Disney World Resorts are about a 2½-hour drive from Ponte Vedra. Amelia Island, with its Bausch and Lomb Tennis tournament, is just 1 hour north.

Weaknesses

There's not much that's negative about this northern Florida location. It's not the tropics of South Florida, and a jacket may keep you from missing the fun at the beach in January and February. Although there is a wide selection, many of the neighborhoods are too pricey for the average budget.

FYI

Check out these sources for additional information: Ponte Vedra Chamber of Commerce (www.pontevedra chamber.com or 904-285-2004), the *Ponte Vedra Recorder* (www.pontevedrarecorder.com or 904-285-8831), and the *Florida Times-Union* (www.jackson ville.com or 800-553-0541).

St. Augustine

The next stop when traveling south along the First Coast is the charming city of St. Augustine, the site of the first successful European settlement in the United States (settled by the Spanish in 1565) and known as "Ameri-

ca's oldest city." Henry Flagler brought the Florida East Coast Railway to St. Augustine. Flagler and the railway are actually credited with the expansion and development of the entire east coast of Florida, from Jacksonville to the Florida Keys.

Historic St. Augustine, with its pedestrian St. George street, Castillo de San Marcos National Monument (the oldest stone fort in the United States), and Ponce de Leon's Fountain of Youth Discovery Park are found within a city that has very successfully combined the old with the new. The original 1888 Casa Monica Hotel has been restored and provides world-class accommodations in the center of the city. Historic Flagler College, the Lightner Museum, and lots of boutiques, art galleries, and restaurants are just a stroll away. This historic city, with its horse-drawn carriage rides and beautiful sunsets over the bay, has a lot to offer. There is even an outlet mall close by. However, it is actually the natural beauty of old Florida with its beaches and boating that make this town a great place to live.

One notable neighborhood in St. Augustine is Palencia (www.vivapalencia.com or 877-245-3390). This community brings to mind the word *palatial*. It's a beautiful Arthur Hills golf-course community with a 40-acre village center and amenity-laden clubhouse. With a location near historic St. Augustine, schools, shopping, and the Ponte Vedra beaches—and with the Mayo Clinic close at hand—you may never have to leave St. Augustine! A variety of home styles are available in this 1,450-acre development, including condos, townhomes, single-family homes, and lots. Condos begin in the high $200,000s, townhomes in the upper $400,000s, single-family homes from the $600,000s, and estate lots from the high $300,000s.

Palm Coast

REPORT CARD

Overall rating:	B+
Climate:	B+
Cost of living:	A
Health care:	B
Transportation:	A-
What's to do:	B

Palm Coast, once described as a diamond in the rough, can now be described as a city discovered! Located about an hour's drive south of Jacksonville, halfway between quaint St. Augustine and lively Daytona Beach, the population of Palm Coast has doubled since the 2000 census. From the exit off Interstate 95, you can be on a golf course, boating on the Intracoastal Waterway, or strolling on the beach within 10 minutes. Three airports triangulate Palm Coast, with Jacksonville International 75 minutes north, Orlando 90 minutes west, and Daytona 30 minutes south. Developed by ITT in the 1970s as a planned community, Palm Coast incorporated as a city December 31, 1999, yet retains the feel of a small town.

Relatively unknown, Palm Coast has the amenities of a resort area—beautiful beaches with cinnamon-colored sand, great boating with access to the beautiful Palm Coast Marina, endless hiking and biking trails, and many championship golf courses. Its location above the frost line precludes Palm Coast from becoming a mecca for snowbirds, creating a community that is less transient than many in Florida. Things are happening in Palm Coast. The amenities and neighborhoods are in place and a new town center (1,500 acres) is currently under construction and will be home for city hall, many businesses, offices, and shops, all helping to make Palm Coast a very desirable place to live.

What's It Like Outside?	Jan.	Apr.	Jul.	Oct.	Rain (in.)	Snow (in.)
Average high (°F)	71	84	89	75	50	0
Average low (°F)	50	65	72	57	–	–

Most rain falls during the summer months in the form of afternoon thunderstorms.

Who Lives in Palm Coast?

More than 72,000 people live in an area that covers about 50 square miles. The median age of a Palm Coast resident is 51, and 15 percent of the population is between 55 and 64 years old. About 85 percent of residents are Caucasian, 10 percent African-American, and 5 percent Hispanic. According to the Census Bureau, Flagler County was the fastest-growing county in the nation in 2004, 2005, and 2006.

What's the Cost?

The cost of living index in Palm Coast is 107. The mean selling price of a single-family home is about $253,000. Palm Coast offers a good mix of single-family homes, condominiums, and rentals.

What's to Do?

There are year-round outdoor activities, including biking, hiking, boating, golfing, fishing, beach sports, and tennis. State parks and wildlife preserves are plentiful in Flagler County. The Washington Oaks Gardens State Park spreads over more than 390 acres, from the Atlantic Ocean to the Matanzas River.

Disney World is an easy 90-minute drive, so it's a possible day trip when the grandchildren visit. Titusville, about an hour south of Palm Coast, is home to the Kennedy Space Center. St. Augustine, about 25 miles north, the nation's oldest city, is a great place to find a gourmet restaurant or a bargain at the Designer Outlet Mall. From St. Augustine, you are a short drive from the World Golf Village and the World Golf Hall of Fame. If you are a sports enthusiast, Daytona Beach and NASCAR are neighbors of Palm Coast, about 25 miles south, or you can travel to Jacksonville for a Jaguars football game. If you're a patron of the arts, visit the Jacksonville Symphony or the Florida Theater in Jacksonville.

Meet your neighbors on Fridays at an outdoor farmers' market at Flagler Beach in Veterans Park. Enjoy fresh produce, bright flowers, and fantastic crafts.

Where Are the Jobs?

Palm Coast is the home of Sea Ray Boats and Palm Coast Data, two of its major employers. The construc-

---

The European Village opened in 2005. Beautiful condos sit above some great shops and restaurants. Live music (Elvis on Thursdays) and great pizza make this a fun place to be.

tion, health, and service sectors have had the most growth. Flagler County's unemployment rate hovers around 4 percent.

Where Are the Doctors?

The Memorial Hospital-Flagler opened in the fall of 2002. Services include the Memorial Heart Institute, Memorial Cancer Care Center, Women's Health Care Center, Outpatient Services, and Emergency Medical Care Center. The famed Mayo Clinic is about an hour's drive north in Jacksonville.

Where Are Some Notable Neighborhoods?

Ginn Clubs and Resorts has several communities in Palm Coast. Hammock Beach and Ocean Hammock are contiguous developments on a spectacular piece of property that includes 2 miles of pristine Atlantic beach, an acclaimed Jack Nicklaus Signature Golf Course featuring six holes on the ocean, an oceanfront beach club, and miles of bike paths. Homesites begin in the

$300,000s and can reach well over a million dollars on the ocean. In addition, Ginn offers homesites from the $400,000s at Yacht Harbor Village, at the Conservatory beginning in the $300,000s, the Gardens at Hammock Beach from about $500,000 (www.hammockbeach resort.com or call 888-246-5500) and condos at Yacht Harbor Village start in the $500,000s.

Grand Haven (www.grandhavenfla.com or 800-957-0213) is a must-see 1,500-acre community with great opportunities to purchase a resale (the community is 90 percent sold out). The centerpiece of Grand Haven is a Nicklaus Signature golf course, with three holes overlooking the Intracoastal. Lots are available from the $100,000s; homes from the $300,000s. As far as newer construction, a luxury project (Riverview Condominiums) with views of the Jack Nicklaus Signature Golf offers condos from the high $400,000s.

How Do I Pursue Lifelong Learning?

There are a number of colleges and universities within an hour's drive of Palm Coast, including the Palm Coast

---

Historically, the Jacksonville area has been affected by the fewest number of hurricanes in Florida. Cooler water temperatures and less favorable wind conditions make it more unlikely to sustain hurricane-strength winds. In addition, this part of the state does not protrude into the Atlantic, which makes northeast Florida less of a target for hurricanes.

campus of Daytona Beach Community College. In addition, you can satisfy your intellectual cravings at Bethune Cookman College (Daytona Beach), Embry-Riddle Aeronautical University (Daytona Beach), Flagler College (St. Augustine), Jacksonville University (Jacksonville), University of Central Florida (Orlando and Daytona Beach), and the University of North Florida (Jacksonville).

Strengths

Palm Coast enjoys three seasons and, fortunately for retirees, winter is the missing one! The climate is subtropical, and the population does not double or triple with seasonal tourists. The city is a 30- to 90-minute drive from many of Florida's major attractions when company comes. Crime rates are lower than the national average.

Weaknesses

The closest upscale shopping is in Daytona Beach or in Jacksonville at the Avenues Mall or the St. Johns's Center, which is about 45 minutes to an hour north on I-95. The cultural amenities of a big city are an hour away in Jacksonville.

FYI

Check out these sources for additional information: Flagler County Chamber of Commerce (www.flaglerpc chamber.org or 800-881-1022), Flagler County information (www.flagleronline.com or www.flaglercounty. org,), and *The Flagler Times* (www.theflagertimes.net or 386-446-1659).

THE TREASURE COAST: Vero Beach

Vero Beach

REPORT CARD

Overall rating:	A-
Climate:	A
Cost of living:	A-
Health care:	B+
Transportation:	B
What's to do:	A

Vero Beach is the largest of five incorporated municipalities in Indian River County. Located in the south-central portion of the east coast of Florida, Vero Beach

---

The name Treasure Coast originates from the gold doubloons that washed ashore from sunken Spanish vessels making their way from Havana to Spain in the 1500s.

is part of the Treasure Coast that includes Port St. Lucie, Stuart, and Jupiter Island.

Commercial airline service is provided by Melbourne International Airport, which is located 35 miles north of Vero Beach. Vero Beach Municipal Airport provides service to corporate jets and small aircraft.

If you like water, you will love this part of Florida. It seems water is everywhere, with homes on canals, lakes, the Sebastian River, the Indian River Lagoon, and the Atlantic coast. Golf and tennis are available to everyone in Vero Beach; both Pocahontas Park and Riverside Park offer active tennis programs. The Sandridge Municipal Golf course has received national acclaim as one of our country's best public courses. Indian River County boasts 26 miles of sandy beaches and all the water sports and activities that can be enjoyed in the beautiful Florida sunshine. Most of the rainfall in Vero Beach occurs between June and October.

In 1995, the Cultural Council of Indian River was created to support many area organizations; the Center for the Arts, the Vero Beach Art Club, and the Riverside Theatre are just a few groups that have benefited from the council. The Kennedy Space Center is 70 miles north. *Money* magazine ranked Vero Beach among its "Top Beach Towns." It appears that Vero Beach has it all.

Who Lives in Vero Beach?

More than 130,000 people live in Indian River County, with 17,700 living in Vero Beach. The median age is 48, and more than 40 percent of the population is 62 or older. Vero Beach's population has remained fairly constant for the last several years.

What's the Cost?

The cost of living index in Vero Beach is 102, based on a national average of 100. The average price of a home is about $300,000.

What's to Do?

Water, water, everywhere. With more than 20 parks that have access to the ocean or a lagoon, everyone has entrée to swimming, fishing, kayaking, and boating—virtually every water sport. There are myriad ecological attractions, including Pelican Island National Refuge, the Environmental Learning Center, Riverfront Conservation Area, and Harbor Branch Oceanographic Institution. Visit the

---

Vero Beach is 190 miles south of Jacksonville and 135 miles north of Miami.

UDT Navy SEAL Museum, or join the Vero Beach Art Club, the Theatre Guild, or the Choral Society. Take the grandkids to Orlando; it's only 100 miles away.

Where Are the Jobs?

Services, retail, government, and agriculture account for most of the jobs in Indian River County. New Piper Aircraft is the largest private-sector employer. The unemployment rate is about 4 percent.

Where Are the Doctors?

Indian River Memorial Hospital provides service to the Vero Beach area, and there are a number of emergency-care clinics as well. Holmes Regional Medical Center is in Melbourne, 40 miles away.

Where Are Some Notable Neighborhoods?

Pointe West (www.pointewestflorida.com or 772-794-9912) is a non-traditional community—live, work, and play all in one location. Calton and Southern

Classic homes enjoy golf-course views and are priced from the $500,000s. Enjoy semiprivate championship golf with a learning center, world-class equestrian facilities, and a pedestrian-friendly, practical town center with apartments "over the shops," all in one location. A great addition to Pointe West is The Lakes at Pointe West, described as "a unique retirement campus in a country-club setting" comprised of independent-living apartments, single-family homes, and assisted and memory-care units. For information, go to www.pointe-west.com or call 772-299-7916.

The Indian River Club (www.indianriverclub.com or 800-575-0005) is a gated golf community that holds the distinction of being an Audubon Signature Sanctuary. There are only a few such sanctuaries worldwide. Carriage homes are priced from the $380,000s, with single-family homes starting in the $400,000s and going to a million plus. Lots begin in the $100,000s.

Grand Harbor (www.grandharbor.com or 877-473-4727) offers a resort lifestyle with amenities that include two championship golf courses, a protected

What's It Like Outside?	Jan.	Apr.	Jul.	Oct.	Rain (in.)	Snow (in.)
Average high (°F)	75	85	90	79	50	0
Average low (°F)	53	66	72	60	–	–

marina, a mile of Intracoastal Waterway, tennis, fitness center, and a beautiful beach club. A variety of housing styles are available with prices in the mid $400,000s. Oak Harbor (www.oakharborfl.com) is an independent-living retirement community located adjacent to Grand Harbor and offers its own nine-hole golf course, world-class clubhouse, and health center. Condos, villas, cottages, and homes are also available beginning around $400,000. An assisted-living residence, Somerset House, is a part of this community as well.

How Do I Pursue Lifelong Learning?

Indian River Community College has a campus in Vero Beach. Career training, professional and personal development, customized business training, classes that will transfer to a 4-year university, and free adult education/GED preparation are offered. The Florida Institute of Technology has more than 100 degree programs and is located 35 miles north in Melbourne.

Strengths

Vero Beach is a well-established small town with all the amenities to draw a diverse population. If you enjoy water sports, the arts, the theater, and ecological attractions (not to mention a 7-day-a-week bridge club!), you will want to consider Vero Beach.

Weaknesses

The closest big city is Orlando, about 100 miles away. Miami is 135 miles from Vero Beach. Housing can be expensive in this part of Florida.

FYI

Check out these sources for additional information: Indian River County Chamber of Commerce (www.indianriverchamber.com or 772-567-3491) and the *Vero Beach Press Journal* (www.tcpalm.com or 772-569-7100).

THE PARADISE COAST:
Naples, Bonita Springs, and Sarasota

Naples

REPORT CARD

Overall rating:	B+
Climate:	B
Cost of living:	B
Health care:	A
Transportation:	B+
What's to do:	A

If you are driving south along the west coast of Florida on Interstate 95 on your way to Naples, you will want to exit early and take a look at Bonita Springs. This community just north of Naples has developed so extensively in the past few years that there seems to be no break in development between the two cities. Bonita Springs has great neighborhoods and great shopping (the new Coconut Point is a mixed-use shopping area). The last exit before the Everglades is Naples, considered by many to be the crown jewel of southwest Florida (although a few folks in Sarasota might disagree). Naples is in the subtropical zone, where you'll find a Mediterranean-type climate with warm breezes and endless sunshine. The sugar-sand beaches and the great fishing and boating make Naples an outdoor paradise. This city is also a cultural treasure in southwest Florida. The Philharmonic Center for the Arts, for example, offers more than 400 events each season.

Southwest Florida attracts thousands of snowbirds seeking warmth from the cold winters of "up north," and Naples is the choice for many of them, as well as for retirees looking for a full-time location. You can expect high humidity and late afternoon thunderstorms on a daily basis during the summer. A short jaunt (35 miles) will take you to Southwest Florida International Airport serving Naples, Fort Meyers, Bonita Springs, and Marco Island.

Who Lives in Naples?

The population in Naples is about 24,000. The city of Naples is 1 mile wide and 9 miles long, and runs along the Gulf of Mexico. The population of Collier County, which includes Bonita Springs, is about 300,000 and swells by at least 100,000 when the snowbirds arrive. About 93 percent of the population is Caucasian, 5 percent is African-American, and 2 percent is Hispanic. Naples is one of the nation's fastest-growing metro areas; Collier County grew 65 percent during the 1990s.

What's the Cost?

Naples can be upscale living, that's for sure. Shopping, dining, and housing all lean in the direction of expensive. Browsing for decorator items, furniture, antiques, and clothing in the great boutiques or larger shopping areas of Naples, as well as experiencing the wide variety of cuisine, could qualify as a part-time job. The median sale price of a home for Naples/Marco Island was

What's It Like Outside?	Jan.	Apr.	Jul.	Oct.	Rain (in.)	Snow (in.)
Average high (°F)	74	85	91	85	57	0
Average low (°F)	52	62	75	67	–	–

$529,000 in 2007. The Florida Price Index for Naples, however, is only 107, based on a statewide average of 100. The more reasonably priced homes are farther away from the water.

What's to Do?

The United Arts Council of Collier County is comprised of more than 40 organizations that bring culture to Naples and the rest of the county. The Philharmonic Center for the Arts/Naples Museum of Art entertains residents of Naples with Broadway plays, opera, classical and popular music, lectures, and dance. Or get out of the audience and join one of the many community theaters for a production—either onstage or behind the scenes.

Enjoy the Florida sunshine while golfing, boating, or playing tennis. Watch a swamp buggy race or go fishing. Indulge in a day of shopping, and take a break for lunch in an outdoor café in Old Naples. Experience the beauty of the sun setting over the Gulf of Mexico. Bidding farewell to the sun each day is somewhat of a ritual in southwest Florida; it often includes a glass of wine on the beach! Explore the 1.5 million-acre Everglades National Park—just not all in one day! Ask about their Golden Age Passport, which allows free entry for life, free access to most federal recreation areas, and other discounts to people over 62 for a one-time fee of $10.

Where Are the Jobs?

The major employers are the schools, retail, county government, health care, and tourism. The unemployment rate in Naples is a low 2 percent.

Where Are the Doctors?

The Naples Community Hospital Healthcare System operates two hospitals with more than 500 physicians and 26 outpatient facilities in the area. The prestigious Cleveland Clinic operates in Naples as well.

Where Are Some Notable Neighborhoods?

Building new communities in Naples is becoming more difficult since there is only so much land with that all-important prestigious Naples address. In years past, when Thomas Edison, Harvey Firestone, and Gary Cooper visited, it is said that you could buy a beachfront

---

In Old Naples, all the streets running east to west end at the beach.
Sounds like this is a town that has its priorities straight!

lot for about $125! Prices have increased significantly since then. We included the area north of Naples (Bonita Springs) and even some communities north of Bonita on the outskirts of Fort Myers as part of our Naples discussion. It is a short drive south to enjoy the city of Naples—and the airport is actually closer!

WCI is building communities in and close to Naples including Tuscany Reserve, Manchester Square, Tiburon, Hammock Bay, and Artesia. To take a peek at these neighborhoods, use the WCI Web site (www.wcicommunities.com) or call 800-WCI-4005.

Ave Maria is a new 5,000-acre community (www.avemaria.com or 866-887-1270). Pulte Homes homes will have a large presence here. All manner of housing styles—single-family, townhomes, condos, carriage homes, villas, and a Del Webb active-adult community—are available. The town of Ave Maria is being built in conjunction with the new university of Ave Maria, founded by Thomas Monaghan (he also founded Domino's Pizza). So if you're looking for a new university in a new town with new housing, consider Ave Maria!

About 15 miles north of Naples is Bonita Springs (www.bonitabay.com or 888-875-8782), a great place to live and still enjoy the amenities of Naples. Bonita Bay is a spectacular, 2,400-acre gated community in Bonita Springs with lots of resale homes, villas, and high-rise condominiums starting from $800,000 overlooking the Gulf of Mexico.

Another outstanding property, the Brooks (www.thebrooks.com or 888-875-8782), also in Bonita Springs, is a 2,500-acre development (more than 50 percent remains as open space) that is minutes from the Southwest Florida International Airport. There are many housing options at the Brooks, and there are many resales among its separate communities.

Toll Brothers (www.tollbrothers.com or 239-596-5966), has a new community of 112 single-family homes just minutes from downtown—Firano at Naples. The homes are two to four bedrooms ranging in size from 2,000 to 3,000 square feet and are priced in the $500,000s. Amenities include a clubhouse with swimming and fitness facilities.

March is considered the peak of the tourist season, and the population generally increases by one-third in Collier County, where Naples is located. Approximately 500,000 tourists descend on Naples between January and March.

Another possibility is to head to Marco Island, Florida, about 20 miles south of Naples, but still within Collier County. Marco Island's 6 miles of beach and its more than 100 miles of waterways throughout its 14 square miles enable many homes to have canals in their backyards. With its approximately 15,000 residents (this number will swell by about 20,000 during the winter), this is a laid-back, friendly island, with many people owning second homes and others converting from snowbirds to full-timers. Home prices vary tremendously, depending on type and location, including access to the Gulf of Mexico for your boat.

How Do I Pursue Lifelong Learning?

There are several opportunities for lifelong learning in the Naples area. Florida Gulf Coast University is actually located in nearby Fort Myers and offers noncredit courses in addition to degree courses. Edison Community College offers classes in Naples and Fort Myers. And, of course, there is Ave Maria University, mentioned previously.

Strengths

The subtropical climate in Naples translates to warm, sunny winters, and the city's location on the Gulf Coast translates to breathtaking sunsets. Great fishing, boating, and beaching, coupled with fine dining, shopping on the waterfront, and more cultural events than days in a year, give Naples a well-deserved wonderful reputation.

Weaknesses

Exceptionally hot, humid summer days make outdoor activities somewhat difficult. Traffic and snowbird crowds in restaurants and at the airport make winter months a challenge.

FYI

Check out these sources for additional information: Chamber of Commerce (www.naples-florida.com or 239-262-6376), Naples/Marco Island and the Everglades Web site (www.visit-naples.com or 800-688-3600), and the *Naples Daily News* (800-404-7343).

The Gulf Stream's water generally maintains daytime air temperatures of at least 70 degrees Fahrenheit, thus giving this area the nickname "Gateway to the tropics."

Sarasota

REPORT CARD

Overall rating:	A
Climate:	A-
Cost of living:	A-
Health care:	A
Transportation:	A
What's to do:	A

Located on the west coast of Florida, about 60 miles south of Tampa, Sarasota might have that small beach town/big-city feel you're looking for. Three international airports serve Sarasota County—Sarasota Bradenton International, Tampa International, and St. Petersburg-Clearwater International. Interstate 75 is the main corridor for the southeastern United States and provides easy access to Sarasota for family and friends.

With 35 miles of pristine Gulf beaches and all the amenities of city life, the combination is irresistible for many retirees and young families alike. Sarasota County includes the communities of Sarasota, Englewood, North Port, Venice, and St. Armand's Circle, as well as the barrier islands of Casey Key, Lido Key, Longboat Key, and Siesta Key. More than 60 public and private golf courses and white, powdery sand beaches not more than a 15-minute drive from almost anywhere in the county make enjoying the tropical weather a snap! If you are looking for more than sun and sand, Sarasota is also known as the cultural coast of Florida.

From June through September, rainfall averages about 8 inches per month.

Who Lives in Sarasota?

The population of Sarasota County is about 366,000, with about 55,000 in the city of Sarasota. About 45 percent of the population is 45 or older; about one-third of the residents are 65 or older. About 92 percent of the

What's It Like Outside?	Jan.	Apr.	Jul.	Oct.	Rain (in.)	Snow (in.)
Average high (°F)	72	82	91	85	60	0
Average low (°F)	51	60	73	65	–	–

population is Caucasian, 4 percent African-American, and 4 percent Hispanic.

What's the Cost?

The cost of living index in Sarasota is 107, compared to an average of 100. The median cost of a home in 2007 is about $300,000, a decline of about 90 percent from 2006.

What's to Do?

Sports fans will have an opportunity to enjoy some old-fashioned baseball every February and March when the Cincinnati Reds come to Sarasota for spring training, the Pittsburgh Pirates are in Manatee County, and the Yankees and Devil Rays hold camp in Tampa. If baseball's not your game, enjoy Reggae by the Bay at Marie Selby Botanical Gardens or check out the Sarasota Film Festival. You can also enjoy performances at the Van Wezel Performing Arts Hall, the Asolo Theatre Company, the Sarasota Ballet of Florida, the Florida West Coast Symphony, the Jazz Club of Sarasota, or the Ringling Museum of Art. Visiting the 30 renowned art galleries is always stimulating and especially fun on the one Friday night a month when the galleries host the artists and local musicians and serve wine and hors d'oeuvres. This is just a sampling of the indoor activi-ties that might appeal to you in Sarasota. The beautiful white sand beaches and the Gulf of Mexico should take care of any additional spare time, unless, of course, you want to go shopping and out to dinner on St. Armand's Circle!

Where Are the Jobs?

The major employers in Sarasota are related to education, health care, social services, and retail. Sarasota is also home to many corporations, including AM Engineering, ASO Corporation, Boar's Head Provisions, and PGT Industries. The unemployment rate in Sarasota County is about 2 percent.

Where Are the Doctors?

There are close to 70 hospitals in the Tampa Bay/Sarasota region. Sarasota Memorial Health Care System has more than 800 beds and is the second largest acute care center in any public hospital in Florida.

Where Are Some Notable Neighborhoods?

Lakewood Ranch (www.lakewoodranch.com or 800-30RANCH) is an award-winning, 7,000-acre master-planned community situated on the line between Sarasota and Manatee Counties. There are more than 30 neighborhoods located in seven residential villages with prices ranging from the $200,000s to well over a million dollars. Everything is provided in one location: recreation, schools, shopping, and restaurants—even a polo club and an osteopathic medical school! An assisted-living facility, the Windsor of Lakewood Ranch, is also located here, making Lakewood Ranch a great place to live for almost everyone!

Rive Isle (www.riveisle.com or 914-776-1729). This promises to be an extraordinary property, with private boat docks and direct access to the Gulf of Mexico. Lots are priced from the $300,000s on its 225 acres located north of Sarasota.

University Park (www.universitypark-fl.com or 800-394-6325) is conveniently located between Sarasota and Bradenton, just west of I-75. This community is composed of individual neighborhoods with a great variety in style and cost: Kenwood Park from the $600,000s, Grosvenor Gardens from the $800,000s, and Wimbledon beginning in the $1 million range. All neighborhoods enjoy the four-star golf course, 11 lighted tennis courts, and the social amenities of the clubhouse, which offers duplicate bridge, bocce ball, bingo, and a book club.

Rosedale (www.Rosedalegolf.com or 800-881-9080), located in Bradenton and only 15 minutes from the Sarasota airport, is comprised of detached, single-family, maintenance-free homes in a master-planned golf and country-club community. New homes are priced from the $600,000s, and resales are available in the $300,000s.

How Do I Pursue Lifelong Learning?

There are an impressive nine colleges and universities in the Sarasota area, including Manatee Community College, Sarasota County Technical Institute, Keiser College, Ringling School of Art and Design, the University of South Florida, and the International College. The International College is the home of the Creative Retirement Center, an Elderhostel affiliate, committed to helping its members enrich their lives by active participation in the process of lifelong learning through the

Don't miss the outdoor farmers' market every Saturday morning from 7 a.m. until noon. Enjoy the Caribbean-style baked goods and the Gulf of Mexico shrimp.

study of history, religion, art, opera, or the American short story (to name just a few).

Strengths

Living in a great climate in the cultural center of Florida, in a real working city that feels like a small town, appeals to many. The beaches (especially Siesta Key) are among the most beautiful to be found anywhere, and the views and sunsets over the water are spectacular. A great airport and easy highway access make travel a breeze.

Weaknesses

The downside to living in paradise is usually cost, and so it is here as well. The average new home on Siesta Key is priced from the $500,000s, and most homes close to the water will be extremely expensive. Some 350,000 tourists descend on the area every winter and create traffic gridlock and long lines at the restaurants. If you are looking for a year-round location, consider spending a few winter and summer months in a rental before you make a full-time move.

FYI

Check out these sources for additional information: Greater Sarasota Chamber of Commerce (www.sarasota chamber.org or 941-955-8187), the *Sarasota Herald Tribune* (www.heraldtribune.com or 941-953-5171), and the *Longboat Observer* (www.longboat observer.com or 941-383-5509).

THE EMERALD COAST:
The Panhandle

REPORT CARD

Overall rating:	B
Climate:	A-
Cost of living:	A-
Health care:	B-
Transportation:	B
What's to do:	B

The Emerald Coast of Florida spans about 100 miles, called the "Miracle Strip," from Panama City west to

---

Siesta Key has some of the most beautiful beaches in the world, and they are often found on the top ten lists of the most sought-after beaches. In addition, there are more than 50 miles of inland waterways and canals for your boating pleasure.

Pensacola. Like pearls on a necklace, towns are strung along the Gulf of Mexico. Communities include Fort Walton Beach, Destin, Niceville, Sandestin, Seaside, Grayton Beach, Seagrove Beach, Santa Rosa Beach, Navarre, and Pensacola. Panhandle beaches are regularly ranked among the best beaches in the country, where you'll find the softest, white-gold sand, and water that really does look like the sparkling gem for which this area is named.

A four-season climate results in quiet, cool winters and a bustling summer tourist season, though the Panhandle is becoming more of a year-round tourist spot. Airports in Pensacola, Fort Walton Beach, and Panama City make the Emerald Coast accessible, but nonstop flights from certain cities are only seasonal. There is a plethora of city, county, state, and national parks. It may be the perfect place if you're looking for a second home, though a number of hurricanes (Opal, Erin, Earl, Georges, Charley, Ivan, and Katrina) have affected the Panhandle since 1995, causing deaths, injuries, and millions of dollars in damages and contributing to beach erosion.

Who Lives in the Panhandle?

The Panhandle's proximity to Georgia and Alabama gives it a real southern flair. The people are unfailingly polite and helpful, and southern accents are not uncommon. The population of the Panhandle is growing; between 1995 and 2005, northwest Florida's population increased by 14 percent. People are younger here than in the rest of the state. In 2005, about 35 percent of the population was under 25, and about 13 percent was 65 or older (compared to 32 percent and 17 percent, respectively). Destin has about 13,000 residents, Fort Walton Beach about 20,000, and the city of Pensacola approximately 54,000. In general, other than the far western counties, the laid-back counties of the Panhandle are not experiencing the rapid growth that many other Florida areas are experiencing. (The rest of Florida's population increased by 24 percent during the same 10-year period.) There's also a strong military presence—both active and retired.

What's the Cost?

Fort Walton's cost of living index is 100, Panama City's is 98, and Pensacola's is 99, based on an average of 100.

What's It Like Outside?	Jan.	Apr.	Jul.	Oct.	Rain (in.)	Snow (in.)
Average high (°F)	61	77	89	80	60	0
Average low (°F)	42	60	74	60	–	–

Panama City is a particularly good bargain for home prices, averaging almost 14 percent below the national average. Of course, there is a tremendous range of prices, from million-dollar homes fronting the Gulf to inexpensive condos in the interior, but the median home cost is about $200,000.

What's to Do?

As would be expected, the Panhandle boasts all things water related, including boating, swimming, and fishing. (Destin is nicknamed the "world's luckiest fishing village.") Other outdoor activities include hunting, horseback riding, hiking, camping, and golfing. There are several museums, including the unique Air Force Armament Museum, a community-theater group in Fort Walton Beach, and a performing-arts center at Okaloosa-Walton Community College. Spend the day strolling around Seville Square, Pensacola's historic district, or enjoying the Gulf Islands National Seashore. Snowbirds longing for a bit of winter sport can watch the Ice Pilots, a minor-league hockey team that plays at the Pensacola Civic Center. The "Big Easy" (New Orleans) is a 4-hour drive from Pensacola, and the Mississippi casinos are fewer than 3 hours from Pensacola. Shop at the Santa Rosa Mall in Fort Walton Beach or the Silver Sands Factory Stores in Destin. A number of entertainment and retail projects are in the planning/development stages on the Panhandle. On a more laid-back note, enjoy a scenic drive: Highway 30A winds along the coast sans advertising, fast-food restaurants, or miniature golf courses. A big plus—construction height along this lovely stretch of road is limited to 50 feet.

Where Are the Jobs?

Service, retail, and government are the three largest job sectors. Eglin Air Force Base, Tyndall Air Force Base, and Whiting Field Naval Air Station are examples of military installations that employ thousands of civilians and contribute to the area's economy and low unemployment rate, which hovers under 3 percent.

Where Are the Doctors?

Sacred Heart Hospital in Pensacola is a 500-bed facility. A 50-bed medical center, Sacred Heart Hospital on the Emerald Coast, opened in Santa Rosa Beach in January 2003. Tallahassee, less than an hour away, has two major hospitals, Tallahassee Community Hospital and Tallahassee Memorial HealthCare.

Where Are Some Notable Neighborhoods?

If you're considering a home in the Panhandle, the largest private landowner in Florida, the St. Joe Company, has a number of developments in northwestern

Florida: Water Color, Water Sound, River Camps, Wind Mark Beach, Summer Camp, South Wood, and White Fence Farms, with prices beginning in the $300,000s (www.stjoe.com or 866-417-7133).

Rosemary Beach (www.rosemarybeach.com or 800-736-0877), established in 1995, is an example of new urbanism, with West Indies–style and southern cottages and homes characterized by small lots, front porches, and interesting architectural touches. An integration of green space, a town center with lofts, a fitness center, tennis, and a neighborhood designed for walking (you can get anywhere within minutes) makes this a most aesthetically pleasing coastal village. According to one Realtor, approximately 85 percent of the homes are either second homes or rentals. Resale homesites begin around $500,000, one-sixth fractional ownership homes start in the $300,000s, and homes fronting the Gulf can cost more than $5 million.

Alys Beach (www.alysbeach.com or 866-732-1760) is located on Highway 30A, in the northwest area of the Panhandle. White walls and white roofs set against the azure skies will create a dramatic contrast in this 160-acre new urbanism community consisting of about 800 residences, including courtyard homes with zero lot lines and multifamily homes. The downside? Homes are expected to fetch upward of $1 million.

If the Panhandle seems like a location you'd want for a primary retirement home, consider living in an area with a sense of community, rather than the condos and homes along the Gulf that are chiefly seasonal or rental homes. There are a number of neighborhoods tucked away from tourist activity, yet close enough that you can enjoy the amenities of a resort town. In Destin, there is the 900-acre Kelly Plantation (www.kellyplantation.com or 800-837-5080), complete with 18 holes of golf, tennis, a fitness and equestrian center, and bay-front property. New homes are priced from $600,000. Regatta Bay (www.regattabay.com or 800-648-0123), also in Destin, is a 525-acre gated golf and country club community on the Choctawhatchee Bay. Wetlands and nature areas are incorporated into this master-planned community, and residences range from condos and golf villas to estate homes; lots are also available. Homes begin in the $600,000s.

On the bay side of Route 98, across from the Hilton Sandestin Beach Golf Resort and Spa, is the Village of Baytowne Wharf, replete with retail, restaurants, condos, townhomes, lodging, and a marina on the Choctawhatchee Bay. There are a number of gated communities near the village center, including Anchorage (condos), the Fountains of Sandestin, and Augusta. Farther inland are towns such as Niceville or Crestview, which are about a half-hour drive from the beaches but are more residential and give more bang for the buck on home prices. For example, the average price of a three-bedroom, two-bath home in Crestview (less than 5 years old), 30 miles inland, is $155,000. Only minutes from the beach, the average three-bedroom, two-bath home in Niceville (fewer than 5 years old) is $240,000.

How Do I Pursue Lifelong Learning?
Several institutions of higher learning dot the Panhandle, including Gulf Coast Community College in Panama City, Troy State University Florida Region in Fort Walton Beach, Okaloosa-Walton Community College in Niceville, and the University of West Florida in Pensacola. There are also several vocational-technical schools. Florida State University is located in Tallahassee, in the big bend area of Florida, about a 45-minute drive from the Gulf of Mexico.

Strengths
The gorgeous beaches and pleasant temperatures are the strong points. A competitive cost of living is also attractive. A number of retail and entertainment facilities are in the planning stages. Plus, it's tough to compete with seeing both the sunrise and sunset over the same glittering body of water!

Weaknesses
The Gulf on one side, and East Bay, Choctawhatchee Bay, and Air Force bases on the other side limit the development of the area (some would consider this a strength). Route 98, although undergoing widening in several places, is the single artery across the Panhandle. Panama City is a big spring-break destination. The area is light on cultural activities, and the hurricane factor can't be ignored.

FYI
Check out these sources for additional information: Crestview Chamber of Commerce (www.crestviewchamber.com or 850-682-3212), Destin Chamber of Commerce (www.destinchamber.com or 850-837-6241), Fort Walton Beach Chamber of Commerce (www.fwb.org or 850-244-8191), Pensacola Chamber of Commerce (www.pensacolachamber.com or 850-

The Panhandle's sand gets its wonderful texture from its amazing journey. Originating in the Appalachian Mountains, the tiny quartz particles are smoothed and polished as they bounce along streams and rivers en route to the Gulf of Mexico.

438-4081), Santa Rosa Beach (www.waltoncounty chamber.com or 850-267-0683), the *Destin Log* (850-654-8400), the *Northwest Florida Daily News* (800-755-1185), and the *Pensacola News Journal* (850-435-8500).

CENTRAL FLORIDA:
The Villages, Ocala, and Gainesville

The cities in central Florida cannot boast an ocean view; however, they do have many other qualities that you might be looking for. Having said "no ocean view," remember, if you are willing to drive a little over an hour, you can enjoy several beaches, including Daytona Beach. In general, central Florida offers a lower cost of living than the coastal areas. A virtual retirement mecca with the best in age-restricted communities can be found here, surrounded by a rural setting complete with horse farms.

The Villages

REPORT CARD

Overall rating;	A
Climate:	A-
Cost of living:	A
Health care:	A
Transportation:	B+
What's to do:	A++

Driving through central Florida and coming upon the Villages, an active-adult community, can be a startling experience. Central Florida reminds you of Old Florida, and in spots the area is very rural and beautiful with a setting of stately oaks, country roads, and horse farms. Not so in The Villages. The Villages is home for about 63,000 residents age 55 and older, and this is the city that never sleeps—well, not very often—because its residents are too busy! Most everyone cruises in a golf cart even if they're not golfers, around the more than 5-square-mile community. It is the preferred method of transportation (tunnels were built so you don't have to cross any major street). You would need a car if you wanted to leave, but most people ask, "Why would you want to leave?" The hospital, churches, shopping, restaurants, schools, golf, swimming pools, polo field, softball fields, movie theaters, and on and on are all within golf-car distance!

Most rainfall occurs in the hot summer months.

Who Lives in The Villages?

This age-restricted community (www.thevillages.com or 800-245-1081) attracts people from all over the country and many from outside the country. The plan is for a population of more than 100,000 when building is complete—only 40,000 more people to go! Most of the residents are white (97 percent), with about 1 percent Hispanic and 1 percent African-American.

What's the Cost?

Using the Florida Price Index, with its average of 100, Sumter County is 95, a little lower than the state average. If you look at housing prices in The Villages, you will see a broad range of style and price. A new patio villa with two bedrooms and two bathrooms (about 1,100 square feet) is priced in the $150,000s. Ranch Homes in the $150,000s, as well as Designer Homes and Premier Homes priced from the $200,000s to the $500,000s are also available. When you request information, you will be given an estimated "Monthly Cost of Living Sheet," based on a $175,000 home.

What's to Do?

This is the best part! When you visit, you will receive *The Villages Recreation News*, and a typical monthly publication is almost 40 pages long! Bridge every day, Big Band Club (a rehearsal band that practices on Wednesday mornings), The Village Harmonica Band, Foreign Film Club, double-deck pinochle, Cloud Chaser (kite flying), Singles (two clubs for singles), tai chi, softball, soccer, Sheldon's Stompers (clogging), travel groups, "Way, Way Off Broadway," pickle ball, tennis, and on and on. There are even two motorcycle clubs, and this is just a sample. There will be no excuse for boredom with the 24 Executive and nine Championship golf courses (open to anyone who lives in The Villages), the swimming pools and fitness centers, and the endless list of activities. And remember, there is live entertainment every night in the Town Square. Yes, every night. Don't forget the movie theaters, restaurants, and shopping in both Town Squares, all within golf-car distance.

Where Are the Jobs?

The Villages, being an actual city, is the main employer, with more than 2,200 people working in some capacity in the town. Public schools are also found within the confines of The Villages, providing a great education for residents with school-age children. A new Super Wal-Mart will also be an employment generator.

What's It Like Outside?	Jan.	Apr.	Jul.	Oct.	Rain (in.)	Snow (in.)
Average high (°F)	68	81	91	83	50	0
Average low (°F)	45	57	71	62	–	–

Where Are the Doctors?

The Leesburg Regional Medical Center and The Villages Regional Hospital provide quality care for the residents of The Villages.

Where Are Some Notable Neighborhoods?

The Villages, spanning more than 23,000 acres, offers a wide variety of home choices to fit your lifestyle. The six unique series of villas and homes let you decide just how much house you want or need.

How Do I Pursue Lifelong Learning?

Central Florida Community College is about 20 miles away in Ocala. Four-year colleges within a 50-mile range include Rollins College in Winter Park and Stetson College in Deland. The University of Central Florida is in the Orlando area, about 60 miles away. With more than 1,000 planned activities per week, there are also many lifelong learning opportunities to pursue right at home!

Strengths

If you are looking for a mild climate; thousands of busy, happy, people (single and married); and an affordable cost of living, this may be the place for you. Restaurants, movies, shopping, medical facilities, and 30-plus golf courses are all within golf-car distance.

Weaknesses

The closest big city and airport are about an hour away.

FYI

Check out these sources for additional information: *The Villages Daily Sun* (www.thevillagesdailysun.com or 800-726-6592) and The Villages Chamber of Commerce (www.thevillageschamberofcommerce.org or 866-489-1856).

true
LIFE **Ann-Marie S. is an author.**

I discovered The Villages in the same way a majority of people find the property—through a friend who lives there. The reason I love it is because it is an adult playground for golf, swimming, tennis, and every other sport and activity you can imagine.

After growing a 20-year-old business, The Villages made me see that working was getting in the way of relaxing. As a direct result of having a second home in The Villages, I am now a golf addict and find that work is getting in the way of golfing.

When they say that the best way to have your children flock home is by having a place in Florida, they were not kidding. We have had more family time in The Villages than ever before. ⓣⓛ

Ocala

REPORT CARD

Overall rating:	A
Climate:	B+
Cost of living:	A+
Health care:	A
Transportation:	B
What's to do:	A-

Ocala is located in north central Florida, about halfway between Atlanta and Miami along Interstate 75. Ocala is horse country, and there are more than 900 beautiful horse farms in Marion County. If you find yourself driving through North Central Florida, taking in the beauty of the green, gently rolling topography, horse farms, and countless old oak trees, you might ask, "Where are we? This can't be Florida!" Oh, but it is! Ocala, a small town in a rural setting, reminds many people of the Midwest or the Northeast. The beaches are 60 miles in either direction, and Orlando, at about 100 miles away, is still accessible when visitors come.

Ocala is a draw for people considering relocation because the city has a great deal to offer, and the cost of living is relatively low. You can be a part of a state-of-the-art retirement community, play a little golf, go fishing, and enjoy college football at the University of Florida in Gainesville, all while living in a laid-back town with a mild, four-season climate. And remember, no hurricanes!

Who Lives in Ocala?

The population of Ocala is about 50,000. The population of Marion County, where Ocala is located, is approximately 290,000. About half the population of Marion County is over 45 years old, with one in four over 65.

What's It Like Outside?	Jan.	Apr.	Jul.	Oct.	Rain (in.)	Snow (in.)
Average high (°F)	66	81	91	81	52	0
Average low (°F)	42	56	70	60	–	–

What's the Cost?

The cost of living is good, reported to be about 94 on the Florida Price Index, compared to a Florida average of 100. The median price for a home in Ocala is $220,000.

What's to Do?

For starters, the 383,000-acre Ocala National Forest is a vast area filled with ecological sites, trails, springs, and lakes for the outdoor enthusiast. Or go camping or canoeing in Silver River State Park. The waters you find in Ocala are crystal-clear rivers and freshwater springs, and there's great fishing and boating on the many lakes and rivers. Visit Silver Springs—Nature's Theme Park—and take a glass-bottom boat to explore the artesian spring system and abundant underwater life. The 47-mile Willacoochee State Trail begins in Citrus Springs and stretches to Dade City for biking, walking, and jogging. Or play one of the area's approximately 40 golf courses within a 30-minute drive.

Enjoy the Victorian homes of the town's historic district, or patronize the Appleton Cultural Center, a complex that includes Ocala Civic Theater and the Pioneer Garden Club and serves as the hub for cultural activities in Ocala. Have lunch at Carmichael's Café and enjoy the art museum in the afternoon. The Ocala Civic Theater has presented almost 400 productions and performs for more than 50,000 people each season. You will also find ballet and a variety of musical offerings, from jazz to symphonic music.

Driving to the famous Florida attractions is a popular pastime for Ocala residents. A short drive will take you to Orlando, the Kennedy Space Center, and any number of spring-training baseball games. Ocala is within half a day's drive to any of the Sunshine State's major cities, and Amtrak also serves the area. The Gainesville Regional Airport, a nonhub airport about 40 miles from Ocala, provides the closest air transportation. Four international airports are located within 100 miles of Ocala.

Where Are the Jobs?

The top employers in Ocala are within health care and manufacturing. Private employers include Emergency

---

Definitions of *age-restricted* vary from community to community, but generally, there is a minimum age of 55 (although it may be as low as 50 or as high as 62) for at least one member of a couple. Check age restrictions prior to purchase.

One, Cingular Wireless, Kmart Corporation, Closet Maid, and Lockheed Martin. The unemployment rate is about 3 percent.

Where Are the Doctors?

Several facilities serve the medical needs of Ocala residents, including Munroe Regional Medical Center, Ocala Regional Medical Center, and West Marion Community Hospital. The University of Florida in Gainesville, a 40-minute drive from Ocala, has a teaching hospital as well.

Where Are Some Notable Neighborhoods?

On Top of the World Communities (www.ontopof theworldcommunities.com or 800- 421-4162) is a gated, active-adult community with two 18-hole golf courses available to everyone. The residents have created more than 200 clubs, and you can start one if you can come up with a new idea! Golf, tennis, and fitness, as well as the full-service Circle Square Commons, make living here fun and easy; they're all within walking distance or just a golf-cart ride away. Three neighborhoods—Indigo East, Chandler Hills, and Windsor—offer homes that begin in the $200,000s.

Oak Run Country Club (www.oakrunflorida.com or 800-874-0898) is a gated, active-adult community with recreational facilities, including indoor and outdoor swimming, fitness, and tennis. There are two golf courses, one 18-hole and one nine-hole executive course. Homes (not including lot) are priced from the mid $200,000s.

Stone Creek by Del Web (www.delwebb.com/stone creek or 877-333-5932) is a newer, age-restricted community in Ocala with 4,000 planned residences. Resort-style amenities, including championship golf, heated indoor and outdoor pools, and twelve beautiful lakes make this an exceptional property. Homes begin around $200,000. Spruce Creek (www.sprucecreek.com) another Del Webb active-adult community, has resales only and is located in nearby Summerfield.

There are manufactured-home communities in the Ocala area as well, including Oak Bend (800-354-3636). Homes begin under $100,000 and offer amenities such as a pool, community center, and RV storage.

Often referred to as the "horse capital of the world," Marion County employs about 30,000 people in some capacity in its thoroughbred industry.

Although it's 25 miles north of Ocala, Gainesville is more than a notable neighborhood; it's a college town of nearly 120,000 residents and home to the University of Florida. While it provides excellent health care and has a low unemployment rate (2.4 percent), it does have a higher cost of living (index of 104). A community in Gainesville worth checking out is Haile Plantation (www.haileplantation.com or 800-226-8802). As an example of new urbanism, Haile Plantation offers the possibility of living, playing, and working all in the same place. Homes range from the low $100,000s to more than $600,000.

How Do I Pursue Lifelong Learning?

Central Florida Community College has an Ocala campus, as does Webster University. And of course, the University of Florida is just 40 minutes away.

Strengths

Living in Ocala means warm, sunny Florida weather (without the threat of hurricanes), green grass and oak trees, horses grazing, and freshwater lakes. The cost of living and the active-adult communities are real pulls. The medical facilities are top-notch and include a major university hospital 40 minutes away.

Weaknesses

Ocala does not have a tropical feel; it has few palms and no ocean. The rural setting and the lack of a major airport might make one feel isolated.

FYI

Check out these sources for additional information: Ocala Chamber of Commerce (www.ocalacc.com or 352-629-8051), City of Ocala (www.ocalafl.org), Gainesville Chamber of Commerce (www.gainesville chamber.com or 352-334-7100), the *Ocala Star Banner* (www.star-banner.com or 352-867-4010), and the *Gainesville Sun* (www.gainesville.com or 800-443-9493).

GEORGIA

Capital: Atlanta
Nickname: The Peach State
Motto: "Wisdom, justice, and moderation"
Flower: Cherokee rose
Bird: Brown thrasher
Population: 9,000,000

Fascinating Fact: Coca-Cola was invented in 1886 in Atlanta by Dr. John Pemberton.

Skidaway Island

REPORT CARD

Overall rating:	A-
Climate:	A-
Cost of living:	A-
Health care:	A-
Transportation:	A-
What's to do:	A

When is an island not an island? When it's Skidaway Island, which was probably oceanfront 40,000 years or so ago during the last ice age but is now an inland barrier island surrounded by the Wilmington and Vernon rivers, Skidaway Narrows, and Romerly Marsh. Eight miles long and 3 miles wide, Skidaway Island is a nature lover's dream, with a wonderful state park, great hiking trails, and rich marshland. It is also home to the Landings, a large residential area that's only 12 miles from Savannah.

What's It Like Outside?	Jan.	Apr.	Jul.	Oct.	Rain (in.)	Snow (in.)
Average high (°F)	60	78	91	78	48	0
Average low (°F)	38	54	72	57	–	–

You can have your cake and eat it too. Enjoy the close-by amenities of a wonderful southern city, bask in warm weather, revel in the natural beauty of the island, and have easy access to the area through the Savannah/Hilton Head International Airport.

Who Lives in Skidaway Island?

Skidaway Island, as well as the city of Savannah, are in Chatham County, which has about 240,000 residents; about 19 percent of the population is 55 or older. The composition of the county is about 55 percent Caucasian, 40 percent African-American, and 2 percent Hispanic. On the island itself, there are around 7,000 residents who are 97 percent Caucasian and about 1 percent Hispanic. The median age is 61 years old.

What's the Cost?

The 2006 cost of living index in the Savannah area was 89, based on a national average of 100, and the 2006 median home cost was $217,000.

What's to Do?

Skidaway Island State Park encompasses more than 500 acres of this 6,300-acre island. Swim, picnic, camp, or hike through the forest or along a boardwalk trail through the marsh. Enjoy the flora and fauna of the area; fiddler crabs, herons, egrets, ferns, palmettos, and pines are your companions. The University of Georgia's Marine Extension Center and the Skidaway Institute of Oceanography are on the island, and both are open to the public. Living on Skidaway Island allows you to combine the pleasures of water, wildlife, and a wonderful city.

When you crave city life, drive a short distance to Savannah and take advantage of all that it has to offer. Visit the pedestrian-friendly historic district, explore the sizable number of museums, stroll along the pedestrian promenade at the city market, take a ghost tour, and investigate the old cemeteries, forts, parks, and churches. Savannah has a Greek Festival, Jazz Festival, and Film Festival, just to mention a few of its almost 200 festivals. Attend a live production at the 1,000-seat Savannah Theater, or attend a performance of the Savannah Symphony or Ballet South, followed by some low-country cuisine. Fewer than 25 miles from Skidaway Island (less than 20 from Savannah), you can saunter along the 3-mile swath of beach at Tybee Island.

Where Are the Jobs?

Health care, education, manufacturing, tourism, and retail are among the largest employers. Gulfstream Aerospace Corporation, International Paper, and Great Dane Trailers also employ a sizable number of residents. The unemployment rate is 4 percent.

REYNOLDS PLANTATION: A 10,000-ACRE COMMUNITY

Almost the size of a small town, the 10,000-acre Reynolds Plantation in Greensboro is another location to consider. Although it feels somewhat isolated—it's 75 miles east of the Atlanta airport—the development boasts six golf courses, 80 miles of shoreline on 19,000-acre Lake Oconee, two marinas, a Ritz-Carlton with its attendant amenities (including its 26,000-square-foot spa), more than three dozen resident-run groups, fitness and tennis centers, pools, and hiking trails. A retail and commercial center adjoining the plantation, which opened in 2002, provides necessary services (Publix grocery, anyone?) to the residents of Reynolds Plantation. Real estate within this scenic, tranquil enclave includes single-family homes, attached homes, cottages, condos, and homesites. Lots begin around $115,000, cottages in the mid $200,000s, and homes start in the high $400,000s. For more details, go to www.reynoldsplantation.com or call 800-800-5250.

Where Are the Doctors?

There are several hospitals in Savannah, including St. Josephs/Candler Health System, Memorial Medical Center, and the Georgia Regional Hospital.

Where Are Some Notable Neighborhoods?

The Landings on Skidaway Island (www.thelandings.com or 800-841-7011) is a private, gated community that spreads over almost 4,500 acres. Six golf courses, more than 30 tennis courts, four clubhouses, two deep-water marinas, fitness facilities, swimming pools, social clubs, and hiking trails are found in this coastal development that is the largest one in the Savannah area. Lots and condos on Skidaway Island begin in the $200,000s, town homes start in the $300,000s, and single-family homes begin in the high $300,000s.

Midnight in the Garden of Good and Evil by John Berendt has Savannah as its setting; the film version of Berendt's book, *Forrest Gump*, and the movie *The Legend of Bagger Vance* were filmed there.

How Do I Pursue Lifelong Learning?

There are several institutions of higher learning in the Savannah area, including Armstrong Atlantic State University, the Savannah College of Art and Design, Savannah State University, Savannah Technical College, and South University.

Strengths

Oaks dripping with Spanish moss are just one more thing to admire about this area. Cost of living is within reason, and people are hospitable and friendly. Savannah is a great city.

Weaknesses

What can you say—you're in the South! You'll have heat and humidity in the summer. Statistically, the Savannah area is brushed or hit by a hurricane every 3.7 years.

FYI

Check out these sources for additional information: Savannah Area Chamber of Commerce (www.savannah chamber.com or 912-644-6400) and the *Savannah Morning News* (912-236-0271).

St. Marys

REPORT CARD

Overall rating:	A-
Climate:	A-
Cost of living:	A
Health care:	B
Transportation:	A
What's to do:	B+

Away from it all, yet close to everything—that pretty much sums up St. Marys, a pedestrian-friendly, historic town located on the southeastern tip of Georgia with its Howard Gilman waterfront park on the St. Marys River. St. Marys is close to I-95, Jacksonville International Airport is only 30 miles away, the city of Jacksonville is about three-quarters of an hour drive, and St. Augustine is 1 hour by car going south. Brunswick and the Golden Isles are an hour north. You can also be in Savannah in a little less than 2 hours.

The Kings Base Naval Submarine Base in St. Marys is the home of the Trident Nuclear Submarine; the base employs close to 2,000 military and civilian personnel

---

Juliet Gordon Lowe, founder of the Girl Scouts, hailed from Savannah.

who repair, maintain, and offer other support services for the subs. *Money* magazine has awarded St. Marys several kudos. Past issues named this village "the Number One Small Town in America," ranked it number one on "America's Fifty Hottest Little Boomtowns," and rated it "One of America's Top Places to Live Today." Described as the "gateway to the Cumberland Island National Seashore," laid-back St. Marys is a find for people who are looking for a small town atmosphere with big-time water activities. Yes, there really *is* something about St. Marys!

Who Lives in St. Marys?

St. Marys is located in Camden County. The population is about 16,000 in the town, and 45,000 in the county. Within St. Marys itself, about 75 percent of the residents are Caucasian, 20 percent African-American, 4 percent Hispanic, and 1 percent other races. Sixteen percent of the population is between 45 and 64 years old, and 5 percent are 65 or older. The median age is 28. The population increase has been brisk—20 percent growth since 2005.

What's the Cost?

The median home value in St. Marys is $220,000, and the 2006 cost of living index was 96, based on a U.S. average of 100.

What's to Do?

Lovers of nature can enjoy the Colonial Coast Birding Trail, Crooked River State Park, fishing, boating, golfing, the Okefenokee National Wildlife Refuge, and the almost 20 miles of unspoiled beach on Cumberland Island National Seashore (rated "one of America's Best Ten Beaches" in 2005 by the Travel Channel). Lovers of the past can visit Orange Hall House Museum, the Cumberland Island National Seashore Museum, the Submarine Museum, Oak Grove Cemetery, McIntosh Sugar Mill Tabby Ruins, and several historic churches. Lovers of city life and travel are a reasonable distance

What's It Like Outside?	Jan.	Apr.	Jul.	Oct.	Rain (in.)	Snow (in.)
Average high (°F)	62	77	88	78	48	0
Average low (°F)	42	57	72	62	–	–

from Jacksonville, St. Augustine, and Savannah, and a short drive from the airport in Jacksonville.

Where Are the Jobs?

The service industry, government, health, and retail are the top employers within Camden County. The 2006 unemployment rate was 5 percent.

Where Are the Doctors?

The Camden Campus is part of the Southeast Georgia Health Care system. Built in 1993, it has 40 acute-care beds and provides inpatient, outpatient, and emergency services. More than 60 physicians represent most medical specialties.

Where Are Some Notable Neighborhoods?

Osprey Cove (www.ospreycove.com or 888-871-9555) is a 1,000-acre amenity-laden gated community with access to the St. Marys River and the Atlantic Ocean. Lots, along with a variety of home styles, are available, and there will be more than 900 residences when the community is completed. Prices for homesites range from under $100,000 (interior) to around $600,000 (water access). Homes range from the $300,000s to more than $1 million. Osprey Cove has received accolades from *Where to Retire* magazine, *Golf Digest*, and *Golf Magazine*. A sister community, Winding River, also built by the LandMar Group, will have about 440 homes on 340 acres. Lots begin under $100,000. Contact www.windingriver.info or 866-800-1429 for more information.

Cumberland Harbour (www.cumberlandharbour.com or 888-231-5263) is a water-lover's dream. Situated on a peninsula several miles from St. Marys, this 1,000-acre gated community is bounded by the North River, St. Marys River, and Point Peter Creek, providing access to the Intracoastal Waterway and the Atlantic Ocean. Up and running, under construction, and proposed amenities include private as well as public docks, tennis courts, a pool, fitness center, spa, marina, and walking/jogging/hiking trails. Interior lots begin in the $200,000s.

If condo living is more your style, consider the gated community of Marsh Arbors (www.marsharbors.com or 800-952-1986), with 6 acres overlooking a saltwater

---

St. Marys ranks seventh among small communities with the greatest growth in the number of people older than 55, according to a 2006 *U.S. News and World Report* article.

marsh in St. Marys. Marsh Arbors will offer a clubhouse and pool for its 128 owners. Prices start around $400,000.

Sample home prices within the town of St. Marys include new three-bedroom/two-bath home with pool listed for $219,000 and a 4-bedroom/2-bath home on an acre listed for $349,900.

How Do I Pursue Lifelong Learning?

The Camden Center, part of Coastal Georgia Community College, offers associate's degrees, technical certificates, adult literacy programs, continuing-education courses, and some bachelor's and master's degrees through Armstrong Atlantic State University.

Strengths

The abandoned Durango–Georgia Mill Paper Mill was sold to the LandMar Group, LLC, for the development of a multiuse residential community. Good news for St. Marys! Pleasant weather, small-town charm, picket fences, porches, magnolias, majestic oak trees—these words describe historical St. Marys. The Mayo Clinic in close-by Jacksonville is another plus.

Weaknesses

If New York City is the kind of place you want to call home, St. Marys is not for you.

FYI

Check out these sources for additional information: St. Marys Tourism Council (www.stmaryswelcome.com or 866-868-2199), *St. Marys Magazine* (www.stmarys magazine.com or 912-729-1103), and the *Tribune and Georgian* newspaper (www.tribune-georgian.com or 912-882-4927).

true LIFE Barbara R. discovered St. Marys and fell in love with the town: "I have found peace in St. Marys."

I had never heard of St. Marys, Georgia, but I was hired (through a professional contact) by the owner of the St. Marys Railroad to write a story. On my first visit to St. Marys, I stood in the median in front of a bed and breakfast (that I later bought) and felt the most overwhelming sense of peace overtake me.

On my third visit, I noticed a for-sale sign in

St. Marys is the second oldest town in the United States. (St. Augustine gets the top spot.)

front of the bed and breakfast. I must tell you, I'm not one of those folks who always aspired to run a B and B. It had never entered my mind. My life was perfect as it was. I was living in a million-dollar home on the water in Fort Lauderdale where I had built a lucrative career in advertising and writing. I've owned several ad agencies, published several award-winning business publications, and was a respected leader in the community. I also had a fabulous boyfriend. There was absolutely no reason to disturb my status quo. But a siren call pulled me into making an offer on the B and B. I still cannot explain it. Every day, I would awake and say "What am I doing?" It made no sense at all. Yet my heartstrings kept tugging me to St. Marys. I had no control over the decision. It was like a runaway freight train. I'm the kind of girl who has a 5-year plan and a 10-year plan, and moving to a little coastal town in Georgia didn't figure into either one. But move I did.

For the first time in my life, I had a strong sense of destiny. I, with my best friend, bought the Goodbread House in Historic St. Marys, Georgia, and began my life as a B and B host while continuing to freelance write for clients in South Florida and New York. Every day, I became more and more enchanted with the little coastal town, with its picturesque waterfront and historical setting. The warmth of the people made me eager to get up each day and mingle in the village. At Christmas time, I had to continually pinch myself to remind me I wasn't dreaming. The town lit up with the magic of Christmas like I had never experienced. Carolers roamed the streets. It was like living in a picture postcard or a Norman Rockwell painting. There is a spirit about St. Marys that embraces all who visit and live here. It is truly the "best of the South, and the best of a small town," as the masthead of the new *St. Marys Magazine* proclaims. And guess who the publisher is? You got it. I felt so passionate about how special St. Marys is, I wanted to share it with the world, and so I launched *St. Marys Magazine* to do just that.

About a year ago, I purchased another home

Cumberland Harbour was the site of the 2004 HGTV Dream Home.

around the corner from the Goodbread House, and this is where I intend to move when I'm ready to let someone else enjoy the pleasures of running the bed and breakfast.

Though I still have homes in Fort Lauderdale, the mountains of North Carolina, and eastern North Carolina as well, I consider St. Marys my home . . . for life. When I travel, I'm always eager to return to the tranquility and beauty of this little town. I miss the people. And I miss the spirit that feeds my spirit.

If I could design a perfect town to retire to, it would look and feel just like St. Marys. Ⓛ

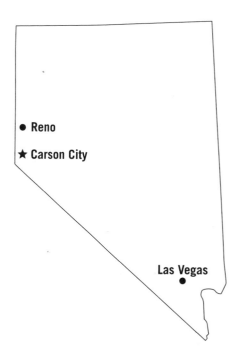

Las Vegas

NEVADA

Capital: Carson City

Nickname: The Silver State

Motto: "All for our country"

Flower: Sagebrush

Bird: Mountain bluebird

Population: 2,400,000

Fascinating Fact: The ratio of slot machines to Nevada residents is about 1 to 10.

REPORT CARD

Overall rating: A

Climate: B

Cost of living: A

Health care: A

Transportation: A

What's to do: A

Las Vegas is located at the southern tip of Nevada between the Sierra Nevada and Wasatch mountain ranges. This big city is described by the Chamber of Commerce as "One city, two stories." On one hand, the entertainment industry and casinos are known worldwide, and the shopping is legendary. On the other hand, Las Vegas is much, much more than its downtown. The mountains, lakes, and desert surrounding the city provide residents with scores of opportunities for recreational activities—more physical than sliding on and off your chair at the casino! Lake Mead, the largest man-made lake in the world, is perfect for water sports, and the fish are biting year-round. Mount Charleston is a great place for snow skiing, and Red Rock Canyon is a photographer's dream and a hiker's paradise. Las Vegas is dotted with dozens of golf courses, and the Grand Canyon is only 300 miles away. McCarran International Airport, one of the 10 busiest airports in the world, has tripled its size since the 1980s, and continues to upgrade and expand its services. Las Vegas enjoys about 320 days of sunshine a year.

Who Lives in Las Vegas?

Nevada is one of our fastest-growing states, and has been for the past 19 years. Clark County is home to 1.4 million people, and the population of Las Vegas is about 576,000. Each month, more than 3.5 million people visit Las Vegas, and the city welcomes about 6,500 new residents a month. Retirees make up the largest segment of people currently moving to Las Vegas.

What's the Cost?

Growth in Vegas has not come cheaply. The cost of living index in Las Vegas is 115, based on a national average of 100. The median cost of a new home is $345,000, and for an existing home, $285,000. Nevada does not have a state income tax. Median household income is about $60,000 a year.

What's to Do?

Blackjack, slot machines, poker, roulette: gambling, gambling, everywhere! Shopping is becoming somewhat of a sport in Las Vegas as well. Try out the Las

What's It Like Outside?	Jan.	Apr.	Jul.	Oct.	Rain (in.)	Snow (in.)
Average high (°F)	56	77	105	84	4	0
Average low (°F)	33	49	75	53	–	–

Vegas Premium Outlets, the World Market Center (furniture—the new High Point?), or the Fashion Show Mall, with a size equivalent to 33 football fields.

Visit Lake Mead, the Hoover Dam, Red Rock Canyon, Valley of Fire State Park, and the Grand Canyon and enjoy all the outdoor activities they have to offer. Or soak in a hot spring at Gold Strike Hot Springs, about an hour from Vegas, after playing some of the 800 holes of golf in the area. But be sure to be back in the city for the evening to enjoy the great restaurants and entertainment, including the new Smith Center for the Performing Arts. Enjoy activities at the seven senior centers throughout the city or the new 180-acre Las Vegas Springs Preserve consisting of trails, botanical gardens, theaters, and museums.

Where Are the Jobs?

Education, gaming, government, medical, high-tech services, retail, and construction are big employers. Las Vegas has a pro-business environment that exempts companies from a variety of taxes. The unemployment rate is under 4 percent.

Where Are the Doctors?

The area is serviced by more than 30 medical facilities and eight hospices. The Nevada Cancer Institute opened in 2005.

Where Are Some Notable Neighborhoods?

Lake Las Vegas (www.lakelasvegas.com or 800-564-1603) is a resort containing 19 different neighborhoods centered on a beautiful 320-acre lake, about 17 miles from the Las Vegas strip. Enjoy the amenities of a Hyatt Regency and Ritz-Carlton, a shopping center, and three world-class golf courses, or build a custom home. There are a variety of housing styles, with prices starting in the $400,000s. Fractional ownership is also available.

Summerlin (www.summerlin.com) is a 22,500-acre master-planned community that is a city as well as a neighborhood. Libraries, schools, houses of worship, medical facilities, a business district, and an amphitheater accompany all the normal bells and whistles of a resort community. With a proposed build-out in 2020, there will be 64,000 residences and about 200,000 residents. Homes, condominiums, townhomes, and custom

Sperling's Best Places (www.bestplaces.net) included Las Vegas among its 2005 "Best Places to Live."

homes are available, and prices begin in the upper $200,000s. Summerlin is about a 20-minute drive from the strip.

Aliante is a community in northern Las Vegas, about 20 miles from the airport and the Las Vegas strip. Aliante is comprised of a half-dozen different neighborhoods built by a half-dozen builders, and includes Sun City Aliante, an active-adult Del Webb community. At Sun City Aliante, seven single-story home designs are available, with prices ranging from the mid $200,000s to the upper $300,000s. For more information, go to www.aliantehomes.com/Aliante or 866-874-6393.

About 50 miles north of Las Vegas, a 13,000-acre master-planned community, Coyote Springs, will begin selling homes sometime during 2008. A golf village, 3,500-seat amphitheater, a 17-acre lake, a school, and a community center will be part of this development. For details, contact www.villagesofcoyotesprings.com or Pardee Homes at 702-614-1400.

A good site with links to many developments in the Las Vegas area is www.greatlasvegashomes.com. You'll get an idea of location, amenities, and prices for more than 30 communities (click on "Las Vegas Neighborhoods").

How Do I Pursue Lifelong Learning?

The University of Nevada, the Community College of Southern Nevada, and Nevada State College enroll more than 60,000 students. There are at least a dozen additional institutions of higher learning in the area, encompassing art, culinary arts, fashion design, and technology.

Strengths

This part of the country is growing at an incredible rate; so much of everything is new—the homes, the roads, the shopping, the people! The sunshine and the entertainment will make this a very popular place for friends and family to visit.

Weaknesses

How much of a good thing is too much? Is Las Vegas growing too fast? Are 45 million visitors a year a few too many? What will that glorious sunshine feel like in July and August? The crime rate in Las Vegas is higher than the national average for both personal and property crime.

FYI

Check out these sources for additional information: Las Vegas Chamber of Commerce (www.lvchamber.com or

---

With its 45 million annual visitors, Las Vegas is the most visited place on Earth (followed by Mecca).

702-735-1616), the *Las Vegas Review Journal* (702-383-0211), and the *Las Vegas Sun* (702-385-3111).

Reno

REPORT CARD

Overall rating:	B+
Climate:	B-
Cost of living:	B
Health care:	A
Transportation:	A
What's to do:	A

Reno is known as the "biggest little city in the world." It sits between the majestic Sierra Nevada Mountains and the Cascade Mountains, which provide a scenic background for the city. The Truckee River winding its way through town and the surprising red-brick construction of the historic section provide quite a contrast to the glitzy casino town that many people envision. Located in the northwestern part of the state, Reno is 230 miles from San Francisco, 470 miles from Los Angeles, and a 45-minute drive from beautiful Lake Tahoe, the largest alpine lake in North America.

The Reno/Sparks/Lake Tahoe area has a lot to offer, with close to 20 world-class ski resorts within a 100-mile radius, more than 40 golf courses, and around 60 gaming locations, not to mention more than 800 restaurants! Summer or winter, inside or outside, you have options, including an international opera company and ballet. The Reno/Tahoe International Airport makes travel to and from this city easy.

After the temperatures hit 90 in the summer, it'll cool off early in the afternoon, and you can expect to be under the covers at night!

Who Lives in Reno?

The population of Reno is 206,000; about 35 percent of the residents are over the age of 45. Approximately 77 percent of the population is Caucasian, 14 percent is Hispanic, 2 percent is African-American, and 5 percent is Asian. The median age is 34.

What's It Like Outside?	Jan.	Apr.	Jul.	Oct.	Rain (in.)	Snow (in.)
Average high (°F)	46	63	90	71	8	26
Average low (°F)	19	29	48	31	–	–

What's the Cost?

Reno's cost of living index is 112, based on a national average of 100. An average single-family home is priced at $301,000. The city boasts more than 100 residential neighborhoods in all price ranges within an easy commute (less than 30 minutes) to downtown and the airport.

What's to Do?

The casinos provide not only gaming but also great entertainment and fine dining. Reno is home to the 80-lane National Bowling Stadium and an IMAX Theater. The National Automobile Museum, the Championship Air Races, and the Reno Rodeo are additional attractions. Or meander along the River Walk that winds along the Truckee River.

For activities of a more cultural nature, patronize an event at the McKinley Arts and Cultural Center or at the Wingfield Park Amphitheater, or visit the Nevada Museum of Art.

Lake Tahoe, about 50 miles away, provides year-round outdoor fun for the entire family. There is skiing and snowboarding in the winter, and Lake Tahoe has about 30 public beaches to help you enjoy water activities in the summer. Flume Trail at Lake Tahoe is rated among the top 20 mountain-bike trails in the United States.

Virginia City, an authentic western town, complete with plank sidewalks and saloons, is 35 miles north of Reno and will give you a real flavor of the Old West. Or take a day excursion to Nevada's capital, Carson City, or travel to Yosemite National Park and enjoy the beauty of the area.

Where Are the Jobs?

The largest employers include education, health care, tourism, and the gaming industry. Many prestigious companies have operations in the area, including Cisco, Microsoft, Oracle, Michelin, and John Deere. The unemployment rate is about 4 percent.

Where Are the Doctors?

Washoe Medical Center, a level II trauma center with more than 500 beds, and St. Mary's Regional Medical Center (around 400 beds) provide excellent care for the residents of Reno. There are additional health facilities, such as the HealthSouth Rehabilitation Hospital and the U.S. Veterans Medical Center.

Reno sits 4,400 feet above sea level and is bathed in sunshine 300 days a year.

Where Are Some Notable Neighborhoods?

Within the master-planned community of Double Diamond Ranch, Tanamera homes (www.tanamerhomes .com or 775-850-4200) offers a selection of four neighborhoods, with prices beginning in the $300,000s. Enjoy 26 miles of walking and biking trails, a clubhouse, pool, and views of the Sierra-Nevada Mountains.

Somersett (www.somersett.com or 800-966-8804) is a master-planned golf community that, when complete, will have close to 2,700 homes, a network of 27 miles of hiking trails, a town center, and 27 holes of golf. Homes are priced from the $300,000s and lots from the $200,000s. Most of the community is multigenerational, but Del Webb has an active-adult community, Sierra Canyon (www.delwebb.com or 866-252-9322) within Somersett. Homes range from the upper $200,000s to the upper $400,000s. As Del Webb's site says, "Reno lies down the hill, Tahoe's just up the river."

How Do I Pursue Lifelong Learning?

Reno offers a number of opportunities for lifelong learning, including Truckee Meadows Community College; Morrison University; the University of Nevada, Reno; and the Career College of Northern Nevada. And don't forget the Reno Professional Bartending School.

Strengths

Three hundred-plus days of sunshine is almost always a good thing, especially when it helps to melt the snow. Access to Lake Tahoe and the ski resorts makes this a great place to enjoy the outdoors. And if you like to gamble, well, watch out!

Weaknesses

Even with a great airport, Reno seems to be a little "out of the way." Evenings are cool or downright cold. Winter will bring snow, and not just to the ski slopes. And if you like to gamble, well, watch out!

FYI

Check out these sources for additional information: Reno-Sparks Chamber of Commerce (www.reno sparkschamber.org or 775-337-3030), the *Reno Gazette Journal* (www.rgj.com or 775-788-6200), and the *Reno News and Review* (www.renonewsreview.com or 775-324-4440).

NEW MEXICO

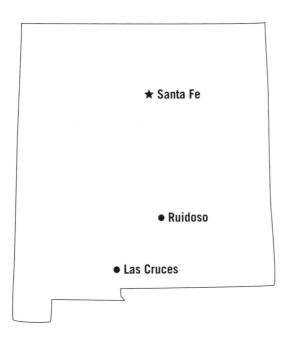

Capital: Santa Fe

Nickname: Land of enchantment

Motto: "It grows as it goes"

Flower: Yucca

Bird: Roadrunner

Population: 2,000,000

Fascinating Fact: Santa Fe, with an altitude

of 7,000 feet, is the highest state capital in the nation.

Las Cruces

REPORT CARD

Overall rating:	B+
Climate:	A
Cost of living:	A
Health care:	B+
Transportation:	B+
What's to do:	B+

Las Cruces means "the crosses" in Spanish and is thought to have been named after the crosses raised in remembrance of those who died during an 1830s raid by the Apaches. Las Cruces is the second largest city in New Mexico (after Albuquerque), the fastest growing area in the state, and it's less than an hour's drive from Mexico. The airport in El Paso, Texas, is also about 60 minutes away. The rugged Organ Mountains and the meandering Rio Grande bound the city. A strong agricultural base of cotton, chili peppers, and pecans is related to Las Cruces's location in the fertile Mesilla valley.

Money, Where to Retire, Family Digest, and *Hispanic* magazines have all rated Las Cruces among their top places to live and/or retire.

Las Cruces has cultural and educational amenities, coupled with a competitive cost of living, nice climate, and scenic beauty. Having celebrated its 150th anniversary in 1999, Las Cruces is growing rapidly yet retains its Old West flavor.

Average relative humidity is a pleasant 27 percent, and Las Cruces boasts 350 days of sunshine a year.

Who Lives in Las Cruces?

The population is close to 90,000, with 15 percent of residents 62 years or older. Anglo, Hispanic, and Native American cultures predominate.

What's the Cost?

Las Cruces is a good value, with a cost of living index at 99, compared to a U.S. average of 100. The median home price is $168,000.

What's to Do?

Activities include playing virtually year-round golf, mountain hiking and biking, and exploring historic sites and museums, such as the Branigan Cultural Center or the Farmers Ranch and Heritage Museum. The adobe buildings and plaza in the close-by community of Old Mesilla make it the top visitor destination in southern New Mexico. Day trips include the Gila Cliff dwellings, recreation areas such as Elephant Butte Lake and White Sands National Monument, and the Juarez City Market in Mexico. Theater, symphony, art galleries, and ballet round out the cultural offerings. And of course, the Mexican influence is a bonus for people who love Mexican food!

Where Are the Jobs?

The largest employers are affiliated with education, health, and government. The unemployment rate for the Las Cruces metropolitan area is around 4 percent.

Where Are the Doctors?

The Memorial Medical Center, Memorial Health Plex, Mt. View Regional Medical Center, and Mesilla Valley Hospital, as well as several clinics, serve Las Cruces. There are approximately 400 physicians in 30 specialties in town. Assisted living, Alzheimer's care, and home-health care are also available.

What's It Like Outside?	Jan.	Apr.	Jul.	Oct.	Rain (in.)	Snow (in.)
Average high (°F)	59	77	97	77	9	3
Average low (°F)	27	42	62	44	–	–

Where Are Some Notable Neighborhoods?

The big push for growth is to the east and north of the city. Sonoma Ranch (www.sonomaranch.com or 877-700-7210) is an example of a golf-course community located east of Las Cruces, with the jagged Organ Mountains as the backdrop. Begun in 1999, this planned community covers more than 900 acres, and the first two phases alone are zoned for more than 3,000 residences. There is a mix of residential styles, and commercial and professional amenities will also be integrated into the community. Homes begin in the $200,000s and zoom to about $1 million. Within the confines of Sonoma Ranch is the gated Boulders, an active-adult community with its own golf course and clubhouse. Homes begin in the $300,000s. For information on the Boulders, contact Sonoma Ranch.

You can travel northwest, cross the Rio Grande, and arrive at the community of Picacho Hills (www.picacho hillscc.com), a private country-club community located in the hills above Las Cruces. Here, you'll find panoramic views of the city and the mountains, though the part of the city you go through to get to Picacho Hills is not very attractive. Although Picacho Hills has been around for about a decade, there is still a lot of building going on with many homesites available. Land/home packages start in the $200,000s.

Organ Mesa Ranch offers homesites beginning under $200,000. There are covenants, but no time frame in which to build. Contact www.organmesaranch.com or 505-382-0264.

How Do I Pursue Lifelong Learning?

New Mexico State University and Dona Aña Branch Community College provide adult and continuing-education classes in addition to credit classes and degrees. The Munson Senior Center, Eastside Community Center, and Mesilla Park Recreation Center also offer a wide array of programs.

Strengths

Cost of living, transportation, scenery, and climate are all pluses. Medical facilities are good. The fact that Las Cruces is the fastest-growing city in New Mexico—and one of the fastest growing in the United States—is no accident!

Weaknesses

Downtown Las Cruces is not that attractive and lacks a central business district, but a master plan has been developed to address its shortcomings. Although the crime rate is higher than the national average, Las Cruces was ranked the number one safest city in 2006 for a medium-size city by Bestplaces.net and Farmer's Insurance Group.

FYI

Check out these sources for additional information: Chamber of Commerce (www.lascruces.org or 505-524-1968), relocation guide (www.lascrucesrelocation.com), visitors' guide (www.lascrucesvisitors.com), the *Las Cruces Bulletin* (www.lascrucesbulletin.com or 505-524-8061), and the *Las Cruces Sun News* (www.lcsun-news.com or 505-541-5400).

Ruidoso

REPORT CARD

Overall rating:	B-
Climate:	B+
Cost of living:	B
Health care:	B-
Transportation:	C
What's to do:	B-

Ruidoso is a small, laid-back town (except in summer), located in south-central New Mexico. Its 7,000-foot altitude provides a cool but fairly mild climate with low humidity; beautiful aspens and evergreens afford a different look from much of New Mexico's desert flora. Ruidoso snuggles at the base of 12,000-foot Sierra Blanca in the Sacramento Mountains.

The town is an outdoor playground; in fact, its nickname is the "year-round playground of the Southwest." Skiing, hiking, fishing, golfing, and horse racing are on the menu of activities. There are also several museums, two casinos, and the Spencer Theater for the Perfoming Arts (with Dale Chihuly glass installations). The town is fairly isolated. The nearest interstates are more than 100 miles away, Las Cruces is a 2½-hour drive, and flying in or out of Ruidoso using a major airport is a hike. Albuquerque International Airport is about a 4-hour drive, and El Paso International Airport is more than 2 hours away. However, there is proposed service by American Airlines between Dallas/Forth Worth and the Sierra Blanca Regional Airport, about 20 miles from Ruidoso.

Who Lives in Ruidoso?

The area is experiencing a lot of growth both in full- and part-time home buyers. The predominant influx is

What's It Like Outside?	Jan.	Apr.	Jul.	Oct.	Rain (in.)	Snow (in.)
Average high (°F)	45	62	82	66	23	47
Average low (°F)	19	27	47	30	–	–

from Texas and California, but more people are moving to Ruidoso from all over. The village of Ruidoso has about 9,000 permanent residents (it's estimated this will double by 2025), but this number can swell to 40,000 on summer weekends, as people escape the heat of the Southwest for this cooler mountain town, many coming to enjoy the horse racing. About 20 percent of the population is at least 65 years old, and the median age is 46. Between 1990 and 2000, the population increased by about 70 percent. About 78 percent of the population is Caucasian, and about 18 percent is Hispanic or Latino.

What's the Cost?

The median household income in Ruidoso is about $40,000, and the median price of a single family home (three-bedroom/two-bath) in Ruidoso is about $200,000. Although exact numbers aren't available, according to one Realtor, the cost of living "is cheaper than California, but more expensive than west Texas."

What's to Do?

If you want to hit the slopes, Ski Apache is owned and operated by the Mescalero Apache tribe. It's open between Thanksgiving and early spring and boasts the largest lift capacity in the state. Or take in a horse race and wager a few bets at the Ruidoso Downs Race Track and the Billy the Kid Casino. Golf, fishing, camping, and hiking are available in Ruidoso as well as nearby towns. If you're looking for something more elegant, enjoy a ballet or the symphony at the Spencer Theater for the Performing Arts. The beauty of Lincoln National Forest and White Sands National Monument can be appreciated year-round.

Where Are the Jobs?

Tourism, real estate, retail, local government, and health care are the largest employers. The unemployment rate for Lincoln County in 2006 was 3.3 percent.

Where Are the Doctors?

The Lincoln County Medical Center has a hospital, clinic, and nursing home associated with it. Home-health care is available, as well as a mental-health program for seniors. The medical center is operated by Presbyterian Healthcare Services of Albuquerque, and medical specialists are provided to Ruidoso when necessary.

Ruidoso's Lincoln County is the birthplace of Billy the Kid, Smokey Bear, and Kit Carson.

Where Are Some Notable Neighborhoods?

There are a number of new developments in the pipeline in Ruidoso. Two that are underway:

River Crossing (www.rivercrossingatruidoso.com or 866-209-6913) is a 14-acre development in downtown Ruidoso consisting of 102 condos in four buildings, with residences beginning in the $500,000s. The retail part of the community contains three restaurants, an art gallery, and shops and offices. A planned River Walk will wind its way through River Crossing.

Rainmakers Golf and Recreational Community (www.rainmakersusa.com or 866-700-8439) is a 525-acre master-planned, gated community just north of Ruidoso offering townhomes, patio homes, and lots, with prices for patio lots under $100,000, and half-acre lots in the $100,000s. Plan on $225 per square foot and up to build your home. The golf club is private and limited to 550 memberships. Rainmakers advertises itself as "environmentally responsible," and it has been named a member in the Audubon Signature Program (the first member in New Mexico), a reflection of this community's sensitivity to nature.

Alto Village and Alto Lakes Golf and Country Club is a bit north of Ruidoso, and homes are available starting around $300,000. Average prices for a home in Ruidoso run about $200,000, and there are a number of manufactured homes in the area in the $100,000s.

How Do I Pursue Lifelong Learning?

Eastern New Mexico University offers 2-year degrees at its Ruidoso community college location, along with vocational classes and community education classes. Online courses and noncredit courses are also available.

Strengths

If you're into the outdoors and are looking for small-town western living in a beautiful, secluded setting with a mild climate, Ruidoso may be your place.

Weaknesses

Although it's growing, Ruidoso's isolation could be a negative factor (or a strength, depending on your personality). The mixture of manufactured homes next to single-family homes might be a concern to some. Health care could be an issue if there are complex medical prob-

---

**Ruidoso comes from the Spanish word for "noisy" and refers to the small
Rio Ruidoso River that flows through the village.**

lems. If you're a big-time shopaholic, you may have to leave town to really feed your addiction.

FYI

Check out these sources for additional information: Chamber of Commerce (www.ruidosonow.com or 877-RUIDOSO) and the *Ruidoso News* (505-257-4001).

Santa Fe

REPORT CARD

Overall rating:	A-
Climate:	B
Cost of living:	B
Health care:	A
Transportation:	A
What's to do:	A

Founded in 1610, Santa Fe is the oldest state capital in the country. It's nestled in the foothills of the Rocky Mountains at an elevation of 7,000 feet. Located in a valley above the Rio Grande and surrounded by thousands of acres of national forest, it is a 37-square-mile city and has a full-service airport 60 miles south in Albuquerque. If you want a day at the beach, it will be necessary to drive 12 hours to either Padre Island in Texas or Los Angeles. That's the bad news. Everything else about Santa Fe is good news! You will enjoy four seasons, with at least partial sunshine 300 days each year. This high desert country is greener than most due to the ample rainfall and melting snows. If you like a lot of space, the population of the entire state of New Mexico is 2 million (close to the population of Houston, Texas)!

With horse racing, hiking, biking, river rafting, cycling, and skiing, not to mention golfing 365 days a year, you'll never have a dull moment. If outdoor adventure is not your thing, the variety of cultural opportunities in Santa Fe is vast. The opera performs at an outdoor theater and is almost never interrupted by weather. The Santa Fe Symphony Orchestra and Chorus and the Desert Chorale provide a year-round calendar of great musical events. Walking from the main, downtown plaza in any direction will take you past sculpture gardens, tons of art galleries, an impressive number of museums, and Native Americans selling handcrafted jewelry. With more than 200 restaurants,

The 2006 *Condé Nast Traveler* Readers' Choice Awards voted Santa Fe the number two city to visit in the world.

you'll never want to cook again (if it weren't for the great cooking schools in downtown Santa Fe). With one to two million tourists each year, too many visitors could be your biggest problem.

Who Lives in Santa Fe?

About 26 percent of the 70,000 people living in Santa Fe are over the age of 55. About 50 percent of residents are Hispanic, 47 percent are white, and 3 percent are American Indian.

What's the Cost?

Santa Fe's cost of living index is 172. The cost of housing is the main culprit, with the median price of a home about $470,000. The southwest area of Santa Fe has the most reasonably priced homes, with a median of $285,000, while the tonier southeast area's median home price is $749,000.

What's to Do?

Santa Fe appears to offer more opportunities to active retirees than a city four times its size! Art classes and cooking classes are available if you're looking for a new challenge. Music, theater, and dance thrive in Santa Fe year-round. The Santa Fe Opera, Chamber Music Festival, Sangre De Cristo Chorale, Shakespeare in Santa Fe, and the Santa Fe Festival Ballet are just a sampling of what the city has to offer. With 250 art galleries and museums, people who love cultural endeavors will certainly get their fill. A new civic center is replacing the Sweeney Convention Center.

For the outdoor enthusiast, there are several exceptional public golf courses in the area, as well as the opportunity for fly-fishing, rock climbing, snow skiing, snowboarding, river rafting, horseback riding, hiking, bicycling, and more. Take a day trip to one of eight Northern Indian pueblos, or volunteer with the Literacy Volunteers of Santa Fe or the Food Brigade of Santa Fe. The only limiting factor is your energy level!

Where Are the Jobs?

Government (local, state, and federal), along with retail, tourism, health care, and construction are the biggest

What's It Like Outside?	Jan.	Apr.	Jul.	Oct.	Rain (in.)	Snow (in.)
Average high (°F)	40	60	91	63	14	32
Average low (°F)	19	35	57	38	–	–

employers in Santa Fe, though one in six people is employed in the arts. Unemployment averages around 3.5 percent. The Santa Fe City Council voted to enact a minimum wage of $8.50 per hour for most private-sector employers in 2006, which will gradually increase to $10.50 per hour by 2008.

Where Are the Doctors?

Santa Fe has four hospitals; the largest is St. Vincent Hospital, with about 270 beds, and it is the only level III trauma center in northern New Mexico. St. Vincent is nonprofit, nonaffiliated, and proudly states its mission "to care for all the people of Santa Fe, northern New Mexico, and southern Colorado regardless of their ability to pay."

Where Are Some Notable Neighborhoods?

Aldea (www.aldeadesantafe.com or 505-438-2525), on the northwest side of Santa Fe, is a neo-traditional village designed by acclaimed new urbanist architect Andres Duany. Homes are gathered around a central commercial and civic plaza. The community includes a mix of housing types, priced from around $400,000, and homesites around $200,000.

The master-planned development of Tierra Contenta (www.tierracontenta.org or 505-471-4551) will have almost 3,800 residences on 1,400 acres when complete. This is a city initiative to provide affordable housing, a major issue for Santa Fe. Tierra Contenta also features more than 300 acres of open space connected by pedestrian and bike paths.

Las Lagunitas (www.laslagunitas.com or 505-857-9566) is a private, gated community several miles south of Santa Fe that includes natural spring-fed ponds, family picnic areas, and private parks, as well as more than 130 acres of open space. Homesites begin around $200,000.

Las Campanas (www.lascampanas.com or 866-401-3578) is the premier private, gated golf community in Santa Fe, set at the southern tip of the Rocky Mountains. About 1,700 homes are planned on 4,800 acres.

The architecture of Santa Fe is very distinctive. The Spanish pueblo style predominates, and strict building codes require all new buildings to be constructed of adobe or adobe-looking material in varying earth tones.

Amenities include two Jack Nicklaus Signature golf courses, an equestrian center featuring a 30,000-square-foot indoor riding rink, and a spacious spa and tennis facility with an outdoor pool and indoor lap pool. Homes, mainly resales, begin in the $800,000s. Pricey, but beautiful.

How Do I Pursue Lifelong Learning?

A number of educational opportunities await you in Santa Fe. The College of Santa Fe is near the top of *U.S. News and World Report*'s list of best regional liberal arts colleges in the West, St. John's College awards both bachelor's of arts and master's of arts degrees, Santa Fe Community College offers a variety of programs as well as classes just for seniors, and New Mexico Elderhostel provides educational and travel opportunities for seniors 55 and older.

Strengths

The beauty of Santa Fe is surpassed only by its multitude of museums, festivals, art galleries, restaurants, music, and theatrical performances. If you're the outdoors type, stay in good shape for all the adventures that await you. Enjoy all four seasons and the low humidity.

Weaknesses

The architecture is fabulous, but housing prices are high. Though it melts fairly quickly, there is snow, and you'll need that winter coat.

FYI

Contact Santa Fe Chamber of Commerce (www.santafe chamber.com or 505-988-3279) and the *Santa Fe New Mexican* (www.freenewmexican.com or 800-873-3372).

The Georgia O'Keeffe Museum in Santa Fe is the home of the world's largest permanent collection of works by Georgia O'Keeffe. Although O'Keeffe was born in Wisconsin, she lived the latter portion of her life in New Mexico, inspired by the area's beauty.

NORTH CAROLINA

Capital: Raleigh

Nickname: Tar Heel State

Motto: "To be, rather than to seem"

Flower: Dogwood

Bird: Cardinal

Population: 8,700,000

Fascinating Fact: Fayetteville is home to the first miniature-golf course.

Asheville

REPORT CARD

Overall rating:	A
Climate:	B
Cost of living:	B
Health care:	A
Transportation:	A
What's to do:	A

Nestled between the Blue Ridge Mountains and the Great Smoky Mountains, Asheville is viewed by many to be a near-perfect retirement location, whether you're married or single. The city sits at an elevation of 2,200 feet on a plateau divided by the French Broad River and surrounded by beautiful mountains with elevations of 5,000 feet and more. Asheville is said to be a "manageable size" with the advantages of big-city amenities. It's 125 miles west of Charlotte, 113 miles east of Knoxville, and 200 miles north of Atlanta. It's the largest city in western North Carolina, and it is the regional center for manufacturing, transportation, health care, banking, professional services, and shopping. Asheville frequently appears on many "best" lists (including *Money*, *AARP*,

Asheville Regional Airport is served by US Airways, Continental, Delta, Northwest, and United.

Forbes, Consumer Report, and *Men's Journal*) and has been given the moniker the "Paris of the South" for its art and architecture.

The mountains and rivers provide outdoor enthusiasts with wide-open spaces for white-water rafting, kayaking, canoeing, rock climbing, and hiking. There are more than 250 waterfalls in western North Carolina, and you can see them by heading to the Blue Ridge Parkway for hiking trails, including those at Craggy Gardens, Great Smoky Mountain National Park, Yellowstone Falls, and Graveyard Fields. But if the shore is really your thing, it's about a 5-hour drive to Myrtle Beach, South Carolina.

Asheville could be called a college town. Although not the home of a major university, several colleges have a real presence here. The North Carolina Center for Creative Retirement (NCCCR) is located at the University of North Carolina, Asheville.

The mild, four-season climate appeals to most people, with the exception of the 16 inches of snow and the possibility of black ice on the mountain roads when the temperatures hover around the freezing point.

Who Lives in Asheville?

Asheville's population in 2005 was about 72,000, and 90 percent of residents are Caucasian, 7 percent African-American, and 3 percent Hispanic. The median age is 39, about 20 percent of residents have a college degree, and the over-50 population has increased about 20 percent since 1999.

What's the Cost?

Asheville's cost of living index, based on a national average of 100, is 101 (2006). The average home price in 2006 was $282,000, and average rent for a two-bedroom apartment in 2006 was $780.

What's to Do?

If you imagine yourself taking to the trails with a group of new friends for a trek through the Blue Ridge Mountains to absorb the beauty of the fall colors or the new spring wildflowers, Asheville may be the spot for you. Just call Asheville Parks and Recreation Outdoor Programs and sign up for Senior Treks or Hikes for Seniors, offered every Friday. If you are someone who enjoys

What's It Like Outside?	Jan.	Apr.	Jul.	Oct.	Rain (in.)	Snow (in.)
Average high (°F)	46	65	83	71	46	16
Average low (°F)	26	41	62	42	–	–

winter, there are more than eight resorts/spots for snow skiing, snowboarding (you, too, can be one of the "grays on trays"), and snow tubing around Asheville. Why not try your hand at rock climbing at Looking Glass Rock, about an hour from Asheville, known as the best rock-climbing spot in the state? If that sounds a little strenuous, you might like to try rockhounding: looking for rubies, sapphires, and other precious stones. Whitewater rafting, kayaking, canoeing, and floating are popular water activities in Asheville.

If you are ready to volunteer, try the World Market, a nonprofit, volunteer-based program that helps market handmade crafts from low-income craftspeople in developing nations. Or shop at the Woolworth Walk, where more than 150 artists and artisans make and sell fine arts, crafts, and jewelry.

History, art, and music are a big part of what makes Asheville a special place to live. The Carl Sandburg Home is located here, as is the Biltmore Estate. The latter covers 8,000 acres, including 75 acres of gardens, a winery, and the 250-room Biltmore Inn. Pack Place is home to the Asheville Art Museum, Colburn Earth Science Museum, Diana Wortham Theatre, Health Adventure, and YMI Cultural Center. Indoors or out, summer or winter, you will find plenty to do and new adventures in Asheville.

Where Are the Jobs?

The top employers include Mission Health and Hospitals, Buncombe County Public Schools, Ingles Markets, and the county government. The unemployment rate is about 4 percent.

Where Are the Doctors?

Mission Health and Hospitals provides virtually all medical and surgical services, and Mission Children's Hospital is western North Carolina's only children's hospital. There are several other hospitals/medical centers within 20 miles of Asheville.

Where Are Some Notable Neighborhoods?

We would be remiss if we did not mention two delightful towns that are close to Asheville that you may also want to consider: Brevard and Hendersonville.

Brevard is small (6,800 residents), charming, and beautifully situated among the streams, forests, and waterfalls of the Blue Ridge Mountains. Thirty-five miles southwest from Asheville, the town is known for its music and fine arts (it's home to Brevard College) and boasts that it averages only 5 days of snow per year.

Hendersonville is about 25 miles south of Asheville and has an attractive historic downtown with antique stores, specialty shops, and restaurants. A number of festivals and events are offered year-round. This scenic mountain town has about 12,000 residents, and the presence of Blue Ridge Community College adds vitality to the area.

Brevard and Hendersonville are only 20 miles apart. In Hendersonville, check out Champion Hills (www. championhills.com or 800-633-5122) as a neighborhood. Homes begin in the upper $300,000s, and lots start around $100,000.

The Cliffs (www.cliffscommunities.com or 866-649-3779) is actually seven communities: the Cliffs at Walnut Cove, the Cliffs Valley, the Cliffs at Glassy, the Cliffs at Keowee Falls, the Cliffs at Keowee Springs, the Cliffs at Keowee Vineyards, and the Cliffs at Mountain Park. The developments are located between Asheville and Greenville, and they offer the unique premise of access to all of the amenities (including golf courses) with your membership. So you'll be able to play the seven golf courses; stroll the pedestrian village; utilize the medical concierge services and the Wellness centers,

marinas, equestrian centers, restaurants, clubhouses, and pools; hike 25 miles of trails; and participate in the 500 activities that are offered! Homesites are available from the $300,000s, and homes from the $700,000s. Choose from lake, golf, meadow, and mountain views on 10,000 acres. The Cliffs Community closest to Asheville is the Cliffs at Walnut Cove.

Reynolds Mountain (www.reynoldsmountain.com or 800-497-VIEW) is a 4-mile drive from downtown Asheville. The 250-acre, five-neighborhood community doesn't offer the typical amenities (fitness center, golf course, tennis, etc.) of many developments but does offer spectacular mountain and city views, and a 16-acre nature preserve. Lots, villas, townhomes, and custom homes are available, with homesites starting in the $300,000s, and homes from the $800,000s.

The Residences at Biltmore (www.residences-asheville.com or 888-577-1670) bills itself as a "concierge condo," with services such as shopping, limo service, and dog walking arranged on an à la carte basis. The community is a reincarnation of the Biltmore Garden

---

Cashiers is a bit off the beaten track (about 75 miles from Asheville), but communities such as Chinquapin and RiverRock are being developed in this spectacular area of the Blue Ridge Mountains.

Apartments, and it will have 114 fully-furnished condos with the kind of upscale touches—granite countertops, stainless steel appliances, hardwood flooring—affluent boomers have come to expect. Studios to three-bedroom suites are available, with prices beginning around $200,000. For someone looking for a second home with turnkey access, this could be a contender.

A number of communities close to Asheville seem particularly suited to second homes. One example is Mountain Air (www.mountainaircc.com or 800-247-7791). In a hurry to get there? Fly (yes, there's a runway!) into this self-contained, 1,300-acre development, located in Burnside. In addition to the amenities that are almost taken for granted these days (golf, pool, fitness), Mountain Air also offers two on-site naturalists and an organic garden. These kinds of outdoor pursuits are among the newer enticements developers are using to attract more people. Mountain Air, about 55 percent completed, will take another decade or so to build up to its ultimate 450 residences. Lots begin under $200,000, condos are in the $300,000s, and homes start in the $500,000s. Mountain Air is about a 40-minute drive from Asheville.

The Preserve at Little Pine (www.littlepine.info or 866-658-8441) is for people *really* pining to get away from it all, and for those without motion sickness or fear of heights. Located 15 minutes from the town of Marshall, about 40 minutes from Asheville, and about 25 minutes from Hot Springs, you'll be rewarded by breathtaking views, peace and seclusion, and low density—only 120 homes spread over 1,800 acres. Lots range from $125,000 to $700,000.

How Do I Pursue Lifelong Learning?

The University of North Carolina (UNC) at Asheville (www.unca.edu or 828-251-6140) is one of only six public universities in the country classified as a National Liberal Arts University and has received accolades from the Fiske Guide to Colleges, the Princeton Review, and *U.S. News and World Report*. The North Carolina Center for Creative Retirement (NCCCR) is a part of UNC Asheville. The NCCCR serves as a "laboratory for exploring creative and productive roles for a new generation of retirement-aged people, many of whom blend education with postretirement careers." NCCCR offers some interesting ways to get ready for the second half of your life: College for Seniors, Transitions for Boomers, Creative Retirement Exploration, and Leadership Training for Older Persons.

Montreat College is a private Christian college located 15 miles east of Asheville. Western Carolina

University, Warren Wilson College, and Asheville-Buncombe Technical Community College are additional options for those interested in pursuing lifelong learning opportunities.

Strengths

The mountains, valleys, lakes, and streams provide unparalleled beauty and a real feast for the eyes. Asheville is the regional hub for western North Carolina, and the town itself offers great shopping, restaurants, theater, and music. The neighborhoods are surrounded by forests and often have great mountain views. Mild summer temperatures make outdoor activities a pleasure and promote a healthy lifestyle. Asheville is also known as a welcoming town for singles.

Weaknesses

Seeing the words *black ice* and *mountain roads* in the same sentence may strike fear in some! Winters are mild, but certainly not free of snow and ice. Housing costs can be high, and some of the neighborhoods seem isolated, although they are not far from town.

FYI

Check out these sources for additional information: Asheville Chamber of Commerce (www.ashevillechamber.org or 828-258-6101), travel information (www.explore asheville.com or 828-258-6101), North Carolina Center for Creative Retirement (www.unca.edu/ncccr or 828-251-6140), the *Asheville Citizen-Times* (828-252-5611), and the *Mountain Xpress* (828-251-1333).

The Research Triangle (Raleigh, Durham, and Chapel Hill)

REPORT CARD

Overall rating:	A
Climate:	B+
Cost of living:	B
Health care:	A+
Transportation:	A
What's to do:	A

The Research Triangle, or Triangle, gets its name from the geographic region anchored by three outstanding

---

Can you define *half-back*? Half-back refers not only to football, but also to retirees coming "halfway back" from Florida and settling in central North Carolina to escape the heat in South Florida!

universities: University of North Carolina (Chapel Hill), Duke University (Durham), and North Carolina State (Raleigh). These universities and several other institutions of higher learning help define this area. There is a greater concentration of PhDs in the Triangle than just about anywhere in the world! Residents are often involved in lifelong learning and are stimulated by the vitality of the students in these college towns. At the center of the Triangle is 7,000-acre Research Triangle Park, founded in 1952, and home to more than 140 companies that employ roughly 45,000 people.

Air transportation is a snap. The Raleigh-Durham International Airport is located in the heart of the Research Triangle, equidistant from downtown Raleigh and Durham.

Living here lets you get to the beaches of the Atlantic or the Blue Ridge Mountains of western North Carolina in just a few hours. And living near the center of the state means few hurricane watches and no mountain roads with black ice!

The Research Triangle has received impressive accolades over the years, including "best" listings from *Where to Retire* magazine, *Forbes, Money, USA Today,* and AARP.

Who Lives in the Triangle?

Chapel Hill is the smallest of the three cities with a population of about 53,000.

Residents of Chapel Hill are 78 percent Caucasian, 11 percent African-American, and 7 percent Asian, with a median age of 28. Durham is the home of 198,000 people, with approximately 48 percent Caucasian, 46 percent African-American, and 4 percent Asian.

Raleigh has a population of 317,000, with about 70 percent Caucasian, 23 percent African-American, and 7 percent Hispanic. The median age is about 30 for both Raleigh and Durham.

What's the Cost?

The Raleigh-Durham area has a cost of living index of 96 and 102, respectively. Chapel Hill's cost of living index is 113. The average home sells for $263,000, but housing costs and rents are higher in Chapel Hill than

What's It Like Outside?	Jan.	Apr.	Jul.	Oct.	Rain (in.)	Snow (in.)
Average high (°F)	50	72	88	72	42	4
Average low (°F)	30	48	68	47	–	–

in Raleigh or Durham. Median family income is high—around $70,000, perhaps proving that education pays.

What's to Do?

University sports come to mind—the North Carolina State Wolfpack, the Tar Heels of UNC, and the Duke Blue Devils . . . just their names can make you think of basketball and their team colors! There are other sports teams in the Triangle, however, including the Durham Bulls, a minor-league baseball team that has been a Triangle tradition for more than 100 years. The Carolina Hurricanes, an NHL team, also resides here.

The universities are also a resource for nonsports activities. Duke Continuing Studies offers hundreds of classes for retirees, including molecular biology, belly-dance fitness, and photo editing. Music and theater are part of each campus and help enrich the lives of everyone in the area.

Raleigh is known as the "Smithsonian of the South." It is the home of several outstanding museums, including the North Carolina Museum of Natural Sciences, the North Carolina Museum of Art, and Exploris—a global interactive museum. The North Carolina Symphony, the Opera Company of North Carolina, and the Carolina Ballet make their homes in Raleigh as well.

The Morehead Planetarium and the North Carolina Botanical Gardens are in Chapel Hill, as are the quaint shops on Franklin Street. The Eno River provides opportunities for canoeing and floating, and there are miles of hiking trails around the river. The Festival on the Eno brings great music to the river every year on the Fourth of July. Jordan Lake and Falls Lake, with miles of shoreline and beaches, set the scene for all types of water-related activities. Add about two dozen local public golf courses and a mild, four-season climate, and you will find that spending quality time outdoors is a breeze.

Where Are the Jobs?

The list is impressive. The largest employers are the universities and the hospitals. (The area ranks in the top ten for physicians per capita nationwide.) You will surely recognize these well-respected corporations operating in

---

Volunteerism is alive and well in the Triangle. The YMCA Service Corps of Retired Executives (SCORE) and the Retired Senior Volunteer Program (RSVP) are both very active organizations in the area.

the Triangle: SAS Institute, BASF, IBM, Wyeth, General Electric, Cisco Systems, GlaxoSmithKline, and Nortel Networks. The unemployment rate for the area is 3.3 percent.

Where Are the Doctors?

Duke University Medical Center, recognized as one of the world's best health-care providers in publications such as *Time* and *U.S. News and World Report*, serves the Triangle with three of the finest hospitals in the state: Duke University Hospital, Durham Regional Hospital, and Raleigh Community Hospital.

Where Are Some Notable Neighborhoods?

Relocating to the Triangle could be a difficult (but fun) task because there are so many options from which to choose. With three cities, all university towns with great amenities, deciding which one to live in may be tough. Should you live on a tree-lined street in the historic section of Chapel Hill within walking distance of shopping and the university? Or choose a lakeside setting in the rolling hills of Durham or Raleigh with nature surrounding you? It could be a daunting choice.

The Preserve at Jordan Lake (www.thepreserve.ws or 919-545-8811) is a magnet for retirees. This community is located in the middle of the Triangle region around a 14,000-acre lake, which means that swimming, boating, and fishing may compete with your tee times. The championship Davis Love III golf course adds to the beauty of the area. Prices for homesites begin under $200,000, and homes begin in the mid $500,000s.

In Raleigh, the Wakefield Plantation (www.wakefieldplantation.com or 919-488-6300) is set on 2,200 acres and includes a Hale Irwin, 18-hole Tournament Players Club golf course, as well as swimming, and tennis. Villas, townhomes, and single-family homes are available from around $140,000 to $4 million.

Governor's Club (www.governorsclub.com or 800-925-0085) in Chapel Hill is a community that is a must-see, even if you are just looking! The rolling hills are enhanced by 27 holes of Jack Nicklaus golf, wooded trails, swimming, wellness center, and a spectacular golf clubhouse. Homesites begin under $100,000, and homes are priced from around $200,000 to $4 million.

In close by Cary, North Carolina, a new community called Amberly is taking shape. A multiuse Residents' Club, Town Center, and a variety of neighborhoods consisting of condos, townhomes, single-family homes, and custom-built homes will be available in this 1,000-acre development. Five builders, including Del Webb, will be represented. If you're interested in an active-adult community, Carolina Preserve by Del Webb will be part of Amberly, with homes ranging from the $200,000s to the $400,000s. The University of North Carolina Health Care Centers will provide fitness and wellness programs to residents of Carolina Preserve. For more information on Amberly, go to www.amberly.com or 877-426-2375; for info on Carolina Preserve by Del Webb, go to www.delwebb.com or 866-330-9322.

How Do I Pursue Lifelong Learning?

If you plan to take classes as part of reprogramming your time after retiring, the offerings for seniors in the Triangle may overwhelm you. But remember, they can be noncredit, without homework or prerequisites. All that is necessary is the desire to learn.

North Carolina State offers the Encore Center for Lifelong Enrichment. A wide range of classes are offered, and if you're over 65, you can get tuition waivers on credit courses on a space-available basis. As mentioned earlier, Duke and UNC also have extensive course listings.

Strengths

Central North Carolina, with its rolling hills, beautiful lakes, and mild four-season climate, attracts many who want to work, as well as many who don't. If you are looking for more than just sunny days and great scenery, you will find it here. The universities provide a stimulating atmosphere, and the health care is hard to beat.

Weaknesses

If the beach is a priority, you have to drive a few hours to get there. Housing in Chapel Hill can be pricey. The college students often gobble up the part-time jobs and may compete for restaurant tables. Traffic can be an issue.

FYI

Check out these sources for additional information: Chapel Hill-Carborro Chamber of Commerce (www.carolinachamber.org or 919-968-6874), Greater Durham Chamber of Commerce (www.durhamchamber.com or 919-682-2133), Greater Raleigh Chamber of Commerce (www.raleighchamber.org or 919-664-7000), and the *Herald Sun* (www.heraldsun.com or 800-672-0061).

Wilmington

REPORT CARD

Overall rating:	A-
Climate:	B+
Cost of living:	A
Health care:	A
Transportation:	B+
What's to do:	A

Wilmington has a lot going for it—proximity to the ocean, an attractive downtown area located on the Cape

Fear River, the University of North Carolina Wilmington, an easily accessible airport, rich history (the city is 250 years old), a growing population, and a stable economy. Wilmington is North Carolina's major port, and manufacturing, service jobs, and tourism contribute to the town's vibrancy. When you add in Wilmington's four-season mild climate, and consider adjoining Brunswick County's dramatic expansion, it wouldn't be difficult to want to call the Wilmington area home. If you're among the majority of retirees who plan to work in some capacity, *Forbes* magazine rated Wilmington number 19 among smaller metro areas in its 2005 list of "Best Places for Business and Careers," and the May 2006 issue of *Budget Travel* lauded Wilmington as one of "four friendly cities" where "you can walk everywhere you want to go."

Who Lives in Wilmington?

Wilmington has a population of about 95,000, and New Hanover County has approximately 180,000 residents. About 23 percent of the population falls between 40 and 60 years of age. Close to 74 percent of the population is Caucasian, 22 percent African-American, and the remaining percents are represented by Hispanics, American Indians, Asians, and other races. Wilmington's residents are fairly well educated, with 31 percent of those over 25 years old having a bachelor's degree or higher, compared to a U.S. average of 24 percent.

What's the Cost?

In 2006, Wilmington's ACCRA cost of living index was 101, based on a national average of 100. Housing costs for Wilmington are a little less than the national average (95 based on a national average of 100).

What's to Do?

The large historic district hugs the Cape Fear River and boasts mansions, landmark buildings and churches, restaurants, and shops. Tour the battleship *North Carolina*, visit one of Wilmington's many museums—including the Children's Museum, Railroad Museum, Louise Wells Cameron Art Museum, Latimer House Museum, and the Cape Fear Museum—or attend a performance of the Wilmington Symphony Orchestra or Opera House Theatre Company. Are you a festival lover?

Wilmington has been called "Hollywood East," reflecting the large number of movies (more than 185) filmed here, including *Divine Secrets of the Ya-Ya Sisterhood, Forrest Gump, I Know What You Did Last Summer, Sleeping with the Enemy, Titus, Blue Velvet, Waking Ned Devine, Before Night Falls, Firestarter,* and *Bread and Tulips.*

Attend the Azalea Festival, Earth Day Festival, River-fest, Scarecrow Festival, or the Cape Fear Crime Festival. Enjoy a carriage ride through town, or take a tour on a trolley car. Enrich your mind through some college courses. And it's less than a 2-hour drive to Raleigh.

If your tastes run more to water-oriented activities, you're in luck. The Cape Fear Coast offers Carolina Beach State Park (don't forget to look for the Venus fly-traps), Kure Beach, and Wrightsville Beach. Beaches range from unspoiled to boardwalks and mini-golf. There's something for everyone.

Where Are the Jobs?

The top several employers in Wilmington include the New Hanover Health Network, New Hanover County Schools, GE, University of North Carolina Wilmington, and the county and state government.

Where Are the Doctors?

The New Haven Regional Medical Center acts as a referral center for the region, and it is also a teaching hospital. It's comprised of three hospitals, two of which are located in Wilmington. The center has more than 20 operating rooms, a significant number of specialty centers, and the only open-heart surgery program in the area. The Wilmington Treatment Center treats adults with alcohol and/or drug dependency. There are three additional hospitals within a half hour drive—J. Arthur Dosher Memorial Hospital, Pender Memorial Hospital, and Brunswick Community Hospital.

Where Are Some Notable Neighborhoods?

The Greater Wilmington area is exploding with new, master-planned communities. You can go in almost any direction (well, except east, which would plop you into the Atlantic Ocean) and find large, developing neighborhoods. Within Wilmington itself, check out the Country Club of Landfall (www.countrycluboflandfall.com or 910-256-8411), a lovely 2,200-acre gated golf and tennis community on the Intracoastal Waterway, and only 5 minutes away from Wrightsville Beach. Homesites begin in the $200,000s, and homes start in the $400,000s and reach more than $3 million. If neo-traditional is more your thing, check out 400-acre Mayfaire (www.mayfairetown.com or 910-256-5829), with its combination of condos,

What's It Like Outside?	Jan.	Apr.	Jul.	Oct.	Rain (in.)	Snow (in.)
Average high (°F)	56	74	89	75	54	2
Average low (°F)	35	52	71	54	–	–

single-family homes, and apartments, anchored by its pedestrian-friendly town center brimming with stores, offices, a 16-screen movie theater, shops, and hotels—and Wrightsville Beach is only 3 miles away. Condos begin around $400,000. The Mayfaire Web site sums up this lifestyle succinctly: "Shop. Dine. Live. Work. Play. Stay."

If 5 minutes or 3 miles is still too far from the ocean for you, and you're willing to travel to neighboring communities for most goods and services, head north about 80 miles and check out the seaside town of Emerald Isle (www.emeraldisle-nc.org or 252-354-3424). This tranquil, 5.6-square-mile residential barrier island with about 4,000 permanent inhabitants (which swells to 50,000 during peak season) emphasizes zoning and controlled growth to maintain its family image. Purchase a condo for about $300,000, or an oceanfront residence beginning around $800,000.

About a 30-mile drive northwest of Wilmington (and 90 miles from Raleigh) is River Landing (www.river landing.com or 888-285-4171). This 1,400-acre gated development in small-town (about 3,500 residents) Wallace, North Carolina, has won a number of awards for its golf courses and was featured in *Where to Retire* magazine as one of "America's 100 Best Master-Planned Communities" in 2004. Lots begin around $60,000, and homes are available from $300,000. The community is about 10 years old.

South of Wilmington is Brunswick County, where most of the building action is taking place, with many communities clustered between Wilmington and the South Carolina border. Southport, a quaint fishing village 30 miles south of Wilmington, has an attractive historic downtown area, and the beautiful St. James Plantation (www.stjamesplantation.com or 800-245-3871) is just 5 miles away. Located on the Intracoastal Waterway, with a private beach club, golf course, and marina, you can purchase a homesite beginning around $120,000, and choose among condos, townhomes, patio homes, and single-family homes (condos in the $200,000s, and homes in the high $300,000s). (Southport is also where you catch the ferry to spectacular Bald Head Island. See page 275 for a description of this residential island where cars are not allowed.)

Southwest from Wilmington in Shallotte is the community of Rivers Edge Golf Club and Plantation. The "river's edge" referred to is the Shallotte River (www.riversedge-nc.com or 800-789-0353). This development is located a bit inland, about 30 minutes from Wilmington to the north or Myrtle Beach to the south, with homesites starting in the $200,000s. Additional master-planned, amenity-laden communities in Brunswick County in various stages of development include 2,000-acre Sea Trail (www.seatrail.com or 888-260-2284) in Sunset Beach, containing a large conference center on the premises and, also in Sunset Beach, Ocean Ridge Plantation (www.oceanridge.com or 800-556-6570), a 2,000-acre enclave consisting only of single-family homes.

How Do I Pursue Lifelong Learning?

The University of North Carolina Wilmington, Shaw University, and Cape Fear Community College provide opportunities for lifelong learning.

Strengths

For people who love the water, living in a city nestled between a river and the sea is appealing. Having the ocean, city, and airport all close to one another is an asset as well. And there is a lot to do and see. Wilmington is a fairly large city, but it retains the flavor of a small town. There is a *lot* of development happening in the greater Wilmington area; your biggest challenge may be choosing a neighborhood from among so many options.

Weaknesses

The crime rate in Wilmington is higher than the national average. Statistically, Wilmington gets brushed or hit by a hurricane every 4 years.

FYI

Check out these sources for additional information: Greater Wilmington Chamber of Commerce (www.wilmingtonchamber.com or 910-762-2611), *Star-News* (www.wilmingtonstar.com or 910-343-2000), and the University of NC Wilmington's paper the *Seahawk* (www.theseahawk.com or 910-962-3229).

OREGON

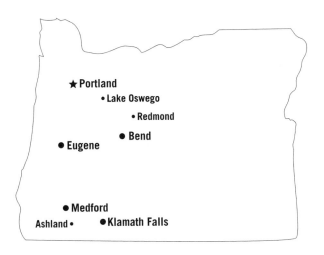

What comes to mind when you think of central and south-central Oregon? If you're not familiar with this part of the state, *sunshine* may not be the first word to pop into your head. The delightful, high-desert, low-humidity climate of this area is compliments of the rain shadow provided by the snow-capped Cascade Mountains, resulting in only ten inches of rain annually and around 300 sunny days a year. A second word associated with this area might be *outdoors*. Indeed, the areas of Redmond, Bend, Medford, Ashland, and Klamath Falls lend themselves to an active lifestyle, with their astounding beauty contributing to the lure of the four-season climate. Add in the vibrant city of Portland with its neighboring community of Lake Oswego and the college town of Eugene, and there are many attractive possibilities for relocating to Oregon. And there is no sales tax in Oregon!

Central and South Central Oregon

REPORT CARD

Overall rating:	B
Climate:	B+
Cost of living:	B-
(except for Klamath Falls, which is a B+)	
Health care:	B+
Transportation:	B
What's to do:	B+

What's It Like Outside?	Jan.	Apr.	Jul.	Oct.	Rain (in.)	Snow (in.)
Average high (°F)	40	57	81	62	10	31
Average low (°F)	23	30	46	32	–	–

* These averages are for Bend, but statistics for Redmond vary by only a little. Snow tends to melt quickly without much accumulation.

Central Oregon

Who Lives in Central Oregon?

When we say central Oregon, we're referring to Bend and Redmond. And when we say central Oregon, we're talking about growth! The population of this area (which of course includes more than just Bend and Redmond, but they are the two places we'll be discussing) increased by more than 50 percent in the decade between 1995 and 2005. This trend will continue, with an anticipated rise in the population by more than 60 percent in Bend between 2005 and 2025, and an almost 120 percent surge in the number of residents predicted in Redmond during that time frame. Accolades for central Oregon and its inclusion on many "top" or "best" lists for working, living, retiring, skiing, golfing, etc. in such publications as *Where to Retire* magazine, *Forbes*, *Money*, *Golf Digest*, and *Ski Magazine* has alerted many people to the desirability of this area.

The population in central Oregon is more than 91 percent white, 3 percent American Indian/Alaskan native, 2 percent a mixture of two more races, less than 1 percent African-American, and other races round out the total. Both Bend and Redmond are located in Deschutes County, which has a population of 140,000; this is expected to swell by more than 60 percent by 2025.

The median age in Bend is 35 years, yet its attractiveness to retirees is reflected by its number of residents ages 45 to 54, which is higher than the national and Oregon state averages. Bend's population in 2005 was 70,000, and Bend is one of the fastest growing cities in the United States. The city is about 30 square miles, and it is 3,600 feet above sea level.

Redmond, Bend's neighbor 15 miles to the north, has about 22,000 residents, and it is situated on a plateau 3,000 feet above sea level. Its median age is 33.

What's the Cost?

Based on a national cost of living index average pegged at 100, Bend's cost of living index is 104, and Redmond is below the national average at 96. Bend's median home cost is $328,000, and Redmond's is $238,000. The median income (family of four) in 2006 was $59,000, compared to a national average of $66,000.

What's to Do?

If you're into the great outdoors, you may have found nirvana. As far as the white stuff goes, Mt. Bachelor Ski

---

The largest herd of commercial reindeer in the world is located only 2 miles from Redmond. Ho ho ho!

Resort offers downhill skiing, snowboarding, snowshoeing, snow tubing, and cross-country skiing on its almost 3,700 skiable acres at one the largest ski resorts in the Pacific Northwest. Since Mt. Bachelor is located in Bend, you can golf in the morning at one of the more than 20 public courses and ski in the afternoon! Hiking, biking, fishing, rock climbing, rafting, camping, and caving are additional popular pastimes. If you're exhausted from too much activity, take a leisurely stroll around Mirror Pond in Drake Park, located in Bend's historical downtown district, or shop and take in a movie and lunch at the Old Mill District (previously the site of a lumber mill), also in Bend. The cultural festivals and events, the Les Schwab Amphitheater (Lynyrd Skynyrd, anyone?), and the High Desert Museum will help satisfy more musical and cerebral pursuits.

Portland is about 150 miles from Redmond, 130 miles from Salem (the state capital, as you know, if you remember your geography), and 125 miles from Eugene, home to the University of Oregon. The city of Redmond owns and operates Roberts Field, the airport for Central Oregon. The four-carrier (Delta, Horizon Air, United, and United Express) airport currently offers flights to Los Angeles (new in 2006), Portland, Seattle, San Francisco, and Salt Lake City.

Where Are the Jobs?

Unemployment in the Deschutes area was 4 percent in 2006. The major employers in the central Oregon area include the St. Charles Medical Center, Les Schwab Tire Center (free plug: We had a flat on our rental car in Bend and had it towed to Les Schwab. We were on our way within an hour; they literally run to your car to assist you), Bright Wood Corporation (lumber re-manufacturer), and Sunriver Resort.

Where Are the Doctors?

St. Charles Medical Center in Bend has about 250 physicians representing forty specialties/subspecialties, and St. Charles Medical Center in Richmond has about 40 physicians representing a dozen specialties.

Where Are Some Notable Neighborhoods?

The central Oregon region has a number of developments to consider. Eagle Crest, located in Redmond about 5 miles from downtown Bend, offers 54 holes of golf, swimming, a day spa, 15 miles of hiking/biking/walking paths, fractional ownership, rental property, and a 100-room inn (some units are pet-friendly) as well as homesites, townhomes, lots, and custom homes on

---

Portland was rated as one of the top 10 "Most Literate Cities" for 2006.

1,700 scenic acres. The Falls at Eagle Crest, an active-adult community within Eagle Crest, has its own clubhouse, and residents can enjoy the other amenities the resort offers. Other neighborhoods within Eagle Crest include Vista Rim, Desert Sky, Creekside Village, and Scenic Ridge. Resale homesite prices start in the $200,000s, and homes in the $350,000s. Contact www.eagle-crest.com or 800-340-8172.

If you want to live in the thick of things, take a look at Mill Quarter, within walking distance of the Old Mill District and downtown Bend. Most of the development is sold out, and remaining townhomes begin at a pricey $1.2 million. However, resales are available (www.millqtr.com or 541-322-4058).

Northwest Crossing is an attractive new urbanism development (see page 287 for a description of new urbanism) in Bend, with a total of 1,100 homes planned on 450 acres over the next several years. Many of the homes are certified "Earth advantage," which means they boast features that promote healthier indoor air, greater energy efficiency, and sensitivity to environmental concerns. Practically, this translates to such things as compact fluorescent-light fixtures, whole-house ventilation, and solid wood flooring. Home prices begin around $400,000 and approach $1 million. Contact www.

northwestcrossing.com or 541-388-1992 for additional information.

River Canyon Estates in Bend is a master-planned community built by D.R. Horton (www.drhorton.com or 541-617-1019), with homes beginning in the $300,000s and escalating to the $900,000s. A clubhouse with a fitness center, tennis courts, and a pool are among the amenities you can enjoy in this community.

Examples of home prices outside of master-planned communities include a three-bedroom, two-and-a-half bath home near a park for $215,000 in Redmond and a three-bedroom, two-bath home in Bend for $250,000.

Fifteen miles south of Bend is Sunriver, a 3,300-acre, 35-year-old resort development that is also a self-contained community with its own landing strip. Many second-home owners live in Sunriver, with condos available in the $200,000s. For information, contact www.sunriver-resort.com or 800-801-8765.

Here's how Gail and Jim K. found Bend.

Bend, Oregon—Bend, where?? It was 1991, and we had 2 weeks of vacation remaining and no set

---

Oregon and New Jersey are the only two states that have laws banning self-serve gasoline.

LAKE OSWEGO

"Welcome to Lake Wobegon, where all the women are strong, all the men are good-looking, and all the children are above average." Garrison Keillor's quote describing this fictitious town could be altered to read "Welcome to Lake Oswego, where all the amenities are close, all the vistas are lovely, and all the elements for a great place to live are above average." Although we're cheating here (Lake Oswego is only 15 minutes south of Portland and not in central Oregon at all), we had to throw in this community of 36,000 that is only 1½ hours from the ocean, 30 minutes from the airport, about an hour's drive from skiing (Mt. Hood), and less than an hour's trip by car to Salem. All this in a town on the Willamette River that has about a dozen parks, is revitalizing its downtown with the lifestyle center of Lake View Village that wraps around 400-acre Lake Oswego, and offers condos that begin in the $100,000s and escalate to estate homes in the millions. *Budget Travel* published an article about Portland entitled "Can a Place Be Too Perfect?" With criticism like that, no wonder this part of Oregon is a popular place for relocation! And with tourism and Intel as major employers, the Portland area has a diverse economy.

plans. In *Sunset Magazine* we saw an advertisement for central Oregon—sunshine, lakes, hiking, golfing, skiing, fishing, camping, bicycling, rock climbing, and boating. We packed the camping gear and the golf clubs and took off on an adventure from San Francisco to parts unknown in Oregon. In the back of our minds we were thinking long-range—retirement. We drove north and decided to explore the central part of the state. Stately ponderosa pine trees, lowly juniper trees, high desert sagebrush, bitterbrush, and rabbitbrush, the Cascade Mountain range, Mt. Bachelor (skiing), Broken Top, the Three Sisters, Mt. Jefferson, Three Fingered Jack, Black Butte were all sights to be seen on the trip.

Bend's population was about 26,000 or so at that time. Bend has a delightful downtown area—numerous restaurants, small shops, and friendly staff—people say hello on the street! There is also Drake Park overlooking Mirror Pond, with views

MORE FOR YOUR MONEY

Prineville, 15 minutes from Redmond and 30 minutes from Bend, is a small but growing community of about 9,000 residents with housing prices that haven't escalated as quickly as those in Bend and Redmond. A new community, IronHorse, will be developed over the next 2 decades and will be a mixed-use community with almost 3,000 units planned on more than 1,000 acres. In additional to housing, IronHorse will contain shops, open spaces, trails and parks, a school, and a civic center. Brasada Ranch, a resort community under construction, will ultimately have 900 residences on 1,800 acres. Additional communities are planned for this area. They are worth checking out if Bend and/or Redmond feel too crowded or financially out of reach.

of Mt. Bachelor. We stopped by a Realtor's office to pick up a housing brochure and hit if off immediately with the Realtor. The next day we went back and set up a date and time to see property the following week. We had fallen in love with Bend. But we also took a trip to Portland and explored some of the other areas in Oregon as well. It took us 1½ days of house hunting and we were Oregon homeowners. Our home is north of town, on 2½ acres with a view of the Cascade Mountains. But we were not retiring for another 4 years!

We went back to San Francisco and advised our friends and family of our impending move . . . in 4 years. "But who do you know there?" "No one—except our Realtor!" "Are you nuts?" "Maybe, but we don't think so!"

Fast forward to 2006. We have owned our home for 15 years and have lived in it for 11 years. We hail from North Adams, Massachusetts, and Denver, Colorado. Our friends in Bend are from all over—Bend and Portland, Chicago, San Diego, Los Angeles, San Francisco, Seattle, Florida, Montana, New York, Pennsylvania, Hawaii, Hong Kong, and Ireland, among many others. What makes this a special place? Number one, the people; we have enjoyed meeting and making new friends throughout the years here. We joined a private golf club, got involved, and volunteered. We enjoy the local community theater, the Central

Oregon Symphony (which is outstanding), the Cascade Music Festival in the summer, as well as free concerts in Drake Park or in the Old Mill District. The High Desert Museum is unique and tops our list when we have visitors. The art galleries are impressive, as are the local artists.

Although we've both gone back to work part-time, we still golf, entertain, participate in gourmet groups, go for walks with the dog (which we need to do after the entertaining and gourmet eating!), volunteer, and continue to explore Oregon and the Pacific Northwest.

Bend, Oregon, has made the list of top places to retire in several magazines. Although the population has increased to 70,000 plus, we still believe our choice was the right one. We would not change a thing! ⓛ

How Do I Pursue Lifelong Learning?

Central Oregon Community College (COCC) has campuses in both Bend and Redmond and offers degree programs, enrichment classes, and continuing education. Oregon State University has a campus in Bend as well (in Cascades Hall on the COCC campus).

Strengths

Outdoor recreational activities are outstanding, and the central Oregon scenery is a feast for the eyes. You can ski and golf in the same day! College towns are always a plus, and there is no sales tax in Oregon.

Weaknesses

Housing costs have soared in Bend and Redmond, driven by people escaping higher-priced areas and the sheer number of people flocking to central Oregon. According to a 2006 Global Insight/National City Report, Bend's housing is overvalued by a hefty 76 percent. Ah, the price of popularity! You'll also have at least a 2-hour drive if you're hungry for the arts and culture of a larger city.

FYI

Check out these sources for additional information: Bend Chamber of Commerce (www.bendchamber.org or 541-382-3221), Bend Visitor and Convention Bureau (www.visitbend.com or 877-245-8484), Redmond Chamber of Commerce (www.redmondcofc.com or 541-923-5191), Central Oregon Visitors Association (www.covisitors.com or 800-800-8334), the *Bend Bulletin* (www.bendbulletin.com or 541-617-7833), and the

---

Note to Republicans: Politically, Ashland is considered very liberal.

Redmond Spokesman (www.redmondspokesman.com or 541-548-2184).

South-Central Oregon

Who Lives in South-Central Oregon?

Medford, Ashland, and Klamath Falls are located in south-central Oregon. Medford and Ashland are only 20 minutes apart from one another, and Klamath Falls is a little over an hour's drive east of Ashland. California is a close neighbor to the south—fewer than 20 miles from Ashland or Klamath Falls. Rogue Valley International-Medford airport is serviced by four air carriers—Skywest-United Express, Horizon, America West, and Skywest-Delta, and it offers flights to eight hubs. A new control tower and new terminal are under construction, with completion targeted for 2009. Medford's population is about 71,000, with 86 percent of the population Caucasian, 9 percent Hispanic, 2 percent American Indian, and the remainder other races or a combination of races, and the median resident age is about 37.

Ashland is a city of more than 20,000, and its composition is changing to reflect the influx of retirees to this desirable area (about 15 percent of the residents are over 65 years old). Demographically, Ashland is about 92 percent white, 4 percent Hispanic or Latino, 2 percent Asian, 1 percent Native American, and the balance is made up of other races or a combination of races. Ashland was rated as the top place in *Money* magazine's "Best Places to Retire 2005."

Klamath Falls has a population of about 20,000, with about 85 percent of the residents Caucasian, 9 percent Hispanic or Latino, 1 percent Asian, 1 percent African American, and the rest other races or a mixture of races. Klamath Falls has an airport, Kingsley Field, which presently offers flights to and from Portland on Horizon Air. Daily nonstop service to San Francisco via United Express is being investigated. Klamath Lake, located in Klamath Falls, is the largest natural lake in the Pacific Northwest. As is true of Redmond and Bend, many Californians are moving to this part of Oregon (particularly Medford and Ashland).

What's the Cost?

Housing costs have driven up the cost of living in the Medford/Ashland area. In 2005, *Newsweek* ranked Medford number two in the United States for investment property (investors account for close to one-fourth of home

---

Klamath Falls is named after the Klamath Indians, the first inhabitants of the area.

purchases), and a 2006 National City Corp/Global Insight report declared Medford housing overpriced by 64 percent. Between 2002 and 2005, the average home price in East Medford (the more affluent area) skyrocketed by more than 70 percent—from $189,000 to $328,000. Ashland's prices rose from $294,000 to $466,000 during the same period. Based on a national average of 100, Medford's cost of living index is 116, and Ashland's is 135. Klamath Falls has a cost of living index of 95.

What's to Do?

Again, think of the great outdoors—and we do mean great! The Mount Ashland ski area receives an average of 300 inches of snow a year and offers 23 runs, with the longest being a mile, as well as chute skiing. Visit magnificent Crater Lake National Park (Oregon's only national park), golf on one of the area courses, camp, fish, go boating, hike, enjoy cross-country skiing—well, you get the idea. The outdoor activities are endless, and the scenery is spectacular.

Arts and culture are alive and well in Ashland. The world-famous Ashland Oregon Shakespeare Festival (OSF) is the country's largest regional theater, presenting 780 performances annually with 360,000 attendees. Tour Ashland's galleries during the First Friday art walk, or stroll through 100-acre Lithia Park after you've visited the many boutiques and restaurants in downtown Ashland.

Five miles west of Medford, the Britt Festivals, held in nearby Jacksonville, in a natural amphitheater, offers a full spectrum of musical performances as well as dance, comedy, and educational programs during the summer. Medford, with its COSTCO, Starbucks, and Rogue Valley Mall, provides the day-to-day shopping opportunities.

Klamath Falls is heaven for birders; it has the largest number of bald eagles in the Pacific Northwest. There are also antique and craft stores, bookstores, art galleries, restaurants, and a trolley, and it has a much more rural feel to it than Medford or Ashland. Construction is underway to expand and utilize the downtown more

What's It Like Outside?	Jan.	Apr.	Jul.	Oct.	Rain (in.)	Snow (in.)
Average high (°F)	47	63	87	68	18	4
Average low (°F)	29	35	50	36		

*These numbers are for Ashland, but Medford and Klamath Falls vary only by several degrees—except for Klamath Falls which gets 40 inches of snow each year.

effectively, and Klamath Falls is experiencing a bit of a boom as more planned communities are built and new businesses move into the area.

Where Are the Jobs?

Agriculture and tourism are two big drivers of Medford's economy. Harry and David (you may be familiar with their Royal Riviera pears), employs about 1,700 workers, supplementing that with an additional 11,000 seasonal employees. The Rogue Valley Medical Center, also in Medford, employs more than 1,300. The Medford school district is also a sizeable employer, with more than 1,000 employees. Ashland is home to Southern Oregon University, a public liberal arts and sciences university with about 6,000 students and 650 faculty and staff, and the Oregon Shakespeare Festival, which employs around 250 people. The Ashland school district, the Ashland Community Hospital, and the tourism industry are also major employers in Ashland. In Klamath Falls, Merle West Medical Center has more than 900 employees, and Jeld-Wen (products include doors and windows) and the school district are the other big employers.

Where Are the Doctors?

The Rogue Valley Medical Center (Medford) is the regional referral and trauma center and offers services including neurology, rehab, diabetes, cardiovascular, orthopedic, and oncology care. Hospice, home care, and the area's only neonatal-care unit are also part of the 300-plus-bed RVMC. Ashland Community Hospital is a 50-bed acute-care facility; a new diagnostic and surgery center just opened in 2006. Merle West Medical Center (Klamath Falls) has more than 170 beds, and it includes a cancer treatment center, cardiac rehab, home-health services, physical therapy, and an ICU. It has undergone recent renovations.

Where Are Some Notable Neighborhoods?

We've already mentioned that housing prices are steep in the Medford/Ashland area. If you can afford it, living in Ashland but having the amenities of Medford (COSTCO, Starbucks, etc.) only 20 minutes away makes a great combination. Mountain Meadows (www.mtmeadows.com or 800-337-1301) is an active-adult community on 40 acres in Ashland that is considered

---

You won't find any falls in Klamath Falls; they disappeared when the Link River was dammed in the 1920s.

one of the "100 Best Retirement Communities in America" by *Where to Retire* magazine. The National Council on Seniors Housing named it the "Best Small Retirement Community in America," touting its "customized options for seniors, its aging in place program, it neo-traditional site plan, its amenities package, its on-site owner and staff, and its phasing of development stages." Examples of cost: a two-bedroom, one-bath home for $248,000 and a three-bedroom, two-bath home for $479,000. You can even rent on a trial basis to see if it's the perfect place for you.

There are no new, large, master-planned communities in Ashland, but other housing examples include a three-bedroom, two-bath downtown condo for $398,000 or, at the other end, a four-bedroom, five-bathroom 6,750-square-foot house for $3.4 million (on .35 acres).

If you're looking for a laid-back, nature-oriented way of life, the Running Y Ranch in Klamath Falls is a place to consider. It's on *Where to Retire* magazine's list of "100 Best Retirement Communities in America" and *Golf Digest* ranked the Running Y's golf course among the "Top 100 Golf Courses in America." Two hours from Bend and a little over an hour from Ashland, the Running Y offers townhomes, homes, cabins, and lots, as well as a lodge, golf, spa, equestrian facilities, fitness center, pool complex, and ice arena. Homesites in the Meadows at Running Y begin around $140,000, resale chalets around $350,000, new townhomes in the $400,000s, and resale townhomes in the $300,000s. Begun in 1996, the community will have approximately 900 homes on 3,600 acres.

In addition to the Running Y, and only 2 miles away, another Jeld-Wen Community, Ridge Water, is developing. Contact information is for the Running Y (www.runningy.com or 888-797-2624) and Ridge Water (www.discoverridgewater.com or 800-569-9015). Smaller and older homes are actually available for under $100,000 in Klamath Falls.

How Do I Pursue Lifelong Learning?

We've already mentioned Southern Oregon University in Ashland, and Rogue Community College has its Riverside Campus in downtown Medford. Medford is also home to Pacific Bible College, whose mission is to "prepare ministry students, laypersons, business professionals, homemakers, and missionaries for effective service in the 21st century by establishing a vibrant personal faith in Jesus Christ coupled with a clear and biblical worldview."

Klamath Falls makes lifelong learning easy with access to Klamath Community College, a 2-year college that was chartered in 1997 and moved onto its permanent campus in 2000. The Oregon Institute of Technology's main campus is in Klamath Falls. This 3,400-student, 190-acre campus offers a number of bachelor's degrees, including a wide range of health programs. Distance education is also available through OIT.

Strengths

Outdoor pursuits surrounded by natural beauty with a temperate climate is the south-central Oregon area's strong suit. Lifelong learning opportunities are accessible in Medford, Ashland, and Klamath Falls. There's a relaxed atmosphere for people who are seeking this lifestyle. Ashland's downtown area is particularly appealing.

Weaknesses

Access to a major airport from any of these cities is a hike of several hours. If you crave the cultural amenities of a major city, you may find south-central Oregon, particularly Klamath Falls, a little light in this area. Housing prices in Medford and Ashland are high.

FYI

Check out these sources for additional information: the Chamber of Medford/Jackson County (www.medford chamber.com or 541-779-4847), Ashland Chamber of Commerce (www.ashlandchamber.com or 541-482-3486), Klamath Chamber of Commerce (www.klamath.org or 541-884-5193), *Mail Tribune* (www.mailtribune.com or 541-776-4411), the *Ashland Daily Tidings* (www.dailytidings.com or 541-482-3456), and

the Klamath Falls *Herald and News* (www.herald andnews.com or 541-885-4410).

SOUTH CAROLINA

Capital: Columbia
Nickname: Palmetto State
Motto: "Prepared in mind and resources"/ "While I breathe, I hope"
Flower: Yellow jessamine
Bird: Great Carolina wren
Population: 4,300,000
Fascinating Fact: The shag is the official dance of South Carolina.

Aiken

REPORT CARD

Overall rating:	B+
Climate:	B+
Cost of living:	A
Health care:	B+
Transportation:	B
What's to do:	B+

With its small-town ambience and the arts and culture of a larger city, Aiken may be the perfect place for you if you're looking to live inland in a quaint, equestrian-friendly area with a mild climate. Aiken is located about 15 miles east of Augusta, close to the Georgia/South Carolina border—an attraction for people who have no desire to live on the coast. The town was named for William Aiken, president of the South Carolina Canal and Railroad Company. As wealthy residents from Charleston visited Aiken to escape the heat of the coast and marshes, and affluent New Yorkers built lavish estates for winter getaways (and brought their horses for polo), Aiken grew. The town was viewed as a health resort and was once considered the "sports center of the South." The building of a cotton mill in 1845 and an electric power plant in the 1950s contributed the necessary industrial base for Aiken to flourish.

Considering its charming historic downtown area, wide boulevards rife with flowers, laid-back atmosphere and scenic beauty—the entire city has been named an arboretum—it's no wonder Aiken is one of the fastest growing cities in South Carolina. Yes, you may be achin' for Aiken (sorry, we couldn't resist!).

Who Lives in Aiken?

The city of Aiken has a population of about 25,000, and Aiken County has approximately 135,000 residents. About 40 percent of the population is 45 years of age or older, and the median age is 40. About 67 percent of the population is Caucasian, 30 percent African-American, and the remaining percents represented by Hispanics, Asians, and other races.

What's It Like Outside?	Jan.	Apr.	Jul.	Oct.	Rain (in.)	Snow (in.)
Average high (°F)	56	77	92	77	52	Trace
Average low (°F)	32	49	70	50	–	–

What's the Cost?

The Aiken/Augusta area cost of living index is 89, based on a national average of 100. Within South Carolina, Aiken had the largest increase in the number of houses sold in 2005—50 percent—largely due to the increasing number of retirees moving to the area. The average sale price of a home in Aiken was $244,000 in 2006.

What's to Do?

Aiken is often equated with horses. So in addition to participating in equestrian sports, visit the Thoroughbred Racing Hall of Fame, located on the grounds of Hopeland Garden, along with the Carriage Museum and Doll House Museum. The Aiken Center for the Arts, the Aiken Community Playhouse, the Aiken Historical Museum, viewing notable estates and cottages, and the symphony, ballet, and opera can satisfy your artistic and cultural cravings. Explore the 2,000-acre Hitchcock Woods, one of the largest urban forests in the country. Once you've taken a horse-drawn carriage and enjoyed the wildflowers, gear up to enjoy the more than 170 other parks in Aiken! A trip to the ocean or to the big-city amenities of Atlanta, Charleston, Charlotte, or Savannah will involve a 2- to 3-hour drive. Airport service is convenient. Augusta and Columbia are both under an hour's drive, and Charlotte International Airport is less than 2 hours away.

Where Are the Jobs?

Top employers in the Aiken area include Westinghouse Savannah River Company, Aiken County Public Schools, Bechtel Savannah River Company, Avondale Mills Inc., and Dixie-Narco, Inc.

Where Are the Doctors?

Aiken Regional Medical Centers include a 269-bed community hospital with all private rooms. (Universal Health Services, Inc. is the hospital-management company for Aiken Regional Medical Centers and is an AARP "Featured Employer.") University Health Care Systems (Augusta) has more than 500 rooms and about 500 medical staff members.

Where Are Some Notable Neighborhoods?

A number of homes are available in Aiken for under $200,000. Large, master-planned communities in or near Aiken include 2,300-acre Woodside Plantation

---

Aiken has been on "top" lists in *Money* and *Where to Retire* magazines.

(www.woodsideplantation.com or 800-648-3052), 1,150-acre Cedar Creek (www.cedarcreek.net or 800-937-5362), and the 4,000-acre Mount Vintage Plantation in North Augusta (www.mountvintage.com or 888-271-3330). All three of these communities have the amenities you'd expect—golf, swimming, hiking, tennis, fitness centers, nature trails, community activities, etc. Woodside Plantation is within Aiken, Cedar Creek is about a 10-minute drive from the historic town center, and Mount Vintage is about 25 miles away—more isolated and offering some equestrian homesites. Lots and homes are available at all three locations, with prices dependent upon size and location. For example, lots in Woodside Plantation start around $30,000 and homes about $200,000; Cedar Creek offers homesites beginning around $100,000, and homes around $300,000; Mount Vintage has homes in the $400,000s. Prices escalate from there.

How Do I Pursue Lifelong Learning?

Aiken offers two opportunities to pursue lifelong learning: the University of South Carolina Aiken and Aiken Technical College, a comprehensive 2-year college that also offers transfer programs for people wishing to continue their educations at 4-year institutions.

Strengths

Aiken is a charming, historic town with reasonable prices. Many retirees are finding Aiken is a great place to live.

Weaknesses

It's a hike to the ocean and to cities other than Augusta. The federally owned Savannah River Site has been designated a Superfund site by the Environmental Protection Agency. The site, which is about 20 miles south of Aiken, produced nuclear materials for the defense industry.

FYI

Check out these sources for additional information: Greater Aiken Chamber of Commerce (www.aikenchamber.net or 803-641-1111), City of Aiken (www.aiken.net or 888-AikenSC), *Aiken Standard* (www.aikenstandard.com or 803-648-2311), and the *Augusta Chronicle* (http://chronicle.augusta.com or 706-722-5620).

Charleston and the Low Islands

REPORT CARD

Overall rating:	A-
Climate:	B
Cost of living:	B
Health care:	A
Transportation:	A
What's to do:	A

The Charleston area, with its coastal islands of Kiawah, Seabrook, Sullivan's Island, and the Isle of Palms, presents a winning combination—island living coupled with the rich history and cultural opportunities of a city with a nice climate. The three islands are about 20 miles away from Charleston and boast beautiful beaches, abundant wildlife, and breathtaking marshlands. Charleston is regarded as the "cultural capital of the South," and justly so. It is an attractive tourist destination, with its several million annual visitors contributing around $5 billion annually to the economy.

This area of the country is often described as "low country." This means that the approximately 200 miles of low-lying land between Charleston and St. Marys, Georgia, is intricately linked with lakes, marshes, and ocean.

Who Lives in Charleston?
The city of Charleston's population is about 97,000. About 65 percent are Caucasian, 30 percent African-American, and 2 percent Hispanic. Average household income is about $43,000.

What's the Cost?
The cost of living index for the Charleston metro area is 99, based on a national average of 100. The average price of a home in the Charleston area is $260,000.

What's to Do?
Art, theater, ballet, the symphony, museums, restaurants, shopping, and the Atlantic Ocean, combined with mild weather, provide the ingredients for a rich, active lifestyle. Parks, gardens, the Francis Marion National

What's It Like Outside?	Jan.	Apr.	Jul.	Oct.	Rain (in.)	Snow (in.)
Average high (°F)	58	76	90	77	50	Trace
Average low (°F)	38	54	73	56	–	–

Forest, plantations, Fort Sumter and other historic landmarks, architectural tours, and the aquarium will help keep you busy as well.

Where Are the Jobs?

The largest employers include the military, health care, and the school system. Bayer, Dupont, Westvaco, and Alcoa also provide a sizable number of jobs. Unemployment in South Carolina is around 6 percent.

Where Are the Doctors?

You'll find medical facilities almost everywhere you look in Charleston. Hospitals include Bon Secours-St. Francis Xavier Hospital, Charleston Memorial Hospital, Medical University of South Carolina Medical Center, Roper Hospital, and East Cooper Regional Medical Center (in Mt. Pleasant), to name a few. There is a naval hospital and a Veterans Affairs Medical Center as well.

Where Are Some Notable Neighborhoods?

Del Webb is building an active-adult community on about 400 acres, called Del Webb Charleston, consisting of 1,000 single-family homes in Summerville, about 25 miles from Charleston. Prices to be determined; presales will begin in 2007. Contact Del Webb at www.delwebb.com or 866-224-4508.

A second active-adult community to consider is the 200-acre Elms of Charleston (www.elmsofcharleston.com or 800-237-3460). Located in North Charleston, the Elms offers more than a dozen different home designs of patio homes, garden homes, or villas; prices range from the mid $100,000s to the mid $300,000s. Community amenities include maintenance of lawns, exteriors, and common areas and a club and fitness center and à la carte home health care.

Prices on the low islands vary widely: $14,000 for a one-bedroom/one-bath condo on Seabrook Island, $600,000 for a three-bedroom/two-bath single-family residence on Kiawah with a wooded lot, and up to $8 million for an estate home on the ocean.

Sullivan's Island doesn't allow condos, nor does it have motels or hotels. It's listed by *Forbes* as one of the most expensive zip codes in the United States; the median home price in 2005 was $1.22 million!

Isle of Palms residences have large price ranges too,

Charleston was listed as one of five "Dream Towns" by *AARP* magazine in 2006.

including fractional ownership. About 5,000 people call the Isle of Palms home. Wild Dunes is a 1,600-acre gated community on the northeast tip of the Isle of Palms with golf, tennis, and its own harbor. Prices begin around $500,000 for a condo and can escalate into the millions for oceanfront property. There are vacation rentals, interval ownership, and year-round residences.

Daniel Island is a 4,000-acre island town located 15 minutes from Charleston with its own businesses, shops, schools, and neighborhoods. Daniel Island isn't on the ocean, but it is bordered by the Wando and Cooper rivers and Charleston Harbor. Homesites start around $200,000 and go up to $900,000. Residences range from around $200,000 for a downtown condo, townhomes start in the $300,000s, and homes range from $400,000 to more than $5 million. Check out www.danielisland.com or 800-958-5635.

How Do I Pursue Lifelong Learning?

The College of Charleston, the Military College of South Carolina (the Citadel), the Medical University of South Carolina, and Charleston Southern University are all located in Charleston.

Strengths

Beach river living with a charming nearby city is a strong pull. The cost of living is reasonable (unless you want a house on or near the ocean, which of course many people do!).

Weaknesses

Summers are hot and humid, and you'll need to like a city steeped in Southern tradition!

FYI

Check out these sources for additional information: Metro Charleston Chamber of Commerce (www.charlestonchamber.net), the *Post and Courier* (843-577-7111), and the *Charleston Regional Business Journal* (www.charlestonbusiness.com or 843-849-3100).

The Family Circle Cup, the longest-running tennis tournament for women, has its home on Daniel Island.

Hilton Head Island

REPORT CARD

Overall rating:	B+
Climate:	B+
Cost of living:	C
Health care:	A-
Transportation:	B+
What's to do:	A

This beautiful, foot-shaped barrier island is located off the Atlantic coast of South Carolina and is wildly popular with permanent residents and visitors alike. Hilton Head Island is located 90 miles south of Charleston and 45 miles north of Savannah, Georgia.

An English sea captain named William Hilton gave the island its name in 1663. The development of the island began 50 years ago by Charles Frazier, an ardent environmentalist, and most folks believe he would be amazed and delighted to see Hilton Head today. The blue heron, dwarf deer, and alligators coexist with the human urban environment as a result of very careful planning by city officials. Keep your binoculars handy; there are more than 250 species of birds on the island.

This 12-mile-long barrier island with its semitropical climate has much to offer in the way of sun and sand. The island is connected by an intricate system of bike paths, and when a traffic jam is reported, it could be made up of bikers! Bicyclists are found on the beach when the tide is low, and there are never tie-ups on the hard-packed, extra-wide beaches of Hilton Head Island. Other outdoor activities include tennis, boating, fishing, crabbing, and did we mention golf? There are more than 20 golf courses on the island, most of which are public, and dozens more in proximity to the island.

The history, ecology, and art of the low country can be explored in many museums located throughout the island. US Airways Express flies directly onto the island from Charlotte, and the Savannah-Hilton Head Island International Airport is 45 minutes away and is serviced by many of the major airlines.

Who Lives on Hilton Head Island?

The population of Hilton Head Island is about 39,000 year-round residents and more than 150,000 summer residents. About 82 percent of the population is Cauca-

What's It Like Outside?	Jan.	Apr.	Jul.	Oct.	Rain (in.)	Snow (in.)
Average high (°F)	59	79	89	78	47	0
Average low (°F)	40	56	74	58	–	–

sian, 9 percent are Hispanic, and 9 percent are African-American. The median age of residents is 46, and it's an educated population—about 80 percent have a college degree. Visitors number more than 2.5 million each year.

Hilton Head Island is in Beaufort County; the Beaufort area population has increased a hefty 13 percent in the past 5 years.

What's the Cost?

The cost of living index on Hilton Head Island is 141, based on a national average of 100. The median price of a home is $431,400 (the U.S. median is $217,900).

What's to Do?

Let's start with the obvious: the beach! The water temperature is warm from April to September and almost bathlike in July. At low tide, this exceptional beach is up to 600 feet wide and hard-packed enough to ride a bike or play soccer, baseball, or football on. Low tide brings waves gentle enough for a toddler to enjoy.

Residents and tourists alike spend time whale watching, crabbing, kayaking, parasailing, or choosing their favorite yacht (to dream about) at Harbor Town. Hilton Head Island is a top tennis destination, with 300 courts and more than 20 tennis clubs. Golf is king, and a big event is the Verizon Heritage PGA Golf Tournament at the Harbor Town Links in Sea Pines, and there are dozens of golf courses in and around the Island. Hungry or have an urge to shop? Enjoy the 200 restaurants and bistros or patronize the 100 or so boutiques and stores throughout Hilton Head Island. Located in the heart of the island is the Arts Center of Coastal Carolina, the centerpiece for visual and performing arts. The center includes a 350-seat center-stage auditorium and a permanent art gallery. The Hilton Head Island Orchestra, Choral Society, Dance Theater, and the Barbershoppers provide musical entertainment year round. The Coastal Discovery Museum offers exhibits, classes, tours, and cruises to help visitors understand the history and ecology of the island. The Hilton Head Art League supports the visual arts and maintains a gallery that showcases the work of its member artists.

Where Are the Jobs?

The big industries on the island are tourism and real estate. The Beaufort County School District, medical

---

The Prince of Tides by Pat Conroy was set in the Colleton River marshlands of this area. Conroy lives on nearby Fripp Island.

centers, and Hargray Communications also employ a sizable number of people. Beaufort County's 2006 unemployment rate of 4.6 percent was the lowest in South Carolina.

Where Are the Doctors?

Hilton Head Medical Center and Clinics, a privately owned acute-care hospital, serves the island, along with a number of urgent-care centers and medical centers. Beaufort Memorial Hospital, 40 miles away, has more than 150 board-certified specialists. It's the largest medical facility between Savannah and Charleston, and it's one of the few hospitals in the country with its own boat dock! Islanders also utilize the Memorial Health Medical Center in Savannah, Georgia, which is less than an hour away. The Volunteers in Medicine uses retired nurses, physicians, and dentists to run a free health clinic for those without access to health care.

Where Are Some Notable Neighborhoods?

The island was originally developed with the concept of gated golf communities within the confines of 11 "plantations." These plantations are named after the southern farms that once occupied them; rice, cotton, and indigo have been replaced with expensive homes, bike paths, restaurants, and full-time residents. Sea Pines was the first plantation to be developed on Hilton Head Island and has the longest stretch of beach of any of the 11 plantations. Finding a place to live on any of these plantations is rewarding but challenging. There are many options for the prospective buyer: some new construction, some teardowns, resale lots, homes, and condos. Off the island, in Bluffton, lots of new construction is springing up. If you can live with a 30-minute drive to the beach, you should take a look at the many off-island communities this area has to offer. We'll take a look at some on- and off-island possibilities.

On the Island

Long Cove is a residential area that does not allow short-term rentals. Of the 569 homesites on 600 acres, around 400 are complete and occupied. All available lots are resales at this time. The number-one ranked golf course in South Carolina is within this private, gated community, and membership is automatic for all property owners and includes use of the tennis courts, deep-water docks, pool, and clubhouse. You'll find lots priced from the $300,000s and resale homes priced from $700,000.

Sea Pines Plantation covers 5,200 acres on the south end of the island and offers 54 holes of golf, a 605-acre wildlife preserve, 5 miles of Atlantic Ocean beaches, miles of great bike paths, wonderful shopping, and fine dining. It's easy to see why new property is hard to find in Sea Pines! Resales include villas and townhomes as well as single-family residences, priced from the $200,000s to over $8 million.

Spanish Wells Plantation is a wonderful Hilton Head Island community offering a variety of housing possibilities, from expensive estates to more modest homes. Many residences have deep-water lots with private docks; lots from around $500,000 and homes from around $600,000.

Off the Island

This area is experiencing a big building boom. Prices can be lower than on the island. Here are a few examples.

Sun City Hilton Head (www.delwebb.com or 800-978-9781) is an active-adult community that's located in Bluffton, 13 miles east of Hilton Head. With two 18-hole golf courses, two fitness centers, four swimming pools, tennis courts, hiking trails, and many clubs, this Del Webb retirement location has something for everyone. About 6,000 homes of a planned 8,500 to 9,000 total homes are completed on 5,600 acres. Homes begin under $200,000.

Heritage at New Riverside (www.heritageatnewriverside.com or 843-338-3688) is a 900-home community located in Bluffton with walking paths, dog park, butterfly gardens, clubhouse, and aquatic center. Home prices begin around $200,000.

Hampton Pointe at New River (www.hamptonpointe

sc.com or 866-375-8655) is located 20 minutes outside of Hilton Head Island in Hardeeville, South Carolina. This Toll Brothers country-club community offers homes beginning in the $300,000s, and lots beginning in the $100,000s.

Looking for something different? Check out Palmetto Bluff (www.palmetto-bluf.com or 866-316-5262), a 20,000-acre community in Bluffton with very low density; a total of only 2,800 homes are planned. Three rivers with more than 30 miles of frontage surround Palmetto Bluff. Neighborhoods consist of "compounds" with up to 30 acres, estate homesites from 1 to 8 acres, and village homes with in a variety of sizes and designs, with lots as small as one-quarter acre. Located 15 miles from Hilton Head Island and 20 miles from Savannah, homesite prices start around $300,000. The nature preserves, golf course, inn, spa, and quaint village center make this community a visual treat.

 Carol W. chose Del Webb's Sun City Hilton Head. Here's why.

In May 2001, my husband of 32 years and I flew from our home in Cincinnati to Hilton Head Island, South Carolina, to attend the wedding of our youngest son, who had recently graduated from college. Our son's new in-laws were living in

Sun City Hilton Head, and the wedding took place at Sun City's Riverbend, a lovely neighborhood within this active-adult community. Riverbend is situated on the banks of a beautiful marsh. The guests sat on lawn chairs under a cloudless sky with the heady aroma of gardenias filling the air, and massive live oaks draped with Spanish moss towered overhead.

My husband and I stayed several days at Sun City after the wedding and dreamed about the possibility of retiring in this paradise. Just days after the newlyweds returned from their honeymoon, my husband suffered a massive heart attack and died instantly; my life was turned upside down. All I could think of was to leave our home of 20 years filled with memories derived from raising our family in Cincinnati. I wanted to start over where the constant reminders could be left behind and remain wonderful memories.

Our children live all over the United States, from Massachusetts to Arizona, and from Minnesota to South Carolina. We lived in many states during my husband's career as an aerospace electrical engineer. I loved living in New Orleans, Fort Walton Beach, and Cape Canaveral. I enjoy the ocean and decided I wanted to be near at least one

of our children. I chose to move to South Carolina and fulfill the dream my husband and I had of moving to Sun City Hilton Head.

What a delightful choice—the beach, the wonderful amenities of Sun City, the glorious climate, and a place where all of my family members and friends want to visit! It is truly paradise. My transition from being married, raising six children, enjoying a 40-year career and suddenly being alone was not easy. I had to start my life all over again, all by myself, but I am surrounded by wonderful friends and family who have made it possible for me to fulfill this dream.

I have no regrets about moving from Cincinnati; I don't miss the snow and ice or the hustle and bustle of a large metropolitan area. Savannah is 20 minutes away from Sun City Hilton Head, Charleston is an hour and a half, the beach is 15 minutes, and the airport is 45 minutes away. What more could you ask for? ⓛ

How Do I Pursue Lifelong Learning?
Hilton Head Island has its peer-organized/taught Lifelong Learning of Hilton Head Island, Inc. with low membership fees ($25) and tuition ($30 to $50 for unlimited classes).

The University of South Carolina Beaufort has a south campus located in Bluffton. Its campus in Beaufort also offers the Osher Lifelong Learning Institute, where volunteers teach classes and the more than 800 members can take a variety of unlimited classes for a $25 annual membership fee and reasonable registration fees. They are also associated with the TraveLearn Network, affording the opportunity to combine travel with learning.

Strengths

This island has the feel of a huge family resort. The two and a half million tourists who visit yearly are mostly families, and they contribute to the energy of the town. The beach is like no other if you like to play on the sand and not just recline with a good book. The beauty of the moss-covered live oaks, the many lagoons (some with alligators and some without), and the exquisite birds and other wildlife make Hilton Head Island a special place. If you are looking for a four-season climate with a short, mild winter, Hilton Head Island might be it!

Weaknesses

The island itself is a bit remote, and the traffic generated by the tourists is a thorn in the side of the full-timers. Many of the homes are rental properties, and the price of buying a home or villa makes this community unrealistic for many. The summers are hot and humid, and several major hurricanes have hit South Carolina.

FYI

Check out these sources for additional information: the Hilton Head Island/Bluffton Chamber of Commerce (www.hiltonheadisland.org or 800-523-3373) and the *Island Packet* (www.islandpacket.com or 843-706-8100).

TENNESSEE

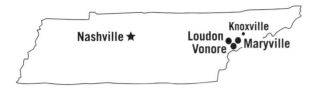

Capital: Nashville

Nickname: Volunteer State

Motto: "Agriculture and commerce"

Flower: Iris

Bird: Mockingbird

Population: 5,960,000

Fascinating Fact: Tennessee is bordered by eight states.

Greater Knoxville Area

REPORT CARD

Overall rating:	B+
Climate:	B+
Cost of living:	A
Health care:	A-
Transportation:	B+
What's to do:	B+

If you don't live there or aren't into Elvis, country, or bluegrass music, Tennessee seems to be one of those states you never read or hear much about. Maybe it's because there are only three large cities in the state—Memphis, Nashville, and Knoxville. If you're considering relocating, though, you may want to change that thinking pattern.

The eastern section of Tennessee nestles in the foothills of the Great Smoky Mountains, close to Knoxville and the University of Tennessee. This area basks in the beauty of the Appalachians, is a haven for outdoor enthu-

---

Maryville is on a number of "best of" lists. It placed among the top dozen recommended places in *Money* magazine. The A&E (Arts & Entertainment) channel named Maryville one of the "Top Ten Cities to Have it All," and the National Strategy Group called it one of "America's Select Cities."

siasts, enjoys a four-season climate with fairly mild winters, and has the additional lure of Great Smoky Mountains National Park, Gatlinburg, and Dollywood. Snow tends to melt quickly because of the milder temperatures. McGhee Tyson Airport is a dozen miles south of Knoxville, is serviced by seven airlines, and has more than 120 daily departures and arrivals. Depending on the source(s) of your retirement income, the Volunteer State may rank in the upper echelons of states offering the best financial deals.

Who Lives in Eastern Tennessee?

The Knoxville area contains a number of smaller towns you may want to consider for retirement, including Vonore (1,200 residents in fewer than 9 square miles), Loudon (4,500 residents in 9 square miles), LaFollette (8,000 people in a little less than 5 square miles), Lenoir City (7,300 people in a little more than 6 square miles), Maryville (population of 23,000 in 13 square miles), and Oak Ridge (about 27,000 residents in 86 square miles), and Knoxville itself has a population of about 175,000 in 93 square miles.

What's the Cost?

Knoxville ranks an attractive 88 (based on a national average of 100) on the 2006 ACCRA Cost of Living Index. In addition, the Tax Foundation (www.tax foundation.org) analyzes states by tax burden, and Tennessee comes out smelling like a rose (or should we say an iris, the state flower?). In 2006, it had the fourth-lowest tax burden, considering only state taxes, compared to the other 49 states. Tennessee is often touted as a retiree-friendly state and, depending on where your income comes from, the facts may support that contention. In 2005, the average price of a home in Knoxville was $185,000, well below the national average. Sweet!

What's to Do?

Think outside: boating, fishing, hiking, enjoying wildlife, tennis, year-round golf, swimming, Great Smoky Mountains National Park (with its whitewater rafting, camping, and horseback riding), Ober Gatlinburg Ski Resort and Amusement Park . . . your imagination is your only limit.

Oak Ridge is also known as the "Secret City." During WWII, it was one of the sites for the Manhattan Project.

The University of Tennessee provides cultural opportunities, and Knoxville itself offers shopping, dining, museums, historic sites, theater, ballet, and opera.

Where Are the Jobs?

There are a number of large employers in the Knoxville area, and the area enjoys a stable economy due to its diverse employment base. Health care (Covenant, University of Tennessee Health System, and St. Mary's Health System) is a biggie, as well as the University of Tennessee, the U.S. Department of Energy, Wal-Mart, and the Knox County School System. Unemployment for the Knoxville metropolitan statistical area (May 2006) is a comfortable 3.3 percent.

Where Are the Doctors?

There are several good health-care options, including the University of Tennessee Medical Center (a teaching hospital with more than 600 beds), Blount Memorial Hospital (330 beds), Baptist Hospital, Fort Sanders Medical Clinics, and St. Mary's Health System.

Where Are Some Notable Neighborhoods?

The 16,000-acre Tellico Lake (although its shape reminds one more of a river than a lake) was created by the completion of the Tellico Dam by the Tennessee Valley Authority and is located about 30 miles southwest of Knoxville and close to the cities of Maryville and Lenoir City. Three neighborhoods of note are located on Tellico Lake.

Tellico Village (www.tellico-village.com or 800-Tellico) has been around since 1986, encompasses about 4,600 acres, and presently has about 3,000 homes and townhomes. Homes can be found from the $250,000s, with those on the lake commanding $700,000 or more; interior lots start around $35,000, golf-course lots are in the $100,00s, and lakefront lots average around $450,000. All properties are within a mile of Tellico Lake. Amenities include three golf courses, tennis courts, three clubhouses, a marina, fitness center, shopping centers, hiking trails, and two swimming pools. Tellico Village is located in the city of Loudon.

What's It Like Outside?	Jan.	Apr.	Jul.	Oct.	Rain (in.)	Snow (in.)
Average high (°F)	45	70	87	70	48	12
Average low (°F)	26	44	66	46	–	–

Rarity Bay (www.raritybay.com or 800-287-0032), also in Loudon, encompasses 960 acres and is the newer of these three developments on Tellico Lake. There is an equestrian center located just inside the entrance of this lovely community, beyond which is the gatehouse. There will be approximately 1,600 residences when the community is completed. Villas, homes, and condos are available, with prices starting below $300,000 for the condos and lots under $150,000. Private and community docks, golf, a clubhouse, dining, swimming, tennis, and hiking trails will help keep you entertained.

Rarity Pointe (www.raritypointe.com or 800-287-0032) is a 1,000-acre peninsula community on Tellico Lake with 1,000 residences planned. Located between Lenoir City and Maryville, and 10 miles southwest of Knoxville, this developing neighborhood will have a golf course, lodge, yacht club, spa, and walking trails. Homesites, custom homes, condos, and villas are available. Fairway homesites begin in the $300,000s, and waterview homes start in the $400,000s.

In addition to Rarity Bay and Rarity Pointe, Rarity Communities offers several other communities in eastern Tennessee and plans to develop at least a dozen more over the next decade. The communities are designed so that there is something for virtually everyone's budget. The community with the lowest price point is Rarity Ridge (www.rarityridge.com or 888-587-4343). Located in Oak Ridge, a notable technology center, it's 20 minutes from Knoxville and a half hour from the airport and from the Great Smoky Mountains National Park. This 1,500-acre new urbanism community, on the Clinch River, offers a variety of homes beginning around $200,000 as well as a community marina, tennis and volleyball courts, swimming pool, a health club, and a town center. Rarity Ridge will have 4,000 residences in total, and it is a relative bargain.

Rarity Mountain, Rarity Meadows, Rarity Club, and Rarity Oaks are additional Rarity Communities under development. Check the Rarity Community Web site (www.raritycommunities.com) to access all their developments.

The Villages at Norris Lake (www.villagesatnorrislake.com or 866-956-5263) is a secluded community built by Land Resource Companies. This 615-acre community is a mixture of full- and part-time residents,

Great Smoky Mountains National Park is the most visited national park in the country.

situated 10 miles from the town of LaFollette and 30 miles north of Knoxville. This is really a place to get away from it all. Planned amenities include a waterfront park, a 600-slip marina, clubhouse, swimming, tennis, RV and boat storage, and nature trails. Norris Lake is a gorgeous 34,000-acre lake with 800 miles of shoreline. A total of 585 homes are planned, and there is no time frame in which you have to build. Homesites begin in the $50,000s.

Finally, although it's a bit of a cheat to include in the greater Knoxville area (it's 75 miles west of Knoxville), we'd feel remiss if we didn't mention Fairfield Glade, a community that is a virtual city—it has its own zip code—as well as a resort. With a long list of amenities including five golf courses, 12 tennis courts, 11 lakes, two marinas, and a health and wellness center (that's just a start), the community also has nine churches on its property as well as a shopping center, library, its own fire department, paramedic team, and ambulance, and more than 50 clubs and organizations for you to join. Located on more than 12,000 acres on the Cumberland Plateau with more than 6,000 residents (not including timeshare owners), this is a self-contained community. Homes can be purchased for under $200,000, and lots begin around $10,000. Contact Fairfield Glade at www.fairfieldglade.net or 800-383-7600.

How Do I Pursue Lifelong Learning?

Several options for lifelong learning in eastern Tennessee include the University of Tennessee in Knoxville with its 29,000 students; Maryville College, a private liberal arts college in Maryville, with about 1,150 students; and Pellississippi State Technical Community College, which serves about 7,000 students in Knoxville. All are places to get an intellectual lift.

Strengths

Financially, including taxwise, Tennessee is a bargain relative to many other locations (of course, as we always caution, you have to see how the tax structure affects *your* particular circumstances). The state has tremendous natural beauty and provides lots of opportunities for people who love the great outdoors.

In 2006, *Forbes* ranked Knoxville number five for "Best Places for Business and Careers," and Salary.com rated it third in the United States for affordability.

Weaknesses

If you have to be near the ocean to be happy, keep in mind it's about a 7-hour drive to get to the Atlantic and 9 hours to the Gulf of Mexico. Although there is a lot of development going on in eastern Tennessee, some of the towns where these new communities are located are small and may lack some of the amenities that people from larger cities are accustomed to having.

FYI

Check out these sources for additional information: Knoxville Chamber of Commerce (www.knoxville.org or 800-727-8045) and the *Knoxville News Sentinel* (www.knoxnews.com or 865-523-3131).

TEXAS

Capital: Austin

Nickname: The Lonestar State

Motto: "Friendship"

Flower: Bluebonnet

Bird: Mockingbird

Population: 22,000,000

Fascinating Fact: Texas has 90 mountains that are at least a mile high.

Texas Hill Country

REPORT CARD

Overall rating:	B+
Climate:	B+
Cost of living:	A
Health care:	B+
Transportation:	B+
What's to do:	B+

Texas Hill Country is the name given to the 14,000 square miles in the middle of the country's second-largest state. This area of Texas is named for its rolling, relatively rugged hills. Juniper, cypress, and oak trees, a riot of spring wildflowers (the state flower is the bluebonnet), valleys, bountiful wildlife, caves carved out of limestone, and numerous lakes, streams, and rivers pepper the landscape. The scenic beauty of this area and the agreeable weather (compliments of a higher elevation) also contribute to its uniqueness. When you add in vineyards, shopping, the opportunity for intellectual pursuits, accessible airports in San Antonio and Austin, and an abundance of outdoor activities, you may find the perfect retirement spot among the 50 or so cities and towns that are part of Texas Hill Country. Everything really may be better with bluebonnets on it!

Who Lives in Texas Hill Country?

A few towns to consider in this area of Texas are New Braunfels (including the charming village of Gruene—pronounced "green"), Kerrville, and Fredericksburg. New Braunfels is close to San Antonio (about 35 minutes away), Kerrville is about an hour to San Antonio and 2 hours to Austin, and Fredericksburg is about a 1½ hour drive to San Antonio or Austin.

New Braunfels has a population of about 45,000, with the majority of the population either white (63 percent) or Hispanic (35 percent). Kerrville has approximately 22,000 residents, with around 73 percent white and 23 percent Hispanic. Fredericksburg is the smallest town, with its 11,000 residents mainly white (82 percent) or Hispanic (17 percent).

New Braunfels has the youngest residents (median age 36 years), while the median age in Kerrville is 45 and in Fredericksburg it's 47. The predominant ancestry in all three places is German. Much of the population growth in Texas Hill Country is due to an influx of retirees, according to demographic research by Steve Murdoch of the University of Texas.

What's the Cost?

Based on a national cost of living index average pegged at 100, Kerrville's cost of living index is 95; New Braunfels and Fredericksburg are also below the national average. San Antonio's median home cost is $180,000 and Austin's is $230,000.

The state's name originates from the Hasinai Indian word *tejas*, which means friends or allies.

What's to Do?

This area of Texas has a lot going for it. The town of New Braunfels has the village of Gruene within its city limits—about the cutest place you've ever seen. Visit Gruene Hall and listen to some real Texas music in the oldest dance hall in Texas, stroll through the pedestrian-friendly town with shops named Gruene with Envy and Tavern in the Gruene (remember, it's pronounced "green"), and stay a night in the Gruene Apple B and B (one of the authors stayed in the "Shady Lady" room). The fact that there are 25 river outfitters located in or close to New Braunfels reflects the importance of the Guadalupe River and other rivers and lakes in Hill Country. Tubing, rafting, fishing, canoeing—all things water-related are available. Visit the Natural Bridge Caverns, the Museum of Texas Handmade Furniture, or the McKenna Children's Museum (great place when the grandkids visit). As they say, "In New Braunfels, *ist das leben schoen*!" (In New Braunfels, the living is good!)

Kerrville has an active arts and cultural scene, offering the Museum of Western Art, the Hill Country Museum, the Kerr Arts and Cultural Center, Point Theater, Playhouse 2000, Symphony, and Performing Arts Society. Fairs and festivals, tennis, parks, hunting, and water activities help round out the things to do. It's also a college town, with Schreiner University, a liberal-arts college, located here.

Known as the "city of steeples" for its large number of religious buildings, Fredericksburg also offers wineries, art galleries, museums, golf courses, parks, theater (including a children's theater), and tons of opportunities for an active outdoor life. Or stroll through the quaint downtown district and enjoy the historic homes while you shop (and take a break at the Rather Sweet Bakery and Café with a Big Hair lemon tart).

Of course, if you're looking for big-city life, you can visit San Antonio with its River Walk and the Alamo (it's the most visited city in the state) and Austin, the "live music capital of the world"—visit the pink-granite statehouse and marvel at the 1.5 million Congress Avenue bats. And as a feast for your senses, follow the self-guided Wine and Wildflower Trail (www.texaswinetrail.

What's It Like Outside?	Jan.	Apr.	Jul.	Oct.	Rain (in.)	Snow (in.)
Average high (°F)	58	77	92	78	32	Trace
Average low (°F)	32	52	69	53	–	–

* These averages are for Kerrville, Texas, but New Braunfels and Fredericksburg vary by only a few degrees either way.

com) and indulge in the famous Texas Hill Country peaches.

Where Are the Jobs?

Unemployment in the Central Texas area is 4 percent. The major employers in the Austin area include the state government (Austin is the capital, after all!), health care, school system, Dell, IBM, and Motorola. Large San Antonio employers include the South Texas Medical Center, federal government (due to the several military bases), communications, the United Service Automobile Association (financial services), and tourism.

Where Are the Doctors?

There are a number of options, from smaller (the Hill Country Memorial Hospital serves Fredericksburg and the surrounding area, McKenna Memorial Hospital in New Braunfels, and Sid Peterson Memorial Hospital in Kerrville) to the larger medical facilities of North Austin Medical Center, Seton Healthcare Network, and the University Health System. No matter what your concern, there's a doctor or medical facility to meet your needs.

Where Are Some Notable Neighborhoods?

If you're looking for large, master-planned communities in Texas Hill Country, consider Cordillera Ranch (www.cordilleraranch.com or 888-667-2624) in the small town of Boerne (fewer than 6 square miles, and around 8,000 residents). Cordillera Ranch is 25 miles northwest of San Antonio and 30 miles southeast from Kerrville, and offers 1- to 10-acre lots on 8,600 gorgeous acres. The average density is targeted at 4.8 acres per lot, with more than 300 acres of open space and parks and over 7 miles of trails. Amenities include golf, tennis, a spa, a social club including formal and casual dining, a pool, a 35,000-square-foot clubhouse, and homesites begin around $125,000.

Comanche Trace (www.comanchetrace.com or 877-467-6282) has garnered praise from *Where to Retire Magazine* (cited as one of "America's Best 100 Master-Planned Communities") and *Golfweek, Golf Digest*, and *Travel and Leisure Golf* for its (surprise!) golf. With more than 1,100 acres, 900 planned residences, and about an hour's drive from San Antonio, there are homes and homesites for all budget levels. Housing styles include

---

Money magazine ranked Boerne number three in fastest job growth and number 48 in their list of top 100 "Places to Live 2005."

casitas, golf villas, cottages, garden homes, and large single-family homes. Lots begin under $100,000, and homes start in the high $200,000s. In addition to 27 holes of golf, you can also enjoy swimming, tennis, casual and fine dining, and fitness programs. Construction in Comanche Trace will continue until 2011.

If it's active-adult living you're looking for, check out a new (opened in 2006) Del Webb community, Hill Country Retreat, a 2,000-home community in San Antonio located within the master-planned community of Alamo Ranch. Contact Del Webb at www.delwebb. com or 877-933-5932 for more information.

Many existing homes in the communities of Kerrville, Fredericksburg, and New Braunfels can be found for less than $200,000.

How Do I Pursue Lifelong Learning?

You'll be able to quench your thirst for knowledge in a variety of settings. A short list includes the University of Texas (at San Antonio and Austin), St. Mary's University, Trinity University, Texas Culinary Academy, Austin Community College (Fredericksburg), Alamo Community College (New Braunfels), and Schreiner University (Kerrville). A large number of community, 4-year, and technical colleges throughout the area will make lifelong learning an easy goal to accomplish.

Strengths

The Texas Hill Country offers a reasonable cost of living, scenic beauty, and lower humidity and temperatures than other parts of Texas. Enjoy a friendly, small-town atmosphere in New Braunfels, Kerrville, and Fredericksburg while benefiting from the closeness and amenities of Austin and San Antonio, along with their airports.

Weaknesses

With all the pollen from the pine and oak trees, people often report new allergies. And no big surprise—you're a hike from the ocean. The beautiful Padre Island National Seashore is about a 3-hour drive from New Braunfels.

FYI

Check out these sources for additional information: Kerrville Chamber of Commerce (www.kerrvilletx.com or 830-896-1175), New Braunfels Chamber of Commerce (www.nbcham.org or 800-572-2626), the town of Gruene (www.gruenetexas.com or 830-629-5077), the Fredericksburg Chamber of Commerce (www. fredericksburg-texas.com or 888-997-3600), the *Fredericksburg Standard* (www.fredericksburgstandard.com or 830-997-2155), the *Kerrville Daily Times* (www.daily times.com or 830-896-7000), or New Braunfel's *Herald-Zeitung* (www.herald-zeitung.com or 830-625-9144).

VIRGINIA

Capital: Richmond

Nickname: Old Dominion State

Motto: "Thus always to tyrants"

Flower: Dogwood

Bird: Cardinal

Population: 7,600,000

Fascinating Fact: Eight presidents were born in Virginia, and seven are buried there.

Charlottesville and Williamsburg

REPORT CARD

Overall rating:	B+
Climate:	B
Cost of living:	B
Health care:	A-
Transportation:	A-
What's to do:	A-

"Virginia is for lovers." This has been this state's advertising slogan since 1969, but is Virginia for retirement as well? We think so.

Situated halfway between New York and Miami, Virginia boasts good highways, about a dozen commercial airports, and is close to 60 private aviation airports as well as railway and ferry service. Its location, according to Virginia's Visitor Information Center, enables you to drive to any city east of the Mississippi in less than a day. Beaches, mountains, parks, gardens, skiing, colleges, factory outlets, theme parks, museums, battlefields, historic buildings—Virginia is a smorgasbord of things to do and see.

Money magazine listed Williamsburg on its 2006 list of "Best Places to Retire," and Charlottesville has been cited on "best" lists by *Money* and *Kiplinger's Personal Finance.*

We especially like two places in Virginia: Charlottesville and Williamsburg. Let's take a look at these two locations and see if you too think that "Virginia is for retirement."

Charlottesville, centrally located in Virginia on the Rivanna River, is situated at the foothills of the Blue Ridge Mountains, about 100 miles southeast of the nation's capital. Its residents enjoy four distinct seasons, numerous parks, a low unemployment rate, and the prestigious (not to mention beautiful) University of Virginia. The area is noted for its horses, fox hunting, and fruit orchards. Old estates and the rolling countryside are visual feasts. The Charlottesville-Albemarle Airport provides nonstop service, mainly to cities on the east coast.

Steeped in history, Williamsburg is the colonial capital of Virginia. You can be at the beach or skiing within an hour, take classes at the College of William and Mary, or go to Norfolk, 35 miles away. Shopping in Williamsburg is legendary. There are outlets galore, craft and pottery shops, and boutiques, and even though there are about 700,000 yearly visitors to Colonial Williamsburg, you'll enjoy small-town living (on fewer than 9 square miles) in this scenic area. Newport News/Williamsburg Airport, Norfolk International Airport, and Richmond International Airport service the area.

Who Lives in Charlottesville and Williamsburg?

Of the approximately 55,000 residents of Charlottesville, about half are between the ages of 20 and 45, with a median age of 26 years. About 70 percent of the population is Caucasian, 22 percent African-American, and 3 percent Hispanic. About 40 percent of the residents have at least a bachelor's degree.

Williamsburg has about 11,000 residents, with an average age of 36. About a fourth of the population is older than 45. Caucasians represent about 80 percent of the population, African-Americans about 13 percent, and Hispanics approximately 3 percent. Almost three-quarters of Williamsburg's residents have completed at least some college.

What's the Cost?

In Charlottesville, the median household income is $44,000; in Williamsburg, it's $42,000. Unemployment in Williamsburg is about 6 percent. The median price of an existing home is about $390,000. For Charlottesville, unemployment is a low 2 percent, and the median cost of a home is $280,000. Both Charlottesville and Williamsburg have overall costs of living that are higher than the national average (137 for Williamsburg, and only slightly higher—102—for Charlottesville).

What's to Do?

There is a full menu of activities to choose from in either town (good use of the word *menu*—Williamsburg has 500 restaurants within a 15-mile radius). Both offer art, culture, and history. Charlottesville offers Monticello, James Monroe's home, the pedestrian-friendly Downtown Mall, concerts, museums, wineries, diverse dining, and the University of Virginia. Williamsburg offers the colonial experience, Busch Gardens and Water Country USA, the nearby Jamestown Settlement, historic plantations, Yorktown, shopping, and the College of William and Mary.

Of course, outdoor activities such as golf, rafting, fishing, hiking, tennis, biking, and canoeing are available in both Charlottesville and Williamsburg. Wintergreen—an all-seasons resort with skiing, golf, nature hikes, rock climbing, and a spa—is only about 30 miles from Charlottesville and 150 miles from Williamsburg.

Where Are the Jobs?

Not surprisingly, the largest employers in Charlottesville are involved with the University of Virginia. The public-school system in Charlottesville, the health-care system, State Farm Mutual Insurance, and Northrop Grumman are also large employers. In Williamsburg, the Colonial Williamsburg Foundation, Colonial Williamsburg, the College of William and Mary, and Anheuser Busch, which operates Busch Gardens and Water Country USA, are the large employers. The Anheuser Busch Adventure Parks Web site specifically solicits older workers (www.becjobs.com).

Where Are the Doctors?

Charlottesville is home to the premiere University of Virginia Health Sciences Center and the Martha Jefferson Hospital, in addition to several clinics. Williamsburg has Sentara Williamsburg Community Hospital and Eastern State Hospital (which emphasizes mental-

What's It Like Outside?*	Jan.	Apr.	Jul.	Oct.	Rain (in.)	Snow (in.)
Average high (°F)	45	69	88	70	47	23
Average low (°F)	26	45	66	47	–	–

*This is for Charlottesville.

health care), urgent-care facilities, and Williamsburg and Norge medical centers.

Where Are Some Notable Neighborhoods in Charlottesville?

Four Season Charlottesville (www.khov.com or 866-568-4553) is an active-adult community close to the city of Charlottesville and about a dozen miles from scenic Skyline Drive, 2 hours to DC, an hour to Richmond, and 1½ hours to Dulles airport. Single-family homes in the $300,000s are available, and amenities include a clubhouse with tennis courts, fitness center, indoor/outdoor pool, and ballroom.

Glenmore (www.glenmore.com or 800-776-5111) is 8 miles east of Charlottesville in Keswick. This gated community of more than 1,000 acres provides country-club living as well as an equestrian center. Homesites begin in the $200,000s, and residences range from the $400,000s to a few million.

There are also many lovely, older homes in the area.

Contact the chamber of commerce (www.cville chamber.org or 434-295-3141) to get a recommendation of a Realtor.

Where Are Some Notable Neighborhoods in Williamsburg?

Colonial Heritage (www.colonialheritageva.com or 866-456-1776) is Williamsburg's only gated, active-adult community. This 700-acre neighborhood, with home prices beginning in the $300,000s, has a golf course, athletic club, tennis, hiking trails, and clubhouse.

Ford's Colony (www.fordscolony.com or 800-334-6033), a gated community stretching over almost 3,000 acres, has been around for approximately 25 years but is still developing. With a planned total of 2,400 homes, you can find a home or homesite in this beautiful award-winning enclave of three golf courses and five-star dining. Homesites begin in the $100,000s, and homes—courtyard, patio, villas, townhomes, and single-family homes—begin in the $300,000s and escalate to

What's It Like Outside?*	Jan.	Apr.	Jul.	Oct.	Rain (in.)	Snow (in.)
Average high (°F)	51	68	90	68	39	10
Average low (°F)	34	48	82	60	–	–

*This is for Williamburg.

a few million. About one-third of the residents are retired, with the other two-thirds semiretired or still working.

(true LIFE) How Jennie and Bob C. decided on Ford's Colony in Williamsburg as their retirement location.

Having relocated a number of times during Bob's career, Jennie and Bob didn't feel there was any one logical place to retire. They discussed desires and options and agreed on a few things: It made sense to have only one home in order to more easily establish a local social network and avoid issues relating to absentee ownership. And since they were going to build their dream home, they wanted to be in it full-time! Jennie loves the beach and Bob loves golf, but neither relished the thought of having sand in virtually everything they own. Having a change of seasons was also important, as was avoiding the extreme temperatures of the far north or south.

With all that in mind, they decided to seek an area that gave them that nebulous but important "right feel" but "would not be in the middle of other people's vacations."

As a result, Bob and Jennie narrowed their search to North Carolina and Virginia and found Ford's Colony in Williamsburg. The area appealed to them for a number of reasons: It isn't a large population center, so it fit their size requirements; it has a terrific local college (William and Mary); it is a magnet for tourists, which has the benefit of supporting a good selection of restaurants and a number of excellent golf courses (the traffic that tourists bring can be avoided by local residents); it enjoys a strong sense of community spirit; the Richmond airport is less than an hour away; and Bob and Jennie found the residents of Williamsburg open, accepting, and welcoming.

By discussing what they wanted in their ideal location, Jennie and Bob were able to shape what their retirement location should look like and geographically shrink the potential places down to a manageable search.

How long did their search take? It lasted a little over a year, but Bob and Jennie started the process almost a decade in advance of Bob's expected retirement so that they wouldn't feel any pressure to make a decision before they knew they had found what they were looking for. (tL)

How Do I Pursue Lifelong Learning?

Both of these towns provide ample opportunities for lifelong learning, which is one of the reasons we recommend them.

As already noted, Charlottesville is home to the University of Virginia, founded by Thomas Jefferson in 1819. A variety of noncredit courses are offered through the university's School of Continuing and Professional Studies. Piedmont Virginia Community College and the Institute of Textile Technology also have homes in Charlottesville.

Williamsburg has its own historic college, the College of William and Mary, as well as Thomas Nelson Community College and Christopher Newport University, both a little more than 20 miles away.

Strengths

If you're a history buff, either Charlottesville or Williamsburg could be a good fit. Milder winters, yet four distinct seasons, are also appealing. Add scenic, small-town living in college towns, and did we mention history? If you love the beach, Williamsburg is about an hour away from Virginia Beach. And if you love books,

Charlottesville, according to *American Profile* magazine, is credited with having "more households per capita engaging in 'avid book reading' than any other place in the United States."

Weaknesses

You'll have to travel to get to a larger airport. If you are snow averse, some white stuff does fall in both these towns, and there's more of it in Charlottesville than in Williamsburg. To get to a beach from Charlottesville, you'll need to travel more than 2 hours. The cost of living index for both places is higher than the national average, and traffic can be daunting at times.

FYI

Check out these sources for additional information: Charlottesville Chamber of Commerce (www.cville chamber.org or 434-295-3141), Williamsburg Area Convention and Visitors Bureau (www.visitwilliams burg.com or 800-368-6511), the *Charlottesville Daily Progress* (www.dailyprogress.com or 434-978-7283), and the *Williamsburg Daily Press* (www.dailypress.com or 757-247-4800).

ANOTHER AREA TO CONSIDER: THE DELMARVA PENINSULA

Delaware, Maryland, Virginia—combining the names of the three states into one word, "Delmarva," is a clever way of describing the coastal part of these three mid-Atlantic states that are bounded by water. The Delaware River, Delaware Bay, Chesapeake Bay, and Atlantic Ocean surround the peninsula; actually, it's technically an island, since this piece of land stretching about 180 miles long and 60 miles wide can be accessed only via travel over or on water.

A favored area for people looking for a beach getaway within hours of the eastern cities of Norfolk, Richmond, Baltimore, and the DC metro area, the Delmarva Peninsula is booming with new development for both full- and part-timers. James Michener's *Chesapeake* and Marguerite Henry's *Misty of Chincoteague* helped popularize this region that is known for tourism and fishing.

Here are several communities that may be of interest.

Bay Creek (www.bay-creek.com or 800-501-7141) is a 1,700-acre community in Cape Charles in the southwestern corner of the Delmarva Peninsula and will have a total of approximately 2,700 residences when completed. Five miles of shoreline, a marina, Nicklaus and Palmer golf courses, a resort hotel, and a community center with a wellness facility, tennis courts, and swimming pool are either in place or being developed. Lots begin in the $40,000s and rise to more than $1 million, depending on the view. Residences consist of townhomes, duplexes, condos, and estate homes, and prices start around $200,000.

Glen Riddle (www.glenriddle.com or 866-753-2636) is located in Berlin, Maryland, less than an hour's drive from Ocean City. This gated, horse-themed community (Man O' War and War Admiral were raised on the grounds that are now Glen Riddle) has 36 holes of golf and a Ruth's Chris Steak House inside the golf clubhouse. Additional amenities include a marina with access to the Atlantic, tennis, a community clubhouse with pools and a fitness center, hiking trails, and forest preserves. Home styles include condos, townhomes, and single-family homes, with prices starting in the $400,000s. There will be a total of 650 homes on Glenn Riddle's 1,000 acres when construction is completed.

Coastal Club (www.delwebb.com or 888-755-7559) is a new Del Webb active-adult community opening in 2008 in Delaware between Lewes and Rehoboth, just 5 miles from the glittering Atlantic. With a total of 630 planned residences consisting of single-family homes and attached villas, the development will have walking paths, ponds, and streams throughout, as well as a clubhouse containing a multipurpose ballroom, arts and crafts room, fitness facility, an outdoor pool, and tennis courts. Prices have not yet been established for Coastal Club.

The Peninsula on Indian River Bay (www.peninsuladelaware.com or 866-PEN-DELA) is a stunning 775-acre enclave in Millsboro, Delaware, with a total of 1,400 homes and amenities galore—a Jack Nicklaus Signature Golf Course, community club, outdoor and indoor pools, fitness center, spa, nature center, tennis, restaurants, and even a water-taxi service to Bethany Beach. (Rehoboth Beach is a 5-minute drive.) Custom homes, townhomes, villas, and condos are available within Peninsula's nine neighborhoods, and build-out is anticipated in 2011. Starting prices for homesites are around the $400,000s. Condos also begin in the $400,000s; townhomes in the mid $500,000s; villas from about $600,000; and a custom home including lot will set you back around $1.1 million.

Bayside (www.livebayside.com or 877-436-9998) is located in Selbyville, a 15-minute drive from the beach in Fenwick Island, Delaware. This master-planned community offers amenities such as golf, tennis, a fitness center, hiking, water sports, and a beach shuttle (Memorial Day through Labor Day), and it will also have a town center with a grocery store, bank, restaurants, spa, movie theater, and boutiques. Begun in 2004, there will be more than 1,600 residences upon anticipated completion of the development in 2014. Bayside is located on more than 850 acres. Homes include condos, townhomes, duplexes, and single-family homes with almost 30 different floor plans from which to choose. Prices begin around $400,000 and escalate to $1 million or more.

WASHINGTON

Capital: Olympia
Nickname: The Evergreen State
Motto: "By and by"
Flower: Pink rhododendron
Bird: Willow goldfinch
Population: 6,300,000
Fascinating Fact: Starbucks had its beginnings in Seattle.

Bellingham

REPORT CARD

Overall rating:	B
Climate:	B
Cost of living:	A-
Health care:	B
Transportation:	B
What's to do:	A-

Bellingham is located halfway between Seattle and Vancouver on the northern edge of Puget Sound, the last city before the Canadian border and about 20 miles away from our northern neighbor. Bellingham's active waterfront includes Squalicum Harbor, the second-largest harbor in Puget Sound, home to 2,000 boats and the hub for port services. Passenger ferries leave from Bellingham ports for Victoria, British Columbia; the San Juan Islands; and Alaska. Three freshwater lakes and several streams add to the beauty of this area. *Money* magazine had this to say about Bellingham: "There are few places where you can walk out of a 20-story build-

Bellingham is listed among *Money* magazine's 2006 top cities for "cleanest air," and it was ranked second by *Forbes* on its 2006 list of "Greenest Cities."

ing, cast a line into a creek, and catch a salmon. Bellingham is one."

The historic Fairhaven district is a real draw for people looking for pubs, boutiques, and shops. Western Washington University, with its renowned outdoor sculpture collection, provides cultural events year-round, contributing to Bellingham's vibrancy. The climate is very mild, though it tends to be rainy. Majestic 10,000-foot Mount Baker and all that it has to offer is just an hour away.

A push is on to transform 140 acres along Bellingham's waterfront over the next 2 decades. Shops, homes, offices, a marina, and parks will be part of this new city community, injecting additional energy into the downtown area.

Bellingham has an average of 93 days of rain a year. But the good news is that between March and September, it rains fewer than 3 inches per month. The warmest day in July rarely exceeds 80 degrees.

Who Lives in Bellingham?

The population of Bellingham is about 73,000, with 18 percent age 55 and over. The median age is 31, and 90 percent of the residents are Caucasian, 5 percent Asian, 3 percent Native American or Alaska Native, and 2 percent African-American.

What's the Cost?

Bellingham's cost of living index is 110, based on a national average of 100. The cost of groceries is a little higher than the national average at 108, as is health care, which is 109. The cost of purchasing a home has escalated in the past few years; the median price is now around $250,000. There is no state income tax in Washington.

What's to Do?

Every Memorial Day, weekend teams of athletes assemble from around the world to participate in the 82.5-mile relay race from Mount Baker to the shore. This Ski to Sea festival puts competitors to the test in all areas of outdoor activity: cross-country and downhill skiing, running, mountain biking, canoeing, and sea kayaking. If you are more than just a "weekend warrior" athlete, you'll have the remainder of the year to enjoy these activities in Bellingham! If golf is your game, there are

---

For all you gardeners out there, the growing season in Bellingham begins in April and continues into October.

plenty of public courses, one described as "sculpted in the windswept, wide open Scottish tradition." About an hour east, in the beautiful Cascade Mountains, you will find the Mount Baker Ski Resort with its fantastic skiing, remote snowmobiling in the winter, and excellent hiking and biking in the summer.

In addition to the natural beauty of the area, Bellingham has many cultural offerings. The Whatcom Museum of History and Art, built in 1892, consists of a four-building campus that includes a children's museum. The Mount Baker Theater, a local treasure, has been in the business of producing local theater and hosting professional touring acts since 1927. The downtown is full of specialty shops, fine restaurants, coffee shops, and art galleries and has a manageable small-town feel. The Northwest Washington Fair, a tradition dating back to 1872, is an outdoor event that showcases local music and art.

Two scenic drives have their beginnings in Bellingham. For exceptional views of Samish Bay, the San Juan Islands, and the Olympic Mountains, take State Route 11 or the Chuckanut Drive. If you are in the mood for waterfalls, vineyards, and mountains, take State Route 542, the Mount Baker Scenic Highway.

Where Are the Jobs?

Bellingham's major employers include Western Washington University, St. Joseph's Hospital, and the Bellingham schools. Bellingham's unemployment rate is about 3 percent.

Where Are the Doctors?

St. Joseph's Hospital, with more than 250 beds, is a non-profit facility that provides a complete array of emergency and diagnostic services, as well as a cardiac care unit.

Where Are Some Notable Neighborhoods?

About 30 minutes north of Bellingham is the resort/golf/spa community of Semiahmoo (www.semiahmoo.com or 800-278-7488). Custom homes and condos are available; lot prices begin in the $200,000s.

What's It Like Outside?	Jan.	Apr.	Jul.	Oct.	Rain (in.)	Snow (in.)
Average high (°F)	45	55	70	55	36	7
Average low (°F)	40	40	50	40	–	–

Other homes available in Bellingham are priced from $150,000 to several million. Cost depends on the view and the location; prices soar when property is waterfront.

How Do I Pursue Lifelong Learning?

Western Washington University is home to 13,000 full- and part-time students. The university plays an active role in the life of the community and provides many cultural opportunities for the residents of Bellingham, including dramatic presentations, concerts, and other educational programs. The Whatcom Community College and Bellingham Technical College also serve the community. The Bellingham Senior Center offers programs for its more than 1,200 members.

Strengths

You won't find extreme temperatures in Bellingham, and the rainy days are not common during spring and summer. You can enjoy the natural beauty of the surrounding mountains, lakes, and ocean, and opportunities for outdoor recreation are endless. Bellingham has many large-city amenities but maintains a small-town ambience.

Weaknesses

Bellingham is a bit out of the mainstream since it's located in the far corner of the Pacific Northwest and at least an hour from a major airport. (It does have a small regional airport serviced by Horizon Air/Alaska Air.) Transportation to other parts of the country may take extra time and money. To paraphrase the Carpenters, if rainy days and Mondays always get you down, 93 days of rain a year may be too much!

FYI

Check out these sources for additional information: Bellingham/Whatcom Chamber of Commerce (www.bellingham.com or 360-671-3990), the *Bellingham Herald* (www.bellinghamherald.com or 360-676-2600), and the *Bellingham Business Journal* (www.businessjournal.org/bbj or 360-647-8805).

Reader's Digest, AARP, CNN, and *Money* magazine have all put Bellingham on their "Best Places" lists.

Port Townsend

REPORT CARD

Overall rating: B

Climate: A-

Cost of living: B

Health care: B

Transportation: C

What's to do: B

Located in the northeast corner of Washington's Olympic Peninsula, Port Townsend is one of only three U.S. Victorian seaports listed on the National Historic Register. With the Olympic Mountains on one side, Port Townsend Bay on the other, and the Strait of Juan de Fuca to the north, Port Townsend is surrounded by water.

Visitors take a step back in time just walking around this quaint, historic town. So many of the Victorian homes and buildings are restored and open for lodging that Port Townsend is sometimes thought of as the unofficial bed-and-breakfast capital of the Pacific Northwest. Most travel to and from Port Townsend is on the Washington State ferries. Although no longer the thriving seaport it was in the 1800s, its commerce is still centered on manufacturing, tourism, and timber.

Whether hiking in Olympic National Park, boating on Puget Sound, bird-watching in the Dungeness River Center, or whale-watching in the San Juan Islands, residents soak up the natural beauty of the area and enjoy the mild climate provided by the rain shadow of the Olympic Mountains (in other words, the mountains help to block the rain). The Pacific Ocean helps to moderate the temperatures throughout the year, and the Olympic Mountains provide the barrier that results in much less rainfall than is the norm for the Pacific Northwest.

Who Lives in Port Townsend?

Port Townsend has a population of approximately 9,000, with about one-third of the residents over the age of 55. The median age is 46, and about 95 percent of the residents are Caucasian, 1 percent African-American, 2 per-

What's It Like Outside?	Jan.	Apr.	Jul.	Oct.	Rain (in.)	Snow (in.)
Average high (°F)	44	59	76	61	18	4
Average low (°F)	30	33	53	45	–	–

cent Native American and/or Alaska Native, and 2 percent Asian.

What's the Cost?

Although specific numbers are unavailable, the cost of living is considered lower than the national average. Depending on location, home prices can be reasonable (a four-bedroom/two-bath in Port Townsend lists for $225,000) to high (a three-bedroom/two-bath in planned community Kala Point lists for $625,000).

What's to Do?

With so much water around, the obvious outdoor, water-related activities spring to mind, including boating, hiking along the lakes and coastlines, and fishing. You can do all of these things in town or close by in Olympic National Park, with its 900,000 acres of land and 60 miles of Pacific coastline.

In addition to the natural beauty of the area, Port Townsend, known as "the city of dreams," was a national prizewinner for its Main Street program of renovating and restoring historical buildings. Many art galleries, clothing boutiques, and fine restaurants are housed in these historic buildings. The Chetzemoka Park, named for the Native America chief Chetzemoka, is one of two dozen city parks in Port Townsend. This park has something for everyone: beach access, hiking paths, a 1905 bandstand, gardens, a picnic area, and a children's playground. The Port Townsend Marine Science Center offers visitors a hands-on marine-life experience. There are music festivals to enjoy, featuring fiddle music, jazz, and country blues.

Although not considered a major wine-producing area, Port Townsend's wineries produce some outstanding wines as well as a few unusual ones: Strawberry rhubarb and plum wines are available for the tasting if you take the winery loop driving tour.

For a small town, Port Townsend has a lot to offer.

Where Are the Jobs?

Jefferson County's largest manufacturing employer, Port Townsend Paper Corporation, is located here. This is also a major boatbuilding and logging town. Health care and tourism are the other large employers. The unemployment rate is about 5 percent.

Take a drive through Kala Point and Cape George to experience the natural beauty of this heavily wooded area. You'll be impressed with the majestic mountain panorama and views of the sparkling waters and rugged coastline of the Pacific.

Where Are the Doctors?

The medical needs of Port Townsend are served by Jefferson General Hospital. There are also several health clinics in Port Townsend.

Where Are Some Notable Neighborhoods?

You will not find retirees living in Port Townsend in one particular area as there are no planned retirement communities per se. Some will choose to live in a Victorian home or a bungalow in town that is close to restaurants, movies, and shopping. Others will choose the seclusion and wide-open spaces of the country, while still others prefer a planned community open to all age groups.

There are two planned communities for all ages close to town. Kala Point (www.kalapoint.net) is 6 miles from Port Townsend and is situated on almost 400 acres with 1½ miles of sandy beach. The community includes swimming pools, boat docks, hiking trails, and some beautiful views. Lots are available from about $100,000, and there are a variety of residences with condos in the $200,000s and homes in the mid $300,000s. You'll need to contact a Realtor in the area for available lots and homes.

Cape George, another private community, has a full-service marina and breathtaking views. Lots are available from around $100,000, and homes begin in the $300,000s. Again, contact a Realtor for more information.

Looking for something a little more out of the ordinary? (Think communes, now called cohousing communities). Check out Port Townsend Eco Village (www.keeskolff.org), "a community of people dedicated to living in harmony with each other and with the Earth, exploring together ways to live more sustainably." The community is in the process of forming, so contact them through their Web site for more information.

Another area to consider is Port Ludlow. Located just 25 minutes south of Port Townsend, this is a 2,000-acre planned residential and resort community. Port Ludlow Associates (www.ludlowhomes.com or 888-694-6477) developed the land, owns the resort, and also builds some of the homes in the neighborhoods, which are both single-family and townhomes. A newer offering is Olympic Terrace Two, with homes priced from the upper $400,000s. Residents enjoy 27 holes of golf; a 300-slip, full-service marina; and the Resort at Port Ludlow. Property owners enjoy automatic membership in the owner's association, which includes membership in the

---

The *City Guide to Port Townsend* states, "Jobs are scarce, so creativity is encouraged."

beach club with more than 1 mile of sandy beach, tennis, squash, pickle-ball courts, and heated indoor and outdoor swimming pools, as well as preferential annual rates at the golf course.

How Do I Pursue Lifelong Learning?

Several opportunities for higher education are available in the Port Townsend area, including Peninsula College at Port Townsend, a comprehensive community college. The Community Learning Center (360-379-5610), a Washington State University cooperative extension in Port Hadlock, offers classes toward several 4-year degrees. Distance learning through the University of Washington is another option (800-543-2320).

Strengths

The charm of living in a small town is magnified by the fact that the entire town is part of the National Historic Registry. The Victorian homes, the restored Main Street, and the busy harbor, all accented with a backdrop of majestic mountains, make this a beautiful location for retirement. The climate is very mild, with little rain and even less snow.

Weaknesses

The ferry system may not be considered a desirable mode of transportation for some (although others may love it).

Sometimes you can detect the smell from the paper plant. Port Townsend is remote. For some, that is part of its charm, but for others, it's not! If you need a job, pickings are pretty slim.

FYI

Check out these sources for additional information: Port Ludlow Chamber of Commerce (www.portludlow chamber.org or 360-437-0120), Port Townsend Chamber of Commerce (www.ptchamber.org or 360-385-7869), the *Port Townsend & Jefferson County Leader* (www.ptleader.com or 360-385-2900), and the *Peninsula Daily News* (www.peninsuladailynews.com or 800-826-7714).

Sequim

REPORT CARD

Overall rating:	B
Climate:	A
Cost of living:	B
Health care:	C
Transportation:	B
What's to do:	B

Sequim, pronounced "skwim," is one of Washington State's most popular retirement locations. The Sequim-Dungeness Valley is located between the Olympic

Mountains and the calm waters of the Strait of Juan de Fuca. Because of Sequim's location in the rain shadow of the Olympics (where the mountains block the rain), the city enjoys mild year-round temperatures and an average rainfall of only 17 inches, much less than in other cities in the Pacific Northwest. The sun shines at least part of the day about 300 days a year, and if it's overcast in Sequim, it's raining for sure in Seattle and the surrounding areas! But Sequim has more to offer than climate. The city has more than 160 service, fraternal, and special-interest groups, offering something for everyone. The senior center is a great place to meet people and sign up for a trip to Victoria, British Columbia, enjoy an art class, or take aerobics or yoga. Golf can be played year-round on any of the three golf courses in the valley—Dungeness, Sunland, and Sun Ridge.

The Dungeness Spit is the world's largest sand spit at 5 miles long. This narrow ribbon of sand, which projects into the Strait of Juan de Fuca, has been designated a national wildlife refuge and is home to the Dungeness crab. It is a popular location for clamming, boating, kayaking, and horseback riding. The Railroad Bridge Park, habitat for 250 bird species, has been named Washington State's first Audubon Center.

Who Lives in Sequim?

There are about 26,000 people living in the Sequim-Dungeness Valley, with about 5,000 people living in the city. Within the city limits, 55 percent of the residents are 55 years of age or older, and the median age is 59. Nearly 95 percent of the population is Caucasian, 2 percent are Native American or Alaska Native, and 2 percent are Asian.

What's the Cost?

The cost of living is a little lower than the national average, which is helped by the lack of a state income tax. The average new, three-bedroom home will cost about $202,000. There are several manufactured-home communities in Sequim. If you'd like to live in a country-club/golf-course setting, the prices will be higher, from the $200,000s and up.

What's to Do?

This is a very laid-back, quiet community, with no tall buildings in sight. Walking on the sandy shores of the Dungeness Spit, clamming, sea kayaking, fishing, and enjoying golf any day, year-round, top the list of things to do. Gardening is very popular due to the sunshine

---

Sequim means "quiet waters" in the native language of the S'Klallam tribe.

and extra-long growing season. Residents of Sequim treasure their slow-paced life, knowing they can travel to Port Angeles or take a trip on the Washington State ferries to Seattle to enjoy the amenities of city life. If you love lavender, you're in luck. Sequim calls itself "the lavender capital of the United States" and has an annual lavender festival that draws people from all over. Or enjoy an open-air market featuring local produce and crafts every Saturday morning from April through October. You can also go skiing in the almost 1-million-acre Olympic National Park or gamble at the Seven Cedars Casino.

Where Are the Jobs?

Getting a job is not out of the question, but the job market is tight. Look for work opportunities in the service areas: health care, schools, or tourism. The unemployment rate is about 6 percent.

Where Are the Doctors?

A full-service medical center, the Olympic Medical Center (OMC), is located in Port Angeles, about 20 minutes away, and provides all the hospital needs for the Sequim area. Some services are available in Sequim through the OMC—lab services, physical therapy, radiation/oncology, and health education. Specialists from Seattle come to OMC often to serve the residents of the area.

Where Are Some Notable Neighborhoods?

While there are no huge, gated golf communities being built in Sequim, there are many established neighborhoods with some lots available for new construction as well as resales. Take a look at SunLand Golf and Country Club (www.sunlandgolf.com or 360-683-7473), the newer Sunland North (www.sunlandnorth.com or 866-525-7294), or close-by Bell Hill and Happy Valley. Prices begin around the $200,000s and increase to more than $2 million.

How Do I Pursue Lifelong Learning?

Peninsula College is part of the state community-college system and offers adult classes in Sequim and also at the main campus in Port Angeles, including Elderhostel programs.

What's It Like Outside?	Jan.	Apr.	Jul.	Oct.	Rain (in.)	Snow (in.)
Average high (°F)	57	56	72	59	17	0
Average low (°F)	24	39	46	42	–	–

Strengths

Living a quiet, slow-paced lifestyle away from the big city but still close to city amenities appeals to many seniors. Add 300 days of sunshine, scenic beauty, and affordability, and you have a winner.

Weaknesses

Some may feel that traveling to Port Angeles for hospital care is a negative. Others may feel that taking a ferry to the city sounds like a lot of trouble! And still others may feel the slow, quiet lifestyle—even in such a beautiful place—lacks excitement.

FYI

Check out these sources for additional information: Sequim-Dungeness Chamber of Commerce (www. cityofsequim.com or 800-737-8462), the *Peninsula Daily News* (www.peninsuladailynews.com or 360-452-4507), and the *Sequim Gazette* (www.sequimgazette.com or 360-683-3311).

ISLAND LIVING IN WASHINGTON STATE

The San Juan Islands, Whidbey Island, and Bainbridge Island

Finally, we'll take a look at three of the islands of Washington State. We're deviating from our normal pattern of describing a city, because, frankly, these places are different and don't lend themselves to that format. The big question is, do you want to live on "island time" and rely on ferries for transportation to and from your home?

The state of Washington has several islands that lie in the far northwestern corner of the United States and one close to Seattle worth considering for relocation. Fidalgo Island, about 90 miles from Seattle, is the easternmost island in what is known as the San Juan chain of islands. It's known as the "drive-to" island and is home to the Washington State Ferry Terminal. The only other islands accessible by car are Whidbey Island at Deception Pass (the northern edge of the island) and Bain-

---

Because of its plentiful sunshine, Sequim has earned the nickname "Banana Belt."

bridge Island (which is close to Seattle). Most residents of Whidbey and Bainbridge travel by ferry, and the remaining Washington State islands are accessible only by ferry or small private planes or charters.

The Washington State ferries are the main mode of transportation for the islands, and they are considered part of the state highway system. Actually, the Washington State ferry system is the largest in the United States, carrying about 25 million passengers a year, more than some major airports!

If you are a person who is always in a hurry and feels the need for speed, you may find ferry travel a challenge. There are many drawbacks to overcome—waiting in line, mechanical problems, rising costs, and huge crowds, not to mention the 30 minutes to 2 hours it may take to get from place to place.

Fortunately, the positive side of traveling on these ferries far outweighs the negative for the millions of passengers traveling each year. When you look around, the veteran travelers are playing cards with their kids, reading, enjoying a snack or a beer from the restaurant, and taking in the amazing natural beauty that is part of every ferry crossing: the snow-capped Olympic Mountains, Mount Rainier, the blue-green water, rocky beaches, and the trees that have given this state its nickname, the Evergreen State. There is always something extraordinary happening: eagles soaring, whales breaching; this is not your everyday mass transit! If you can picture yourself relaxing and enjoying the ride, explore this part of the country for retirement.

Friday Harbor, San Juan Island

The San Juan Archipelago consists of about 700 islands, only about 170 of which have names. Only four islands are populated enough to have ferry service: San Juan, Orcas, Lopez, and Shaw. Friday Harbor, located on San Juan Island, which is about halfway between Vancouver Island and the Washington State mainland, is the business hub and county seat for San Juan Island. This quaint, historic fishing village has a population of 2,200 (total population of San Juan Island is about 6,500) and is a destination for visitors or retirees looking for a getaway.

Surrounded by ocean waters and mountains, Friday

Washington State maintains the largest fleet of ferries (both passenger and auto) in the United States and the third largest in the world.

Harbor's daily temperatures rarely dip below freezing or rise above 80 degrees. The people who live here take advantage of these mild temperatures and the 250 days of sunshine while enjoying activities centered on the outdoors: watching Orcas and other marine and land animals, scuba diving, sailing, sea kayaking, and bicycling. The interior of the island has a diverse terrain where you will find lakes, prairie land, lavender and alpaca farms, vineyards, and beautiful parks. Lime Kiln State Park is the only whale-watching park in the contiguous United States. If you tire of outdoor activities, Friday Harbor has a theater, art galleries, fine restaurants, and plenty of shopping. Don't miss the Saturday morning outdoor farmers' market and the musicians in the parks.

There are no large, gated golf communities currently under construction (although there is plenty of golf). When you look at the real-estate ads, you read enticing descriptions of panoramic vistas, pastoral acreage, views of the San Juan Channel and Mount Baker, and waterfront estates with docks. Residences are listed from around the $300,000s to the millions.

The Friday Harbor Clinic has family physicians and provides emergency care; if a hospital is needed in an emergency, however, patients are airlifted to Anacortes or Bellingham. Most residents pay for an insurance policy that provides their family with MEDEVAC helicopter service.

Living on an island accessible only by air or water means getting away from it all for sure. The beauty of the San Juan Islands is breathtaking, as are the ocean temperatures if you're a swimmer! Seattle is only a few hours away if you need a big-city fix, but the cost of living is higher on the islands than in surrounding areas of the state.

Whidbey Island

Whidbey Island, the longest island (55 miles) in the continental United States, is also located at the northwestern tip of Washington State, with the Cascade Mountains to the east and the Olympic Mountains to the west. The Olympic Mountains protect Whidbey from temperature extremes and excessive rainfall. Temperatures rarely fall below freezing in the winter and rarely rise above 80 in the summer. Rainfall varies from 18 inches to 28 inches, thanks to the rain shadow provided by the mountains.

Receive Washington ferry schedules on your cell phone; set your mobile Web browser to www.goyoura.com.

The total population of Whidbey Island is about 72,000 people, with Oak Harbor, home of the Naval Air Station, the largest community. The Naval Air Station is the island's largest employer. Boeing Company's large plane plant in Everett is a short commute from Whidbey. Oak Harbor is a bustling small town, with busy streets, fast food, a historic section called Pioneer Way, and City Beach, a park right downtown for swimming and recreation. Oak Harbor's public marina is home to Whidbey Island Race Week, one of the top 20 sailing regattas in the world.

Deception Pass State Park is Washington's most popular state park, with freshwater swimming and a sandy beach at Cranberry Lake, 38 miles of trails, boat ramps, complete camping facilities, and an underwater park for scuba diving.

Driving around the island (don't worry about getting lost, as one road connects the entire island), you will find much smaller communities, such as Coupeville, with about 1,700 people, and Langley, with about 1,100 residents. Langley, sitting on a bluff overlooking the southeastern shore of Whidbey Island, is a quaint small town complete with art galleries and home to the island's art council. Enjoy shopping, dining, or a stroll on the beach in this village by the sea.

Whidbey Island General Hospital, located in Coupeville, has more than 50 beds and a 24-hour emergency room. The Whidbey branch of Skagit Valley College offers 2-year associate's degrees, and Western Washington University has a branch campus in Oak Harbor.

There are plenty of opportunities to purchase a part-time or full-time residence on Whidbey Island. Oak Harbor has homes listed from $200,000 and also for $600,000 and into the millions on 2-plus acres with water and mountain views. Useless Bay Colony (love that name!), located near Clinton on the southern end of the island, is an existing community with a golf course and a country club and several hundred homes already built. Homes are for sale from the $400,000s, although those residences with some acreage and great views of the Sound and the mountains will have much higher price tags. Condominiums are also available from the mid $300,000s, some with golf-course views and others with water views.

For more information on real estate in Whidbey Island, contact a realty company such as Whidbey

---

Washington State (particularly around the San Juan Islands) is rated among the best places for scuba diving in North America by *Scuba Diving* magazine.

Pacific Realty (www.whidbeypacificrealty.com or 800-543-5405).

Many working people live on Whidbey Island. The ferry commute is like any commute to a big city; at peak times it's awful, but midweek or midday it's a lot more enjoyable than other types of mass transit—fast (relatively) and exceedingly beautiful.

Bainbridge Island

Bainbridge Island, known as a "suburb" of Seattle, is home for some 22,000 people, half of whom commute to Seattle on a daily basis. The commute, by ferry, takes about 35 minutes. The homes in this Seattle suburb are expensive, with a median value of $436,000. The climate is mild, but unlike the other islands protected by the Olympic Mountains, Bainbridge has more rain and snow (about 38 inches of rain and 11 inches of snow each year). The average temperature in the summer is 70 degrees and during the winter, 42 degrees.

If you plan to work in Seattle or visit the city amenities regularly, Bainbridge has a lot to offer as a home base. You can enjoy walking on the beach, kayaking, bicycling, hiking, or golf. There are art galleries, antique shopping, island-grown produce at a weekly farmers'

market, a historical museum, and a performing-arts theater. Olympic College opened a branch campus 15 miles from Bainbridge Island in 2004. You may not need to go to Seattle after all!

FYI

Check out these sources for additional information: San Juan Island Chamber of Commerce (www.sanjuan island.org or 360-378-5240), San Juan County Visitors Bureau (www.guidetosanjuans.com or 888-468-3701), and the *San Juan Journal* (www.sanjuanjournal.com or 360-378-5696).

Connect to Whidbey newspapers (www.whidbeynews times.com or 360-675-6611 and www.southwhidbey record.com or 360-221-5300), and Island Transit (360-678-7771). Contact Bainbridge Island Chamber of Commerce (www.bainbridgechamber.com or 206-842-3700) and the Bainbridge Island Review (www.bain bridgereview.com or 206-842-6613).

HONOR ROLL

In keeping with the report-card motif, we thought it only fitting to create an honor roll of the places we found

---

Money magazine ranked Bainbridge Island number two on its 2005 list of "Best Places to Live."

to be particularly outstanding or unique. Although we realize that priorities and values differ, and that there is no perfect place, this is our alphabetical top ten list of retirement locations.

1. Asheville/Hendersonville, North Carolina: scenic mountains, small towns with big-city amenities, single friendly, great summer golf

2. Bend, Oregon: spectacular beauty, walkable downtown, nirvana for people who love the outdoors.

3. Fort Collins, Colorado: 300 days of sunshine, low humidity, college town, outdoor lover's paradise, regional medical center

4. Greater Knoxville area: lots of small-town living, gorgeous lakes, college area, Great Smoky Mountain National Park, can find a home regardless of budget

5. Panama (country): lower cost of living, friendly people, gorgeous scenery, perfect for people who want a really new experience

6. Ponte Vedra, Florida: variety of housing styles, 30 minutes to everything, few seasonal tourists, upscale area with great shopping

7. Prescott, Arizona: beautiful freshwater lakes, cool summer days, small western town, known as "everybody's hometown"

8. San Luis Obispo, California: almost perfect weather, 10 miles to the Pacific coast, vibrant downtown, college town

9. Santa Fe, New Mexico: pedestrian friendly, vital arts community, great southwestern cuisine, mild climate with close proximity to skiing

10. Wilmington, North Carolina: the airport, historic downtown area, and beaches are all within 20 minutes of one another; college town

A SECOND HOME

We mentioned near the beginning of this chapter that some people who will keep their primary residence might be interested in a second home. Here is a list of possible locations. Of course, any of the places already recommended could be considered for a second home as well, just as these places could be your ideal setting for a primary home.

Q: "Why are you moving out of your house?"
A: "Because, according to statistics, most accidents happen at home."

Escape from the City

These places could be a drivable distance from your primary residence or a reasonable drive from a major airport.

* Bethany Beach/Rehoboth Beach, Delaware
* Breckenridge, Colorado
* Lake Norris, Tennessee
* Lake of the Ozarks/Branson, Missouri
* Long Beach Island, New Jersey
* Poconos, Pennsylvania

Sunbirds

If you're looking to escape the heat and humidity of the summer months, one of these towns might fit the bill.

* Quebec City, Canada
* Charlevoix, Michigan

* Door County, Wisconsin
* Petoskey, Michigan
* Reno, Nevada

Snowbirds

If the winters are too cold for you, then head south. Located below the frost line, these places will provide sun and warmth during the coldest of months.

* Boca Grande, Florida
* Sarasota, Florida
* Jupiter, Florida
* Cabo San Lucas, Mexico
* Bonita Springs, Florida

6

WHAT ARE SOME NICHE RETIREMENT LIFESTYLES?

"Choose to live in a place where your eyes are always open to the positive possibilities."
—*Ralph Marston*

For some people, choosing a new retirement spot is much more about lifestyle than about location. If you're looking for a way of living, rather than a particular place, here are some niche retirement lifestyle choices that may appeal to you.

ACTIVE-ADULT COMMUNITIES

Age-qualified, age-restricted, age-targeted, or active adult—are different ways of saying "Life is great." If you're tired of hearing the pitter-patter of little feet in your existing community or longing to be surrounded by like-minded neighbors, you may want to explore living in

an active-adult community. If a more age-homogeneous lifestyle with facilities and social activities that allow you to do as much or as little as you'd like sounds like your cup of tea, there are many choices, some probably close to your present home. Some of these communities have age restrictions, such as that at least one resident must be 55 or older and that no one under 19 may live full-time in the community. Other communities are marketed to people over 50, without age restrictions. There are about 2,000 active-adult communities in the United States, and this number is increasing.

Today's active-adult community residents are more affluent, more educated, more computer literate, more intellectually curious, healthier, and more physically active than ever. Most active-adult communities have a wide range of housing types and price points; homes can often be purchased beginning around $200,000. Below are some of the "big guns" in active-adult living.

Del Webb, now owned by Pulte Homes (www.del webb.com or 800-808-8088), is the country's largest builder of active-adult communities for people 55 and better. There are three types of Del Webb communities: active adult (which are age restricted), country club (which feature a resort setting), and family living (which cater to all ages). Amenities may include golf, tennis, fitness centers, swimming, special-interest clubs, and numerous planned activities. Del Webb's communities are located in 22 states: Arizona, California, Colorado, Connecticut, Delaware, Florida, Georgia, Illinois, Indiana, Maryland, Massachusetts, Michigan, Nevada, New Jersey, New York, North Carolina, Ohio, Pennsylvania, South Carolina, Tennessee, Texas, and Virginia. More than 200,000 residents live in Del Webb communities.

Hovnanian Enterprises (www.khov.com or 877-HOV-HOME), building communities since 1959, has active-adult communities in Arizona, California, Maryland, Minnesota, New Jersey, North Carolina, Pennsylvania, South Carolina, Texas, Virginia, and West Virginia.

Leisure World, a concept that began in California in the 1950s, has several active-adult communities; they are located in Mesa, Arizona; Laguna Woods and Seal Beach, California; Silver Spring, Maryland (near Washington, DC); and Lansdowne, Virginia. All Leisure Worlds have gated security, full-time professional management, and a plethora of facilities and activities that cater to virtually every desire and need. The Leisure World in Laguna Woods incorporated as a city, becoming one of California's newest (in terms of cities) and oldest (in terms of population) places! For more information, contact the individual Leisure World locations.

Lennar Corporation (www.lennar.com or 305-559-4000) is another formidable presence in the active-adult niche and offers communities in 14 states. Again, amenities reflect a resort lifestyle.

Robson Communities (www.robson.com or 800-732-9949), headquartered in Arizona, has five com-

---

Check out www.retirementresorts.com for the "World's Finest Active-Adult Retirement Living," according to the Senior Housing Hospitality Institute.

munities: Robson Ranch (Texas), Robson Ranch (Arizona), Quail Creek (Arizona), Pebble Creek (Arizona), and Saddle Brooke (Arizona). Amenities may include golf, fitness facilities, swimming, tennis, organized activities and clubs, shopping, medical facilities, banks, etc. More than 30,000 people call a Robson community home.

Sun City Center (www.suncitycenter.com or 800-633-0871) is a self-contained, 45-year-old community located between Tampa and Sarasota, Florida. Originally developed by Del Webb, it is now managed by Florida Design Communities. Sun City Center has about 17,000 residents out of a planned 20,000, with build-out anticipated in 2010. Sun City Center provides more than 200 activities and clubs. Condos, duplex villas, and single-family homes range from the $100,000s to around $500,000. Golf carts compete with cars as the prime mode of transportation. There is something for everyone in this all-inclusive retirement city, including an assisted-living facility and skilled nursing care along with churches, medical facilities, shopping, restaurants, a post office, and a security force.

AWAY-FROM-IT-ALL ISLANDS

Does the idea of seclusion, a laid-back lifestyle, and limited access appeal to you? If so, you may wish to investigate island living. Refer to the South Carolina and Washington sections of Chapter 5, or check out some of these island towns, which are more get-away-from-it-all than others.

Bald Head Island (www.baldheadisland.com or 800-804-9826) is on the southeastern tip of North Carolina, where the Cape Fear River meets the Atlantic. Development is allowed on only 2,000 of its spectacular 12,000 acres of marsh, tidal creeks, and forests. Four-and-a-half hours from Charlotte, the island does not permit cars; electric carts, bikes, and feet are the modes of transportation. Access to Bald Head Island is via a 20-minute ferry ride from Southport, North Carolina, or by private boat. Bald Head Island's beaches (there are 14 miles of them) have been included among the top 20 beaches in the United States in annual rankings. Additionally, the island offers golf, restaurants, and shopping (but not too much—after all, this section is called "Away-from-It-All

---

Remember the days of communes? Well, it's now called cohousing or collaborative housing. If you're interested in this type of niche living, contact the Cohousing Association of the United States (www.cohousing.org or 314-754-5828).

Islands"). Neighborhoods include Harbour Village, Cape Fear Station, and the Hammocks (interval ownership). Prices vary, depending on location. Serenity can be expensive. For example, an oceanfront five-bedroom/ five-bath home is listed for $2,350,000; a 4-week interval ownership of a two-bedroom, two-bath home is offered for $125,000; and lots on the island begin in the $300,000s.

Daufuskie Island is located about 50 miles east of Savannah, Georgia, and 100 miles south of Charleston, South Carolina. Daufuskie Island (it means "sharp feather" or "land with a point") is surrounded by the Atlantic Ocean, the New River, Cooper River, Calibogue Sound, and Mongin Creek. As with Bald Head Island, cars are not allowed; there is no bridge to this island. There is a lot of discussion about the future development of this 6-mile long and 3-mile wide island of 500 full-time residents, and right now, prices are good, if a community without automobiles appeals to you. Lots begin around $50,000, villas begin in the $300,000s, and homes begin around $500,000.

San Juan, Lopez, Orcas, Whidbey, Camano, and Shaw islands are some of the many islands in Washington State near Seattle. Located in Puget Sound, these Pacific Northwest islands are accessed by water and/or air and allow cars. For example, on Orcas, lots can range from $150,000 to $18.5 million, and residences cost from $200,000 to $20 million (yes, that zero belongs there). For more information, check out www.sanjuanweb.com or see Chapter 5.

If you *really* want to get away from it all and live like Gilligan, go to www.privateislands.com and buy your own! How about 2-acre Little Gauldling Cay in the Bahamas for $600,000 or a more than 60-acre island off the coast of Maine for a cool $3.25 million?

COLLEGE TOWNS

Question: Where can you be assured of plenty of cultural activities, stimulating intergenerational discussions, sports, entertainment, restaurants, bookstores, libraries, stable housing prices, a well-educated community, and perhaps top-notch medical facilities? Answer: college towns. For people who would rather hit the books than hit a golf ball, it's worth considering. For many baby boomers, living in an academic community provides the

---

Another active-adult community that is a city is The Villages in Central Florida.
Read about it on page 168.

vitality of college life without the hefty tuition. Colleges are responding to this trend with lifelong learning opportunities for retirees, such as the North Carolina Center for Creative Retirement in Asheville and the almost 100 peer-driven Osher Learning Institutes at various college campuses nationwide. In addition, essentially all state universities offer reduced or free tuition (space permitting) and auditing of classes for people desiring knowledge (without the exams!). Contact the admissions office or continuing-education office for specifics. (Also, check out Chapter 2 for more information about lifelong learning.)

Approximately 60 colleges and universities across the United States have developed communities to attract retirees, and about the same number are examining the possibility of doing so. The concept is not new—more than 25 years ago, Indiana University built Meadowood Retirement Community for retired faculty and staff—but the idea has become more encompassing. Many alumni return to their old college stomping grounds; after all, their college years were some of their best years! (And, as a gentleman at one of our seminars commented, "College towns also have pretty girls and cheap beer!")

Some college retirement communities require entrance fees as well as monthly fees. (The entrance fee is often partly or fully refundable upon leaving the community.) Just as you might pay more for a house located on a golf course or lake, you may pay more for housing with access to a college campus. Some communities are continuing care retirement communities. (For a discussion of CCRCs, see below.) with housing ranging from independent living to assisted living. Regular housing in the college town of your choice may be an attractive financial alternative if you don't desire a CCRC. If your plans don't involve purchasing a home, however, finding rental property could be difficult because of stiff competition from students, who also compete for part-time jobs.

Kendal Corporation (www.kendal.org) manages a number of retirement communities associated with colleges, including Hanover, New Hampshire (2 miles from Dartmouth); Oberlin, Ohio (1 mile from Oberlin College); Granville, Ohio (2 miles from Denison University); Lexington, Virginia (close to Washington and Lee University and the Virginia Military Institute); and Ithaca, New York (2 miles from Cornell University and Ithaca College).

Other college retirement communities include Oak Hammock (a CCRC) at the University of Florida in Gainesville; University Commons at the University of Michigan (offers condos for alumni and retired faculty); Holy Cross Village at Notre Dame (offers independent living through skilled nursing and memory care); Villa

St. Benedict (a CCRC) at Benedictine College in Lisle, Illinois; Classic Residence by Hyatt (a CCRC) at Stanford University in Palo Alto, California; University Place (a CCRC) at Purdue in West Lafayette, Indiana; Capstone Village at the University of Alabama in Tuscaloosa; and the Village at Penn State in State College, Pennsylvania.

If you want to get in on the (almost) ground floor of a new university and town, consider Ave Maria University. Thomas Monaghan, founder of Domino's Pizza, is building Ave Maria University, a Catholic university 17 miles east of Naples, Florida. Just over 100 students began the fall 2003 session at the university's temporary site. The new town of Ave Maria will be integrated into the Ave Maria campus, with a total of about 11,000 households on 5,000 acres.

CONTINUING CARE RETIREMENT COMMUNITIES

If you're looking to make only one move that will provide for whatever care needs may develop, a continuing care retirement community may fit the bill. A CCRC offers a continuum of care and allows you to "age in place"; you can segue from independent living to assisted living to nursing care, all within the same facility. A variety of housing options are usually available, and there is often a community dining area where you can purchase meals if you wish. If your goal is to remain in the same geographic area, the sizable number of these facilities throughout the country may enable you to stay close to your present community, yet receive the help you need.

There is a menu of choices in CCRCs. Residences may be condos, apartments, single-family homes, or duplexes. In general, residents may either pay an entrance fee along with monthly fees or be charged a monthly rental fee that covers certain services. CCRC contract options are typically either extensive (monthly payments stay the same regardless of services), modified (a set number of days of nursing care is provided, beyond which the resident is financially responsible), or fee for service (you pay à la carte for nursing services and other health-related costs). In some CCRCs, domiciles can be passed on to heirs; in other communities, a portion of the entrance fee is refunded if the resident leaves or

Hint: Consider buying into a newer active-adult community if you're younger. People tend to stay once they move in, so the older communities have a much higher average age than a newer one!

refunded to his or her estate if he or she passes on. CCRCs can be pricey; if you are in poor health, you could pay a hefty entrance fee for little time. There is often a wait to get into these types of communities, although more are opening all the time. Here's a sampling of a few.

Carlsbad by the Sea (www.carlsbadbythesea.com or 800-255-1556) is located on the Pacific Coast in the delightful village of Carlsbad, California, north of La Jolla and Del Mar. This 4-acre CCRC has 148 independent-living apartments (some oceanfront or with an ocean view), 13 assisted-living studio residences, and a 33-bed care center. A full complement of services and amenities is provided in this intimate, scenic setting. Two commuter rail lines in Carlsbad facilitate travel. At Carlsbad by the Sea, entrance fees for residential living range from the $199,000s to $614,000, and monthly fees from $2,490 to $4,450. An additional person is $825 per month. The Care Center operates on a daily fee of $236 to $337. There is no Alzheimer's facility.

Twin Lakes (www.twinlakes.org; click on "Twin Lakes" under "communities" or 513-247-1300) is located on 56 acres in Montgomery, Ohio, and borders the Vil-lage of Indian Hill, both upscale suburbs of Cincinnati. Twin Lakes is affiliated with the United Methodist Church and is open to anyone 62 years or older. The 400-resident community has 115 villa homes, 91 apart-ments, and a health-care pavilion with 27 assisted-living units and 38 full-care nursing accommodations. There is no Alzheimer's facility. Twin Lakes is located close to shopping, dining, and parks, as well as the amenities of downtown Cincinnati.

Classic Residence by Hyatt (www.hyattclassic.com or 800-421-1442) entered the retirement community arena in 1987. Classic Residence by Hyatt has 21 upscale retirement communities in 11 states. As an example, Bentley Village in Naples, Florida, provides a contin-uum of care and, in addition, offers an Alzheimer's/memory support-care facility. Its 156 acres include apartments, homes, golf, lakes, walking paths, and a 400-seat auditorium. Plus, you're minutes away from Naples, an outstanding location in its own right. On average, monthly fees at these communities range from $2,500 to $5,500, depending on residence and level of care, and entrance fees range from $215,000 to more than $4 million.

The Commission on Accreditation of Rehabilitation Facilities (CARF) offers online searches of accred-ited CCRCs by state or province (www.carf.org or 866-888-1122).

CRUISE THROUGH RETIREMENT—LITERALLY!

What if you could sail the seven seas and never leave your house? Imagine having a home in dozens of countries! If this intrigues you, consider *The World of ResidenSea*. *The World* is a 44,000-ton Norwegian-built, 12-story luxury ship that has a crew of 250, about 200 residents and guests, and 165 one-to-three room apartments and studios. The cost of a home on *The World* ranges from around $850,000 to $7.3 million (not counting maintenance fees), and the ship has all the amenities of a gated community—including a country club! *The World* had its maiden cruise in March 2002 and travels the globe, stopping for a night or two in ports from A to Z—Athens, Barcelona, the Canary Islands—you get the idea. (Contact www.aboardthe world.com or 800-547-0727 for more info.)

With the successful concept of a ship as a floating home established, several additional in-the-water communities are in the planning stages. Four Seasons has commissioned a 96-apartment, 43,000-ton ship offering full or fractional ownership on a 50-year leasehold basis, with the level of services and amenities you'd expect from a Four Seasons property. Construction of the Four Seasons Ocean Residences, which will travel around the globe, is planned to commence in 2007. Tentative prices are $4.1 million for a full residence and $400,000 for a fractional ownership. (Contact www.oceanresidences. com or 305-438-7447 for more info.

The *Magellan* is the brainchild of Randall B. Jackson, a Phoenix real-estate developer. (Jackson's inspiration for this luxury vessel occurred while cruising through the straits of Magellan with his family.) Still in the preconstruction phase, plans for the *Magellan* include a 70,000-ton ship boasting not only the usual amenities but also an observatory (staffed by an astronomer) and a marina. The 200 homes on 15 decks begin at $1.9 million for full ownership and $160,000 for fractional ownership. Of course, don't forget the monthly assessments (beginning at $8,000). The ship, slated to launch in 2009, will stop at more than 150 ports per year. (Contact www. residentialcruiseline.com or 480-497-8833.)

Another residential ship with a target launch of 2008 is the *Orphalese* (named after the city in *The Prophet* by Kahil Gibran). Two hundred fully-furnished homes will be available, ranging in size from 1,000 to 4,000 square feet, priced from $1.8 to $10 million, with monthly fees beginning at $2,500. There will be an additional 265 staterooms for regular cruisers. You can enjoy the 80,000 square-foot mall in between visiting 200 ports per year. The itinerary of the *Orphalese* is event-driven rather than destination-driven. (Contact www.theorphalese.com or 888-287-7447 for more info.)

The most ambitious project under consideration is the *Freedom Ship*, which, as its Web site states, "is actually nothing more than a big barge." Although not off the ground (er, water?), CEO Norman Nixon envisions a slow-moving city that circumnavigates the globe once every 3 years, spending 30 percent of the time moving and 70 percent of the time offshore from major cities. Not only would the 4,500 foot-long *Freedom Ship* have residential, commercial, and hotel properties onboard, there would also be schools, parks, an airport, and medical facilities to serve its total population of 100,000. (Contact www.freedomship.com or 941-539-6824 for more info.)

On a smaller scale, Condo Cruise Lines International (www.condocruiselines.com or 888-897-0690) is purchasing medium-size cruise ships (10 to 15 years old) and retrofitting them as fully-furnished condos, which are priced from the $350,000s to $1.3 million. The ships cruise the world and returns to their home port (San Francisco) once every two 2 years. You can rent your condo when you're not in it. When the ship is retired (after 10 to 30 years of cruising), it will become a floating hotel.

So if you like the idea of traveling the world without ever leaving home, and you have the considerable funds to pay for this type of lifestyle, you may want to consider a seagoing city.

GAY AND LESBIAN COMMUNITIES

According to the U.S. Census, almost 3 million gays and lesbians turned 55 in 2005; by 2010, that number will be closer to 4 million. Many gays may feel that a traditional active-adult community or other communities may not welcome them. To serve this growing niche market, a number of gay/lesbian communities are now open, are being developed, or have been proposed. Here are a few examples.

"Assisted Living at Sea"? Lee Lindquist and Robert Golub published an article in the *Journal of the American Geriatrics Society*, concluding that for people who needed some assistance with food preparation, house-cleaning, and access to medical care, it could be just as cost-effective, and provide a better quality of life, to live on a cruise ship as to live in an assisted-living facility. A hypothetical 80-year-old woman, for example would pay $228,075 in an assisted-living facility compared to $230,497 on a cruise ship over a 20-year time span. Food for thought!

The Palms of Manasota (www.palmsofmanasota.com or 941-722-5858) is in Palmetto, Florida (between Sarasota and St. Petersburg). Its Web site calls it "America's first gay and lesbian adult-living community." This 30-acre community began in 1997. New lake-view villas are available for $300,000.

The Resort on Carefree Boulevard (www.resortoncb.com or 239-731-6366), for women only, is located in Fort Myers, Florida. The community has 278 manufactured homes and a number of RV sites. Homes begin below $200,000, and typical lots are under $100,000.

Birds of a Feather (www.flock2it.com or 888-425-3121), a 140-acre development, is right outside Santa Fe, New Mexico (in Pecos). Homes are in the $300,000s (excluding lot prices). Home building began in 2006, and community amenities such as a fitness center, library, and community garden are planned.

Rainbow Vision Properties (www.rainbowvisionprop.com or 505-474-9696) built 40 club condos, 20 independent-living condos, 60 independent-living rental apartments, and 26 assisted-living rental apartments on 13 acres in downtown Santa Fe, New Mexico. Condo prices are in the $200,000s, not including membership fees. This community welcomes gays, lesbians, and straights. Amenities will include a fitness center, spa, and wellness services. Rainbow Vision Properties will break ground on a new community in Palm Springs, California, in the near future.

Stonewall Communities (www.stonewallcommunities.com or 617-570-9090) is in the planning stages of Stonewall at Audubon Circle (Boston area), and the Lundberg Group (www.ourtownvillages.com) is also developing gay and lesbian communities.

Wilton Manors, in Broward County, Florida, is known as an extremely gay-friendly city. Approximately 35 to 40 percent of its residents are gay.

FREE LAND COMMUNITIES

You've heard the saying "There's no such thing as a free lunch." Well, what about free land? In an effort to reverse population losses, some small towns are giving away lots and providing other incentives for people to move to their communities. You won't be going to a stadium-style theater for a movie, and you won't be getting a latte from Starbucks, but if you like small-town living and harsh

---

To compare facilities covered by Medicare or Medicaid, log on to the government's Web site, www.medicare.gov, then click on "Compare Nursing Homes in Your Area."

winters, this might be your ticket! Several communities in Kansas (www.kansasfreeland.com) and North Dakota (www.prairieopportunity.com) are extending these offers.

GOLF COMMUNITIES

Itching to trade in the weed whacker for a Big Bertha? If you want to focus on the fairways, consider living in a golf-course community. Even though the number of golfers in the United States (about 27 million) has remained relatively stable over the past several years, the number of courses has increased. Even those who aren't golfers like to live where they can see lots of green grass and open space for which they're not responsible! For specific information on golf-course communities, click on www.golfcoursehome.net or www.privatecommunities.com (click on "golf courses"). For golf-course communities with home prices starting at $1 million or more, or lots beginning at $750,000 or more, go to www.luxury golfhomes.net.

You could also check out World Golf Village (www.wgv.com). Located less than half an hour south of Jacksonville, Florida, the community boasts two championship golf courses: the King and Bear (designed by Arnold Palmer and Jack Nicklaus) and the Slammer and Squire (for which Sam Snead and Gene Sarazen were consultants). Here, you not only play golf, but can also eat at a number of golf-themed restaurants, sleep, think, and shop golf. Homes range from condos to estate homes to Glenmoor, a retirement community whose offerings range from independent living to 24-hour nursing care. Condos at World Golf Village begin in the $200,000s, patio homes in the $300,000s, and single-family homes in the $300,000. The Cascades, an active-adult community, offers single-family homes in the $300,000s. The World Golf Hall of Fame is located here, and the 30,000-square-foot PGA Tour shop offers about any golf-related accessory imaginable. Contact the Neighborhoods at World Golf Village (904-940-5000) or Glenmoor Adult Retirement Community (800-471-2335).

Or, if you're truly a diehard, live where the best-rated golf courses are located. *Golf Digest* ranked "America's 100 Greatest Golf Courses" for 2005 to 2006. Go to www.golfdigest.com (click on "courses" under "rankings"). *Golf* magazine published its "Top 100 Courses You Can Play

---

Looking for golf on a smaller scale? Myrtle Beach is considered the mini-golf capital of the world with more than 60 miniature golf courses; the U.S. ProMiniGolf Association is located here.

2006 to 2007" rankings—access www.golfonline.com and put "top 100 courses you can play" into the search site. If you'd like to play at the best private courses, perhaps you can find a member who could take you as a guest; failing that, some of the courses (about 20) offer charity benefits that you may be able to attend.

MARTHA STEWARTVILLE

If Martha Stewart is your house goddess, you can live in a Martha-inspired community.

Stewart and KB Homes have joined forces to build a number of developments based on her own homes. Seven new neighborhoods are in the works in four states—California, Georgia, North Carolina, and Texas. Homes begin around $200,000. For more details, go to www.kbhome.com or call 800-KB-HOMES.

ON THE ROAD AGAIN

Over one million Americans call their RVs home. The largest contingent of recreation-vehicle owners is 35-to-54-year-olds. If you're itching to be on the road, there are a few things to consider. Full-time RV living offers flexibility and convenience and the opportunity to visit many places; you can take your pets with you, provide your own guest quarters when you visit others, and meet lots of interesting people. It's also a lifestyle to consider if you're single. A full-size motor home costs about $100,000 and gets around 7 miles per gallon. However, living the nomadic life makes it more difficult to form a social-support system and to develop deep and lasting friendships. There are several practical issues to address as well.

Tax considerations. Where will income from pensions and dividends be taxed? How do you determine your domicile? (See www.newrver.com/taxation.html for an excellent explanation of some of the tax issues affecting full-time RV living.)

Connections. It can be difficult to stay in touch. Cell phones, message and mail-forwarding services, and wireless technology make it easier to keep tabs on others (and to let them keep tabs on you!).

Illness. This is a real worry, since many insurance policies don't take kindly to illness on the road. Even with coverage, it's often difficult to find a doctor and get an appointment. The Escapees RV Club offers a CARE (Continuing Assistance for Retired Escapees) Center in Livingston, Texas. It's "designed for RVers whose travels

---

Sixty percent of residents living in golf-course communities don't play golf.

are permanently ended because of age or temporarily interrupted because of an illness." See www.escapees care.org or call 936-327-4256.

Stuff. For some people, the biggest drawback to living in an RV is lack of space. Of course, you can always rent storage space or lockers, but most find they have to live without their souvenirs.

Burnout. Discovering the right pace is critical. Generally, staying in the same place for at least a week will help prevent burnout.

Breakdowns. Thomas H., an RVer for many years, gives this advice: "Remember that you are in a house never meant to be on wheels and that you are traveling on wheels never meant to hold a house. When you marry the two, something is going to break as you travel down the highway. My wife and I have tried to take the mental frustrations out of the equation by simply looking at problems as part of the challenge of RVing—i.e., hey it's part of the trip! Luckily we have never broken down in an isolated area, mainly because I spend money up front on making sure my unit is well serviced by a local dealer whom I have trusted for the past 10 years."

If you think you'd like life on the road, you may want to take a test drive first. For example, you could rent an RV through Cruise America (www.cruiseamerica.com) for 7 nights in the southern United States in June 2007 for about $1,800. This includes a standard RV, an estimated 700 miles of travel (you're reimbursed or charged for the difference upon return of the RV), kitchen equipment, linens, liability insurance, and damage deductibles.

true LIFE **Bill M. lives in Newport Beach, California, and is the owner of a company that provides plastic containers to major corporations. Bill and his wife, Kathy, have owned motor homes for more than a decade, and here are his thoughts about RVing.**

Here I am, driving my motor home to Las Vegas (for work, honest), contemplating retirement. I've just turned 57, and this retirement idea seems to be on my mind. My decision is easy. When the time comes, my wife and I will be hitting the road. For us, traveling in our motor home is the answer. We have owned motor homes for the past 14 years and

Many, but not all, Wal-Marts allow you to park your RV for free. For a list of free (or nearly free) sites, go to www.freecampgrounds.com.

are convinced this is the key to happiness when we retire. If you can say yes to any of the following statements, then motor-home retirement may be for you, too.

❋ You want to see this country up close and personal.

❋ You want to travel at your pace, coming and going when you want.

❋ You want to renew old acquaintances and make new ones.

We've covered about 150,000 miles and can't wait to get the next 100,000 miles under our wheels. This is a very spontaneous way to live, see old friends, and make new ones. Hope to see you on the road! Ⓛ

ROOM SERVICE, PLEASE! OR, LIVING IN A HOTEL

Yearning for a roast beef sandwich at 2 a.m.? Call room service! Need reservations for that trendy new restaurant? Call the concierge! How would you like valet parking, housekeeping, fitness facilities, and the other amenities of a fine hotel just a phone call or steps away? Well, you could consider living in a hotel

(or at least having the same privileges). Here is a sampling of full-time/shared-ownership (also called fractional ownership) opportunities available in fine hotels that you could call home. Warning: Luxury doesn't come cheap! Prices are easily a 20 to 25 percent add-on to comparable residences not located on a hotel campus.

Four Seasons (www.fourseasons.com or 800-819-5053) has private residences and shared-ownership properties available both within and outside of the United States. Properties are located in California, Wyoming, Mexico, Arizona, Colorado, Florida, Texas, Costa Rica, Barbados, Ireland, and Canada.

Ritz-Carlton (www.ritzcarlton.com or 800-241-3333) also provides the option of purchasing a residence or sharing ownership, both within and outside of the United States. Owning a residence is possible in 12 states and the District of Columbia, and five countries outside of the United States. Sample costs: A private residence at Kapalua Bay in Hawaii is $3.9 million, and fractional ownership is offered from the $300,000s.

SINGLES TOWNS

If you're single and wish to relocate, what considerations should you weigh? Of course, whether you're part of a couple or going it alone, the same things—agreeable climate, ample cultural and recreational opportunities, good medical facilities, reasonable cost of living—are desirable. If you're unattached, however, you might want to look for specific places known to be hospitable to singles. These places tend to provide opportunities for singles to make new friends and create social-support structures. Consider areas that are growing rapidly. People new to an area tend to be more receptive to making new acquaintances than are those whose social circles have already been firmly established. Here are several suggestions for places particularly amenable to singles.

Asheville. Located in beautiful western North Carolina, Asheville has a four-season climate, the University of North Carolina-Asheville campus, and many opportunities to get involved.

Las Vegas. Beyond the strip, Las Vegas has affordable housing and a reasonable cost of living. About one-third of Las Vegas's population is retired, and there is a good job market. The desert beauty of Red Rock Canyon; boating, swimming, and fishing in Lake Mead; and the Hoover Dam are all a short distance away. Excellent transportation and numerous volunteer opportunities are also available.

Naples. With its 7 miles of beach on Florida's west coast, Naples is upscale and cosmopolitan with an abundance of arts, entertainment, shopping, activities, and attractions.

Sarasota. As part of Florida's "cultural coast," this shining jewel on the state's west coast is "sophisticated yet laid-back, elegant, fun-loving, and dedicated to the arts," according to its Web site.

RV living. Approximately 10 percent of people in RV parks are single, so this could be an option if this type of living appeals to you. If you're a single woman, there is an organization especially for you: Rving Women, which has about 5,000 members (www.rvingwomen.com or 888-557-8464).

In general, if you're single, you might consider active-adult communities with their organized activities and/or gated communities for safety. Also, and perhaps most important, remember that a positive mental attitude will contribute to your enjoyment—wherever you decide to live!

According to *Forbes*, the top 10 "Best Cities for Singles 2006" are: Denver/Boulder, Boston, Phoenix, San Francisco/Oakland, New York, Raleigh/Durham, Seattle, Austin, Washington/Baltimore, and Miami.

NEW URBANISM

Would you like to live, play, and work (if you're considering working!) all in the same place? If so, new urbanism (with its neo-traditional or traditional neighborhoods) may be for you. This style shares several principles: It is pedestrian friendly, which reduces residents' need for cars; offers a mix of shopping, homes, and offices; offers a variety of architecturally interesting housing designs with homes close to the street and lots of porches; and features narrow roads. New urbanism stresses increased density so that most everything is within a 10-minute walk. A neo-traditional neighborhood will have a well-defined edge to it—no bleeding into the next town or neighborhood. Its supporters claim the creation of compact, integrated villages fosters a sense of community, is environmentally friendly, raises the standard of living, and provides a better quality of life.

This type of neighborhood (old new urbanism!) can be found around the world in places like Capri, Venice, and Florence. In the United States, cities such as Annapolis, Maryland; Alexandria, Virginia; St. Augustine, Florida; and Washington, DC, reflect this type of configuration. There are approximately 600 of these neo-traditional neighborhoods either built or being developed in the United States. Here are some sample towns that exemplify new urbanism.

Celebration, Florida (www.celebrationfl.com or 877-696-TOWN). Just south of Orlando, Celebration is now more than 15 years old. Developed by the Disney Corporation, it really sparked the new urbanism movement in the United States. A total of 12,000 residents is expected by completion of the community. Housing possibilities include apartments, terrace homes, bungalows, garden homes, cottage homes, townhomes, village homes, and estate homes. (One of us thought it was the perfect community; the other thought it was too Stepfordlike.) Example of price: A resale condo in the downtown area is listed for $375,000, while a three-bedroom, two-bath, single-family home is offered for $439,000.

Habersham (www.habershamsc.com or 877-542-2377). Located 8 minutes from Beaufort, South Carolina; 30 minutes from Hilton Head Island, South Carolina; and 1 hour from Charleston, South Carolina, and Savannah, Georgia, Habersham's location is great. The Habersham Creek encourages boating, fishing, and swimming. Available homes, including lofts, townhomes, flats, and single-family homes, begin in the high $400,000s, and homesites begin in the $100,000s.

I'On (www.ionvillage.com or 866-330-8200). This is a 243-acre neo-traditional neighborhood in Mount Pleasant, South Carolina, 10 minutes from Charleston.

This development, which will ultimately include about 760 homes, began in 1997. Lots begin in the $200,000s, and available homes start in the $600,000s. Porches are at least 8 feet deep to encourage rocking-chair action and socializing with neighbors.

Seaside (www.seasidefl.com or 866-891-4600). This is where the new-urbanism movement was born. Located on Florida's panhandle on the Gulf of Mexico, Seaside was the setting for the movie *The Truman Show*. Developed on 80 acres and begun in 1981, Seaside has 430 cottages, many of which can be rented. Want to purchase a cottage? Sale prices range from $1 million and up, with condos and townhomes also available.

Sunset Island. This 37-acre neighborhood in Ocean City, Maryland, nudges up against the Assawoman Bay and is two blocks from the Atlantic Ocean. A mix of condos, townhomes, and single-family homes makes up this almost 600-unit property. Prices for condos begin in the upper $400,000; townhomes, in the upper $400,000s; and new single-family homes from $1 million. A fishing pier, green spaces, a beach, pool, and walking paths are incorporated into the planning. Contact www.sunsetislandocmd.com or the three builders (Main Street Homes, 410-524-1245; NV Homes, 888-348-6060; and Ryan Homes, 888-343-7926).

 true LIFE **Beth M. and her husband, Brian, own a second home in Sunset Island.**

My husband and I bought a house at Sunset Island about 3 years ago. We decided to buy the house with my husband's brother and his family. Between the two families, there are 12 of us, so we needed plenty of space. As children, both my family and my husband's family grew up going to the Delaware shore. We spent our summers there going to the beach and hanging out with friends and family; it was wonderful. We wanted to give our children the same experience that we enjoyed growing up.

Ironically, I always felt that Ocean City had grown too much and was too busy and overcrowded until Sunset Island was developed. Sunset Island is a private island located on the bay, at 67th Street in Ocean City, Maryland, but seems a world away from the commotion of downtown OC. We have incredible views of the bay, and the beach is only 2 walkable blocks from our house. The gated community is built in neo-traditional streetscapes with sidewalks, front porches, alleyways, rear garages, and a number of community boat slips. This style gives the community a warm, welcoming feeling. The clubhouse has a workout facility as well as indoor and outdoor pools. The kids also enjoy the interactive fountain, crabbing and fishing piers, private beaches, community store, and more.

We feel very lucky that we have such an incredible place to retreat to, and it is only 2½ hours away from our primary home in Maryland. It's a place where our children can build their own beach memories and learn to love the summers like we did. Ⓛ

PARK YOUR PLANE

If you're really in a hurry to get home, consider one of the 500 or so fly-in communities. Airstrips can be found in a number of developments, including Fox Harb'r in Wallace, Nova Scotia; Sunriver in Oregon; the Ocean Reef Club in Florida; Pauma Valley Country Club in California; Mountain Air in North Carolina; Aero Estates in Texas; Edgewater Estates in Idaho; Spruce Creek in Florida; and Jumbolair Aviation Estates in Florida (where John Travolta has a home and parks his 707 and Gulfstream jets). For more info, go to www.livingwithyourplane.com or www.airporthomes.com.

SPRING-TRAINING TOWNS

Ah, baseball, the great American pastime (although this is now a subject of debate). If you're a die-hard fan of the game, you could consider living where one of the major-league baseball teams conducts spring training. By moving to Florida, you could travel to about two-thirds of the spring-training sites and also see the Florida Marlins and Tampa Bay Devil Rays at home when the regular season begins. Anne Marie and Joseph A. of Silver Spring, Maryland, were so enamored with their beloved Baltimore Orioles that they purchased a condo in Fort Lauderdale so they wouldn't miss any of the action!

For schedules, tickets, and restaurant and hotel information regarding spring training, get *Spring Training* magazine (919-967-2420) or log on to www.springtrainingmagazine.com. Batter up!

WATER, WATER EVERYWHERE

Looking to live on the water, but on a smaller scale than *The World of ResidenSea*, the *Freedom Ship*, or one of the other proposed residence ships? If you love the water, aren't susceptible to motion sickness, and think traveling where and when you'd like would be heaven, entertain the notion of trading in your home and car for a boat. Financial aspects of living aboard vary widely, as maintenance costs, insurance, and fees to dock your boat expand dramatically as the size of the vessel increases. Resources include Living Aboard (www.livingaboard.com or 800-927-6905; they also have a magazine), the

Seven Seas Cruising Association (www.ssca.org or 954-771-5660), and books on the topic.

Judee and Tom S. live aboard. Here is an e-mail they sent out to friends describing a typical day on their sailboat, the _Cheshire Cat_.

Tom and I get up with first light, so the very first thing we do—after getting dressed, but before breakfast—is to raise the anchor. This is just about the time the sun is pulling itself up out of the water too.

Hauling up the anchor brings up, over the bow and onto the deck, a lot of black, sticky, mucky, yucky mud.

(One time, when Tom pulled up the anchor, he also pulled up with the mud a long, long, very, very thin something that looked like a piece of string. Except this piece of string wiggled on its own, curving and winding itself into a little doodle. One end might have been a head, because it seemed to look this way and that as if to ask, "Where am I?" We had never seen anything like this little creature before. I felt something akin to Jacques Cousteau aboard Calypso! I wondered if this skinny piece of string had eyes. I thought that after the anchor was up, I'd look at it more closely with a magnifying glass, and I went back to my station at the wheel. _Too bad I didn't let Tom know about this important research effort. Before I got back to the little whatever-it-was, Tom had flicked it overboard. Darn!)_

Can't travel with a dirty _Cat_, so once the anchor is up, it's my job to clean the deck while we start traveling. I use a canvas bucket attached to a rope, dip it into the water, haul it up hand over hand, and swish it on the deck. About 20 dips and "swashes" will do it. And all the while, I'm enjoying the sunrise too.

The winds are usually calm in the morning, so Tom runs the motor for about an hour to recharge our batteries. As soon as the wind picks up, we raise the sail and turn the motor off.

(OFF is what we love best and work toward. The moment OFF happens is pure relief! Like when you take a pair of ski boots OFF!)

Sometime between ON and OFF, I go down below to make breakfast.

(This can be a little exciting when a big yacht or a sports fisherman zooms by. Tom usually sees the disaster coming and yells a warning: "Hold on!" I capture the styrofoam box of eggs, the carton of milk, and the bottle of chili sauce in a quick embrace. Then the boat heaves, bounces, and rocks and everything I didn't grab or was afraid to hug—like our steaming cups of *coffee—slippy-slide, topple over, or simply slosh on the counter top that has turned into a teeter-totter. The bacon and eggs on the stove, however, are safe. The stove is gimbaled and knows how to rock and roll and stay flat at the same time.)*

After breakfast I do dishes, then I tidy up down below. Sounds familiar, right? Nothing too exciting.

We move toward lunch at an average of 5 knots. About 6 to 8 hours after starting out, we get to where we've planned to get to—a whole 25 to 30 miles down the way.

(Think about it: A car could get that far in 30 minutes!)

What do we do with all this travel time?

Not much. Whoever's at the helm is kept busy, and whoever isn't at the wheel is a second pair of eyes. You're both playing the buoy game. It's a matter of matching the numbered buoys along the Intracoastal Waterway to the numbered buoys on the chart. The challenge is to keep all the green buoys on one side, the red ones on the other (except when you're in a river, and then rules about which ones are on the right and which ones are on the left can change). In between the buoys the water is supposed to be deep enough for you to travel. Outside of the buoys, you could go aground.

You can win this buoy game only if you stay between the green ones and the red ones—and you don't bump into one of either color.

Actually, sailing the ICW is harder than sailing in the ocean, because the ICW is comparatively narrow, often twisting, sometimes busy, and usually shallow. And if you don't see a buoy, or at least know on your chart where a buoy is supposed to be, and know for sure where you are in relation to that buoy, you're in trouble.

You also have to keep up with such trivia questions as how deep is the water you're in.

(It's a little scary when our instruments show we're moving at 8 knots through 6 feet of water. It's even more exciting when the depth sounder suddenly drops to 4.1, the Cat's *5-foot keel digs in, and we come to a sudden stop. Correction: Make that a thud and stop.)*

Besides the buoy game, we also play the bridge game. Most of the bridges crossing the ICW are 65-footers. We pass under without a care. But a lot of the bridges are lower than the *Cat's* mast is high, so we have to plan and time our approach. Then, when we're in sight of the bridge, we use the VHF radio to call the bridge tender to request an opening. Playing the bridge game is a lot like doing a crossword puzzle. If you get it right, you're home free.

(But if you get it wrong, you're in for a little excitement while you—and a bevy of other waiting boats—cool your keels. For example, consider this word puzzle for the Wappoo Bridge on the Stono River a little south of Charleston.

Per our cruising guide:

Wappoo Creek Bridge. RESTRICTED. From April 1 to May 30 and October 1 to November 30 M-F, closed 6 to 9 a.m. and 4 to 6 p.m. Opens on the hour and half hour from 9 a.m. to 4 p.m. Weekends and holidays opens on the hour and half-hour from 9 a.m. to 7 p.m. From December 1 to March 30 and June 1 to September 30 M-F, closed 6:30 to 9 a.m. and 4 to 6:30 p.m. On request all other times.

Took awhile to decipher the rules, but we did. Since we're going through on June 3 and we'll get to the bridge sometime after 9 a.m., all we have to do is ask for an opening. We rounded a bend and saw the bridge at exactly 9:32 a.m.

"We'd like to request an opening," we radioed the control tower.

The bridge tender, seeing that we were still a few minutes away, radioed back: "I'm sorry, Captain, the next opening will be at 10 a.m."

Why the problem? Because the guidebook was wrong. The puzzle was missing a piece. $%^#@!)

In between playing the bridge game and the buoy game, we just sit—engulfed in togetherness.

We talk. We plan our day, the next season, or the year ahead.

We listen to music, tune the radio to NPR to get a take on what's happening in the real world, point to dolphins, notice boat names, check the tides and the weather, and for the most part, simply watch the changing shoreline scroll by.

(We do say "I love you" quite often. But then, you sure wouldn't want to be doing this with someone you didn't! Yet, it's still quietly exciting! After 46 years of marriage and 10 years of being within 30 feet of each other, it's still amazes me how many times each day we exchange this vow.)

When we get to where we're going, (exhausted even though we have been doing practically nothing), it's tea time. Only after a rejuvenating cup of tea will we start to do whatever there is to do wherever we are.

More nights than not we spend at anchor in a cozy, not-very-busy cove. In that case, we stay barefoot and aboard, perhaps go for a swim *(I try not to think about that little skinny wormy thing)*, then take a sun shower on deck. I'll cook a nice, big dinner. We'll have *(homemade!)* bittersweet chocolate truffles, Jell-O, or berries and cream while we watch the sunset. Lately, we've had some spectacular moonrises.

After dark, we usually read, play Sequence (Skip-Bo is no longer our favorite), or fire up our computers.

(One night in Florida or maybe Georgia, I was topsides, in the cockpit, surrounded by pitch-black darkness. Every so often I heard a loud "Puff-f-f" close to the boat, as if someone were blowing air out of a snorkel.

"Listen! A dolphin!" I said to Tom.

A while later, there was a big splash off toward the marshy shore.

"An alligator!" said Tom to me.

Now why would I ever, in the future, even give a second thought about that little skinny slimy wormy thingy?)

If there's a town along the ICW that we'd like to see, we usually arrange for a slip in a marina. In that case, after tea, we'll haul out and unfold our bikes on the dock, dress up (a little or a lot depending), pedal into town, and probably dine out. While we're in town, we fit in the necessities, like doing the grocery shopping, getting a haircut, or finding a doctor or dentist.

(Transporting a hundred-plus dollars worth of groceries on two little bikes can be what you might call
"exciting." And it does take a certain amount of courage to sit down and have a perfect stranger start working on your hair, your teeth, or whatever hurts. And sometimes, in town, the strangest things happen. For instance:

Tom's lower back was acting unkindly last winter. While we were in Naples, we asked the dockmaster to recommend a walk-in clinic. Off we went on our bikes. Found the clinic. Signed in. Waited for our randomly assigned doctor.

Three minutes into the examination, the doctor mentions that he also has a boat—a catamaran. Two minutes later, he is talking about sailing in Maine last summer with his wife and three boys. Something clicked in my memory. We exchanged boat names— and confirmed that last summer the Cheshire Cat *and* Wind Song *had crossed paths at least five or six times!)*

Whatever have I been thinking of! That's it! We do have excitement aboard the *Cat*. Regularly!

The excitement we have comes from encounters of the nicest kind: *people!*

We meet a lot of interesting boat folk as we move along. And the biggest thrill is when we meet them again. It's always a thrill to bump into "boats" we met 2 days ago, last month, or last year. It's an even bigger thrill to happen upon a boat you cruised with to the Bahamas 6 or 7 years ago! Or came down the New York Barge Canal with 10 years ago!

Yes, you meet boats. The identity of the people who live on a boat is one and the same as the name of their boat. Mary and Craig are *Rum Tum Tiger*. Jacques and France are *Yallah!* Jim and Joyce are *Flying Fortress*. Don and Ruth are *Odyssey*.

To say the name of the boat is to remember not only the people but in one swift image to remember how and where we met, where they hail from, what we did together, and where they were headed when we last saw them.

It's a fact of cruising. If you sail near, anchor with, or dock close to a boat for 2 days in a row, you're friends. You arrange to get together for happy hour. Over wine and cheese and sea stories, you exchange boat cards and e-mail addresses. The odds are good that you'll bump into each other again.

It's amazing how small a world it is out here.

And it's even smaller when friends like you keep in touch.

Hugs,

Tom and Judee (who are known as the *Cheshire Cat*) ⓉⓁ

We've explored some niche retirement lifestyles, and the previous chapter looked at particular places within the United States, but if you want to consider relocating outside the U.S.A., then the next chapter is for you!

WHERE SHOULD YOU MOVE?

Recommended Locations Outside the United States

"Two roads diverged in a wood, and I—I took the one less traveled by, and that has made all the difference."
—Robert Frost

It's estimated that three to six million Americans live abroad, but how many people retire to another country? It's a good question, and one for which there is no definitive answer. The Social Security Administration sends about 400,000 Social Security checks out of the country each month, although it's estimated that many additional Americans living in another country have their checks deposited directly into a U.S. financial institution. *Where to Retire* magazine estimates that about 460,000 Americans are retired outside of the United States.

Perhaps the more important question is *why* consider relocating outside the United States? For many, money is a big incentive. Living in a low-cost-of-living country can stretch your retirement dollars. For others, becoming immersed in a different culture is exciting, becoming proficient in another language is enticing, and living in a locale with perfect weather and a laid-back approach to life is attractive. Some people feel safer escaping a high-crime area in the States or they are intrigued by the novel recreational and cultural opportunities a new country has to offer. Many people who retire to another country have had positive experiences through travel, work, or study abroad. Others are ready to embrace a completely new way of life during the second half of their lives. The shrinking of the world through communications, computers, and improved transportation makes living abroad a more attainable possibility for many.

If having a home in another country sounds like a good idea, you'll need to prioritize your preferences and needs, suggests *International Living* magazine. Think about these factors when considering another country: proximity to North America, cost of living, language barriers (if any), tax ramifications, recreational/cultural amenities, safety and political stability, medical care, climate, infrastructure (communications, roads, etc.), and special incentives for those who relocate. For example, if you never want to see another blizzard in your life, that would help narrow your list of possible locations. If you plan to stay only for several years and are in good health, top-notch, nearby medical care may drop to the bottom of your list.

Here are some additional points to think about when contemplating another country for relocation.

Your personality. This may be the biggest issue. Remember, you're moving to another country, one with its own concepts of time, social interactions, politics, and ways of doing things. You can't expect the experi-ence to be like moving to another area of the United States. If you live by the phrase "Don't sweat the small stuff," you're a much likelier candidate. If you're a type A personality, easily frustrated when appointments and schedules aren't kept, moving outside the United States—particularly to a Latin or southern European country that honors the tradition of an afternoon siesta—could be frustrating. (Of course, if that's your personality, living in the United States is probably frustrating as well!)

Health care. In general, health care tends to be less expensive in foreign countries. Doctors' visits, prescriptions, and hospitalizations can cost less than comparable U.S. medical care. In many cases, however, your medical insurance will not be honored outside of the United States, and Medicare won't cover you. You'll need to find out whether the insurance available in the country you're relocating to will serve your needs and whether you're eligible for low-cost government health plans; you might also be able to obtain national coverage in conjunction with private insurance.

Some countries have socialized health plans that will

If cost of living is your *primary* criterion for relocating, you'll be interested in Mercer Human Resource Consulting's 2006 ranking of 144 cities on six continents. The least expensive city in the world is Asuncion (Paraguay), followed by Buenos Aires, Montevideo, and Caracas. Moscow ranked as the most costly.

cover you once you've lived as a full-time resident for a set number of months. If you need to purchase international health insurance, consider Allnation Insurance Company (www.allnation.com or 800-342-0719), BUPA International (www.bupa-intl.com or +44-0-1273-208-181), or Health Insurance 4 International Travelers (HI4.com or 877-982-5200). As with all insurance policies, there are exclusions, deductibles, and different levels of coverage, so be sure to read the fine print before signing up. You may also want to include medical-evacuation coverage, which will cover transportation to an appropriate medical facility—even to the United States, if necessary. Health-care quality can be excellent or poor (often within the same country); this is an important area to research.

Money matters. If your income and assets are in dollars, the amount available to you to spend will be tied to the exchange rate of your newly adopted country. If the dollar is strong, your purchasing power will also be strong; if the dollar is weak, your financial base will be weakened. You may want to set up a bank account at a local institution and keep several months' worth of expenses in that country's legal tender as a hedge against currency swings.

Although you may be living outside of the United States, you are still responsible for filing U.S. federal tax returns because you are still a United States citizen, which, don't forget, also entitles you to U.S. embassy privileges abroad. (Even if you renounce your U.S. citizenship—which we are not advocating!—you can still be subject to the U.S. tax code for an additional decade after renunciation because the IRS will assume you are trying to avoid your tax liability.) You may also have to pay taxes in the new country as well. In some cases, you may be eligible for tax credits, deductions, or exclusions under U.S. and international tax laws. If you're seriously considering a move to a particular place, your best bet is to meet with both a tax professional in the new country who has expertise working with expatriate Americans and a U.S. tax planner with expertise in international tax. The four major U.S. accounting firms—Ernst and Young LLP, PricewaterhouseCoopers, KPMG LLP, and Deloitte and Touche LLP—are good resources. When determining your budget for living in the new country,

---

Two suggested companies if you're interested in a retirement relocation tour: International Living (www.internationalliving.com/events) or a tour with author Christopher Howard (www.boomersabroad.com/howardtours.html).

don't forget to plan for trips back to the United States.

Legalities. What type of visa or residency permit is required? Can you become a citizen? How do you (and can you?) finance and purchase real estate? (This is a huge issue; people have lost their homes or have had to repurchase them due to changing political winds.) Do you need a work permit if you'd like to start your own business or get a job? What are the requirements for a driver's license? Can you take your pet with you? To help answer these questions, contact the embassy of the country where you're considering relocating or its closest consulate. "Foreign Consular Offices in the United States" can be accessed online at http://www.state.gov/s/cpr/rls/fco/. You can also contact the U.S. Department of State Bureau of Consular Affairs at 202-647-4000. They produce a number of helpful pamphlets and provide assistance to people considering moving outside the United States and to those already living outside the United States.

Before deciding on a place to live, learn as much as you can about the country: Talk to a number of real-estate agents, view actual properties to get the lowdown on where to live (if purchasing, **be sure to buy what you see, not what is promised**), and rent for several months to get a real feel for the place. Remember, different times of the year can feel distinctly different. Hurricane season in September may make you forget about those warm, sunny days in February when you knew your old neighbors back in Boston were digging out from under a nor'easter! Contact expatriates (U.S. citizens living in the places you're interested in). To communicate to expatriates over the Internet, try a Web site such as www.liveabroad.com or www.expatexchange.com.

Countries with large numbers of U.S. citizens frequently have a U.S. chamber of commerce or organizations or clubs for Americans that can provide information. The Department of State produces data sheets on many countries called "Consular Information Sheets"; they include topics such as geography, government structure, safety, entry requirements, medical information, and real-estate purchasing requirements. Of course, many books and magazine articles have been written about living in other countries; see the reference list for this chapter for some suggestions. The Association of Residents of

---

The Web site www.retiringsinglesoverseas.com/retire/ (free membership at press time) does have finding Mr./Ms. Right as part of its mission, but it also focuses on singles traveling, investing, and living in a foreign country.

Costa Rica has developed a list of questions you should ask if you're considering locating to a foreign country. Their valuable "Relocation Checklist" is located in on page 437.

Which countries outside the United States are best? Of course, *best* is a subjective term, but *International Living* publishes a yearly Global Retirement Index that attempts to quantify countries' infrastructures, health care, climates, costs of living, retiree benefits, safety, freedom, and culture and entertainment. Their 2006 top 10 countries? Panama, Malta, New Zealand, Uruguay, Mexico, France, Romania, Argentina, Malaysia, and Ecuador. Needless to say, this list is colored by the reviewers' biases, as is any list of what is best, including our lists throughout this book! Now that you're aware of some of the particulars involved in moving to another country, let's take a look at a few specific desirable locations, as well as issues unique to each, such as how to purchase property, become a resident, and access health care. Based on our own Western slant, we suggest three countries to consider if you'd like to retire abroad: Costa Rica, Mexico, and Panama. Let's take a closer look.

COSTA RICA

Capital: San José
Population: 4,075,000
Natural Resources: Hydropower
Industries: Textiles, clothing, fertilizer, plastic products, construction materials, food processing, and microprocessors

Costa Rica abolished its army in 1948.

Costa Rica

REPORT CARD

Overall rating:	B+
Climate:	A
Cost of living:	A
Health care:	B+
Transportation:	B-
What's to do:	B

What country has fantastic weather, gorgeous scenery, a stable democratic government, a high standard of living, relatively low unemployment, a 96 percent literacy rate (defined as the percentage of the 15-and-older population who can read and write), and one-fourth of its land set aside as protected areas? It's Costa Rica.

Costa Rica (Columbus named this country "rich coast") has more than four million people in an area a little smaller than the state of West Virginia (just under 20,000 square miles). This Central American country is located between Nicaragua to the north and Panama to the south and is bounded by the Pacific Ocean on the west and the Caribbean Sea on the east. Although Spanish is the official language, English is very commonly spoken in this highly educated, highly Catholic (more than 75 percent) country.

Costa Rica is a democratic republic with a president, a cabinet chosen by the president, a legislative assembly, and a supreme court. The country is comprised of seven provinces: Alajuela, Cartago, Guanacaste, Heredia, Limon, Puntarenas, and San José.

The international airport in San José makes Costa Rica very accessible from the United States, and major carriers include American, Continental, United, and Delta. The improvements and enhancements to the second major airport, Liberia International, on the Pacific coast, opens up this desirable country even more. And a third international airport, in the Osa Peninsula area, is being considered.

If you already know some Spanish or want to learn it and are ready to think metric, consider Costa Rica!

Who Lives in Costa Rica?

About 94 percent of Costa Ricans are Caucasian (this includes Mestizos, those with Native American–Spanish

---

International Living magazine ranked Costa Rica 81 out of 193 countries in its "2006 Quality of Life Index."

lineage), African-Americans make up about 3 percent of the population, and Chinese people and people indigenous to Costa Rica make up about 1 percent each. It's estimated that 250,000 foreigners, mostly from North America, live full-time in Costa Rica. About 20 percent of the population is below the poverty line, compared to 12 percent in the United States.

What's It Like Outside?

Costa Rica, located 8 to 11 degrees above the equator, contains coastal plains, rain forests, river valleys, and mountains. Whether you experience the subtropical or tropical climate of Costa Rica is a function of elevation rather than season. The central highlands remain in the 60s and 70s, while the coastal regions vary between the 70s and 80s. The dry season runs from December to April, and the rainy season from May to November. This is a bit simplistic, however, since rainfall can vary from more than 220 inches on the Caribbean coast to fewer than 60 inches in the northern part of the Pacific coast. In the wettest areas, it tends to rain at night (à la Camelot!).

The country is part of the Pacific "Ring of Fire" and experiences tremors from time to time. Arenal, Irazu, Rincon de la Vieja, Poas, and Tenorio are among Costa Rica's active volcanoes, and there are about 60 extinct or dormant volcanoes. The last major earthquake, 7.4 on the Richter scale, was in 1991, killing 27, injuring 400, and leaving 13,000 homeless.

With its biodiversity of flora and fauna, its protected land, and its topography, Costa Rica is an environmentalist's dream.

What's the Cost?

It's not as expensive to live in Costa Rica as it is in the United States, but the difference is not enormous. Housing is more reasonable, although prices have been steadily escalating as more people become aware of Costa Rica as a desirable place to consider for relocation. Prices on the beach can vary substantially, from fairly reasonable to "a bundle."

For some items, such as automobile and boat parts (which may also be harder to get), you will pay more, but the cheaper labor costs result in about the same

---

Using New York City as a base with a score of 100 points, the 2006 Mercer Human Resource Consulting Cost of Living Survey rates San José, Costa Rica, as a 58; Cleveland, Ohio, a 70; Washington, DC, a 77; and Miami, Florida, an 84.

repair costs as in the States. Cars (new or used) are also pricier. On the other hand, groceries are only about two-thirds of what you'd pay in America, and you can have a full-time maid for about $250 per month. Utilities, dining out, and lodging are also not as expensive as Up North. Property, corporate, and personal taxes are low, and there is no tax on money earned outside of the country. But the sales tax is a hefty 13 percent on most goods and services.

Lifestyle choices will determine how much it costs to live, of course, but a reasonable estimate for an average North American moving to Costa Rica would be somewhere around $2,500 a month, according to "The Real Costa Rica" Web site.

The official currency is the Costa Rican colon, although a double economy with the dollar exists. An inflation rate of 11 percent is estimated for 2007.

What about Property Ownership?

The short answer is "yes, but." Buying property in Costa Rica can be straightforward in some cases but more complicated and convoluted in others.

There are three main categories of buying and owning property in Costa Rica. Fee simple ownership is the most comprehensive type of ownership, where foreigners enjoy the same rights and protections as Costa Rican nationals. Titles are registered in the Registro Nacional, along with any liens, judgments, or mortgages. Then there are the properties that are not titled (and have no recordings at the Registro Nacional). In some cases, legitimate ownership can be traced back through private documents; in other cases, ownership is basically through squatter's rights. Most land in Costa Rica is this untitled land, and sifting through the process to establish legitimacy can be difficult. Some real-estate professionals caution that these types of properties should be completely avoided.

The third property category is beachfront. Also called Maritime Zone lands or concession properties, they are handled quite differently. Some of this land (the first 50 meters from the average high tide line) cannot be owned at all; it's public and no permanent structure can be placed on it. The next 150 meters may be leased or a concession for it granted, generally for 20-year, renewable periods. The owner may build on the property, assuming he or she obtains the proper permits. Rights may also be transferred. One important caveat: Unless you have been a resident for 5 years, you are not allowed

---

Don't go to Costa Rica expecting pure white-sand beaches; sand colors range from beige to almost black.

to register beach property in your own name. You can, however, register it through a Costa Rican corporation with an agreement with the Costa Rican shareholder(s) that he/she/they will endorse the shares over to you at settlement so that you end up with all the shares; or, a legal trust may be set up by attorneys, accomplishing the same result.

Bottom line: Buying property or having concessions or leases on beachfront property is not uncommon. Be sure to hire an attorney who specializes in real-estate issues to help you maneuver through the purchase of such a significant investment. A good commercial Web site with information on real estate is www.osapeninsula.com (click on "Buying/Owning—Rules of the Road").

What's to Do?

Costa Rica is an ecological wonderland and a premiere ecotourism destination. The country has a dozen or so climate zones, and you can travel from rainforest to volcano to savannah to beach in the course of a day. The variety of plant and animal life is astounding, with more than 1,000 species of orchids and butterflies, almost as many bird species, and many different reptiles, amphibians, fish, and mammals. It's estimated that 6 percent of our planet's biodiversity is in Costa Rica! Surfing, white-water rafting, fishing, kayaking, snorkeling, swimming, sunbathing—all things water related are high on the list of things to do. The bounty of national parks and preserves, volcano-watching, rainforest canopy tours, horseback riding, hiking, and golf help round out the outdoor activities.

You could also take advantage of the universities, colleges, or technological institutes in Costa Rica, including distance education through the Universidad Estatal a Distancia in San José. Classes, however, will almost certainly be taught in Spanish, so make sure your language skills are sharp!

Cultural opportunities exist, but not on a grand scale. There is some live theater, the symphony, several art galleries, and museums. Movie houses, fiestas, casinos, bars, and restaurants are also available. Soccer (called football) is the main sport. There are a number of clubs, including the Rotary, chess, Internet, and singles' clubs for expatriates in Costa Rica, and volunteer activities are plentiful. San José's downtown is compact enough to be pedestrian friendly.

With a maximum width of 161 miles, you can enjoy a spectacular sunrise and sunset in the same day on different coasts of Costa Rica, and with more than 700 miles of coastline, a great water view isn't a problem!

What about Employment?

Unemployment in Costa Rica hovered around 7 percent in 2005. Tourism, agriculture, fishing, forestry, and commerce are the biggest industries. With the arrival of a number of multinational companies (MNCs) in Costa Rica, bilingual or English-speaking employees are hired to work in customer service or call centers that are being established at a rapid pace.

Can you work in Costa Rica? When you first apply for residency, you are usually granted conditional permanent residency; after a specified period of time, you may then apply for permanent resident status. Once you attain this level (it may take 5 years or so), you can live and work in Costa Rica without any restrictions. Many Americans, however, do not want to work at the low wages paid to Ticos (as Costa Ricans are also known), since salaries are much lower than in the States. Prior to obtaining permanent-residency status, it is illegal for foreigners to work, unless a Tico can't fill the position. There are many opportunities for volunteer work though.

What about Immigration Requirements?

If you want to check out Costa Rica for retirement, you can enter the country with a passport and stay for 90 days; if you want to say longer as a tourist, you need to apply for an extension through the Office of Temporary Permits in the Costa Rican Department of Immigration. Requests are evaluated on an individual basis.

If you're seeking residency (which doesn't affect your U.S. citizenship), you need to apply to the Costa Rican Consulate in Washington, DC, which serves all states as well as the District of Columbia (202-328-6628). It normally takes about 4 months to process residency applications, but it may take as long as a year. Documentation needed as part of this process includes a police certificate of good conduct issued within the past 6 months from the area in which the applicant has lived for the past 2 years, birth certificate, marriage certificate (if applicable), and income certificate. If retired, you must demonstrate that you receive at least $600 per month income from a pension or qualified retirement

A good source of information and help if you're considering Costa Rica is the Association of Residents of Costa Rica (ARCR). For $100 per year (nonresident rate), you receive *El Residente* magazine as well as assistance with legalities, insurance, work permits, real-estate advice, social activities, and more. Contact them at www.casacanada.net or 506-233-8068. They also offer free seminars (locations vary) on relocating to Costa Rica.

plan outside of Costa Rica, or from interest and/or dividends from dollars deposited in a Costa Rican government bank. You must reside in Costa Rica at least 4 months a year. This is to meet eligibility requirements in the pensionado category. There are additional categories with requirements for residency, including annuitant income status, investor status, and entrepreneur status. For example, with the annuitant or rentista status, another common way for retirees to achieve residency in Costa Rica, the person applying for residency must demonstrate that he or she has outside investments that will guarantee a monthly income of $1,000 a month for 5 years. The rentista must also live in Costa Rica for at least 6 months a year.

Some laws have been proposed, however, that would remove the rentista status and increase the monthly income requirement from $600 to $1,000 for pensionados and from $1,000 to $3,000 for rentistas. Contact the Costa Rican Consulate for further information.

Where Are Some Notable Neighborhoods?

Certain areas of Costa Rica seem to attract more Americans than others. One popular area is around the capital, San José. The town of Escazu is fewer than 4 miles from downtown San José; Rohrmoser, La Sabana, and Pavas are also located near the city. Santa Ana and Ciudad Colon are a little farther away from San José; Ciudad Colon is an option if you'd like to live halfway between the beach and the city. San José and the surrounding Central Valley area is where you'll find the major services and infrastructure in Costa Rica.

Do you think life really is better at the beach? The Pacific coast is less humid and more populated than the Caribbean coast, so you may want to concentrate your search there. A lot of development is going on as the country gets ready for its share of the close to 80 million retiring American baby boomers. A town to consider on the northwest Pacific coast is Tamarindo, which is located on what is known as Costa Rica's "Gold Coast." In Tamarindo, you'll find a number of activities as well as a regional airport, and Liberia International airport is less than an hour away. There are a number of beaches (*playas*) with growing populations. Playa Hermosa, Playa Flamingo, and Playa Grande are all to the north of Playa Tamarindo; Playa Nosaro and Playa Carrillo are to the south. Moving along to the more remote, but beautiful, Nicoya Peninsula, consider Tambor, which is more of a resort community, or perhaps Playa Montezuma. Natural beauty and better access to this area are positioning it to really take off.

The central Pacific coast has Playa Jaco, Playa Herradura, and Manuel Antonio. Playa Jaco is more of a tourist area; since it and Playa Herradura are easily accessible from San José, they are popular beaches, and a good number of Americans live there.

If you possess a pioneer spirit (not to mention a four-wheel-drive vehicle and the zest to live on the wild side), look at the Osa Peninsula, home to Corcovado National Park, which *National Geographic* has called "the most biologically intense place on Earth." An 8-hour drive from San José, this area is a feast for the eyes, but it's not for those who need pampering. Puerto Jimenez is a little town in the Osa Peninsula that could do the trick. A proposed international airport in this area will ease the difficulty of accessing it.

As in any other place, housing costs and choices can vary tremendously from location to location. A few examples: Apartment rentals in the San José suburbs run between $300 and $650 per month. To rent a home would be a few hundred more dollars per month. A two-bedroom condo in desirable Escazu, with 24-hour security, underground parking, pool, and private jogging trail is listed in the upper $200,000s. A single-family home in Escazu, built in 2000 with three bedrooms and two baths in a gated community is listed for $170,000.

Some Pacific coast prices include: Near Tamarindo, a new three-bedroom home with a swimming pool and garage on a half-acre lot lists for $375,000, whereas the asking price for a home with a spectacular Pacific ocean view is $985,000. Playa Hermosa has a resort area called Los Suenos (www.lossuenosresort.com), which boasts a marina, golf course, beach club, and Marriott Hotel, while the Central Pacific area of Jaco is home to the new St. Regis Resort and Residences (www.stregis-residences.com), with over a mile of Pacific coastline, and elevations ranging from sea level to 900 feet. Condo/hotels, villas, and estate homes will be surrounded by a 250-acre wildlife reserve. Prices vary, with residences beginning in the mid $300,000s and escalating to more than $2.5 million. Build-out is projected in 2009.

Four Seasons has a residence club at Peninsula Papagayo in Guanacaste, in the northwest corner of Costa Rica, offering waterfront condos on a fractional ownership basis. Interested in purchasing a condo or home? Prices range from around $1 million to $12 million. Two other upscale amenity-laden communities in Guanacaste are Hacienda Pinilla (sample prices: half-acre plus lots with views of the golf course and ocean listed from $70,000 to $600,000) and 2,300-acre Reserva Conchal, a community with a 25-year build-out time

---

Costa Rica and the United States have similar infant-mortality rates and life expectancies.

frame with prices beginning in the $70,000s. Contact Hacienda Pinilla at www.haciendapinilla.com and/or Reserva Conchal at www.reservaconchal.com.

On the Osa Peninsula, 130 mostly forested acres is listed for $350,000, but beach property would be much more expensive.

If considering a property purchase, be sure there is available water, adequate space for the location of a septic system, access to gravel roads year-round (flooding could be an issue), and that the site is away from lowlands, mangrove swamps, protected areas, and wetlands. You can (and should) haggle over prices. Again, be sure to enlist professional help prior to any real-estate purchase and hire a good title company to ensure legitimate ownership rights. Real-estate fraud is not uncommon.

How Is Costa Rica's Health Care?

One of the many positive aspects of living in Costa Rica is the caliber and affordability of its medical care, including dental care, which is about 30 percent less than dental care in the United States. The health system can be accessed through several avenues. You can go the private, pay-as-you-go route for doctors' visits and hospitalization at a much lower cost than you'd find in the States (a private hospital room averages about $140 per day). For about $55 per month, you can participate in the government-sponsored health plan, CCSS. Although the quality of care is good, the wait for appointments and the abbreviated office visits may not be as much to your liking. There is also government health insurance through Instituto Nacional de Seguro (INS), which is widely accepted by Costa Rica's health-care industry and ranges from $900 to $1,700 annually. Or choose a combination of private pay and public access. Many doctors have their own private practices in addition to their public service. See doctors at a more leisurely pace for routine visits and pay them out of pocket, but use your coverage for expensive procedures.

The World Health Organization released a study that compared health systems in 191 countries based on eight criteria, including cost, access, and level of care. In this list, Costa Rica ranked 36th. (The United States ranked 37th.)

How Safe Is Costa Rica?

The violent-crime rate is low, but muggings and thefts do occur. People should exercise the same caution they would in any big city or tourist area: Don't walk alone in deserted areas, don't leave valuables in your car, park in secured lots, patronize licensed taxis, and don't exchange money on the streets (where you are more likely to encounter credit-card fraud and/or counterfeit money).

Of course, no place is crime-free, so just keep your wits about you.

Strengths

People are friendly, and Costa Rica is receptive to foreign residents. The nice climate, good standard of living at a lower cost (if you avoid expensive areas and shop locally), stable government, fairly low crime rate, and good medical care all combine to make Costa Rica a real contender for retirement living. Your pets are allowed if you have a veterinary certificate. To drive, you need only your American (or international) driver's license while visiting on a tourist visa; when you obtain residency, you can use your American license to apply for your Costa Rican license. And you can drink the water! If you're a nature lover and a person of simple pleasures, Costa Rica could be for you.

Weaknesses

On the other hand, patience is not only a virtue in Costa Rica, it's a necessity. Red tape is a given, and things promised on a certain day may or may not materialize.

Your day could be consumed renewing a driver's license, or it may take an hour in line for your turn at the bank. Roads are not very well-maintained—many are unpaved—so watch out for the potholes! It may be difficult to really get to know Costa Ricans, particularly if you don't learn the language and you choose to live in the areas heavily populated by other Americans.

MEXICO

Mexico was ranked number five (out of 28 countries) in *International Living* magazine's "2006 Annual Global Retirement Index," 32nd (out of 193 countries) in its "2006 Quality of Life Index," and was rated "Best Foreign Country for Retirees" by *Kiplinger's* magazine (2006).

Capital: Mexico City
Population: 107,450,000
Natural Resources: Timber, natural gas, petroleum, copper, silver, gold, lead, and zinc
Industries: Tourism, tobacco, mining, petroleum, iron, steel, food and beverages, clothing, and durable consumer goods

Mexico

REPORT CARD

Overall rating:	B
Climate:	A-
Cost of living:	A
Health care:	B
Transportation:	B
What's to do:	B

If you're willing to venture outside of the United States for relocation after retirement, you have only to look south of our country's borders to find some attractive alternatives. We've addressed Costa Rica, now we'll turn our attention, as Frank Sinatra sang, "South of the border, down Mexico way."

Imagine Texas, and then imagine Texas times three. That's about the size of Mexico—around 760,000 square miles. Mexico is bordered by the United States to the north, Belize and Guatemala to the south, the Gulf of Mexico and the Caribbean Sea to the east, and the Pacific Ocean to the west. The population is spread out among this country's rugged mountains, high plateaus, deserts, and lowlands. Depending on location, you can experience desert or tropical conditions. The country has 31 states and one federal district, governed by a president (Felipe Calderon since 2006, in a hotly contested election), a supreme court, federal and local courts, and a congress consisting of a senate and federal chamber of deputies.

How many Americans live in Mexico? Estimates from the U.S. State Department range from 600,000 to 1 million (full and part-timers), which makes it the most popular foreign residence for U.S. citizens. Mexico is reachable by car from the States, and when you add the ease of access to a lower cost of living, delightful weather,

---

Keep in mind that your body may require some time to acclimate to the higher altitudes in the central plateau area. Mexico City, for example, has an elevation of more than 7,500 feet—about a half-mile higher than Denver.

scenic beauty, democratic government, rich culture and history, friendly people, laid-back lifestyle, good medical care and infrastructure (high-speed Internet is available most places Americans live), and access to most of the goods and services you'd find in the United States, you may have found a winner!

Who Lives in Mexico?

The median age in Mexico is 25, and the population is growing annually at about 1.2 percent. About 6 percent of the population is over 65 years of age, while more than 64 percent is between the ages of 15 and 64. The majority of the population (89 percent) is Roman Catholic, while 6 percent are Protestants, the next largest religious group. Ethnic groups include Amerindian-Spanish (60 percent), Amerindian or mostly Amerindian (30 percent), Caucasian (9 percent), and 1 percent "other."

Culturally, a high value is placed on family life, but there are sharp class divisions, and about 40 percent of Mexico's citizens live in poverty (compared to 12 percent in the United States). Life expectancy averages about 75 years (compared to 78 for the United States). The literacy rate (defined as the percentage of the 15-and-older population who can read and write) is about 92 percent (compared to 99 percent in the United States).

What's It Like Outside?

Location (altitude and latitude) dictates climate in Mexico. The central plateau, which makes up about two-thirds of the country, enjoys cooler temperatures and lower humidity because of the elevation; annual average temperature is around 65 degrees, although the evenings can be chilly. Along the lowlands of the coast, it's hot and humid, with an average temperature ranging from 80 degrees on the Yucatan peninsula to 68 degrees on the northwest coast.

The rainy season runs from May to October, and rainfall varies with topography. In the central plateau region, annual rainfall varies from 20 inches in the north to 35 inches in the south, and some of the precipitation may actually be in the form of snow. (As a benchmark, think of New York City, with its annual rainfall of about 50 inches). The Sierra Madre Occidental snakes down the western side of Mexico, and the Sierra Madre Oriental is

---

How to get title insurance? Two suggestions (both American companies): Stewart Title Company (www.stewart.com or 800-729-1900) or First American Title Insurance Company (www.firstam.com/title-intl/mexico.html or 214-979-0003).

found on the eastern side. These mountain ranges block some of the rain in the central portion of Mexico.

On the Caribbean side of Mexico, the warm water and northeast trade winds result in larger rainfalls—20 to 60 inches, depending on the place (the northern Yucatan tends to get the least rain). The Pacific and Gulf of Mexico coasts get from 10 inches to 60 inches; rainfall is more plentiful the farther south you go, and the presence of the Sierra Madre Occidental range behind sections of the western coast also contributes to higher rainfall. Hurricanes along the coastal areas, volcanoes and earthquakes toward the central and southern part of Mexico, and tsunamis (tidal waves) on the west coast are some of the natural disasters you could be exposed to while living in Mexico. But heck, we have the same stuff in the United States!

How Much Are Property Taxes in Mexico?

Property taxes are less than those in the States, but, according to Raoul Rodriguez-Walters, a U.S.-certified financial planner with offices in Mexico, there is no easy answer to this question. Rodriguez-Walters notes that property taxes are regulated at the local level, and each Mexican state is free to decide how the property tax will be assessed, how often it will be updated, what the mill rates are, if taxes are based on declared value in the deed, or if a new formula will be devised. Some jurisdictions send out property-tax bills and others do not (you'll need to go to the municipal tax office and ask at least once a year). Some jurisdictions exempt the first (number can vary) pesos from tax, others provide no subsidy at all. Again, our advice is to seek professional help in these matters.

What's the Cost?

The cost of living is lower in Mexico than in the United States. Over the past several years, prices have increased in Mexico, particularly for housing, but if your source of income is based on U.S. dollars, your money will go farther here. The peso is the basic unit of money in Mexico, and there are currently about 11 pesos to a U.S. dollar.

Food (especially fruits and vegetables), utilities, phar-

To find a qualified Mexican real-estate attorney (called a "notary"), contact the Embassy of Mexico in Washington, DC, or one of the Mexican consulates located throughout the United States. Go to www.mexonline.com/consulate.htm for a listing. The phone number of the Embassy of Mexico in Washington, DC, is 202-736-1000.

maceuticals and medical costs, alcohol and tobacco, clothing, home insurance, property taxes, and repair services are cheaper, and there's no need for heating or air conditioning in many regions of the country. Gas averages about $2.20 a gallon. As far as building costs are concerned, labor costs are lower, but material costs are higher. In addition, homes in the areas with the most foreigners are more expensive.

According to Mike Nelson, author of *Live Better South of the Border*, multiplying your present expenses in the United States by 75 percent (excluding the purchase of a home) gives you an idea of what a comparable lifestyle in Mexico would cost. Nelson feels that $2,500 a month would be about the average amount a single person would need to live—$3,500 for a couple (2006 figures). Nelson adds that home prices have doubled or tripled in the tourist areas within the past few years, and that housing prices on the Baja Peninsula can rival those of California. Renting in Mexico, however, is still reasonable.

What about Property Ownership?

Yes, you can buy property in Mexico, and no, it's not always simple (sigh). When purchasing real estate in Mexico, you want to be sure to get title insurance and hire a competent attorney to review everything. That being said up front, we would also strongly advise against purchasing *ejido* land. What does this mean?

Ejido land is large parcels of land the Mexican government originally gave to farmers, Indians, and peasants, who could then farm or build on it but did not own the land or have title to it. It was communal property, with many sharing the same piece of land. Some foreigners have been evicted from their land or homes because they bought *ejido* property that turned out, of course, not to be theirs. Beginning in 1992, *ejido* land could become regularized, meaning that those who used the land could convert it to private property so they could benefit from its sale. This process is complex and can easily take a year or more to complete properly (keep in mind that all the people who used the land have to come to a consensus). If the regularization process on the land you buy was not done properly, guess what—you won't really own it. How do you make sure the land you're buying is not *ejido* land? Be sure you're dealing with a reputable developer, have an attorney check the public records to see if the title is clear and there are no

---

Although it's only been in Mexico since 1991, Wal-Mart is the largest private employer and the biggest retailer in the country.

liens on the property, and get title insurance. In other words, we suggest you avoid purchasing *ejido* property.

When buying property, you also need to know that foreigners cannot directly own land within about 31 miles of the coast (this land, of course, is wildly popular) or within about 62 miles of the country's borders. There is, however, a legal way to circumvent these restrictions (isn't there always?). It's called a trust deed, or *fideocomiso*. An authorized Mexican bank retains the deed to the restricted property, but the beneficiary of the trust has rights to the land (the beneficiary can use, rent, sell, or transfer the rights to another party) for up to 50 years. The trust deed can also be renewed by the beneficiary. It costs about $3,000 to set up the *fideocomiso*, then there is an annual fee of about $500.

Purchasing nonrestricted properties in Mexico results in simple-fee titles. If you're not paying cash, you can get mortgages through some Mexican as well as U.S. companies, but interest rates tend to be higher on loans for property outside of the United States. It's also worth knowing that escrow is not commonly used, and that real-estate agents in Mexico are generally not licensed nor regulated as they are in the States. However, in October 2006, the National Association of Realtors (NAR) signed a reciprocal membership agreement with AMPI (Asociacion Mexicana de Profesionales Inmobiliarios) so members of Mexico's AMPI will become certified NAR Realtors. This is a positive step toward making real-estate purchases easier and less risky in Mexico, and it also makes it easier to make real-estate deals on both sides of the border. At the risk of sounding like a broken record (or should we say CD!), the best advice is to get expert help from a Mexican notary (attorney), and again—don't forget the title insurance. (Stewart Title Company, www.stewart.com or 800-729-1900), is an American company that offers this service in a number of countries, including Mexico.)

If you want to rent before you buy (it's always a good idea to do a test run if you're considering a place for relocation), you need to do your homework and nail down where you think you want to live. Once you've whittled down your search of possible areas, ask the

---

Caution: Mexican law recognizes squatter's rights, so if you purchase property be sure no one is already living in it, and be sure to visit frequently or have someone check on it for you to ensure it doesn't become occupied by a squatter. In some cases, homeowners have spent thousands of dollars going through the Mexican courts to try and remove squatters from their land.

locals and any friends/acquaintances in the area and look at ads and at the classified sections of the newspapers. You may also go through a real-estate agent; one source is the Mexican Association of Real Estate Professionals (www.icrea.org will direct you to AMPI agents). You can also do Internet searches for property or take a look at our resource list for this section at the back of the book, but this is only a starting point. As we mentioned before, renting is reasonable in Mexico.

What's to Do?

Mexico enjoys a diverse topography and rich history. Explore one of the many archaeological areas, including the Mayan sites of Tulum, Coba, and Chichen-Itzá, or examine the Aztec excavations at Cuexcomate and Capilco in Morelos, one of Mexico's 31 states.

Or travel from jungle to desert to the warm aqua waters of the Caribbean. Spend a lazy day on the beach, go golfing, celebrate at one of the many Mexican festivals, or visit the magnificent Copper Canyon. Attend the ballet or a concert, wander around a museum or an art show, and follow it up with a meal that emphasizes corn, beans, tomatoes, chilies, and fruit. In Mexico City,

be sure to see the National Palace, which also displays murals by Mexican artist Diego Rivera.

What about Employment?

You can work in Mexico if you have the required permits from the Mexican government and are sponsored by a company, are sponsored by people who require particular skills, or are an investor starting up your own company. According to Mexperience (www.mexperience.com), teaching English as a foreign language (with the proper certification), consulting, or setting up a restaurant or bar are common jobs for foreigners. If you desire to work in Mexico and establish permanent residency, you need to apply for an active immigrant permit and meet the requirements outlined above. Contact the Mexican consulate in your state (http://www.mexonline.com/consulate.htm). The laws regulating working in Mexico are strict; they have been enacted to preclude foreigners from taking jobs away from Mexican nationals.

What about Immigration Requirements?

What if you don't want to work, but do want to become a permanent resident? In that case, you would apply for

---

La Paz was known as "the city of pearls" for many years, until disease wiped out the oyster beds in the mid-1900s.

a retiree immigration permit. In order to qualify, you must be at least 50 years of age and have monthly income from abroad that is at least 400 times the daily minimum wage and 200 times the daily minimum wage per month for each dependent (this is the current formula). At the current requirements, a single retiree would need an income source of about $2,000 a month. There are other types of permits too—for journalists, artists, ministers, and investors, for example. Again, contact the Mexican consulate in your state for more information.

Where Are Some Notable Neighborhoods?

We have identified several places to begin your search in Mexico, and they do tend to be where most Americans relocate. These areas are more expensive because they are more popular among foreigners, so if your (admirable) goal is to completely integrate yourself into the culture, you will want to do some additional research (refer to the references for this chapter). Otherwise, here are some places to consider.

Baja Peninsula

The Baja is hot, and we mean that both literally and figuratively! Building is booming on this 876-mile long arid, largely mountainous peninsula comprised of the Mexican states of Baja California Norte and Baja California Sur (translation: north and south lower California). The Baja is bounded on the north by the U.S.-Mexican border, on the west by the Pacific Ocean, and on the east by the Sea of Cortez (also called the Gulf of California). Many new developments are springing up, enticing foreigners (particularly those from the United States) seeking primary as well as secondary residences. It's no big surprise that Baja California has the highest per-capita income among the Mexican states.

The capital city of Baja California Sur, La Paz, (which means "peace" in Spanish), is home to three developing communities: Paraiso del Mar, Pedregal de la Paz, and Marina Costa Baja. Each of these has a different flavor. **Paraiso del Mar** (www.paradiseofthesea.com or 888-201-2825) occupies 1,700 acres on the tip of a peninsula a half mile across the bay from La Paz and has 5 miles of beach with a marina, stores, and restaurants in addition to the

---

Loreto Beach was named by *National Geographic Traveler* as one of the magazine's top six adventure beach towns in their September 2006 edition.

country-club amenities of a golf course, pool, tennis courts, and spa. Ground floor condos begin around $230,000, and homes start in the $300,000s (not including any lot premiums). Access to Paraiso del Mar is via ferry or car.

Pedregal de la Paz (http://osmx.com/pedregal_lots.htm or 702-425-6048) is a gated community, with a total of 48 lots available, overlooking the Bay of La Paz. There is no time frame in which you must start to build, although once you do begin, you need to complete your home within 2 years. (An architectural review committee will review house plans and elevations.) Cobblestone streets, a marina, concierge service, and dining are planned. The development is not directly on the bay; it is across the street on the side of a mountain. Lots begin around $100,000 U.S.

Marina Costa Baja (www.marinacostabaja.com or 866- 899-7567), which opened in 2005, has condos, villas, a hotel, a 250-slip marina, shops, and restaurants on the Sea of Cortez. One and two-bedroom condos begin in the mid $200,000s. A hillside bluff on the other side of the street has condos and casitas, providing panoramic vistas of the turquoise water.

La Paz itself is a coastal town, located on the eastern side of the peninsula on the beautiful Sea of Cortez. This port city (there is an oil refinery and electric power plant here), with its waterfront *malecon* (boardwalk) in the vibrant downtown area, is also home to the University of South Baja California. La Paz is a fast-growing Mexican city (second only to Tijuana), with a population of about a quarter of a million people, about 4,000 of whom are American. *Money* magazine rated La Paz as one of the best places to retire, stating, "For those who love magnificent seaside sunsets, sugary beaches, sailing, diving—and the ability to stretch a retirement dollar—La Paz is a superb choice." The nonstop flight from Los Angeles to La Paz, Mexico, is about 2 hours.

Los Cabos (the Capes), also in Baja California Sur, is located at the southern tip of the Baja peninsula. The municipality of Los Cabos includes the towns of Cabo San Lucas and San Jose del Cabo, separated by an 18-mile corridor of hotels, golf courses, restaurants, and developments. Cabo San Lucas and San Jose del Cabo are really a "tale of two cities." Cabo San Lucas is much more Americanized, with Costco, Guess, Quicksilver, McDonald's, Subway, Ruth's Chris Steak House, a 10-screen theater . . . you get the idea, and the prices in Cabo San Lucas

Check out the *Gringo Gazette* online (the English-language newspaper of the Baja) at www.gringogazette.com.

reflect this American slant. San Jose del Cabo is more of a "real" Mexican town (like La Paz) and is the seat of government for Los Cabos. The incredibly gorgeous water off the tip of the Baja—where the Sea of Cortez meets the Pacific—is a huge draw for all things nautical.

There is a lot of development in this area as well. In San Jose del Cabo, **Puerto Los Cabos** (www.puerto loscabos.com or 011 52 624 146-9656) is a newer, huge (2,000-acre), gated master-planned resort community east of downtown San Jose del Cabo. Amenities will include 3 miles of beach, a 500-slip marina, restaurants, a boutique hotel, and two golf courses. Condos begin around $300,000, and homes start in the mid $300,000s. Upon completion (more than a decade away), there will be approximately 6,000 residences.

Other areas of the Baja are also barreling ahead with resort-style communities. Close to Loreto, a quiet, friendly fishing village located midpeninsula on the Sea of Cortez, is **Loreto Bay** (www.loretobay.com or 866-956-7386), an 8,000-acre development melding elements of new urbanism and economic, social, and environmental sustainability. Loreto Bay is slated for approximately 6,000 residences, and the community offers all the amenities you would expect in a resort community. (Delta began nonstop service to Loreto from L.A. in late 2006.)

La Ventana del Mar (www.laventanadelmar.com or 800-455-0119), developed by an American, is a gated community located in San Felipe, a town on the Sea of Cortez; about a third of its 30,000 residents are from the United States, Canada, and Europe. At this time, all sales are resales, but there is talk of future development. With driving times of less than 3 hours from parts of California and Arizona, this is a community that is easily accessed from the United States.

"You're fired!" Yes, even Mr. Trump is getting into the Baja action. He's developing the Trump Ocean Resort Baja Mexico in Rosarito, a 30-minute drive from downtown San Diego. Owners (and guests) will enjoy condos in a north Baja location on the Pacific Ocean with prices ranging from the $300,000s to $1 million. Spas, pools, restaurants, tennis, a fitness center, and spectacular views are part of the property. Contact www.trump-baja.com or 866-858-8736 for more info.

Want to rumble in the jungle? You can purchase a 5-acre jungle lot near Tulum in the Yucatan Peninsula in the $50,000s. Contact Los Arboles Tulum (www.losarbolestulum.com or 512-484-2145— U.S. number—the developer is from Austin, Texas).

Yes, the Baja is hot, and as almost 80 million boomers search for nirvana both at home and abroad, it will get even hotter!

 Here's how Donna H. ended up living in Cabo San Lucas.

Marshall and I spent most of our lives in Southern California along the Gold Coast area. Marshall loves to deep-sea fish and golf, and he found himself making trips to Cabo San Lucas, Mexico, starting in 1959. He purchased a lot on a golf course in Cabo with visions to build some day. We met in 1994, and he could not wait to get me down to the place where he loved to spend so much time.

On my first trip, I instantly fell in love with this paradise. To make a long story short, we got married and a year later decided to build our home on the lot he had purchased in 1991. We built a beautiful home on the sixth green of the golf course. We even made a trip to Guadalajara to seek out traditional furniture to give our home a Mexican feel. We also imported some of our English antiques from the States to give our home an eclectic look. We were also keeping a home in Corona del Mar, California. I had retired, and Marshall was about to retire. We kept going between homes and started spending more and more time in the Cabo home. So we decided to sell our home in California and have one home . . . the one we loved the most . . . in Cabo! We made this move during the summer of 2002.

I must say that after living here full-time for about 3 months, I would ask myself, "What were we thinking moving to a third-world country?" Then as the months passed and we met more and more friends and started a whole new group of friends that mostly revolved around golf, we really started to settle in. I missed U.S. friends at first, but we see our friends more since we moved down here than we did living 20 miles away from them! They come and visit one to two times a year for a week at a time, and the time is truly quality time. We leave Cabo for at least a month or more during the hot summer months to travel or just leisurely

---

If you drive your car into Mexico, you must purchase automobile insurance from a Mexican company. Mexico does not accept insurance issued outside of the country.

drive up the Baja to California to visit friends and family.

In addition to golf, Marshall loves to fish. I might mention that he is a very experienced angler and has won the Bisbee Black and Blue Billfish Tournament (largest billfish tournament in the world) three times in a row. That is quite a feat in itself. So Marshall goes fishing. I join him sometimes when it is nice and calm, and I ride in the bow of the boat and watch the abundant sea life. The water is so beautiful and clear here.

I manage the booth for all the clothing sales for Bisbee Tournament. It is such a fun time of year (late October), and it is fun to see a lot of the same people over and over again. During this time it seems you can just feel the electricity in the air with the all the activities of the tournament, which last for a week.

After living in Cabo for 2 years full-time, enjoying golf and fishing and riding our ATVs, Marshall was beginning to get a bit bored. So he decided to take up real estate to take up just a little of his time. Well, he is now very busy but actually loving it. Properties are exploding in the whole Cabo area. Marshall needed to keep busy and this was the ticket, and the buzz that when people reach retirement they are going to do nothing but golf, etc., isn't all it is cracked up to be. Retired people need to keep busy and active. Keeping your mind busy and remaining in good health and physical condition is very important, especially down here. We've seen too many people get down here, retire, get out of shape, and begin to drink too much. We strive to be the best we can be here in Cabo.

I know a lot of people resist moving to a foreign country because of the language barrier. Speaking fluent Spanish would be a good thing, but this area is pretty much like an extension of Southern California. Most of the Mexicans speak pretty good English. Our "Spanglish" gets us by just fine.

As far as health care, we prefer to use the Mexican doctors at a Mexican hospital in downtown Cabo. We do, however, have health insurance in the States and evacuation insurance to fly us out of the country in case of a major health emergency. Recently, though, international medical insurance

---

International Living magazine calls Mexico "one of the best places in the world for inexpensive, quality dental work."

is becoming available down here, so that is on our list of items to pursue.

And how many Costcos do you know of that have an ocean view? Even Home Depot has as ocean view! Oh yes, getting Costco, Home Depot, and recently Office Depot makes life a bit easier. Plus, we now have nice shopping markets that have opened in the past 2 years. These major conveniences have taken the allure of a small fishing town away, but Cabo's quick growth makes these shopping conveniences a necessity.

So, as you can see, we have adapted quite well in this beautiful paradise. We have hunkered down and made it through hurricanes and have survived the heat and humidity of some of the summer months. We continue to make new friends, both American and Mexican, and we try to give back to this lovely community the wonderful things it gives to us. Waking up in paradise every day gives you a great outlook on every day! ⓛ

San Miguel de Allende. The town, with about 80,000 people (5,000 to 10,000 of whom are expatriates), is in the state of Guanajuanto, north of Mexico City. San Miguel de Allende has an altitude of over 6,000 feet, resulting in wonderful weather. There are many churches, and the town is also known as an arts community. It's home to a huge bilingual library, it has an English newspaper, and it offers many plays and other productions performed in English. San Miguel de Allende boasts more than 30 volunteer organizations as well. There are even the conveniences of a Wal-Mart and Costco 45 five minutes away in Queretaro for those who can't live without them.

As with real estate everywhere, factors such as location, amenities, views, eagerness of the sellers, competition, and condition of the home will affect the asking price. Some recent San Miguel de Allende real-estate prices (in U.S. dollars): a two-bedroom, one-bath condo in a gated community 10 minutes from downtown lists at $109,000; a two-bedroom, one-and-a-half bath lists at $220,000; and a new townhome with two bedrooms, two-and-a-half baths, and three blocks from the town square lists for $345,000. (There are homes exceeding $10 million, as well!) Within the town itself, Villas de Allende is a new community where you can walk to the central plaza in 25 minutes, and residences begin under $100,000 (www. sanmiguelvillas.com or 713-249-2040 in the U.S.).

The winding cobblestone streets of San Miguel de Allende could be a challenge if you have bad knees.

Not far from San Miguel de Allende (actually, about a 30-minute drive north), a new community is being developed—San Gabriel Villas. Advertised as an active-adult community (although there are no age restrictions), this 20-acre, rural, high-desert development will consist of villas and condos, with prices beginning in the $100,000s. Planned amenities include a clubhouse, tennis, swimming, cultural center, driving range, restaurant, and a water-treatment plant. Common green areas make up more than 10 percent of the community. For more information on communities near San Miguel de Allende, including Sonterra (based on new urbanism concepts) and Rancho Los Labrodores, go to www.latin americainsider.com, click on "Hot Properties," and then on Mexico. (*International Living* receives promotional fees from some of these communities, but *International Living* has been in business for almost 30 years and is a respected organization.)

Other places. Additional places touted as potentially good retirement spots in Mexico include Lake Chapala and Ajijic, Mazatlan, Oaxaca, Guadalajara, Queretaro, and Manzanillo.

How Is Mexico's Health Care?

The U.S. State Department's consular information sheet on Mexico states: "Adequate medical care can be found in all major cities. Excellent health-care facilities are available in Mexico City. Care in more remote areas is limited."

People who can afford it avail themselves of private-sector medicine, which provides excellent care. A doctor's visit may cost around $25 to $50; many retirees in good health pay for their health costs out of pocket. This is a gamble, however, if a catastrophic illness occurs. Dental fees are often less than half of what they would be in the States (for example, you can receive a cleaning for around $30).

Prescription drugs can often be purchased for significantly less than their cost in the United States (be sure it's the correct formula and dosage). Be aware that Medicare and Medicaid do not travel with Americans moving to Mexico (although Social Security does), and physicians often require cash up-front. In addition, foreigners may be charged more than locals. It's best to get a written list of the charges prior to any procedure. Foreigners can benefit from Mexico's national health-insurance program, the National Health Program, which is about $300 per year, but under this program, you don't have a choice of doctors (and it would be very helpful to speak Spanish). Some retirees purchase private Mexican health insurance, which runs about $1,000 per year.

Some U.S. companies provide health insurance for those living in Mexico, including insurance covering evacuation to the States. For example, contact: International Medical Group (www.imglobal.com or 800-628-4664). Many expatriates use Mexico's medical services for regular health issues but return to the United States for major surgery.

How Safe Is Mexico?

Crime in the big cites, especially Mexico City, is certainly an issue. Even people who are paid to uphold the law have been implicated in criminal activities. Crime in Mexico, however, is similar to crime in the States: Big cities are generally associated with higher crime rates. Apprehension and conviction rates tend to be fairly low in Mexico, which exacerbates the crime problem.

General guidelines, such as being aware of your surroundings, locking up valuables, not traveling alone, using ATMs cautiously, and avoiding the use of gypsy cabs hold true no matter what country you're in.

The U.S. State Department, in its consular information sheet on Mexico, also suggests that you use toll roads rather than the free roads and travel on first-class buses. The areas featured in our "Notable Neighborhoods" section are considered safe. To read the consular information sheet on Mexico and the warnings for specific areas by the U.S. State Department, go to http://travel.state.gov/travel/cis_pa_tw/cis/cis_970.html or call the Embassy of Mexico to request a copy (202-728-1600).

Strengths

Climate, cost of living, air transportation, urban roads, beauty, a variety of landforms, friendly people, a rich history, gorgeous beaches, and proximity to the United States are all pluses. If the words *serenity, tranquility, laid-back,* and *peaceful* appeal to you, consider Mexico.

Weaknesses

Roads in rural areas are not always good, and in some cases are even dangerous. Pollution is an issue in some cities (particularly Mexico City, which restricts car traffic to help combat pollution); deforestation and the availability of clean water can also be problematic. Taking your American car into Mexico can be complex, as quite a few rules govern this. Choose your medical care wisely; all medicine is not created equal in Mexico. You may need an acclimation period to get used to the higher altitude of some of the central areas, as well as to the different microbes present in Mexico's ice, water, and fresh foods. *Mañana* doesn't always mean tomorrow when you're talking about getting things done. Patience is not only a virtue; it's also a mandatory component of your expatriate personality. Housing prices have escalated, particularly in areas that cater to North Americans.

PANAMA

Capital: Panama City
Population: 3,200,000
Natural Resources: Copper, hydroelectric power, mahogany forests, and shrimp
Industries: Construction and construction materials, milling of sugar, and brewing

Panama

REPORT CARD

Overall rating:	B+
Climate:	B+
Cost of living:	A-
Health care:	B
Transportation:	B -
What's to do:	B+

"A man, a plan, a canal—Panama." You may be familiar with this palindrome (a word or phrase that reads the same forward and backward). But there is nothing backward about this small but vital Central American country roughly the size of South Carolina. Panama offers 1,500 miles of coastline, the second highest number (after Hong Kong) of offshore-registered firms, a democratic government without a military, the dollar as its currency, good infrastructure, and altitudes that range from 0 (sea level) to 11,000 feet. Bordered by the Pacific Ocean on the south and Caribbean Sea (Atlantic) on the north, and situated between Costa Rica on the west and

The United States Embassy in Panama City estimates that 25,000 to 30,000 Americans are living in Panama, and the Panamanian government reports a four-fold increase in American retirees applying for visas in 2005 compared to 2004.

Columbia on the east, Panama is comprised of nine provinces and one territory, and its topography ranges from coastal plains and rolling hills to rugged interior mountains.

Panama was ranked the number one location (for six years running, including 2006) in *International Living*'s "Annual Global Retirement Index." As *International Living* says, "It is quite clear why this country is so appealing for North American retirees: Panama boasts the world's most generous program of special benefits for retirees, it offers easy access from the U.S., its cost of living is low, the landscapes and coastlines are beautiful, its population is friendly and warmly welcomes foreign residents and investors, and its capital, Panama City, is without peer in the region."

With all Panama has to offer, you may decide your plan includes considering this beautiful country for relocation.

Who Lives in Panama?

Most Panamanians (70 percent) are mestizo (a combination of Amerindian and white), 14 percent are Amerindian and West Indian, 10 percent are white, and 6 percent are Amerindian. The predominant religion is Catholic (85 percent). Spanish is the official language, and many residents are bilingual or speak some English, especially in the business, banking, retail, and tourist areas. The median age is young—26 years—and only 6 percent of the population is over 65. The literacy rate is 93 percent.

What's It Like Outside?

Panama's climate is tropical, with a dry season between the middle of December and May and a rainy (often referred to as "green") season running from May until mid December. The rainy season typically includes about an hour-long afternoon shower. Temperatures vary with location. The coastal areas range from the 80s to 90s with higher humidity than the inland mountainous regions, which hover in the 70s. Panama is also hurricane and major-earthquake free.

What's the Cost?

The cost of living in Panama is lower than that in the United States and in Western Europe. Since Panama is a hot retirement location for foreigners, prices have

The origin of the name "Panama" is a little murky. It may come from an indigenous language meaning "abundance of butterflies" or "abundance of fish," or it may refer to a type of tree found in the country.

risen, but it's still possible to live a comparable lifestyle for less. Local food products (vegetables, fruits, beef, pork, and poultry) can be purchased for about half of what it would cost in the United States, and restaurants, insurance, movies, and household/yard help are much less expensive as well. Although gasoline prices in Panama used to be considered high, that is no longer the case compared to the prevailing gas prices in the States. Imported goods are available but no great bargain because of shipping costs, but it's important to note that items you may be used to purchasing *are* available in some places. Sales tax is generally 5 percent, but there may be exceptions (10 percent for hotels and cars, for example.)

The dollar has been Panama's legal tender since 1904, so no reason to change your money. Panamanian coins, called "Balboa," have the same size, heft, value, and metal content as U.S. coins, and can be used in any machine requiring U.S. coins.

Retirees who are Panamanian residents with a *pensionado* visa are treated like royalty when it comes to discounts and incentives. Panama is considered to have the most generous program for resident retirees anywhere. A few examples: 50 percent off admission to movies and sporting events, 25 percent off water bills and phone service, and 15 percent off orthodontic, private clinic, and hospital bills.

Panama is known for its low inflation. Rates were estimated at 2.3 percent in 2007, and 2.8 percent in 2006.

What about Property Ownership?

Purchasing property in Panama is fairly straightforward, and foreigners enjoy the same rights as Panamanians. There are three types of property in Panama: titled property, possession-rights property, and concession property. Titled property is closest to purchasing property in the United States, and you should purchase titled property only. Keep in mind that contracts in Panama are written in the official language, Spanish. It's important to utilize the services of a competent attorney and licensed real-estate broker to be sure all is in order. A list of attorneys is available from the Panama embassy; the e-mail contact is panama-acs@state.gov. Residents don't pay taxes on foreign-earned income.

What's to Do?

Think of Panama and you think of the Panama Canal. Often referred to as the "eighth wonder of the world," this engineering marvel is Panama's most visited site. But there are numerous places to explore and things to do in Panama besides its famed canal. Panama City, the capital, is actually three cities in one—an attractive, cosmopolitan city with skyscrapers hugging Panama Bay;

the original part of the city, with its 16th-century ruins; and the colonial-era Panama, with its Spanish and French influence reminiscent of New Orleans.

If your tastes lean more toward outdoor activities than city life, Panama has it all, and it is well regarded as an ecotourism destination. Diving, sailing, fishing, marine parks, rafting, birding, surfing, kayaking, or just strolling the miles of beaches, watching stunning sunsets, or gazing at magnificent waterfalls are all options. Or trek through one of Panama's national parks, which cover more than a fourth of the land. Imagine—a rain forest within 45 minutes from Panama City! Hike through mountains or saunter through a village such as Boquete—a wildly popular retirement area for Americans, or El Valle—a picturesque town nestled in a 2-mile wide volcanic crater that is also becoming a retirement haven.

What about Employment?

Unemployment in Panama was about 9 percent in 2005, an improvement over previous years. The country is short on skilled labor but has a lot of unskilled workers. Some areas of the country, such as Boquete, have close to full employment.

As in most countries, Panama doesn't want foreigners to take jobs away from its own citizens. If you come into Panama with a *pensionado* visa, you won't be eligible for a work visa to be employed by someone else. However, can you set up your own small business, or perhaps teach English as a second language? The answer is yes, but you'll need to adhere to the Panamanian laws to open a restaurant, have a consulting business, etc. If you're contributing to the country without taking a job away from a Panamanian, it's okay, as long as you follow the rules. And of course, the sky's the limit on volunteering your time and talents.

What about Immigration Requirements?

As we mentioned before, Panama welcomes people who want to spend their retirement money or invest in their country. You can qualify for the *pensionado* program if you're over 18 and have a guaranteed pension from a government agency or a pension from a private company where it can be well documented that you have been and will continue to receive this pension. The amount of a pension must be at least $500 a month (single) or $600 (couple). You must apply for the visa in Panama and preferably be there when it's issued. (It takes about a month for this process through the Immigration Department.)

There are several other types of visas, including personal income, investor, and self-employed or artist visas. For all the details connected with obtaining a visa, contact the Panama embassy at http://usembassy.state.gov/panama or 202-483-1407.

Where Are Some Notable Neighborhoods?

You can pay a lot or a little for housing in Panama—depending heavily upon, as they say in real estate, "location, location, location." Our discussion will focus on the more popular areas for Americans retiring in this country, which, of course, usually means more expensive, since many expats are looking for amenities found in the United States Moving west from Panama City, consider the following.

Tucan Country Club and Resort (www.tucancountryclub.com or 800-456-6016) is a 180-acre, gated golf community located 15 minutes from Panama City and bounded by the Panama Canal and a 900-acre tropical-forest preserve. The golf course is a re-do of a 1940s military course designed by the Army Corps of Engineers. There will be a total of 500 residences by the estimated build-out in 2011, including townhomes, single-family homes, and condos. Prices range from the $200,000s to $1 million. Membership in the country club is required (cost is included in home purchase price), and additional amenities, including a spa and tennis club, clubhouse, shopping arcade, and fitness center are planned. Monthly fees include a homeowner's fee (about $200 per month for a 2,000 square foot home) and resort fee (also about $200 per month). Approximately 80 percent of purchasers at Tucan Country Club and Resort are from the United States.

Altos del Maria (www.altosdelmaria.com or 507-260-4813 in Panama) is truly a mountain lover's dream. Situated between 2,000 and 3,400 feet elevation, this place may be for you if you're more into birds than birdies, and you want to enjoy perpetual springtime temperatures. Altos del Maria seems very remote. It's near the small town of Sora and about an hour-and-a-half drive from Panama City. (It's more than 10 miles just to climb the mountain to get to the community from the turn-in from the town of Bejuco, and it's about a half hour drive to the nearest beach. Although it's a gated community, there are no amenities other than the exquisite views—you literally drive through the clouds—and natural trails. (As an aside, unfortunately the utilities are above-ground.) The 12,500 acres that comprise Altos del Maria have a total of about 1,800 lots, averaging about a half-acre, leaving tremendous green space. Homesites begin in the $30,000s and head north to about $100,000; a resale of a three-bedroom, two-bath home lists for around $200,000.

Coronado (www.coronadopanama.com) is an hour's drive from Panama and is located on the Pacific Ocean. This large, well-established coastal resort community has been around for more than 65 years and offers lots, villas, homes, duplexes, and condos. Some sample prices include: lots beginning in the $50,000s, a new condo located on a golf course listed in the $300,000s, and a resale four-bedroom, three-bath single-family home including golf membership for $225,000. More than 1,600 residences are already constructed in Coronado, and building continues in this 2,500-acre community that also offers a beach club, equestrian center, and onsite pharmacy and supermarket.

Boquete, in the Chiriqui Province, is one of the most popular spots in Panama for Americans who are relocating, and there are more than 20 new communities springing up that reflect this village's popularity. The town itself received recent accolades from *Fortune*, *Forbes*, and AARP as a hot relocation area for Americans. Nicknamed "the city of flowers and coffee," Boquete, about 300 miles west of Panama City and 25 miles north of David (there is a movie theater, a shopping mall, small airport, medical facilities, and some American fast food in David), has a population of about 5,000, and it's estimated about 500 North Americans live there at least part-time. Boquete is in a valley at about 3,000 feet, and the highest point in Panama, Volcan Baru, is close by. Boquete's downtown area is small and walkable, with several restaurants and two grocery stores. The weather is springlike, which includes rain—a lot of rain—about 130 inches a year (compared to New York City at 50 inches). Three examples of communities attracting Americans in Boquete include:

Cielo Paraiso (www.cieloparaiso.com or 011 507 720.2431) is a golf community about 7 miles southeast of Boquete that will have fewer than 200 homes (averaging more than an acre per lot) on its scenic 800 acres (almost 300 acres are set aside as nature and wildlife preserves). Planned amenities include a golf course, clubhouse, boutique inn, pool, tennis, and spa. Canadians Raideep and Colleen Lal are developing Cielo Paraiso. Lots can be purchased beginning around $180,000, which includes membership in the golf and country club.

Valle Escondido (www.valleescondido.biz) is up and running, and within walking distance to town. Shops, a café, an amphitheater, spa, and a nine-hole executive golf course are already a reality, and there will be a total of about 200 villas, condos, and homes in this attractive Spanish colonial-style community designed by an American businessman. Some examples of cost include: a lot for $170,000 and a new three-bedroom, three-bath home for $350,000.

Boquete Country Club (www.boquetecountryclub.com) is a gated community with spectacular canyon and Pacific Ocean views. An equestrian center, clubhouse, spa, fitness center, tennis courts, pool, and walking trails are among the amenities that will be built, and the infrastructure in the community is about 75 percent complete. Townhomes, condos, homes, and lots are available, with condos beginning less than $200,000, and a model home can be purchased for under $300,000. The community is a 5-minute drive from the town of Boquete and a 30-minute drive from David.

 Jane and Eric A. chose Panama for retirement. Here's Jane's story.

Tracy and Andy . . . they're heading off to Panama . . . the country . . . in 5 weeks. To be more specific, they're headed to Boquete, Panama, a quaint little town in the highlands of Panama, located near the eastern border of Costa Rica. My husband, Eric, and I met with them last night, to hear where they're at with their move and to offer to take something to Boquete for them. We'll be traveling to Panama in 3 weeks, first to Panama City and then to David (pronounced DaVeed) before heading to Boquete. Why are we going to Panama? First and foremost, to finalize negotiations to have a retirement home built in Cielo Paraiso—a new golf-course community just outside of Boquete. We are very excited! This process has been about 16 months in the making, and we're eager to move forward.

About 2 years ago, I was at a wedding shower when someone across the room—Tracy—mentioned to someone that she and her husband (Andy) had bought property in Panama and planned to retire there in just over 2 years. I listened intently while Tracy answered the questions the other showergoers were asking, thinking, "This is a place I have to visit." That evening, I mentioned visiting Panama—in particular, Boquete—to my husband. After asking me if I were nuts, he wanted to know "Why?" My thought was that since we hadn't been able to agree on a location to retire within the United States, maybe we should look outside the country. Also, since Boquete has a climate similar to San Diego and sits in a valley similar to towns in Italy or Switzerland, I couldn't imagine why we should rule out such a place, especially since it has a heavy U.S. influence. I was also keeping in mind that my husband wanted to retire in an area with golf, golf, and more golf, while I wanted something picturesque and not enveloped in humidity. (Yes, there's humidity in Panama, but not so much in Boquete.)

Although Eric balked while making the travel arrangements, he went with a fairly open mind, but thinking we'd return home and he'd say: "See, I told you." After a week of visiting a number of towns—some inland and some along the southern part of Panama (as in the Pacific Ocean shoreline)—we came upon Boquete. We weren't there 2 days before we decided we had to live there, on a permanent basis, for ever and ever. (Keep in mind that before we reached Boquete, we'd only heard great things about it from anyone with whom we conversed, be it other travelers, from the United States and other countries, or Panamanians. With our expectations being so high, we couldn't believe what we'd envisioned was the real thing.)

On our return trip, while waiting in Atlanta for our luggage, we ran into another couple who had just returned from Boquete and visited the same places we had. They too found the place spectacular and were interested in the same lot as we in Cielo Paraiso. Maybe because of that, once home, we progressed on making a decision to purchase property in Panama. Fortunately, things in Panama move at a slower pace than in the United States, so we had time to re-evaluate every decision. To date, we have no regrets!

Before our first trip and since, Tracy and her husband have supplied us with lots of information. With all our conversations regarding Panama, and Boquete in particular, we've become friends, rather than acquaintances—friends that we look forward to visiting when we return to Panama in several months, at which time they will be living there permanently. ⒧

How Is Panama's Health Care?

Many physicians are trained in the United States, and medical and dental facilities in Panama City and David are very good. Each province in Panama does have some type of medical care. Medical and dental costs are about a third of those in the United States. Since it's only a 3-hour flight to Miami from Panama City, many retirees living in Panama return to the United States for more serious illnesses. Some hospitals recognize U.S. insurance, and Panamanian government health insurance is available for about $70 a month.

How Safe Is Panama?

The corrupt General Manuel Noriega has been out of power since 1989, when he was arrested following the U.S. invasion of Panama, codenamed "Operation Just Cause."

Crime in Panama City is termed "moderate" by the U.S. Department of State, typical of all metro areas. (We felt very safe walking around both day and evening.) Travel near the Columbia-Panama border is discouraged, due to drug traffickers. Overall, Panama is considered one of the safest countries in Central and South America.

Strengths

Living in Panama requires less red tape than in many other countries. Friendly people, gorgeous scenery, lower cost of living, lower crime rate, desirable climate, plenty of outdoor activities, and good infrastructure are all pluses. The country welcomes foreigners to live, play, and invest. You can drink the tap water here! Life moves at a slower pace. Depending on your personality, this could be a weakness rather than a strength.

Weaknesses

Oversight and management of the country's natural resources needs improvement. Close to a third of Panamanians live below the poverty line, and unemployment and underemployment are high. If you don't have some conversational Spanish, you'll be at a disadvantage, regardless of what you may read to the contrary. If you're planning on going to see major opera or theatrical performances, you're in the wrong place.

PART III

HOW DO YOU ENJOY YOUR RETIREMENT FOR YEARS TO COME?

8

FOREVER YOUNG?

"You can get old pretty young if you don't take care of yourself."
—*Yogi Berra*

Average life expectancy has increased from 49 years in 1901 to 78 years today. And if you are a 65-year-old female, odds are you'll live to 85. What will you do with this gift of 30 or more years?

How can you stay healthy—physically as well as emotionally? Most of us want to live a long, long life. A 2005 Pew Research Survey found that 43 percent of people surveyed want to reach the ripe old age of 100. Of course, we want these years to be better, not just longer. But how do we accomplish that? According to Dr. Walter Bortz, a scientific expert on aging, genes account for about one-fifth of our longevity, and our lifestyle choices account for four-fifths. As Dr. Bortz states, "Living lon-

ger is a choice, not fate. Living longer is active, not passive. You create your own destiny."

The trick, therefore, is to capitalize on those things we can control. How can we be proactive and stave off disease? Does looking better help us feel better? And what are the financial repercussions of living longer? With nursing homes costing an average of more than $75,000 a year, according to a 2006 MetLife Survey, and medical experts bemoaning the shortage of geriatricians, it's in our best interest to remain as healthy as possible. Finally, since death is inevitable (along with taxes, of course!), how can we help our aging parents—and ourselves—prepare for this final act of our lives?

The phrase carpe diem translates to "seize the day" and includes the concept of "eat, drink, and be merry, for tomorrow we may die." So let's start with that thought. How should we eat, drink, and be merry?

"EAT, DRINK . . ."

From Atkins to the Zone, the way you choose to eat really does run the gamut from A to Z! Notice we didn't use the word *diet*. Strike that word from your vocabulary, since it conjures up images of deprivation, and it's often used as a short-term means to achieve a goal of losing weight, followed by a return to old habits. Instead, the idea is to foster a lifelong way of eating that is healthful and makes you feel good.

What is the best way to eat? Needless to say, judging from the millions of magazine articles, scientific studies, news reports, and books on the topic, nutrition is a field with many opinions and a lot of controversy. One reason is that, particularly in the area of losing weight, a certain approach may work for some people but not for others. There is, however, agreement in one area: Obesity is a huge and growing (no pun intended) problem in the United States. About 65 percent of adults are either overweight or obese, and obesity is associated with almost 30 medical conditions, including arthritis, some cancers, diabetes, coronary heart disease, and high blood pressure.

If we assess all the nutrition information that has been generated, several constants emerge.

Calories count. There is one ironclad rule that virtually no one disputes: To lose weight, the number of calories you burn has to exceed the number of calories you eat. To find out how many calories a certain food contains, go to www.caloriecontrol.org. This site also assesses your diet, offers recipes, and provides suggestions and tips for staying (or getting) healthy and fit.

High-quality carbohydrates are better for you. All carbs are not created equal. Think whole grains such as whole-wheat bread, whole-grain pasta, whole-grain cereals, oatmeal, fruits, and vegetables.

Highly processed grains should be avoided. These include white bread, white rice, white pasta, cake, doughnuts, pancakes, waffles, and sugary cereals that aren't whole grain.

Protein is a requirement of a healthy diet. How

As of 2007, the oldest documented living person is 114-year-old Yone Minagawa, a Japanese woman born in 1893.

many grams of protein do you need every day? The answer depends on how active you are. If you're sedentary, you need about .4 gram of protein per pound of body weight. If you are strength-training on a regular basis, you'll need .8 gram of protein per pound of body weight in order to rebuild those muscle fibers you break down during your workout. Lean meats, fish, poultry, dairy products, legumes, and peanut butter are all good sources of protein. Keep in mind that foods that contain protein, water, and fiber have a higher fullness factor—you won't have to return to the fridge as frequently!

There are "good" fats and "bad" fats. Although the mantra has been to avoid all fats like the plague, more recent information has shown that, as with carbs, not all fats are created equal. Fats are necessary in the human body. There are two fatty acids our body can't manufacture: omega-6 (linoleic acid) and omega-3 (alpha-linoleic acid). We call these two "essential fatty acids" because they are essential to our health and life. In addition, fat in food adds flavor and gives us a feeling of satiety, or fullness.

The trick in eating fats is to choose those that are heart healthy, which means those that include monoun-saturated and polyunsaturated (omega-6 and omega-3) fats; these are generally plant-based fats that tend to be liquid at room temperature. You will find them in canola, olive, and safflower oils, as well as fish (we know, not a plant) and nuts. In the United States, our ratio of omega-6 to omega-3 fats tends to be around 20:1; aim for a ratio between 3:1 and 5:1.

The fats to avoid are the saturated fats, which tend to be from land animals and are solid at room temperature (think lard, butter, and the fat streaks in red meat), and tropical oils (palm and coconut oil).

In addition to saturated fats and tropical oils, trans fats are another type of fat to avoid. Trans fats are found in margarine, baked goods, and fried foods. The FDA now requires trans fats to be listed separately on nutrition labels (unless the food is not a significant source of trans fat), which will make it easier to know how many grams of trans fat you're ingesting. Eat as few grams as possible.

Fiber is essential. The American Dietetic Association recommends that we ingest 20 to 35 grams of fiber every day, but most Americans get only about half that. Good sources of fiber include whole grain cereals; legumes

---

The American Institute for Cancer Research reports that from 30 to 40 percent of cancers could be prevented through better nutrition and other lifestyle choices.

such as kidney beans, black beans, and lentils; apples with the peels; and popcorn.

The glycemic index is an important tool. Some carbohydrates cause a rapid rise, then a rapid drop, in blood-sugar levels; these are called high-glycemic foods. Other carbohydrates cause a much slower, more even rise in blood-sugar levels; these are the low-glycemic foods. Studies done at Tufts University and elsewhere indicate that eating high-glycemic carbohydrates can lead to overeating, while other researchers have found evidence linking diabetes and heart disease with high-glycemic patterns of eating. Foods are classified as having a high glycemic index (70 or above), medium glycemic index (56 to 69), or low glycemic index (55 or less). For a list of the glycemic indexes of some common foods, go to http://www.mendosa.com/common_foods .htm or refer to *The New Glucose Revolution Shopper's Guide to GI Values 2006* by Jennie Brand-Miller.

Water is good for you. Water is vital to health, and research presented at the Obesity Society's national convention in 2006 has shown it can also aid in weight loss. Researchers from the Oakland Research Institute in Cal-ifornia found adult women who replaced sweetened drinks with water lost an average of 5 pounds more over a year's time than those who did not replace sugary drinks with water, and women who drank more than 4 cups of water a day lost 2 pounds more (over the course of a year) than those who did not drink as much as 4 cups a day.

Consume alcohol in moderation. There has been a lot of research on the relationship between alcohol consumption and heart disease, and studies demonstrate that moderate drinkers—women who have one drink a day and men who have one or two—have a lower risk of heart disease than nondrinkers. The American Heart Association does not recommend that you start drinking if you do not presently consume alcohol, however, since many more deaths, illnesses, accidents, and tragedies are associated with drinking than with not drinking.

How Much Should You Eat and in What Proportions?

Be proactive about your health, and help stave off disease, by keeping the aforementioned guidelines in mind. But knowing what you should eat is not enough; you

---

You know your chronological age, but what is your biological age? Take the free "RealAge Test" (go to www.realage.com and click on "RealAge Test"), which analyzes your lifestyle choices, and see how you can become younger!

need to know how much protein, fat, and carbohydrate you should consume each day. There are two ways to approach this problem: by understanding what percentage of your total intake each of these nutrients should represent and by using food pyramids, which graphically represent what you should eat.

The recommended percentages of various nutrients will differ depending on what diet you look at. Most, however, tend to emphasize nonprocessed foods, whole grains, and lean cuts of meat. The bestselling entry into the weight-loss melee, *The South Beach Diet*, restricts processed carbohydrates but is more liberal with the complex carbs than is Atkins.

If you go the percentage route, you will first need to know how many calories your body requires each day. There are several ways to calculate this. You can use an online calorie calculator such as www.inch-aweigh.com/dcn.php (click on "Calories Per Day" under "Weight-Loss Tools"), which takes into account gender, age, height, weight, and activity level, then calculates how many calories you need per day to maintain your present weight and how many calories you need if your goal is to lose weight. One pound is equal to 3,500 calories, so reducing your caloric intake (or increasing your activity level) to create a deficit of 500 calories a day will result in a loss of 1 pound per week. For healthy weight loss, don't attempt to lose any more than 1 or 2 pounds per week.

If math isn't your thing—or you have other things to do with your day than count calories—several food pyramids recommend the number of servings and kinds of food to eat. The Food Guide Pyramid is designed by the United States Department of Agriculture (USDA). The current one, revised in 2005, allows you to individualize your pyramid based on age, sex, and activity level. Go to www.mypyramid.gov to input your info.

Walter C. Willett, MD, of the Harvard School of Public Health, developed the Healthy Eating Pyramid (which is illustrated on page 338).

Note that physical activity and weight control form the foundation of Dr. Willett's pyramid. On the second level, whole grains are encouraged, and healthy unsaturated, monounsaturated, and polyunsaturated fats are given a prominent location on the Healthy Eating Pyramid. As far as fruits and veggies go, Dr. Willett excludes potatoes from the recommended vegetables, placing

---

For a comprehensive listing of food values and recommended daily values, enter "nutritive value of foods" into the Google search bar. You'll access the USDA's publication.

them at the top along with sweets and unrefined grains, which are to be eaten sparingly. Dr. Willett views nuts and legumes as healthier forms of protein, so he gives them their own level, and he places fish, poultry, and eggs (he suggests that red meats should be eaten less frequently) on a different level. He recommends fewer dairy products and suggests the use of a calcium supplement. Both pyramids reflect that sweets should be eaten frugally, but Dr. Willett also places foods that either have a high glycemic index or are high in saturated fat at the top of his pyramid. Moderate alcohol consumption is reflected in his pyramid, as is the taking of a daily multivitamin.

What's the moral of the story? You have to figure out what works for you. Keeping in mind the general guidelines discussed previously, healthy eating that keeps you at a good weight and feeling energetic is what works.

How often should you eat? Again, there is no one correct answer. Since it's not so much the frequency as the quality and quantity of what's ingested that counts, the number of meals that prevents you from overeating at the next chow time is the frequency that is right for you.

HEALTHY EATING PYRAMID

From Eat, Drink, and Be Healthy *by Walter C. Willett M.D.,* © *Simon and Schuster, 2001.*

For a creative way of looking at serving sizes (for example, 2 tablespoons of peanut butter is equal to a golf ball), use the Texas A&M University's "Serving Size Stumper" or by putting that phrase that into the Google search bar.

Should You Take Vitamins and Minerals?

Finally, should you take supplements? Many of us do not get the DRI (dietary reference intake; this replaced the RDA—recommended dietary allowance—in 1997) of certain nutrients. As a result, most experts suggest or see no harm in taking a good multivitamin/mineral supplement every day.

One mineral that most Americans don't get enough of is calcium. The most abundant mineral in the body, calcium is responsible for healthy bones and teeth as well as nerve transmission and muscle contraction. Although most calcium is stored in the bones, if there is not enough calcium in our bloodstreams, the hormone parathormone takes it from our bones, increasing the risk of a brittle skeleton. Since absorption of calcium decreases with age, the DRI increases as we get older. The calcium DRI between the ages of 19 and 50 is 1,000 milligrams per day, but that number increases to 1,200 milligrams per day when you hit that magic age of 50. Vitamin D helps our bodies absorb calcium from our digestive tract;

thus, you should choose a calcium supplement that contains vitamin D.

Since adults may absorb only 30 to 50 percent of ingested calcium, try to spread the intake of calcium-rich foods (as well as supplements) throughout the day to ensure the maximum uptake of this important mineral.

Don't completely shun the sun. Our skin makes vitamin D when our bodies are exposed to ultraviolet B rays from the sun (or tanning booths). There has been such an emphasis on preventing skin cancer and wrinkles that cases of vitamin D insufficiency have been on the rise. The darker your skin, the longer you need to be in the sun to make vitamin D, since the pigment melanin (which gives color to the skin) prevents UV absorption. How much time is enough? Several times a week, expose 25 percent of your body (such as your limbs or arms plus your face) for 25 percent of the time it would take for you to start turning pink in the sun.

Heart disease is the number one killer in the United States, and recent research has emphasized the importance of an amino acid called homocysteine in our blood.

A number of other pyramids reflect healthy eating patterns; among these are Asian, vegetarian, Latin, and Mediterranean pyramids. These pyramids reflect actual, healthy, traditional ways of eating. To take a look at some of the alternative pyramids, go to www.oldwayspt.org, and click on "Traditional Diet Pyramids."

The American Heart Association states that too much of it is "related to a higher risk of coronary heart disease, stroke, and peripheral vascular disease (fatty deposits in peripheral arteries)." What does homocysteine actually do? The current thought is that an excess of this amino acid, which is necessary for healthy tissue, can damage blood-vessel linings, leading to the accumulation of plaque, which can block the flow of blood. It has also been implicated in dementia.

Folic acid and vitamins B_6 and B_{12} may break down homocysteine in the bodies of some individuals. Good sources of folic acid include dark green leafy veggies, whole grains, walnuts, and lentils; cereals are often fortified with folic acid. B6 can be found in bananas, nuts, seeds, chicken, and potatoes. Good sources of B_{12} are eggs, poultry, milk, shellfish, and cottage cheese.

The bottom line is that we need to be informed consumers. New research continues to modify, verify, and vilify prior research. Common sense, knowing what works for you, and maintaining a healthy skepticism will probably serve you well in the nutrition arena.

". . . AND BE MERRY"

Exercise can make us merrier, but, as with nutrition, you have to find out what works for you. Do you remember the original 1962 *Twilight Zone* episode "Kick the Can," in which Charles Whitley, residing at the Sunnyvale Rest Home, believed that by thinking young and playing active games (like kick the can), he would truly be young? He was joined by most of Sunnyvale's residents, and indeed, by the end of the show, those who participated in the vigorous game had literally become children once again. (It is the *Twilight Zone*, remember.) What a powerful statement about the effects of exercise!

Activities you enjoy, performed at a regular time, perhaps with another person who also commits to exercising, offer the best chance to make fitness a lifelong habit. Experts often advise that you exercise first thing in the morning, so that later in the day you don't get too tired or overwhelmed with other things to do and let exercise slide. In other words, insert this valuable activity into your schedule, just as you would grocery shopping, meeting a friend for lunch, or going to a movie; no one

---

Your dentist may be able to warn you of an impending stroke! X-rays taken with panoramic machines can detect calcifications in the neck arteries, indicating possible blockages. Alert your dentist to look for this "hardening of the arteries."

can easily find time to exercise. Before embarking on a new exercise regimen or plan, however, it's a good idea to ask your physician to check you out and give you the okay, especially if you have been relatively inactive.

The three pillars of physical fitness are strength training, increasing flexibility, and cardiovascular workouts. Here's a list of some of the benefits of regular exercise.

* Increases feelings of self-worth.
* Reduces LDL ("bad") cholesterol and triglycerides.
* Decreases body fat, including dangerous visceral fat (the fat surrounding organs) that is implicated in diabetes, high blood pressure, and cardiovascular disease.
* Makes your body more sensitive to the effects of insulin, decreasing the chances of developing diabetes.
* Lowers stress levels and relaxes you.
* Helps alleviate moderate levels of depression.
* Elevates mood.
* Improves your appearance.
* Strengthens your heart so it pumps out more blood with each beat, resulting in a lower heart rate and lightened workload on the heart.
* Lowers blood pressure and decreases the risk of stroke and heart disease.

* Raises your levels of IgA (immunoglobulin A), which fights cold viruses.
* Increases muscular strength and endurance.
* Increases lean body mass, which in turn increases the number of calories your body burns at rest.
* Improves joint flexibility, helping to ease joint pain and stiffness.
* Decreases your chances of getting gallstones.
* Adds or slows loss of bone mass (if it's a weight-bearing exercise), reducing chances of osteoporosis.
* Helps prevent fractures of the spine (back-strengthening exercises in particular).
* Results in the production of a natural antibiotic (dermicidin) by sweat glands.
* Improves blood circulation to the prostate gland.
* Lowers the risk of some cancers, including breast, kidney, endometrial, prostate, and colon cancers.
* Allows you to fall asleep more easily and sleep better.
* Improves the efficiency of the lungs, and delivers more oxygen to cells.
* Decreases risk of falling by improving balance and coordination (yoga is particularly effective).
* Suppresses appetite signals from the hypothalamus after vigorous workouts involving lots of heat production.

✳ Hones planning, goal-setting, and decision-making skills.

✳ Increases energy (which may stimulate your sex life as well).

Whew! Although our list is not all-inclusive, you certainly get the idea that exercise is vital to good health!

When we hit our late twenties, we start losing muscle mass—about 1 percent each year. That doesn't seem like much, but by the time we're 50, we've lost approximately one-fifth of our muscle mass—and replaced a lot of that with fat! Since muscle is much more active metabolically (it burns more calories at rest than fat does), this loss, along with a more sedentary lifestyle, accounts for much of the creeping weight gain as we hit middle age. This weight gain is not inevitable; it can be reversed through lifting weights. In many cases, you can use your own body as the weight (think squats and pushups) or use fairly inexpensive free weights. You don't have to join a club and use their machines (although the social aspect of a club or organized class can be a great extrinsic motivator).

To make sure you're using correct form—not only to prevent injury, but also to get the most out of your workouts—it's a good idea to schedule a few lessons with a personal trainer to put you on the right path. Call your local health club for some recommendations. Costs vary, but they run somewhere around $50 an hour. Trainers can come to your home or your health club, or you can go to their place of business.

Dr. Miriam Nelson, director of the Center for Physical Fitness at Tufts University in Boston, recommends three 45-minute strength-training workouts a week and three 45-minute aerobic workouts a week. Alternate your strength-training days with aerobic days. Also, stretching while your muscles are warm will promote the best flexibility. If six days of working out seems daunting, start slowly, and see if you can work up to a higher, more intense level. Keep a list of the benefits of working out to help keep you motivated. If you truly believe in the value of exercise, you'll set aside the time. Exercise is something you can't afford not to do!

Remember that a scale is not the only arbiter of change. Although it sounds like a cliché, muscle does weigh more than fat, so as you're becoming more fit, the numbers on the scale may not change that much even though you're

---

A fascinating study by the Mayo Clinic found the "fidget factor" could be one reason some people stay slender, even if they overeat. Hundreds of calories were burned each day by those who stretched, moved around, were restless, tapped their toes, or twiddled their thumbs.

losing inches. How you feel, how your clothes fit, and how you look naked standing in front of a full-length mirror are better judges of what's going on with your body! Will you be sore? Most likely. But take this as a good sign that you are producing stronger muscles. As your muscles get more powerful, the soreness will decrease. Of course, actual acute pain is a warning signal from your body that something is wrong. Don't overdo it!

Whether you walk (or mall walk), do yoga, bike, take step aerobics, play tennis or other sports, swim, dance, do core training (strengthening your "core" muscles—your abdominal, back, chest, and shoulder muscles), lift free weights, or use machines, there are a host of rewards from regular exercise. The phrase "use it or lose it" truly applies to keeping your body, an incredible machine, in its best possible shape.

Okay, so you're eating right most of the time and you're exercising several days a week, but you still think the way you look on the outside doesn't reflect how young you feel on the inside. Or you want to have your cake and eat it too (then have it removed from your thighs). Should you consider a cosmetic procedure?

"If I Could Turn Back Time . . ." The title of Cher's song captures the essence of cosmetic surgery—turning back the clock to make our outward appearance more closely resemble the (hopefully!) energetic and vital people we feel we are inside. The American Society of Plastic Surgeons (ASPS) reports that in 2006 about 11 million people had cosmetic procedures, including both surgical procedures (such as a tummy tuck) and nonsurgical cosmetic procedures (such as Botox injections).

ASPS statistics indicate that the top five surgical procedures in 2006 were breast augmentation, rhinoplasty (nose reshaping), liposuction, eyelid surgery, and abdominoplasty (tummy tuck). The most common nonsurgical procedures were Botox injections, chemical peels, laser hair removal, microdermabrasion, and hyaluronic acid (skin fillers).

All this nipping and tucking doesn't come without a cost, however. Most cosmetic surgery is considered elective and will generally not be covered by insurance. In certain cases, such as drooping eyelids that interfere with vision, procedures may be covered. Check with your

Bill Phillips, author of the bestselling book *Body for Life*, advocates exercising first thing in the morning on an empty stomach. The idea is that if you exercise first thing, your stores of carbs will be low, and your body will be forced to draw on fats for energy. (One of the authors incorporated this single change into her workout routine and lost 10 pounds over the course of a year!)

insurance company to be sure. Payment options may include paying all fees prior to the surgery, making a deposit when scheduling your procedure and paying a penalty for cancellation, using a credit card, or financing your procedure, sometimes through your doctor's office.

Choosing a physician for surgical cosmetic procedures shouldn't be taken lightly. The best advice is to pick a board-certified plastic surgeon. The rigorous credentialing process to become board certified ensures that the surgeon has the necessary training and expertise. Also, consider where the surgery will be performed. Your surgeon should have hospital privileges at the better medical centers. For more extensive surgeries, a medical center is your best bet. Asking friends for suggestions can also be helpful. Your internist or other physicians you see may be a good source for referrals as well. Whatever you do, don't let price be your only factor in choosing a physician for your cosmetic procedures!

The American Society of Plastic Surgeons provides a free referral service for board-certified surgeons by location or name. Go to www.plasticsurgery.org and click on "Find a Plastic Surgeon" or call 888-475-2784.

Of course, cosmetic procedures won't change who you are, but they may change how you feel about yourself. If you have realistic expectations about the results, are emotionally stable, recognize the inherent risks, can afford it, and know there will be some discomfort and healing time for some of the procedures, it may be something to consider.

Now, let's look at another way of staying "forever young"—nurturing your emotional health. Feeding your body nutritious food and keeping it in good working condition are very important, but you must nourish the brain and spirit as well.

The Importance of Giving

As we pointed out in Chapter 1, social support is one ingredient in the recipe for a happier, healthier retirement and a happier, healthier, longer-living you.

"Live long and prosper." A greeting from Mr. Spock or an attainable goal? A 2006 study published in the *Journal of the American Medical Association* reported that men (only males were involved in this study) who were still exceptionally healthy at 85 were trim and physically active at midlife, used alcohol moderately, were nonsmokers, and were proactive about their health. So cleaning up your act now can pay big dividends later. Here's to the new Middle Ages!

SENIOR EXAMS (OR, TESTS YOU CAN'T STUDY FOR)

What sort of medical tests or procedures should you consider as you grow older? Although frequency and recommended age can vary (depending on your personal history and consultation with your physician), some common recommendations include testing for fecal occult blood (for colon cancer), blood-pressure screening, diabetes testing (fasting plasma glucose), a colonoscopy, cholesterol testing, testing your level of thyroid hormone, having your skin examined for any changes, having regular eye and dental exams, and getting a flu shot. Women should also do breast self-exams and have regular mammograms and gynecological checkups that include a pelvic exam, Pap test, and breast exam. Men should consider a prostate-specific antigen test, as well as a monthly self-examination of the testes. Scheduling physicals on a regular basis can go a long way toward preventive health.

Research published by Stephanie Brown in *Psychological Science* indicates that it may indeed be healthier to give than to receive. Dr. Brown's study found that "mortality was significantly reduced for individuals who reported providing instrumental support to friends, relatives, and neighbors, and individuals who reported providing emotional support to their spouse." In other words, during this 5-year study of older married adults, those who gave their time and support to others lived longer than those who didn't. Lending a helping hand not only helps others, it increases your longevity.

Does Marriage Matter?

Emotional health also benefits from marriage. A recent study from England reported that over a 7-year period, men were more likely to die from being single than from being smokers! Researchers Andrew Oswald and Jonathan Garner from the University of Warwick found that married men had a 6.1 percent lower risk of death than

---

Men account for approximately 9 percent of those who've had cosmetic procedures.

their single counterparts. For married women, the risk of mortality was 2.9 percent lower than for single women. Dr. Oswald summed up, "Forget cash. It is as clear as day from the data that marriage, rather than money, is what keeps people alive." It has been found, however, that unhappy marriages can have a negative effect on health. Depression, ulcers, elevation of stress hormones, increased blood pressure, and even a slower repair of wounds and more cavities have been associated with poor marital relationships. Although the research subjects in these studies were married, it's thought that the same results (good and bad) would also apply to any couple in a long-term, committed relationship.

Controlling Stress

Our ability to deal with the events life tosses our way can affect our sense of well being. Consider these scenarios: buying a new house, caring for elderly parents, becoming a grandparent, beginning a new career, losing money in the stock market, learning a difficult piece on the piano, preparing for the holidays, being involuntarily downsized, and retiring. How we react to each stimulus determines whether it is a "eustress" (good stress) or a "distress" (bad stress) for us. Eustress, a term coined by Canadian scientist Dr. Hans Selye, can be stimulating, challenging, and fun, while distress can lead to negative consequences such as anxiety, irritability, feelings of being overwhelmed, anger, and depression.

When we experience physical or psychological stress, our bodies churn out the stress hormones cortisol, epinephrine, and norepinephrine, which help regulate insulin; increase blood pressure, heart rate, blood-sugar levels, and blood flow to the large muscles; and prepare us for the "fight-or-flight" response to the stressor.

To view the average 2006 costs of various procedures compiled by the American Society for Plastic Surgery, go to www.plasticsurgery.org and click on "Average Surgeon Fees" under "View 2006 Statistics." AARP, in conjunction with Roper Starch Worldwide, conducted a survey to find out who considers cosmetic procedures. It turns out only about one in five boomers is completely satisfied with his or her appearance, and about four in ten boomers are happy with how they look for how old they are. When boomers were asked if they would consider having cosmetic surgery, 14 percent of women and 5 percent of men said yes. If, however, the procedures were free, guaranteed safe, and could remain secret, the numbers who said yes rose to 64 percent for women and 33 percent for men!

Under ideal circumstances, we experience the stress response, we resolve things, and our levels of stress hormones return to normal. The increase in energy we experience was a beneficial evolutionary response that helped our ancestors escape predators. In modern society, however, the stress response is often initiated repeatedly (think of being stuck in traffic or dealing with an intractable illness), and the body is bathed in these stress chemicals often and for prolonged periods of time, perhaps resulting in fatigue, depression, anxiety, irritability, and pain in the muscles and joints. Older people with chronic stress also tend to have higher levels of a chemical called interleukin-6 that is associated with a decline in immune-system function, as well as illnesses such as heart disease, arthritis, and diabetes.

Frequent negative stress, whether physical or psychological, exacts a toll on the body. One way to reduce stress is to try changing your response to the stressor. One person's distress could be another person's eustress. If you can change the way you perceive a stressor, you can deal with the stress more easily and return your body to its normal state more quickly. Let's say you're committed to doing a half-hour talk for the local Rotary, but you're feeling panicked. Using time management to prepare for your presentation, visualizing yourself making a successful presentation, and practicing your presentation until you feel comfortable could change what would be considered a distress, were you to wing it, to a eustress.

Additional techniques for stress reduction include biofeedback, meditation, slow and deep breathing, exercise (particularly yoga, Pilates, and t'ai chi), massage therapy, getting enough sleep, listening to soothing music or a relaxation tape, interacting with others, making a road map for your life and moving forward on it in measured steps, setting priorities, saying no to unwelcome requests, laughing, surrounding yourself with pink (it's calming) or yellow (energizing), connecting or reconnecting with your spiritual side, associating with positive-thinking people, stretching, practicing aromatherapy (especially with lavender), taking some time for yourself each day, avoiding stressful triggers (for example, keeping a book handy to read

Remember that immunizations aren't just for kids. The Centers for Disease Control and Prevention recommends a tetanus/diphtheria booster every 10 years, a onetime pneumococcal vaccine if you're over 65, and a flu shot every year. Check with your doctor to see whether you need an MMR (measles/mumps/rubella), chicken pox, and/or hepatitis B vaccine.

while you're on hold on the telephone), taking a walk, learning something new, playing with a pet, making a list of 10 things you are grateful for, and practicing mindfulness (a term coined by Dr. Jon Kabat-Zinn, founder and director of the Center for Mindfulness at the University of Massachusetts Medical Center, for giving your full attention to what you're involved in at that particular time).

Finally, remember that you are responsible for your own feelings; you are in charge of choosing your response to emotional stimuli. Replace flawed thinking (life "must" be fair; you "must" treat me like a king/queen; I "must" be perfect in all I do) with rational thought processes (I "prefer" that life is fair, but even though it isn't, I can still enjoy it; I "prefer" that you treat me like a queen, but I can't control your actions; I "prefer" that I never make a mistake, but when I do, I know I'm still an okay person). Practicing this kind of thinking is called cognitive behavioral therapy or rational emotive behav-

ior therapy. Try it; it works! But it takes time and practice to replace negative, ingrained thought patterns with newer, healthier ones. The payoff? A lot less stress in your life.

Let's face it—a life that is completely stress-free would be boring, but too much stress is unhealthy.

Avoiding Depression

Depression among older adults is frequently overlooked. In fact, it's estimated that 3 out of 100 people over 65 experience clinical depression. Sometimes there may be no obvious cause for the depression, or it may be the result of a change (decline in health, loss of spouse, retirement, etc.); certain medications may also mimic or cause depression. If you think you or someone you know is depressed, it's important to seek help from your physician or a mental-health professional and to stick with treatment options until a successful one is found.

More reasons to get unrelenting stress under control: The stress hormone cortisol is associated with deep abdominal fat, also called visceral fat, that surrounds organs. This fat, in turn, has been associated with heart disease and diabetes. Cortisol is also correlated with cravings for fats and carbs. Bruce McEwen of Rockefeller University conducted studies that determined that, over long periods of time, cortisol can damage or destroy neurons, or brain cells.

Keeping Your Brain Fit

When we discuss staying forever young, we can't ignore the care of the 3-pound dynamo called the brain. Comprising about 2 percent of our weight but consuming close to 20 percent of our energy needs, this vital organ needs to be kept in the best shape possible. It had been, for about a century, a basic tenet in biology that brain cells don't regenerate—that once the brain matures, we have all the neurons we're ever going to have, and we can only lose them. Research done in the past decade, however, has upended this belief, and we now know that new cell growth has been observed in the most advanced parts of the brain involving learning and memory. So, how do you keep your brain in fighting form?

Researchers from the University of Illinois at Champaign-Urbana presented some interesting findings at the 2006 annual meeting of the *American Psychological Association*. They reported that aerobic activity had both short and long-term effects, including improved mental functioning and a reduced risk of dementia and Alzheimer's. It's thought that physical activity actually affects the brain at the cellular level by providing more blood flow to those areas involved in memory and stimulating the growth of neurons. So aerobic exercise can keep both brain and body buff!

In addition to physical exercise, mental gymnastics may play a role in keeping our brains facile. One type of mental exercise is called "neurobics." A cute play on words, coined by Dr. Lawrence Katz and Manning Rubin by combining the word for brain cells, *neuron*, with the word *aerobic*, as in aerobic exercise, neurobics involves using your senses in ways you usually don't, doing something novel, and/or changing a routine. Switching hands to brush your teeth or to write, learning to play an instrument, studying a foreign language, taking a different route to a frequent destination, or getting dressed with your eyes closed are examples of

---

Visualization or guided imagery can promote faster healing and reduce anxiety when it comes to surgery. Visualizing your operation in a positive way prior to surgery results in less pain, less blood loss, less medication, lower anxiety, and a quicker recovery time. Conditions such as asthma, obesity, and cancer can also be positively affected through visualization or guided imagery. One source of CDs or tapes on this method is *Health Journeys* (www.healthjourneys.com or 800-800-8661).

SYMPTOMS OF DEPRESSION

How can you tell if it's depression? Look for these common symptoms. If they last for more than 2 weeks, see a doctor.

❋ An empty feeling, ongoing sadness, and anxiety

❋ Tiredness, lack of energy

❋ Loss of interest or pleasure in everyday activities, including sex

❋ Sleep problems, including very early morning waking

❋ Problems with eating and weight (gain or loss)

❋ A lot of crying

❋ Aches and pains that just won't go away

❋ A hard time focusing, remembering, or making decisions

❋ Feeling that the future looks grim; feeling guilty, helpless, or worthless

❋ Being irritable

❋ Thoughts of death or suicide; a suicide attempt

Source: U.S. Administration on Aging

---

neurobic exercises; these activities stimulate your neurons and rev up neglected nerve pathways.

More suggestions for maintaining your mental edge: Get sufficient sleep; don't smoke; be aware of side effects of medications; do crossword puzzles, brainteasers, acrostics, and riddles; avoid extreme stress; play bridge or chess; be socially engaged with others; read; listen to music; play board games; garden; dance; and travel. Then, of course, there is the Japanese puzzle craze of Sudoku, or Nintendo's *Brain Age*.

"... FOR TOMORROW WE MAY DIE."

"Nothing in life is certain except death and taxes." A wise man, that Mr. Benjamin Franklin. And we would be remiss, even though the chapter is named "Forever Young," to ignore the situation(s) that many of us find ourselves in—becoming less robust both physically and mentally as we grow older, caring for an aging parent or spouse, placing a spouse in a nursing home or other care facility, grieving over the death of a loved one, and/or making choices/thinking about death and dying for ourselves and others.

Spirituality

As adults begin to confront their mortality, and the daily rat race has faded into the background, religion and spirituality often become more front and center in their lives. A *Newsweek* (2005) survey found that 56 percent of those age 40 to 59 described themselves as both religious and spiritual, and this percent increased to 66 for those over 60 years of age. When asked, "How important is spirituality in your daily life?" 63 percent of people age 40 to 59 indicated it was very important, and 66 percent of those over 60 years of age felt it was very important. The most common reasons for practicing their religion included becoming a better and more moral person, forging a personal relationship with God, finding peace of mind and happiness, providing meaning and structure to life, connecting with something larger than yourself, and being part of a community.

Elder Care

The "sandwich generation" refers to people caught between caring for their children and caring for aging parents. Carol Abaya, columnist and sandwich generation expert (www.thesandwichgeneration.com), has added two new sandwich terms to the menu: a "club sandwich" refers to "those in their fifties or sixties, sandwiched between aging parents, adult children, and grandchildren" and an "open-faced sandwich" is "anyone else involved in elder care." So regardless of which type of sandwich you are or may become, it's helpful to know about some existing resources.

According to Abaya, more than one in four Americans is caring for an aging person in some capacity. Whether you're an in-home caregiver, regularly check in on an elderly person by phone or in the flesh, or coordinate care from a distance, here are a few suggestions for help.

Be sure you incorporate variety and novelty into your brain workouts. You need to cross train your brain like you cross train your body; pursuing a single activity, such as Sudoku, for 5 hours a day doesn't provide the brain with enough different kinds of stimulation. "Use it or lose it" applies as much to the brain as to the body.

REGARDING ALZHEIMER'S DISEASE

Alzheimer's affects about 10 percent of people over 65 and close to 50 percent who reach the age of 85. The destruction and death of brain cells can continue for up to 2 decades and is ultimately fatal. Presently, Alzheimer's cannot be cured or stopped, although certain drugs (such as Aricept) have helped improve memory for some victims. Here is a checklist of common symptoms or potential signs of Alzheimer's.

1. Memory loss. One of the most common early signs of dementia is forgetting recently learned information. While it's normal to forget appointments, names, or telephone numbers, people with dementia will forget such things more often and not remember them later.

2. Difficulty performing familiar tasks. People with dementia often find it hard to complete everyday tasks that are so familiar we usually do not think about how to do them. A person with Alzheimer's may not know the steps for preparing a meal, using a household appliance, or participating in a lifelong hobby.

3. Problems with language. A person with Alzheimer's often forgets simple words or substitutes unusual words, making his or her speech or writing hard to understand. If a person with Alzheimer's is unable to find his or her toothbrush, for example, the individual may ask for "that thing for my mouth."

4. Disorientation to time and place. People with Alzheimer's can become lost on their own streets, forget where they are and how they got there, and not know how to get back home.

5. Poor or decreased judgment. Those with

The Eldercare Locator, sponsored by the Department of Health and Human Services Administration on Aging, provides information on state and area services for the elderly. Enter a topic and zip code on their Web site (www.eldercare.gov), and up pops the list! You can talk to an information specialist at 800-677-1116. You can also look under "Council on Aging" in the phone book for the agency closest to you.

You could hire a geriatric care manager. Whether you are providing care from up close and personal or from afar, these professionals can maneuver through the maze of services an elderly person may require. Although these managers are not federally or state regulated, they are usually licensed in nursing or social work. They can also be expensive, with hourly rates up to $150. In addition, although Medicare or long-term

Alzheimer's may dress without regard to the weather, wearing several shirts or blouses on a warm day or very little clothing in cold weather. Individuals with dementia often show poor judgment about money, giving away large amounts of money to telemarketers or paying for home repairs or products they don't need.

6. Problems with abstract thinking. Balancing a checkbook may be hard when the task is more complicated than usual. Someone with Alzheimer's could forget completely what the numbers are and what needs to be done with them.

7. Problems misplacing things. A person with Alzheimer's may not only forget where the house key is, but may also put things in unusual places: an iron in the freezer or a watch in the sugar bowl.

8. Changes in mood or behavior. Someone with Alzheimer's can show rapid mood swings—from calm to tears to anger—for no apparent reason.

9. Changes in personality. People's personalities ordinarily change somewhat with age, but a person with Alzheimer's can change a lot, becoming extremely confused, suspicious, fearful, or dependent on a family member.

10. Loss of initiative. The person with Alzheimer's may become very passive, sitting in front of the television for hours, sleeping more than usual, or not wanting to do usual activities.

If you recognize any warning signs in yourself or a loved one, the Alzheimer's Association recommends consulting a physician. Early diagnosis of Alzheimer's disease or other disorders causing dementia is an important step in getting appropriate treatment, care, and support.

Reprinted with permission from the Alzheimer's Association

---

insurance may cover some of the services these managers recommend (such as a home health care workers), they usually doesn't cover the managers' services themselves. As with any person you hire, seek recommendations, check references and credentials, discuss fees, be sure the manager is compatible with the elderly person (and with you), and be sure there is a plan in place in case the manager has an emergency or goes on vacation.

The phrase "you're a gem" can have new meaning. A LifeGem "is a certified, high-quality diamond created from the carbon of your loved ones." Prices range from $3,300 to $25,000 and there are also LifeGems for pets. Look at www.lifegem.com for more info.

To find a geriatric care manager, contact the National Association of Professional Geriatric Care Managers (www.caremanager.org or 520-881-8008), or contact the Eldercare Locator, referenced on page 354.

If the elderly person insists on staying in his or her home, but things aren't going well, it can often be difficult for a child to take over the role of parent and offer suggestions. Sometimes a trusted outsider, such as the elder's physician or religious leader, may be able to act as a go-between. By using the Eldercare Locator, you can get a recommendation for an assessment of the person's needs and what has to be done to keep him or her in the home. Otherwise, an agency dealing in adult protection can get involved to take the necessary steps to ensure the person's safety.

Assuming the person doesn't require lots of hands-on care, perhaps hiring a housekeeper, companion, or someone to run errands would work. Seek out recommendations for private hires from friends, colleagues, and professional health workers you may know, as well as from your church or other groups.

But what if the best alternative is moving the person out of the home? There are a few ways you can assess facilities. For example, contact Medicare (www.medicare.gov or 800-MEDICARE) and you'll be able to access all nursing homes that are Medicare or Medicaid certified, find out their staffing and inspection information, general information such as the number of beds and type of ownership, and quality measures (percent of residents physically restrained, percent of residents with pressure sores, percent of residents spending most of their time in a chair or in bed, etc.).

Continuing care retirement communities (CCRCs) are accredited through the Commission on Accreditation of Rehabilitation Facilities. You can see which CCRCs are accredited by logging on to www.carf.org or calling the commission at 888-281-6531. To view checklists for independent living, home care, assisted living, CCRCs, and nursing homes, go to Care Pathways (www.carepathways.com) and click on "Home Care/Facility Checklists" under "Resources." Of course, none of these suggestions should be in lieu of personal visits to the

---

Purchase a casket over the Internet? In 1996, the Federal Trade Commission mandated that funeral homes must accept caskets purchased from other suppliers. This has resulted in real savings (averaging 50 percent or so over funeral-home prices), and delivery is usually guaranteed in 1 or 2 days. In addition, monuments, flowers, urns, vaults, and markers can be ordered online at significant savings.

facility and talking with the residents and their families, professional staff, and other employees.

To find the best physician for your elder, you can follow up on recommendations from friends, colleagues, relatives, and/or other health professionals. A local university medical center, nearby hospital, or the American Geriatrics Society (212-308-1414) are also good sources for referrals. A geriatrician or board-certified doctor with a certification in geriatrics could be an excellent fit.

End-of-Life Issues

Grief and loss are a normal part of life for virtually everyone, yet it's an area that still seems taboo in our society. It's often difficult to find the proper words when consoling someone, and talk of death and last wishes is often avoided, even as a loved one is dying.

If you're married, caring for a loved one, or want to make your own wishes known, a dialogue about the issues surrounding incapacity or death should take place. As difficult as it may seem, set up a meeting time, let the people involved know the topic of discussion, put on the coffee or tea, sit in some comfortable chairs, and start addressing these tough issues. A survey by the National Hospice Foundation found that three-fourths of Americans have not made their end-of-life wishes known through either oral or written communication. As a result, if a loved one is unable to make decisions, others are forced into second-guessing what his or her wishes are, sometimes resulting in anxiety, guilt, or conflict among family members. Assuming you're addressing these issues for yourself, here are some specific suggestions.

Health-care agent. If you become unable to make medical decisions on your own, you want someone to be able to carry out your wishes. Your health-care agent should be someone you trust who has agreed to speak on your behalf and to advocate for you. Health care agent forms can be state specific. Share these forms with your physicians and family members so they know who the health care agent is. See a sample form on page 450.

Durable power of attorney. Just as you may need someone to speak for you medically, you may also need someone to speak for you financially and legally. Durable power of attorney means that the person would represent you while you are incapacitated or until the power

---

Blast your ashes (or a portion of them) into space. James Doohan (Scotty) of *Star Trek* and astronaut Gordon Cooper have both had their ashes rocketed into space. A number of options are available, ranging from $500 to $12,500. Check out www.memorialspaceflights.com.

is withdrawn or you pass away. If you are single, divorced, or widowed, you may want an adult child to act as your durable power of attorney. Some documents combine the durable power of attorney with health-care forms. Durable power of attorney forms can vary by state; they are legal documents and should be carefully worded, perhaps with input from an attorney. You can purchase copies online (by state) through www.Med LawPlus.com or www.FindLegalForms.com. Again, family members as well as your attorney need to be made aware of your durable power of attorney.

Living will/advance directive. Under what conditions do you want to be resuscitated or attached to a respirator? What are your feelings about pain management and palliative care? Do you want to be kept alive no matter what the prognosis? How do you feel about donating your organs? Do you want to die at home or have hospice care, as opposed to dying in a hospital? A living will/advance directive reflects your medical wishes if you are incapacitated. Having your preferences in writing (again, you need to share these with the relevant people) will help your doctor(s), health-care proxy, and family members carry out your desires. Surveys have found that only about one-fourth of people have a living will/advance directive. See a sample of one on page 450, or go to Caring Connections (www.caringinfo.org), then to "Advance Care Planning," and click on "Download Your State's Advance Directives."

Funeral arrangements. Consider leaving written instructions about your final arrangements. What do you want your obituary to say? Do you want an open or closed casket? Or do you want to be cremated or to donate your body to science? Which funeral home should handle your remains? Who should conduct the funeral or memorial service? Who would you like as your pallbearers? Any thoughts on readings, flowers, etc.? Do you already own a cemetery plot? One of the author's fathers had placed his wishes in writing about the things that were very important to him. He had written his own obituary, stressing his love for his wife and children, service to his country, professional accomplishments, and minor-league pitching career; this is what was published. He preferred a certain funeral home (which was used) and stated his desire to die at home (which he did with the help of hospice care).

For help in starting difficult discussions about end-of-life issues, obtain a free copy of the 12-page pamphlet, "Conversations Before the Crisis" by Nancy Carson from Caring Connections (800-658-8898).

Again, let someone (or preferably two people) know about your wishes, or at least where to find them in writing in the event of your passing.

In addition to the forms that deal with end-of-life issues, you need to communicate information about your other records of importance (mortgages, deeds, financial records, will, etc.). We provide a sample form (the Estate Planning Register) on page 459, Appendix 2, that helps you compile, organize, and specify where your documents are located. And don't forget to talk about items that may be meaningful to children or relatives. Asking family members if there are any things (jewelry, furniture, or clothing, for example) they would like after you're gone (and then documenting this in your will) can prevent dissent among relatives later.

Grief and Loss

"Death is a punishment to some, to others a gift, and to many a favor." This quote from Seneca may apply to those who die, but often the living are bereft, with tremendous feelings of sorrow, bewilderment, and loneliness. How to cope? Consider a support group: Churches, hospitals, hospice programs, health providers, and neighbors and friends may be able to suggest a forum in your community. Support groups can help both emotionally and practically. Meeting others who are going through what you're experiencing and getting advice on practical matters can be quite therapeutic. The Internet can be a source of comfort as well; there are many groups you can join online to share your concerns and grief (www.griefnet.org is an example).

AARP is well known for its grief and loss outreach. They offer a grief support line (866-797-2277), a one-to-one peer program that pairs a volunteer who has experienced a similar loss with the bereaved, and a number of grief programs and publications. Contact AARP (www.aarp.org, and enter "grief and loss" in the search bar, or 800-424-3410).

A number of excellent books have been written about grief and loss. We've provided several suggestions in the resources for this chapter.

Boomers will delay the inevitable through better nutrition, exercise, medication, supplements, and behavioral changes. Being a proactive cohort, they will aim for a "good death" for themselves and their loved ones. To paraphrase Dylan Thomas, baby boomers will not go gentle into that good night.

Inside every older person is a younger person—wondering what the hell happened!

9

HOW DO YOU MAKE YOUR MONEY LAST AS LONG AS YOU DO?

"Money is better than poverty, if only for financial reasons."
—Woody Allen

There is a 50 percent chance that at least one of a pair of spouses, 65 years old, will live to 92 and a 50 percent chance that one of them will reach 97, according to the Society of Actuaries. That means that we need to have enough assets when we retire to carry us for many years.

In its 2006 Retirement Confidence Survey, the Employee Benefit Research Institute found that the percentage of people saying that they or their spouses have saved for retirement increased from 65 percent in 2001 to 70 percent in 2006, and 68 percent of today's workers feel secure about having enough money to retire comfortably, compared to only 63 percent in 2001. Even though this survey shows improvement, it also showed that 53 percent of all respondents, and 43 percent of respondents 55 years old or older, had less than $25,000 in savings (excluding the value of their residence and their defined benefit retirement plan). It is no wonder that retirees' number one fear is "running out of money before they run out of life," according to *Advisor Today.*

No doubt, despite its steady recovery, the stock-market drop that began in early 2000 is still taking its toll, causing many to delay their retirements. A national survey by Fidelity Investments of people working who were age 25 or older found that the financial reasons for delaying expected retirement dates ranged from not having saved enough (55 percent) to needing to maintain employer-paid health insurance (34 percent).

In the United States, retirees have traditionally relied on three sources of income: pension benefits, Social Security, and personal savings. Many companies have moved from traditional "defined-benefit plans" to "defined-contribution" plans, such as 401(k)s, which place the onus on the employee for investment decisions and eliminate the risk to the companies that the investment results of the defined-benefit plans will not be adequate to pay the promised pensions. (There's a detailed discussion of these plans beginning on page 374.) And even though Social Security is often viewed as a safety net, more than half of women over 75 rely on Social Security as their chief source of income (54 percent), and Social Security makes up 40 percent of income for women between ages 65 and 74. (Men's comparable percentages are 41 and 30.) Scary statistics, indeed.

So how do you ensure a comfortable retirement? The uncertainty of the stock and bond markets, disappearing pensions, rising health costs, and the insecurity of Social Security's future has made this question more critical than ever for today's retirees.

HOW MUCH MONEY DO YOU NEED TO RETIRE?

In a way, this is a trick question. One rule of thumb says you need only 60 to 80 percent of your current income to retire, since it costs money to make money—workers pay for transportation, a work wardrobe, and meals, plus they pay Social Security taxes and invest in retirement funds. In addition, many retirees have already put their

---

Delaying retirement by 1 year could increase a retiree's annual retirement income by 5 percent on average, and by 25 percent if retirement is delayed by 5 years, according to the Center for Retirement at Boston College.

MYTH VERSUS REALITY

A study by the TIAA-CREF Institute looked at what people predicted they would spend in retirement and compared it to what they really spent. About 56 percent thought their spending would decrease, 36 percent thought it would remain the same, and 8 percent expected they would spend more. In reality, 31 percent spent less, 47 percent had no change in what they spent, and 22 percent spent more. The lesson: Plan, save, and be realistic estimating what you will really spend in retirement.

---

kids through college and plan to downsize their homes. Some experts, however, suggest you may need 100 percent or more of your current income (especially when you first retire) if you still have kids in school, have parents who rely on you for some financial support, have to pay a larger share of your health insurance, plan on traveling extensively or pursuing new interests, would like to eat every meal out, or want to relocate to a more expensive resort-type setting. The real answer to "How much do you need?" is that you can't rely on anyone's rule of thumb; you need to make your own judgments after considering your own retirement plans.

Each of us is different. Some of us are eternally optimistic, while others have a dim view of the world. Some people save money to a fault, while others seem never to have a spare dime. Here's another catch-22: The earlier you start planning for retirement, the better. The earlier you start, however, the less you will know what your specific needs will be down the line. Will you need long-term care insurance? Will you have to move to a home with your master bedroom on the main level for mobility purposes? As you grow older, you will have a much better idea of how you want to live in your retirement years, but if you wait until you are older to start planning for retirement, you will have less time to prepare for it.

The best way to start thinking about retirement is to think about the choices you'll be making. If you are within 5 years of retirement, you probably have a fairly good idea of the lifestyle you desire. You may know you want to work part-time, volunteer, and develop some new skills. You might be trying to decide whether you should relocate to a warmer climate, buy a second home, or downsize your housing in order to travel and spend less time on chores. Each of these decisions comes with some type of cost—financial, emotional, or both.

Many people don't really have a handle on what life is costing them now. We get a paycheck, pay our bills, and if there is anything left over, we spend it or add it to our savings or investments; if we're short, money comes out of savings. Here are some specific things to consider as you think about your financial retirement plan.

Reexamine your 401(k) plan. First and foremost, once you retire, you won't be adding funds to your 401(k) plan anymore. So money may start to come out of it rather than go into it every month.

Reslice the pie. Medical care and medications will likely become a much larger part of your overall expenditures, and the cost of leisure travel, which has held fairly steady in recent years, may spiral upward as the almost 80 million boomers start marching toward postponed vacations. There are many variables to consider—how long you'll live, the return on your investments, future inflation rates, and unexpected retirement expenses, to mention a few.

Reexamine homeownership. Even if your mortgage will be paid before you retire, you will still have real-estate taxes and insurance to pay. If these amounts are currently escrowed and paid for you by the lender, remember to account for them separately when planning for the future. Also, remember that without a mortgage, you will have no mortgage interest tax deduction, so you may see your income-tax payments go up. (See the pros and cons of having a mortgage on page 381.)

Separate the necessities from discretionary expenses. Heat, electricity, telephone, health insurance, food, and car expenses are among the things you might have a hard time foregoing. Vacations, club expenses, hobbies, subscriptions, dining out, entertainment, and charitable contributions are discretionary items and may vary quite a bit from year to year. And don't forget the support you may give to your kids, your grandkids, and maybe even an elderly relative.

Remember important capital items. Do you have several cars now that you will continue to have in retirement? How often will you replace those cars, and what will you spend to do so? Will you lease, borrow, or pay cash? Will your home need improvements (a new roof, landscaping, painting, emergency repairs), and what will they cost? Will you be maintaining two homes? If so, what will be the added cost?

Plan for inflation. It can be your biggest enemy

A savings rule of thumb: Put at least 10 percent of your annual gross income aside for retirement. If you've hit 50 and haven't started saving, increase this to at least 20 percent.

(although making bad investments and spending too much on frivolous things can be just as bad). An unfortunate reality is that many people ignore inflation when calculating what they'll need down the road. This is a huge mistake. While working, your raises generally help you keep up with inflation. When you retire, you need to plan for income increases just to pay for price increases. While inflation has been very low in recent years (prices for the goods we buy have increased about 2.8 percent per year for the past decade), this may not always be so. For example, in 1980 the inflation rate was 13.5 percent—in just that 1 year! And many of the things you will be buying in retirement may increase at much higher rates than the average rate of inflation, with medical care likely leading the pack. Experts estimate health-care costs may increase up to 15 percent annually; they've already outpaced inflation for the past 2 decades.

Decide on a reasonable inflation rate for the sake of projection—say, somewhere between 3 and 4 percent for most of your ordinary expenses, and 10 percent for health care. The following chart, which assumes a 4 percent rate of inflation on purchasing today's equivalent of $25,000 in goods and services, illustrates inflation's tremendous impact.

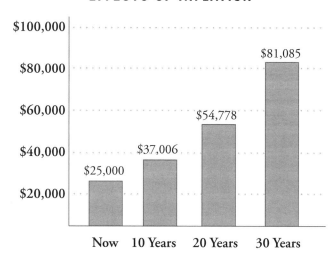

EFFECTS OF INFLATION

Assuming a 4% inflation rate, 30 years from now it will take more than $80,000 to purchase what $25,000 does today!

Anticipate health-insurance costs. They are becoming a huge concern. Currently, Medicare is available at age 65. Whether you retire before or after age 65, you still must anticipate your health-insurance costs. Since many businesses subsidize the cost of health insurance, expect that paying the full amount will cost you much more than the amount currently deducted from your paycheck. You may find that your employer provides

If you're looking to compare health plans, try www.eHealthInsurance.com or 800-977-8860.

some coverage upon retirement, but you need to know which family members are covered and how long that coverage lasts. In recent years, many employers have either completely discontinued or increased the cost of health coverage to their retirees. In the 2006 Retirement Confidence Survey, 68 percent of current workers indicated that neither they nor their spouses expected to have any health insurance from their employers after they retire.

If you need health insurance for someone who has a serious medical condition, your insurance premiums may be considerably higher. (The *Journal of Gerontology* reported that 45 percent of respondents over 70 lost more than half of their retirement income when a spouse became unexpectedly ill with a serious disease. Even when you qualify for Medicare, you may still pay for supplemental coverage and wrestle with the cost of prescriptions, although the new Medicare prescription-drug coverage may help with the cost of prescriptions. (Go to www.medicare.gov to learn about prescription plans and to compare them.) If your health plan now subsidizes your drug costs, that coverage may stop in retirement. In that case, expect your prescriptions to cost up to four times more—out of your pocket.

Consider long-term care insurance. More than 40 percent of Americans age 65 or older will enter a nursing home at least once, with an average stay of 3 to 5 years. Since women live an average of 7 years longer than men, it's more likely they'll end up in a nursing home. The 2006 MetLife Market Survey of Nursing Home and Home Care Costs concludes that the average cost is $206 per day (more than $75,000 per year) for a private room in a nursing home in the United States. However, it is important to check the costs in the area where you intend to live as the cost ranged from $111 per day in Louisiana to $578 per day in Alaska. Keeping inflation in mind, those numbers will boggle the mind 15 to 30 years from now, when boomers may need long-term care.

Among the largest companies selling long-term care insurance are Transamerica, Occidental, GE Capital, John Hancock (Kiplinger's rated it among the best), Unum Provident, MetLife, CAN, and Penn Treaty. There are a lot of questions to ask if you're considering this type of insurance: How long has the company been

---

Excluding long-term care and nursing care, experts estimate a couple retiring at 65 will need about $160,000 to cover insurance premiums and out-of-pocket costs. Drop the retirement age to 60, and that number balloons to $200,000.

around, and how long has it been selling this type of insurance? How healthy are the company's finances? (Check www.ambest.com or http://info.insure.com/ratings/sandp.cfm for financial strength ratings.) What conditions are necessary to qualify for benefits? Is the policy guaranteed to be renewable? Exactly what services are covered (does it cover home care and Alzheimer's, for example)? How long after you need services do the benefits kick in? Is being admitted to a hospital a necessary prerequisite to receiving benefits? What is the benefit period of the policy? Do the benefits keep pace with inflation? Do you need to keep paying the premiums once you start collecting benefits?

Invest less aggressively. Add an element of conservatism to your investment decisions. You will need to make investments, and investments always have risks. The risks could be just temporary declines in the market value of a good company's stock or they could be more severe—bonds defaulting, elimination of a dividend you were counting on for your income, or even bankruptcy. If you place too many large bets, you increase the possibility of a failed retirement plan. Because of this, practice diversification, and plan your investment strategy with prudence; don't put all your dollars into one or two companies; place most of your faith in companies that have successfully weathered the past (especially after the 3 years of investment trauma between 2000 and 2003); and use a mix of investments, such as a combination of bonds, CDs, money-market funds, real estate, and stock, including large capitalization stocks, small capitalization stocks and foreign stocks. Mutual funds are great tools that offer instant diversification within almost all investment-asset classes, but you generally need to use different mutual funds to diversify between investment-asset classes. Don't bet on long shots, or if you must, keep those bets to sizes that you can afford to lose. (For more help with diversification, including a discussion of the new life-cycle funds, see page 388.)

Be careful when selling a business. If you plan to sell your business and use the proceeds from your years of sweat and toil to provide a nest egg for retirement, be sure to plan for contingencies. If you're getting all the cash up front, that's great, but many business sales are structured with payouts lasting 5 years, 10 years, or more. If you have one of these structures, what are you going to do if the new owner fails? Will you be in a position to take back control (and will you even know before it's too late)? How will you replace this cash flow? Are you on the hook for the liabilities of the business because you had to cosign notes pledging some or all of your

---

You can further investigate insurance companies by calling your state's insurance department.

personal assets? Be very careful here, and be sure your accountant and legal advisor explain all the contingencies and risks of the sale agreement.

Reexamine your life insurance. You may be close to dropping that old term life insurance policy because the premium is going up. If you find that your assets and income are adequate and your investments are positioned conservatively, your spouse might not need it. But if you still have debts or your plan looks tight, or if your 401(k) and company stock took a beating in the market, you may want to keep that policy in place to ensure that your spouse's future is secure. (For more on life insurance, see page 383.)

Think about how you think about money. It's an odd statement, but a fairly new area called behavioral economics, which combines psychology with finances, has found that people don't necessarily follow the rules economic theory predicts. For example, people often view a tax refund as found money and treat it differently than they would a paycheck. Or, when asked "Could you comfortably save 20 percent of your household's income at this point in your life?" about half the respondents said they couldn't; but when asked "Could you comfortably live on 80 percent of your household income today?" about 70 percent said yes! Another example concerns an experiment involving an auction for tickets to a Boston Celtics basketball game. Researchers from MIT found that those in the experimental group who were told they could pay with a credit card were willing to bid twice as much for the tickets as those who were told they would have to pay by cash or check. The moral: Think about how you think about money . . . and how it affects your decision-making process.

Adopt a different way of looking at things. Instead of asking how much money you need to retire, you could ask how much you should withdraw from your savings to ensure your money will last as long as you do. Although 4 percent is often used as a rule of thumb, there is considerable debate about the answer to this question, and it depends somewhat on your age when you retire and your life expectancy. One common recommendation is to spend 3 to 5 percent or less of your accumulated savings in the initial retirement year. Obviously, the more you keep invested, the more you will earn for the future. Compounding produces a bigger effect the longer funds stay invested. Then, to keep pace with inflation, increase

---

How long will it take your invested money to double? Using the "Rule of 72," start with the number 72 and divide it by the expected rate of return. For example, if your money is invested at 4 percent, divide 72 by 4 = 18. Thus, it would take 18 years for your money to double.

your withdrawal by the inflation rate for that year. For example, if you spent $50,000 in your first year of retirement in 2007 and inflation was 3 percent that year, you would plan to spend $51,500 in 2008 (3 percent of $50,000 is $1,500). This works out fine if you're earning a good return; but if the market has a bad year, you may have to deny yourself an inflation raise that year to ensure that your money lasts. Or make intermittent adjustments to increase your withdrawals based on inflation—doing so every year could cause the money to run out more quickly. Also, as a hedge against a big market dive, consider putting some funds in a short-term bond fund as a cash reserve and then replenish it by selling longer-term investments, if necessary.

Finally, if you don't mind potentially wild fluctuations in your living expenses, you could take out a fixed percent, say 3 to 4 percent, of your savings balance every year. You probably won't run out of money, but the amount you can spend will vary with the value of your investments. A variation on this is to subtract the annual inflation rate from your annual investment return to determine the percentage of your savings you can spend

for the upcoming year. The bottom line is, if you remove too much of your asset base and inflation is higher than you expect, or your returns are lower, you could easily run out of money before you run out of time to spend it!

Contemplate end-of-life issues. Are you trying to preserve your family's wealth for your children or do you plan to give it away to charity? Or are you hoping to have very little left at the time of your death? Do you have real estate or family heirlooms? Have you developed the tools for your plans to be implemented?

About 60 percent of American adults lack a very important document: a will. If you die intestate (without a will), state law, not your personal wishes, will determine what happens to some or all of your assets. You might be surprised how your state thinks your assets should be divided! A will can also prevent unnecessary expenses for your loved ones. Attorney fees can range from a few hundred dollars for a simple will to thousands of dollars for more complex documents. The use of trusts can save estate taxes, as well as probate costs, and can also enhance the confidentiality of your affairs. If you want to attempt to do it yourself, you can pur-

---

In its 2005 investment guidance, Vanguard provides a chart showing that an investment portfolio should last for 42 years if the annual return is 7 percent and the annual withdrawal rate is 4 percent. Increasing the annual withdrawal rate to 5 percent reduces the duration to 29 years.

chase books or software from a place such as Nolo (www.nolo.com or 800-728-3555), which helps you create or customize a will. Prices range from $30 to $50. If nothing else, trying it yourself first will give you a better understanding of the issues that will arise and the information you will need when sitting down with an attorney, and it may save you some of the cost of a professional's time. Keep in mind that whenever you move to a different state, your will should be reviewed and possibly updated.

Many of the standard estate planning measures are geared toward heterosexual, married U.S. citizens. Others for whom these categories do not apply need to take special care in their end-of-life planning. Special rules also apply to those who live in one of the community property states (Arizona, California, Idaho, Louisiana, Nevada, New Mexico, Texas, Washington, and Wisconsin).

Will your spouse, partner, or some third party make financial or medical decisions for you if you are unable to do so yourself? When life-altering events overtake us, it's often too late to go back and put a plan into action. Refer to Chapter 8 for some practical suggestions and examples regarding a durable power of attorney for finances, choosing a health-care proxy (also called a health care power of attorney), completing an advance directive (also called a living will), and talking about these difficult topics with loved ones. To help you organize and list your important documents, refer to page 459 for an Estate-Planning Register.

WHAT ARE YOUR SOURCES OF RETIREMENT INCOME?

Now that you've thought about some general issues that will affect your retirement planning, you need to think about where the money will come from.

Work

Perhaps you'll be among the majority of boomers who plan to continue working after their primary careers end. This would certainly be a source of income, and it could

---

Rather than prepay funeral costs, preplan with your family and set up a separate account for funeral purposes. If you or a loved one have a prepaid plan already or feel you would like to purchase one, know what protections a reputable funeral home guarantees through the Consumer Preneed Bill of Rights. Contact the National Funeral Director's Association at www.nfda.org or 800-228-6332.

also help with your health-insurance costs. But keep in mind that 40 percent of those who plan to continue working "forever" find they can't because they are downsized, become disabled, or have to care for a ill parent or spouse. So you need a plan B—and maybe plans C, D, and E as well.

Social Security

Available as early as age 62, this government pension fund provides a base-level security net for most people who worked in the private sector and their nonworking spouses (even former spouses). The benefit varies with the number of quarters worked (for which taxes were paid into the Social Security system) and the level of income earned. Be aware that some individuals are not qualified to receive a benefit or will receive only a reduced benefit. This is true of some people who were employed by state and local governments or school districts and who receive pension income from federal or state pension programs, and would otherwise be eligible

to collect Social Security benefits either in their own right or as a spouse or as a widow or widower. There is an offset to the Social Security benefit for a portion of the retirement benefit received from these government plans. Information regarding these offsets is available from the state pension agencies and from the Social Security Administration Web site (www.ssa.gov). Two relevant publications about these offsets are the "Windfall Elimination Provision," SSA publication number 05-10045, and the "Government Pension Offset," publication number 05-10007. Or you can call the Social Security Administration at 800-772-1213.

For people born before 1937, a full retirement benefit is paid if the benefits start at age 65; for the rest of us, the age when full benefits will be paid gradually increases to 67 for those born in 1960 or later. For example, individuals born in 1942 will get full benefits only if they begin taking them at age 65 and 10 months or later. How can you determine your full retirement age? Use the Social Security chart at www.ssa.gov (click on "Plan

The Social Security Administration mails an annual statement of projected benefits to people who are 25 and older and not yet receiving benefits. You may also contact them at www.ssa.gov/mystatement or call 800-772-1213 to request a copy. Keep in mind that the benefits projected in the statement are based on assumptions as to your future earnings, so be sure to read the fine print in order to understand those assumptions.

your retirement," then "Find your retirement age") or call 800-772-1213.

Although retirees can start collecting benefits at age 62, the benefits will be reduced by as much as 30 percent for a retiree born in 1960 or later who retires at age 62, thus requiring them to determine whether a reduced benefit starting earlier is better than a regular benefit starting later. If an early benefit is elected, however, the retiree will receive the reduced amount for the rest of his or her life. Sixty percent of people take their benefits early.

To make things more confusing, if you continue to work after the benefits start, your earnings may increase the amount of your Social Security benefits subject to regular income taxes (see a discussion of this in Chapter 10). In addition, if you're receiving Social Security benefits and working prior to the month in which you reach full retirement age, your Social Security benefits may be reduced to reflect your employment earnings. The reduction is $1 in benefits for each $2 you earn above a limit ($12,960 in 2007) during the years prior to the year in which you reach full retirement age. During the year in which you reach full retirement age,

the formula is more generous, using a reduction of $1 in benefits for each $3 you earn above a limit ($34,440 for those reaching full retirement age in 2007). Also, in the year you reach full retirement age, benefits are reduced only for your earnings prior to the month in which you reach full retirement age. During and after the month in which you reach full retirement age, you are no longer subject to a reduction of your Social Security benefits resulting from your employment earnings.

For example, let's say that Paul S. started collecting benefits of $600 per month ($7,200 for the year) at age 64, even though his full retirement age was 66, and he also worked and earned $20,000 for 2007. Since his earnings were over the $12,960 limit by $7,040, his benefits are reduced by $3,520 because Paul loses $1 in benefits for each $2 he makes over the limit.

Here's another example of how this reduction works in the year during which you reach full retirement age. Assume Karen H. was age 65 at the beginning of 2007 and reached full retirement age in August. She worked from January through July, earning $36,000 while

---

For more information about working and Social Security, see SSA publication number 05-10069, "How Work Affects Your Benefits," at www.ssa.gov. Click on "Publications," then on "Recently Published or Revised Publications," then on "How Work Affects Your Benefits."

receiving $600 per month in benefits. Since her earnings were $1,560 more than the $34,440 limit, her benefits are reduced by $520 because, in Karen's case, the reduction is $1 for each $3 of earnings over the limit. How does Social Security know what you are making? Well, in an ideal world you'd call them and tell them your estimated income for the year, rather than waiting for them to gather the information from income-tax records. They will then adjust your payments accordingly. If you overestimate or underestimate what you make, they will adjust future benefit payment checks or pay you a lump sum, if the situation warrants it, so you're "even."

Company or Government Defined-Benefit Plans

Some companies and many governmental agencies, schools, hospitals, and colleges continue to offer traditional pension plans, also called defined-benefit plans. Most of these plans pay a monthly stipend for life. They may also offer the option of taking a reduced pension payment so that your surviving spouse will still receive a benefit. Usually, this benefit is fixed, although some plans provide inflation protection. Although these plans rarely allow a lump-sum distribution option, some are

now being converted to cash balance plans, which may, in fact, provide for a lump-sum distribution option at retirement.

Other than choosing among the various distribution options and timing when the pension begins, there is little one can do to change the value of a traditional pension benefit. Most benefits are calculated based upon a formula that uses the number of years employed and the average salary level (commonly the average of the last 3 or 5 years of salary prior to retirement). The result is a benefit that could be as much as 50 percent of pay for someone employed for 20 years or even 70 percent of pay for someone who worked 30 years or more. Early retirement provisions may permit a reduced income starting at age 62 (often 80 percent of the age 65 benefit). It's best to check with your employer to determine the various provisions of your plan.

While most people feel that there are no risks associated with pension plans because the primary risk falls on the plan's sponsor to fund the plan enough to provide the guaranteed benefit, there are actually several risks to consider. First, because the benefit is usually fixed, inflation will erode its value over time. Second, many employers are terminating their pension plans and replacing

You can apply for Social Security retirement/disability/spouse's benefits online. Go to www.ssa.gov.

them with defined-contribution plans (see discussion on page 374). A Watson Wyatt study reported that during 2004, 11 percent of Fortune 1000 companies with traditional pensions had either frozen or terminated them, a 6 percent increase from 2001. A third risk is one of benefit reduction should the employer become insolvent. Although a federal pension guarantee program, the Pension Benefit Guaranty Corporation (PBGC), protects worker benefits from such insolvencies, it has an annual maximum limit, amounting to $47,659 in 2006, for workers who retire at age 65 (early retirees have a lower maximum limit), so some expected pension benefits could be lost in the event of a company's demise.

It is also important to understand that you are usually locked into your distribution choices. For example, you may choose to take a pension benefit that is reduced by 20 percent so that it will continue, in the event of your death, for the life of your spouse. If your spouse predeceases you, the reduction will probably not be restored (although some plans do offer restoration options).

Some businesses offer supplemental pension benefits for executive, professional, and/or managerial employees. These come in many forms and are called many different things—top hat plans, nonqualified deferred compensation plans, supplemental pensions, executive pension plans—but essentially, they are promises to pay a pension or lump-sum benefit when the employee attains certain goals, such as a specific length of service or retirement.

These programs are customized to the company or to a particular subset of employees and are not required to provide uniform benefits. Of some concern is that these benefits do not have to be prefunded by the business and are generally not guaranteed by the PBGC. Even if prefunded, these plans are vulnerable if the company experiences a financial decline, and company insolvency may eliminate them, as creditors will have a higher claim on the assets of the employer. For example, when accounting firm Arthur Andersen became insolvent following the Enron debacle, retired partners of the firm lost their pension benefits because the firm's retirement plan was unfunded. (Even if it had been fully funded, the claims of other creditors most probably would have decimated the retired partners' funding.) Another example occurred when a large agribusiness company went into Chapter 11, and executives who had been encouraged to retire

---

For questions about pension guarantees, contact the Pension Benefit Guaranty Corporation at www.pbgc.gov or 202-326-4000.

years earlier with the promise of extra financial support from an executive pension plan found that their monthly checks stopped coming in the mail.

Keep in mind that employer pension benefits are fully taxable and do not survive the death of the employee, unless the retiree has elected a "contingent annuitant" option at the time of retirement. This means the pension is a fixed amount for the retiree and when the retiree dies, the contingent annuitant—normally, the spouse—continues to receive a monthly benefit payment. This payment may be the same as or less than the retiree was receiving, based on the election made by the retiree at the time of retirement. Although this provides desired security in many cases, there is a cost in the form of a reduced benefit from what the retiree would receive if there were no contingent annuitant. For those lucky enough to have both a retirement benefit and a partner, the contingent annuitant decision is one of the most important retirement planning decisions.

A second distribution option that may be available to a retiree is the election of guaranteed payments to himself or herself or to a beneficiary for a specified time period, such as a "10-year certain" benefit. In this case, if the retiree (or the retiree and the spouse) dies, a designated beneficiary would receive up to 120 monthly payments—the 10-year certain benefit—minus the ones received by the primary annuitant(s) prior to death. On the other hand, if the retiree (or the retiree and the spouse) lives beyond the period of the guaranteed benefit, the pension will continue for the balance of the retiree's life—the 10-year certain option just ensures that there will be a minimum of 120 monthly payments to the retiree or the beneficiary.

Defined-Contribution Plans

Another type of retirement plan is an employer-defined contribution plan (also known as profit sharing, 401(k), or 403(b), and money-purchase pension plans). Profit

---

If you own a business, look into making enhancements to your retirement plan in order to increase your retirement savings. This can be especially useful for those business owners who do not have any employees, since pension nondiscrimination rules will generally require that the employees be covered along with the owner. Under the current rules for 2007, businesses like these can defer and shelter from income taxes up to $45,000 per year in a defined-contribution plan and up to the annual amount necessary to fund a pension of $180,000 per year in a defined-benefit plan for the owner.

sharing and money-purchase pension plans represent dollars that your employer has placed into a retirement trust for you on a pretax basis. Section 401(k) plans often include both employee contributions (called salary deferrals) and employer matches, both generally on a pretax basis. When you retire, these funds are available to you to supplement your other retirement income. The funds that your employer put into the plans may be subject to a vesting schedule determined by how long you have been employed (the longest vesting schedules are now 6 years from date of hire). If you have been employed for a shorter period than is required for full vesting, the employer contributions to your account will be reduced or eliminated if you leave the company. However, the dollars you put in the plan through 401(k) deferrals are not subject to vesting; they are yours from day one.

All dollars distributed from retirement plans are usually subject to taxes, but, like everything else in life, there are exceptions. Some plans permit after-tax salary deferrals to be invested, allowing only the earnings to be tax deferred. In this case, distributions of the after-tax contributions are not subject to taxation, but distributions of the earnings on all contributions are. For example, assume Jennifer, age 65, had contributed $31,000 in after-tax contributions to her qualified retirement plan and will receive a joint and survivor annuity of $1,000 per month over both her life and the life of her husband, David, who is also 65. Using IRS-prescribed mortality tables, which show that an estimated 310 monthly payments will be made while either Jennifer or David is alive, $100 of each payment will be tax-free. After 310 monthly payments have been received, each future payment will be 100 percent taxable.

Most people avoid taking a taxable lump-sum payment upon retirement and elect to either take income out of the plan as needed (and be taxed on it as withdrawals are made) or transfer the lump-sum payment (tax free) from the retirement plan to an individual retirement account (IRA) via either a tax-free rollover or a tax-free direct transfer, thus allowing the earnings and

---

Although Susan E., in her grief, failed to roll over a distribution from her deceased husband's qualified pension plan within the required 60 days, her alert CPA realized it was possible to obtain a waiver of the 60-day requirement in those cases where a failure to waive the requirement would be unduly harsh and unfair. Ten months after filing a request with the IRS for another chance to accomplish the tax-free rollover, a new 60-day period was granted.

growth of the plan's assets to go untaxed until withdrawals are made at a later date. A tax-free rollover must be completed within 60 days of the date of the distribution, whereas a tax-free direct transfer of a lump-sum distribution goes directly from the trustee of the original plan to the trustee of the new plan. In some cases where a rollover was not completed within the required 60-day period, it is possible to obtain a private ruling from the Internal Revenue Service, which waives the 60-day period. However, such a private ruling will only be issued in situations where the failure to comply with the 60-day requirement was due to unusual factors that prevented compliance. For more information on lump-sum distributions, see page 391.

Individual Retirement Accounts

Think of traditional IRAs—we'll get to Roth IRAs in a bit—as a tax-deferral wrapper around a pool of investments. The funding may have come from funds transferred from a retirement plan (called a rollover) or from annual contributions, which are often deductible. The annual funding and rollovers can be mixed together in the same account. Once in this pool, the investments enjoy protection from annual income taxes (they are taxed only when funds are distributed). IRAs can also hold some after-tax contributions. These deposits enjoy tax-deferred growth, even though the principal was previously taxed. The IRS has special rules for taking distributions from IRAs containing after-tax contributions. It's the responsibility of the taxpayer to keep good records of such contributions so that no income taxes are paid on the distribution of the after-tax amounts.

Starting in 2006, employers are able to offer 401(k) plans with an option for the employee to contribute on an after-tax basis. Not surprisingly, these new plans are called Roth 401(k) plans and share some of the features of the Roth IRAs, which are discussed below. Since funds are contributed on an after-tax basis, retirement withdrawals are tax-free. The limitations on the annual

---

There has been much discussion about the huge, $10 trillion transfer of inherited wealth from their parents to the baby boomers. As a result, some analysts feel that boomers won't have to worry that much about saving. It turns out that over one-fourth of the largest bequests (those more than $100,000) will end up going to the already wealthiest one-fifth of boomers, and more than two-thirds of us won't get any inheritance, according to the AARP Public Policy Institute. Lesson: Start saving!

amount of contributions to these plans (see discussion below) are the same as for regular 401(k) plans. Additionally, as is the case with regular 401(k) plans, the income limitations that apply to IRA contributions do not apply to Roth 401(k) plans.

Congress has capped the amount of total contributions that can be made in any tax year to both IRAs and 401(k) plans. The limitation on contributions to IRAs will increase from $4,000 in 2006 to $5,000 in 2008. The limitation in 2006 on contributions to a 401(k) plan is $15,000 with adjustments for inflation in future years. Additional "catch-up" contributions are also allowed for people who are 50 or older. For IRAs, the catch-up contribution is $1,000. For 401(k) plans, the catch-up contribution is $5,000.

Roth IRAs

A Roth IRA permits after-tax funding combined with tax-free earnings and tax-free distributions at retirement. People who have more than 10 years until retirement (or until the funds will be distributed) and who qualify to use the Roth IRA will generally find it to be a very effective investment tool offering the ability to achieve tax-free returns.

For example, assume $3,000 is invested in a Roth and a traditional IRA at the beginning of each year for 20 years. Earning an average return of 8 percent each year,

the principal would grow to approximately $148,000 in each account. For someone in the 25 percent marginal tax bracket, the traditional IRA would provide $10,500 per year of after-tax income over the following 20 years, while the Roth would provide about $14,000 of after-tax income per year. The $3,500 lower amount from the traditional IRA is caused by the 25 percent tax on the $14,000 annual distributions, which the Roth IRA does not have.

Disability Income

Most disability income plans terminate at age 65; there may be exceptions, however, such as military disability plans or privately funded disability insurance plans. Payments may or may not be tied into a future pension plan benefit. If they are, the disability payment may end at age 65, but the pension benefit should continue.

Other Investments

Rental real estate, common and preferred stocks, government and corporate bonds, certificates of deposit (CDs), municipal bonds, money-market funds, and bank savings accounts represent the usual final frontier in a retiree's support base, although you may also receive alimony, get an inheritance, or have income from a partnership or other sources.

Each of these can provide income or an income supplement in varying degrees. Some have income-tax advantages. Rental real estate offers tax deductions for depreciation, interest (if there are borrowings), and property taxes. Most common stocks and some preferred stocks currently enjoy a maximum tax of 15 percent on dividends received, and that rate also currently applies to long-term capital gains on the sale of stock (both preferential rates are scheduled to expire on December 31, 2010). Most municipal bonds are free of federal taxation and may be free of state taxation if you are filing a state tax return in the state issuing the bond.

Think of your investments as the engine that will power your retirement income. The larger the engine, the more financial horsepower you will generate to propel your retirement lifestyle.

SO, NOW WHAT?

You've thought about your expenses and reflected on your sources of retirement income. As part of your recipe for a financially successful retirement, you've decided when you plan to retire, determined how much you've saved and plan to save (and how) before you retire, estimated how much your desired lifestyle will cost, guesstimated how long you'll live, factored in the effects of inflation and taxes, and thought about what (if anything!) you want to leave to others when you're gone. Remember that your and your spouse's assets and income may need to last into your nineties. For many, that's a planning horizon of 25 or 30 years or more, maybe equal to your entire working career.

Retirement Calculators

One way to get an estimate of how much money you need to retire is to use a retirement calculator. Although not a perfect tool, it can help you determine a reasonable approximation of what you'll need to satisfy your goals. A few caveats, however: Most calculators assume an average annual return and ignore the fact that investment returns fluctuate (don't we know it!). Thus, even if you achieve your assumed average annual rate of return on your investments, you could achieve a lower return in the early years of retirement and a higher return in the later years, causing you to not meet your goals.

Be conservative when inputting the numbers on a retirement calculator. Err on the low side for rate of return and on the high side for inflation rates, presume you'll live to a ripe old age, and assume you'll need more than the oft-quoted 70 percent of your current income. Play it safe, and plug in 100 percent. Several free calculators to try include: the American Savings Education Council's "Ballpark Estimate" worksheet at http://www. choose tosave.org/asec/ (click on "Ballpark Estimate");

the ING Retirement Calculator at www.ing-usa.com (enter "Retirement Needs Calculator" into the search bar), or the RetireAbility calculator at www.nationwide.com (click on "Get Ready for Retirement?").

Monte Carlo

Another approach to determining how much money you'll need to retire is to use a Monte Carlo simulation. This type of calculation addresses the inherent wide swings of the stock market and doesn't presuppose a fixed annual return. It incorporates more of a bell curve, which the market does not always follow, either. The more complex Monte Carlo simulations, however, generally will allow you to project the success rate of your retirement assumptions.

Try out a retirement calculator using this type of simulation at T. Rowe Price at http://www3.troweprice.com/ric/RIC/. A free Monte Carlo simulator is available at www.firecalc.com. You can also purchase software for Monte Carlo calculations; for example, Efficient Solutions offers a 30-day free trial for MCRetire (www.effisols.com or 203-744-4023), after which you would need to purchase the software to continue using it. Or if you have an account at Vanguard (Vanguard allows free trial of its software), Financial Engines, Morningstar, or Fidelity Investments, you can pay a fee to access their more complex Monte Carlo simulations. Another provider of this software is Analyze Now at http://www.analyzenow.com. Keep in mind, though, that whatever type of forecasting you do, the original assumptions need to be sound in order to increase your probability of success. Remember the axiom: "Garbage in—garbage out."

Maybe You Should Start with Pencil and Paper

You need to be able to estimate how much you are going to spend in retirement as a starting point, even if you use a retirement calculator to project into the future. So before you start, why not complete the worksheet "How Much Do You Need for Retirement?" on page 457. It's a helpful method of determining what you need when you retire and will help you quantify what you're spending now and compare it to what you predict you'll spend in

---

The statistics and probability involved in these Monte Carlo calculations date back to the days of the Manhattan Project, when mathematician Stanislaw Ulam coined the phrase "Monte Carlo simulations" while working on problems associated with the development of the atomic bomb.

retirement. Then you'll calculate your best estimate of your retirement income. Finally, you'll subtract your retirement expenses from your retirement income and see what you get!

It's good to try at least two of the three methods to calculate what you need for retirement (online calculator, Monte Carlo simulation, and/or worksheet). Hopefully, the results are nice, big, positive numbers (meaning an excess of income over expenses). But what if they're not? You'll have to go back to the basics and decide what to do. Maybe your assumptions are faulty: Is your estimated inflation rate too high or the estimated return on your investments too low? If that's not the case, can you work longer before retiring or maybe part-time after you retire? Cut spending before you retire, and save more? Reassess what you need to spend in retirement? What about those discretionary items we mentioned earlier? Can you trim your subscriptions, eliminate some travel, move to an area with a lower cost of living or lower taxes, stay in the same area but downsize your home, consider homesharing, rent out space in your home (if it's legal), cut back on charitable contributions, let your grandchildren pay their own way through college, consider a reverse mortgage (see page 396), or forgo the inheritance you planned for your children? A professional may help you fine-tune your retirement planning. Also, take a look at some of the general sug-

gestions we've made for Growing Your Own Personal Money Tree on page 397.

Finances Not Your Thing?

You may want to bounce your ideas about your retirement goals and ways to reach them off a professional. A certified public accountant with a PFS (personal financial specialist designation), a certified financial planner (CFP), insurance agent, or investment broker might meet your needs. A professional should be able to help you organize your thoughts, give investment and saving advice, and provide insight into the various rates of return and expected inflation factors or other costs you are trying to forecast. If you haven't been actively involved in number-crunching most of your life, the guidance of a professional can be well worth the cost of his or her advice. This cost can vary, of course, depending on the time involved; the scope of the planning project; the size and complexity of your asset base; whether it's a onetime meeting or an ongoing relationship of planning, monitoring, and recommending future adjustments; and how the professional bills his or her time.

Our recommendation would be to start out with either a CPA/PFS or a CFP. After working with you to get your planning done, they may refer you to an investment broker and possibly also to an insurance agent to help you implement your plan. These professionals should be able to provide a comprehensive plan that details which investments you should make and what type of insurance, if any, you need, as well as provide estate planning, tax-saving tips, etc. For help in locating a CPA, contact the American Institute of Certified Public Accountants (AICPA) at 888-777-7077.

If you go with a CFP, recognize that there are several kinds of fee arrangements. A CFP may be compensated by commission, by fee, or through a combination of fees and commissions. Fees could involve charging you an hourly rate, charging by the job (for example, setting up your financial plan), or charging a percentage of the value of your investments (usually about 1.5 percent). Compensation is probably not the best way to choose a CFP. Their reputations and references are usually the best measure. Be aware that some clients—and even some financial professionals—feel there is a conflict of interest when commissions are involved because the planner might be tempted to steer clients toward purchases that involve larger commissions. All planners should be willing to divulge exactly how they are compensated. For fee-based planners, get in touch with the National Association of Personal Financial Advisors (NAPFA), which locates planners by zip code, at www.napfa.org/consumer/index.asp or 847-483-5400.

Of course, as you probably do when searching for doc-

tors, dentists, or other professionals, ask for suggestions from your attorney, friends, neighbors, and colleagues.

NOT QUITE 20 QUESTIONS

Let's take a look at some answers to common questions, which may help shed more light on the thrill of retirement planning!

1. Should You Have a Mortgage?

This is a big question to address in your retirement planning, since you will probably have limited or no earned income from which to pay your mortgage. Having a mortgage is both a financial security issue and an investment issue. Although many think that no one truly benefits by having debt, it really depends on how much the debt costs and what return you get on the funds you borrow. Many people who are used to making real-estate investments look at borrowing funds against the real estate as an acceptable risk. In fact, most investors in investment real estate probably feel that holding debt on that real estate is essential, but keep in mind that a personal residence is not investment real estate and does not generate income to help pay the debt.

You can justify having mortgage debt in retirement if, by borrowing, you invest the dollars not spent on the house generating after-tax returns that exceed the after-tax cost of the mortgage (interest only). Note that your mortgage payment is only part interest, with the remainder being a pay down of debt. So, for example, if you borrow (or continue to have a mortgage of) $100,000 with an interest rate of 5 percent, your cost of borrowing is $5,000 per year. Since the $5,000 is tax deductible, it may be costing you only $4,000 per year after considering the value of the tax deduction (assuming a 20 percent tax rate), for a 4 percent net of tax borrowing rate. Assume you put that money in a common stock or a stock mutual fund with the expectation of receiving a 2 percent annual dividend and of the stock's appreciating at 6 percent per year. Since dividends and long-term capital gains (gains from investments held longer than 12 months) are currently taxed at the maximum rate of 15 percent, there is a net after-tax return of $6,800, or 6.8 percent. So by having that $100,000 mortgage and taking the risk of the stock mutual fund, you could have $2,800 per year of additional cash. Of course, some of this cash may have to be used to pay the principal on the debt, but that is essentially savings for you. Alternatively, if that money were invested in a bank CD with a 3 percent taxable return, you would be paying more in interest than you are receiving in return.

So is having a mortgage worth it? Ultimately, you have to be the judge. Probably a small mortgage in pro-portion to total resources is worth the risk, but certainly heavy amounts of debt would be unwise for a retiree's household.

2. Should You Purchase Long-Term Care Insurance?

The answer is pretty much a catch-22. Some experts feel that if you need to buy it, you probably can't afford it, and if you can afford it, you probably don't need it because you can self-pay if the need arises! There are a few things to keep in mind: The United Seniors Health Cooperative recommends that no more than 7 percent of your yearly income should go toward long-term care insurance.

You should also be aware that since Medicaid is designed for people with little money, a married couple must possess very few assets before it will kick in—that is, spouses are financially responsible for one another. Medicare, on the other hand, doesn't usually cover the type of custodial care that a nursing home provides. Private insurance doesn't cover nursing-home care, other than perhaps some short-term recovery periods. Note, too, that there is often a waiting period (say, 90 days) before your policy covers certain benefits (hospice care and respite services may not have a waiting time).

So what does it cost? Try the LTC calculator at Smart Money.com (put "SmartMoney.com LTC insurance evaluators" into Google). There are two calculators—one that helps you determine if you should purchase LTC insurance, or pay for it out-of-pocket; the other helps you choose a particular policy. Or use the calculator at the Federal Long-Term Care Insurance Program (www.ltcfeds.com, click on "Calculate FLTCIP Premiums" to get a sense of costs).

Using this calculator, a 30-year-old requesting very basic coverage and a 3-year benefit limit of $109,500 would pay $21.40 a month for coverage; a 53-year-old with more comprehensive coverage and an unlimited benefit coverage would pay $176 per month; and a 65-year-old with the same coverage as the 53-year-old would pay $292 per month. Obviously, the type of coverage and your age play a huge role in the size of your premiums.

There is no doubt that long-term care insurance is a facet of retirement planning that needs to be addressed. You may find some consolation in the facts that the average stay in a nursing home is only about 3 years, that only about 5 percent of people over the age of 65 live in a nursing home, and about 25 percent of those over 85 do. Of course, if you have family or children who are willing to take care of you, perhaps this discussion is moot!

3. What Are Some Life-Insurance Guidelines?

The first piece of advice about life insurance is that it should generally not be purchased as an investment nor, if you purchase permanent life insurance, should it be considered forced savings. After all, the life-insurance agent is often paid large commissions when selling you permanent life insurance, and you're also paying for death benefits. These costs come out of your premiums and are not invested. Also, the ability to dip into the cash value of a policy actually equates to borrowing, not tapping into a savings account.

When you think about your retirement lifestyle, it's also time to think about your insurance needs. You may have purchased life insurance in order to replace your income if you died, pay off a mortgage or major outstanding loans, or provide for your children's education. Do you have a big estate or dependent relatives? Do you own a business? Are you married? If you answered yes to any of these questions, you may want to consider whether insurance is for you. Depending on your answers, you may no longer need insurance, you may need less insurance, or you may need more.

There are two basic categories of life insurance. The

Experts predict nursing-home costs will almost triple within the next 2 decades.

first, term insurance, is for a specific period of time, after which you need to decide whether to drop or continue the coverage. Term insurance offers death benefits only; if you die during the term you are insured, your beneficiary gets paid (this money is exempt from federal income tax but not necessarily from estate tax); if you don't die, your beneficiary doesn't get paid. For example, say you are married, you and your spouse are retired, and you have a $100,000 mortgage left on your home which you plan to have paid off in 10 years. Consider buying a $100,000 term-insurance policy and paying annual premiums for 10 years, then dropping the coverage once the mortgage is paid off. Or you might be able to save money by using decreasing term insurance, a policy that provides for a smaller death benefit each year, rather than a constant death benefit. Either could give you the protection you need. Or say you still have debts or your retirement plan looks tight, or your 401(k) and other investments took a beating in the market—you may want to keep a term policy you have purchased in place to ensure that your spouse's future is secure should you die first.

Term life insurance tends to be fairly inexpensive since it's very competitive. Keep in mind, though, that the cost of term insurance is based on your age and health, in addition to the amount of the death benefit, so the older you are, the more expensive the premiums are. You can choose to have the premiums increase each year, or you can choose for them to stay the same for a certain number of years before they increase; neither of these options is necessarily better than the other since a premium that stays level for a number of years will likely be initially higher than one that increases each year. In some cases, companies will pass on their increased costs to you by increasing your premiums, and some require you to prove you're in good health to continue your lower premiums. You may be able to convert your term insurance to permanent insurance.

The other category of insurance, permanent insurance, differs from term insurance in that there is a savings component to it, in addition to a death benefit. You can cash in your policy, you can borrow against it, or you can use it to supplement your retirement

---

Compare insurance policies at sites such as www.reliaquote.com/termlife or www.insure.com (click on "Life Insurance Needs Estimation"). These sites will also help you calculate how much life insurance you need, based upon your circumstances. Another life-insurance needs calculator can be found at http://moneycentral.msn.com (type "Life Insurance Needs Estimator" into the search bar).

income (which is why it's also called cash-value life insurance). Permanent life insurance costs more than term (and will be more expensive the older you are when you purchase it), and don't forget that you're still paying those commissions. (Permanent insurance is more lucrative than term for those selling insurance.) The beneficiary or beneficiaries will receive the death benefit exempt from federal income tax (but not necessarily from estate taxes), the premiums you pay usually do not vary from year to year, and the insurer can't cancel your coverage if you suddenly become a poor risk. The longer your permanent policy is in force, the greater the cash value, since much of the early premiums may go toward sales commissions and other administrative costs. In addition, assuming the dividends are high enough to keep the policy in force, you may ultimately be able to choose for your dividends to pay your premiums.

There are three types of permanent insurance: traditional whole life, universal life, and variable life. In general, whole life is best for the conservative investor; you get a fixed amount of accumulation of cash value over the term of the policy. Universal life is more flexible and allows the insured to adjust the premiums (you may even skip premiums at times, depending on the contract) but is tied to the insurer's success in the markets. And variable life is the riskiest type of permanent insur-

ance—performance of the policy is tied to the investments you choose for your policy.

If you feel you need life insurance, the general rule of thumb is to purchase term insurance if you need it for a period of up to 10 years but to purchase permanent life insurance if your need is for 20 years or more. The murkier part falls between the 10- to 20-year period. For most people, once you hit about 50, the reasons for purchasing term insurance have dwindled, and you're looking more at permanent life insurance. If you are comfortable with your assets and income, and your investments are positioned conservatively, you may not need any life insurance.

Actually, one of the biggest reasons to consider life insurance is to protect your heirs from estate taxes, which can gobble up as much as 45 percent of your assets in 2007 through 2009, and up to 55 percent in 2011 and later years. (Under a quirk in the tax law, there is no estate tax for decedents dying in 2010). To avoid the taxman, consider setting up an irrevocable life-insurance trust, which is not in your name, to protect your heirs. Since you do not own the policy yourself, the death proceeds are not taxable to your estate.

There are other permutations of life insurance, such as increasing and decreasing term insurance, but the bottom line is to determine if you need life insurance, and if so, how much and for how long. The calculators mentioned earlier in this chapter will help you, but your best bet is getting advice from a professional who doesn't have a vested interest in pushing insurance. Don't be talked into purchasing life insurance just to cover your funeral expenses—except, possibly, in the event that your estate will not have any assets available for these costs.

4. How Can You Use Insurance as an Alternative to Electing a Joint and Survivor Payout from a Defined-Pension Plan?

If you have a defined-benefit pension, near the time you start receiving your pension, you must decide to either have either the full pension paid over your life or a reduced pension paid over both your life and that of your spouse. This is not a simple decision because it comes at a cost, usually a permanent 10 to 20 percent reduction in the amount of the pension benefit (depending on your age and the age of your spouse). Once the necessary election has been made, it usually cannot be changed or altered. Therefore, if a life benefit is elected for a spouse but that spouse dies first (or you get a divorce), the pension has been reduced in anticipation of a benefit that never materialized.

One solution to this dilemma is to take the full pension and buy a life-insurance policy on your life, to replace the lost income of the pension in the event that you predecease your spouse. Alternatively, should the spouse die first, or if you end up divorced, the insurance policy can be cancelled since there would no longer be a need to replace the pension upon your death. Or you could keep the insurance policy as a source of a legacy for your heirs. Keep in mind when evaluating this option that the life insurance death benefit payable to your spouse is not subject to either federal estate tax or income tax.

As an example of this strategy, consider George T., age 55, and his wife, Sally. George's company has a defined-benefit plan that will pay him $36,000 per year ($3,000 per month) for the rest of his life when he retires at age 65. He has several choices for providing a continuing benefit for Sally if he predeceases her and is considering the one that will pay her $24,000 ($2,000 per month) for the rest of her life. Under this election, George's pension benefit will be reduced to $28,800 ($2,400 per month). In the event that Sally predeceases George, even very early in his retirement, the retirement benefit would not be reinstated back to the $36,000. Alternatively, assuming he is healthy, George could use the $7,200 difference ($36,000 minus $28,800) to buy a life-insurance policy that would pay $600,000 to Sally in the event of his death. If Sally invested this amount in tax-free municipal bonds yielding 4 percent, she would receive $2,000 per month in income—just what the pension benefit would have been. In addition, her estate would still have the $600,000 for her beneficiaries. Should Sally predecease George, however, George could drop the life-insurance policy and have the full $36,000 available, not just the reduced pension benefit of $28,800.

5. How Do You Determine Your Asset Allocations?

We've all heard the mantra "diversify." How do you decide where to put your money and how much to put there? If there were a magic, definitive answer to this question, this entire discussion would be unnecessary.

The way you divide up your investment portfolio among different asset groups (stocks, bonds, real estate, money markets, cash, etc.) is called asset allocation. Studies of large pension funds over the past 30 years have determined that about 92 percent of the success of your portfolio is due to asset allocation, 5 percent is due to the specific stocks and bonds you choose, and about 2 percent is due to market timing. The other roughly 1 percent? Who knows?

Before deciding on your own asset allocation, however, you need to be able to answer a few questions:

When do you need the money? Are you 15, 10, 5, or just a couple of years away from retirement? Some experts believe that as you get closer to retirement you need to allocate your assets differently; historically, stocks can be volatile, so if you're close to retirement, more money should be put into lower-risk asset classes, such as bonds. Others argue that you continue to invest your entire life, so your asset allocation can remain basically the same. Usually, however, the closer you are to needing the principal, the less risk you will want to undertake.

What type of a risk taker are you? Are you willing to go for aggressive growth? Are you looking to limit your risk? Are you concerned only about security? Or are you somewhere in the middle? Figuring out your personality traits in this area—and deciding whether you want to be risky, conservative, or moderate—will also determine how you invest. On the one hand, some people think they are risk takers, but when they see

---

Harry Markowitz and Bill Sharpe shared the Nobel Prize for economics for their work in asset allocation. Trying to minimize risk while maximizing returns is called modern portfolio theory. Volatility (risk) can be reduced and returns enhanced by adding different asset classes in different proportions rather than just having one asset class (such as large-company stocks).

their stocks plummet, quickly become conservative. People who think they are conservative, on the other hand, may become bigger risk takers when they see they aren't achieving the growth they had envisioned.

What is your financial situation? How much give do you have in your projections? If you have more wiggle room for downturns, you will, of course, be better off than if you have to meet your estimates exactly.

You often hear the word *diversification* mentioned with asset allocation. Even if you were a very aggressive investor, it would still be wise to put some of your money into lower-risk asset classes. Does the phrase "putting all your eggs in one basket" ring a bell?

Conversely, if you're very conservative, you still should not shun all stocks. Following the principles of asset allocation provides the opportunity to maximize returns while minimizing risk but will almost always involve investing in stocks, as well as in bonds. Placing some

money in a more volatile asset group will help you achieve growth, even as you try to minimize risk. Playing it too safe can also allow inflation to erode your nest egg, compromising your retirement lifestyle.

Diversification also means diversity within an asset class. For example, placing all your stock funds into just one company would not be advisable.

So what are some examples of asset allocation? Here are several from Fidelity.com that combine investment styles with time horizons.

1. Eighty-five percent stocks; 15 percent bonds. Consider this plan if you don't need the money for at least 7 to 10 years, and you're a risk taker.

2. Seventy percent stocks; 25 percent bonds; 5 percent money markets. Consider this plan if you don't need the money for at least 7 years, are still fairly aggressive, yet want to balance your risk taking with more conservative asset allocations.

A new type of mutual fund that is getting lots of attention is the "life cycle" or "target-date" fund. These funds take care of the diversifying for you by using an asset mix based on the targeted retirement date and then rebalancing the assets to more conservative investments as that date approaches. For example, such a fund with a targeted retirement date in 2036 might start off with 90 percent in stocks and 10 percent in bonds, and end up with only 30 percent to 50 percent in stocks when that date gets close. The leaders in such funds are currently three major mutual fund groups: Fidelity Investments, Vanguard Group Inc., and T. Rowe Price Group Inc.

SPOUSAL BENEFITS

A spouse is entitled to a Social Security benefit that is, at full retirement age, generally the greater of one-half of the other spouse's benefit at full retirement age or the benefit computed on his or her own working record. If payment of your spousal benefit starts before you reach full retirement age, the amount payable to you will be permanently reduced by a percentage based on the number of months prior to your full retirement age. For example, Mary, who was born in 1947, plans on starting her spousal Social Security benefit at age 62. Since her full retirement age is 66, her monthly benefit will be only 35 percent of her spouse's full retirement-age benefit because she will be getting the benefits for an additional 48 months. For a chart showing the reduction in benefits that start prior to full retirement age (both for benefits based on your own earnings history and for a spousal benefit), go to www.ssa.gov (click on "Plan Your Retirement" and then click on "Find Your Retirement Age").

3. Fifty percent stocks; 40 percent bonds; 10 percent money markets. Consider this plan if you don't need to dip into the principal for at least 4 years but are looking for both growth and income.

4. Twenty percent stocks; 50 percent bonds; 30 percent money markets. Consider this plan if you need some income now, will tap into your principal within the next 2 to 4 years, and are willing to trade greater returns for lower risk.

Of course, none of these examples guarantees any specific return or even success; they're just examples of asset allocations.

What about diversifying within an asset allocation? If you don't have the financial savvy, time, or desire to do this, it's time for professional help. Consider a CFP/PFS or a registered-investment advisor. If you're the do-it-yourself type, you can get help from various sources. Today, virtually every financial institution offers free basic literature on how your assets should be allocated among investments. With a phone call, you can get most of it in print, or, on the Internet, try CNNMoney.com's asset-allocation calculator at www.money.com (type "get the right asset allocation" into the search bar, then click on "calculators," and then on "asset allocator").

6. Should You Take Your Social Security Benefits Early?

It is often better to start taking a reduced Social Security benefit early (at age 62 or later) rather than waiting until full retirement age to start collecting the full benefit. Although several factors enter into this decision, the most important one is often life expectancy. The longer you live, the better it is to be collecting the larger, full retirement benefit; at some point, the full retirement benefits will exceed the smaller early retirement benefits, even though the early benefits would have been paid over more years. If, however, you fail to live long enough to reach the point where the cumulative full retirement benefits exceed the cumulative early benefits, it would have been better to elect the early benefits. (Now, if only we had a crystal ball. . . .)

For example, let's say you were born between 1943 and 1954 and are entitled to receive a Social Security benefit of $22,000 per year at your full retirement age of 66. You retire at age 62 and decide to start collecting Social Security immediately, which means (according to the law) your annual benefit would be reduced by 25 percent to only $16,500 per year; however, you would be collecting it for 4 more years than if you had waited for your full retirement age of 66. If you end up living to age 70 (ignoring cost of living adjustments), you would have received a total of $132,000 by electing the reduced benefit at 62. If, instead, you had waited to take the full benefit at 66, you would have received only $88,000. So you would have made a good choice (of course, you're dead, but that's a separate issue!). At age 78, the two amounts would be equal—in other words, you would have received a total of $264,000 under either option, but keep in mind that the amounts are not really equal at age 78 since it is always better to receive something good sooner, rather than later. So assuming you had selected the early benefit, you still would have made a good choice since, using present value principles, you would have had the use of the money earlier and could have invested it and earned more or used it to avoid interest charges on debt. On the other hand, if you lived to age 85, you would have received a total of $418,000 by waiting to receive benefits at the full retirement age of 66, as compared to only $379,500 if you had elected the age 62 reduced benefit. The better choice in this case would depend on a present value determination, and the answer would depend on what interest rate you select for the calculation.

In addition to life expectancy, several other factors enter into the decision of whether to start collecting Social Security before full retirement age. These other factors include whether your Social Security benefits will be reduced due to a decision to continue working in the years between age 62 and your full retirement age (see the discussion of this earlier in the chapter), the impact of income taxes on your decision (see the discussion on page 418 on taxation of Social Security benefits), the interest rates at which you can invest funds, and whether you are planning for Social Security benefits of two partners where the second partner's benefit is derived from the first.

Although we doubt that delaying the start of Social Security benefits makes sense to very many individuals (except perhaps to those who plan to continue to work between age 62 and their full retirement age), we do want to point out that delaying the start of the benefits beyond your full retirement age can increase your annual Social Security benefit. For those born in 1943 or later, the annual benefit will be increased by 8 percent for each year beyond full retirement age that you delay the starting date (if born in 1941 or 1942, the annual increase is 7.5 percent, and if born in 1939 or 1940, it is 7 percent). Hopefully, it's apparent from the above discussion on electing to receive benefits early that making up for the loss of one year's benefit will take a number of years (more than 12) of collecting the higher benefit just to break even.

So it seems that taking the "bird in the hand" approach of starting the benefit as soon as possible will often result in the greatest benefit for many of us, but a number of factors (health, other employment, income-tax considerations, interest rates, and partner benefits) may also need to be considered before making a choice.

7. If a Lump-Sum Distribution Is Available, Should You Take the Money and Run?

There are really two questions here; the first is whether you should take a lump-sum distribution from a qualified employer plan, and the second is what you should do with the funds if you do take such a distribution.

If the plan in question is a defined-contribution plan—say, a 401(k) plan—that is 100 percent funded, the most likely reason to consider a lump-sum distribution is if you are unhappy with the investment alternatives within the plan. Taking a lump-sum distribution and rolling it over into an IRA will provide you with the many opportunities available for qualified plans. If the plan is a defined-benefit plan, we believe you should give serious consideration to taking a lump-sum distribution whenever it is available, and then roll it over to an IRA. We suggest this because most defined-benefit plans are not fully funded (meaning that the funds necessary to pay out the benefit obligations are not all there). If the employer falls on hard times and cannot continue funding the plan (remember Enron), your full benefit will likely not be paid. Even though defined benefits from a qualified plan are insured by the Pension

Benefit Guaranty Corporation, the amount of the insurance is limited and may not cover your entire benefit. Taking a lump-sum distribution and rolling it over into an IRA ensures that your benefits will be there, no matter what happens to the employer.

In the event you do take a lump-sum distribution from a qualified plan, the next question is what you should do with the money. We believe that you should almost always roll the distribution over to a traditional IRA and then give careful consideration to how the IRA should invest the funds. You should consider making an election to convert the traditional IRA to a Roth IRA, if you are eligible. Under this election you will be taxed on the lump-sum distribution, but future distributions from the Roth IRA (generally after age 59½) will be tax-free. You should consider seeking the advice of a qualified professional, particularly if the amount of the distribution is large, to determine if this election would work for you.

Whenever you are going to receive a lump-sum distribution that you intend to roll over into an IRA, be sure to have your employer do a direct transfer to your IRA, rather than distributing the funds to you. Whenever you receive such a distribution, your employer is required to withhold 20 percent for federal taxes. Even though you can still roll over the entire amount of the distribution (you have 60 days to do it), you will have to compensate for the taxes that were withheld. For example, when Kim T. received a $400,000 lump-sum distribution from her employer, $80,000 (20 percent) in taxes was withheld, leaving a net amount of only $320,000. Since Kim wanted to do a 100 percent rollover into her IRA but did not have any funds of her own, she ended up having to take out a personal loan from her bank for $80,000 so she could complete the rollover. After she filed her income-tax return and received a refund of the $80,000 withheld, she was able to repay the bank loan, but she ended up incurring significant interest costs that could have been avoided if her employer had transferred the $400,000 distribution directly to her IRA. You can get specific answers to questions on IRAs at www.irahelp.com (click on "Forum").

Although the thrill of having all that money at once may be enticing, and it may be tempting to keep it available to meet current expenses or as a safety net rather than rolling it over to an IRA, keep in mind that the distribution represents retirement savings and you may need it to last the rest of your life. If you're not extremely well disciplined, you might chew it up on shopping, traveling, or meeting current expenses (many people do). In addition, and significantly, if you do not roll over the distribution into an IRA, it will be fully taxable at your current tax rates, leaving less to be invested for your

---

A TECHNICAL TIP

A provision related to retirement-plan distributions offers special onetime tax treatment for a lump-sum distribution that includes shares of your employer's stock. Called net unrealized appreciation (NUA), it allows you to receive a distribution of some or all of the shares of your company's stock that you have accumulated in the plan, instead of having the plan sell the stock and distribute the cash, and to pay taxes only on the cost basis of those shares to the plan, instead of on the fair market value of the shares at the time of the distribution. Taxes on the balance of the value of the stock are not paid until it is sold. Assuming the stock is sold at a gain, that portion of the gain realized up to the time of the distribution will automatically be treated as long-term capital gain. Any additional gain will be either short-term or long-term, depending on how long the stock is held after the distribution before it is sold. With maximum federal long-term capital gains rates now at 15 percent, it may be advantageous to use this provision if the employer's stock has appreciated significantly within the plan. Of course, this is an alternative to selling the stock and rolling the cash proceeds completely tax deferred into an IRA. Which of these two options is better requires some detailed calculations.

---

retirement years. Resist the temptation to take a lump-sum distribution without rolling it over to an IRA, even if the dollar amount seems small.

8. What Rules Govern Early Withdrawal from IRAs, 401(k)s, etc.?

Distributions from pension plans (or IRAs) before the account holder reaches age 59½ are generally subject to a 10 percent tax penalty unless the distribution is structured to conform to certain "safe-harbor" rules. Possibly more important is that minimum distributions must start no later than the calendar year following the year you turn age 70½ and then be continued over your life expectancy in order to avoid significant tax penalties for failure to make distributions of the funds.

9. Should You Use a Traditional IRA or a Roth IRA for Retirement Savings?

The single biggest difference between a traditional IRA and a Roth IRA is that a tax deduction is available for contributions to a traditional IRA, assuming you meet the requirements, but the distributions are fully taxable. On the other hand, although contributions to a Roth IRA are not deductible, the distributions are generally not taxable.

In deciding which IRA is better for you, some general guidelines should help. The ability to compound earnings over a number of years and then distribute those earnings tax-free using a Roth IRA is a powerful device for accumulating retirement savings. If you're in a low tax bracket now but think you'll be in a higher tax bracket when distributions will be received, a Roth IRA is likely the better choice. The loss of the tax deduction available when using a traditional IRA is more than outweighed by the tax-free income from a Roth IRA, which you can receive in future years when you expect to be in a higher tax bracket. Even if you will be in the same tax bracket in future years when you receive distributions, a Roth IRA is still likely the better choice, due to the ability to generate compounded tax-free earnings and then distribute them tax-free. The most likely situation in which a traditional IRA could be a better choice is when you are in a higher tax bracket in the year you make a tax-deductible contribution to the traditional IRA than you will be when you receive the taxable distributions. Even in this situation, it is possible that the Roth IRA may still be the better

choice, depending on how many years you will be leaving the funds in the IRA generating tax-free compounded earnings and how much higher your tax rate is expected to be in the year in which distributions are expected to be received. Similar concepts apply to the use of the new Roth 401(k) plans.

Another consideration with respect to using a traditional IRA is that your ability to make a tax-deductible contribution when you are also an active participant in an employer's qualified plan is severely limited. In fact, if you are married and your joint modified adjusted gross income (MAGI)—essentially, your total income with certain adjustments—is in excess of $75,000, your ability to make a tax-deductible contribution to a traditional IRA is affected even if your spouse participates in an employer's qualified plan and you do not. So what are these thresholds that you need to be under in order to obtain a full deduction for a traditional IRA?

a. If you are single, your MAGI needs to be $50,000 or less in 2006 and later years.

b. If you are married filing jointly, your MAGI needs to be $75,000 or less in 2006, and $80,000 or less in 2007 and beyond.

Enough said about traditional IRAs! They will work for some, but the Roth IRA is often the better choice.

But remember, some people are not eligible for a Roth

IRA. If you're single with MAGI greater than $110,000, married with MAGI greater than $160,000, or married but filing separately with MAGI greater than $10,000, you can't put any money into a Roth IRA.

As noted above, contributions to a Roth IRA are not deductible and distributions from them after age 59½ are nontaxable. In order to receive nontaxable distributions from a Roth IRA after age 59½, the IRA must have been in existence for at least 5 years after the first year for which a contribution was made. There are also limited circumstances (such as for first-time homebuyers) in which nontaxable distributions can be received prior to age 59½.

In 2006, up to $4,000 a year can be contributed by each taxpayer to a Roth IRA, and this amount increases to $5,000 for 2008 and beyond. Additionally, if you are over 50 years old, you can also make a catch-up contribution of $1,000 in 2006 and later years. In addition to the above limitations on contributions to a Roth IRA, the contribution cannot exceed your compensation for the year.

Here is how eligibility for the contribution amounts to a Roth IRA is determined.

a. If you are single and make $95,000 or less, you are eligible for the maximum contribution amount. If your MAGI is between $95,000 and $110,000, your maximum contribution is reduced under an IRS-prescribed formula. If your MAGI is over $110,000, no contribution is allowed.

b. If you are married with MAGI of less than $150,000, you are eligible for the maximum contribution amount. If your MAGI is between $150,000 and $160,000, your maximum contribution is reduced under an IRS-prescribed formula. If your MAGI is over $160,000, no contribution is allowed.

c. If you are married and file separately, you are allowed only a limited contribution, and only if your MAGI is less than $10,000.

Although distributions of your contributions made prior to age 59½ would not be taxable, early distributions of the earnings on your contributions generally would be taxed, and, with certain exceptions, there would also be a 10 percent penalty on a distribution of earnings prior to age 59½. You may make contributions at any age with a Roth IRA, but you cannot make a contribution in any tax year in which your MAGI exceeds the allowable limits. Unlike a traditional IRA, for which you have to start making withdrawals at 70½, there is no time at which you are required to make distributions from a Roth IRA.

A final point: If you conclude that a Roth IRA is better for you than a traditional IRA, you are allowed to convert an existing traditional IRA to a Roth IRA as long as your MAGI is under $100,000 (either joint or single, but not married filing separately) in the year of the conversion. Additionally, starting in 2010 this MAGI income limitation is eliminated. Such a conversion, however, means you will be taxed on the entire balance in the traditional IRA as of the date of the conversion, although no penalty will be imposed for early withdrawal. (Starting in 2010, the tax cost of the conversion can be spread over 2 years, if desired.) The decision to convert to a Roth IRA should be based on your current tax rate, your expected tax rate in future years when you will be making distributions from the Roth IRA, and the number of years you will be able to keep the funds in the Roth IRA earning tax-free compounded earnings.

10. In What Order Should You Fund Benefit Plans?

When deciding whether to fund 401(k)s, Roth 401(k)s, traditional IRAs, or Roth IRAs, understanding the differences in tax treatment is important. Most 401(k) funding and traditional IRA funding offers current tax deductions; Roth IRAs and Roth 401(k)s do not. Some 401(k) funding may be supplemented by employer matching dollars, another enhancement. Usually, when all the factors are considered, it is beneficial to fund 401(k) plans first, at least to the extent needed to receive the full amount of an employer match. Then, the next amount of funding is often best put into a Roth IRA (if eligible). If you are not eligible for a Roth, the choice likely reverts to funding a 401(k) to the maximum limit before considering after-tax funding of a traditional IRA.

11. What Is a Reverse Mortgage?

A reverse mortgage is a loan against the equity you have built up in your home. It allows you to receive extra income, and when you die, vacate, or sell your house, the loan is repaid. You must be 62 years of age or older to obtain a reverse mortgage, and the loan applies only to your primary residence. There are several possibilities—you can receive a lump sum, monthly

---

The U.S. Department of Housing and Urban Development (HUD) says that there are about 13 million seniors who are qualified to obtain a reverse mortgage, and the number of seniors taking out a reverse mortgage has grown to 74,000 per year from just 6,600 per year 5 years ago. These numbers will increase substantially as the boomer generation reaches 62, the age at which reverse mortgages are available.

payments, a line of credit, or some combination of these options. The homeowner retains ownership of the home during the reverse-mortgage period. Since these types of mortgages can be complex and involve fees, you need to be comfortable with how the costs stack up against how much you will receive in loan advances and how much equity will remain at the end of the reverse-mortgage period.

There are several types of reverse mortgages, but the only kind insured by the federal government are the home equity conversion mortgages (HECMs). According to AARP's Web site, "HECM loans are the lowest-cost multipurpose reverse mortgages available, and in most cases they provide the largest total cash benefits as well." Other types of reverse mortgages are offered by state or local governments, banks, mortgage companies, or other private lenders.

If you are pursuing an HECM, then by law you must meet with a U.S. Department of Housing and Urban Development (HUD)-approved mortgage counselor ahead of time. For general info, go to www.aarp.org/revmort or call AARP at 888-687-2277; for a list of lenders, contact www.reversemortgage.org; for a list of approved counselors, contact HUD at www.hud.gov (this site is a little tricky—click on "Consumer Info," under "Homes," then click on the link with information about reverse mortgages for seniors). Or you can call them at 202-708-1112.

GROWING YOUR OWN PERSONAL MONEY TREE

Let's face it—if financial planning for retirement was simple, there would be no need to have hundreds of books about the topic or an entire industry built up around it. There are many variables to consider, and a small change—such as a 2 percent difference in the return on your investments, or a 1 percent change in the

---

When paying off loans early, particularly auto loans, watch out for precomputed loans, which provide for interest refunds or rebates when the loan is paid off early. Usually the payoff amounts are determined using a calculation like the so-called "rule of 78s," which accelerates much of the interest into the early months of the loan (as much as three-fourths of the interest may be in the first half of the loan term) and leaves you stuck paying much more interest than if you were paying off a loan with simple interest. The use of the rule of 78s has dwindled in recent years due to legislation that restricts its use.

estimated rate of inflation—can make a huge difference when you're talking time spans of 10, 20, or even 30 years. We've compiled a list of savvy strategies that, whether you're retired or not, can help increase the amount of money available to you. Although each one is relatively simple, instituting just a few can make a powerful difference.

Check your credit report. Your credit score is often used to determine the interest rate for a mortgage or terms of credit for other purchases, such as a car. Three-fourths of Americans don't know this score, or whether it's correct. To order a copy of your credit report, contact Equifax (www.equifax.com or 800-685-1111), Experian (www.experian.com or 714-830-7000), or TransUnion (www.transunion.com or 800-888-4213). Scores may vary from one credit bureau to another, so to be safe, order a copy from all three companies. You can also purchase your credit report from www.myfico.com. If you feel there is an error, you can then ask the company to correct it. Or if you are denied credit, you can ask the company that denied you to divulge the source of the negative credit report. You are then given 30 days to request a free copy of your report from that credit bureau.

Time your car buying. Consider buying a car at the end of the model year, particularly if you're flexible about the model and accessories. Because dealers have lots of inventory, this is a good time for great deals. Also, dealers will often be more willing to deal at the end of a quarter and at the end of the year, when they are trying to meet sales quotas.

Be a shrewd homebuyer. Purchase the least expensive home in a good neighborhood in the best school district. These homes tend to appreciate more quickly, so you get the best return on your investment.

Appeal your property-tax assessment. According to the American Homeowners Association only around 2 percent of homeowners ever appeal this assessment, even though many homes are overassessed. This strategy could be particularly worthwhile when property values are decreasing.

Consider a home-equity loan. Think about getting a home-equity loan (without closing costs) to pay off your mortgage. This might work if your first mortgage balance is fairly low, especially if you can get a fixed rate on the equity loan. You can also use a no-cost, lower-rate equity loan to pay off higher-interest debts, such as credit-card or auto-loan debt. Also, interest on a home-equity loan is often tax deductible, while interest on the credit card and auto loans is not. But don't fall into the trap of financing credit-card or car-loan debt over longer periods just because you are using home-equity loans.

Pay off debts. Which debts should you pay off first?

Start with the ones that have the highest interest rates, particularly if they're not deductible, such as credit cards and auto loans (assuming you have a simple interest car loan). Then tackle student loans, home-equity loans, and mortgages.

Use an Internet bank for your temporary cash investments because they generally pay a higher interest rate and can be set up to allow quick transfers of funds back to your checking account. Two such Internet banks are at INGdirect.com and Emigrantdirect.com

Be sure that your bank is at least giving you a free checking account but also look into the use of interest-paying checking accounts.

Be careful with those credit cards. If you have an introductory low-interest-rate credit card, be wary. Rates often dramatically increase after the initial time frame is over.

If you are paying a high interest rate on your credit card, contact the issuer's customer-service center and ask that the interest rate on your balance be lowered. This is often successful, particularly if you have a good credit rating.

Remember: Little changes add up. In Allyson Lewis's book, *The Million Dollar Car and $250,000 Pizza*, she illustrates how your spending today affects your future financial health. For example, instead of having your favorite Italian carryout once a week, take the $30,

invest it—say, at 7 percent—and at the end of 25 years, you'll have $105,800!

Lower your insurance premiums. Elect high deductibles for car and homeowner's insurance. Use your monthly savings from the lowered insurance cost to save for the deductibles in case of a claim—after the deductibles are set aside, enjoy the savings. If you're over 55, ask for a discount. Make sure your insurance company knows if you have antilock brakes, passive safety restraints, and burglar alarms on your autos and burglar alarms, fire extinguishers, and dead-bolt locks on your home because such devices may qualify you for discounts.

Reduce your life-insurance premiums. Check life insurance policy rates from time to time. Rates may decrease, and you may be able to cancel your policy and purchase another one at a better rate, especially for term insurance.

In the unfortunate event of the death of a loved one, consider buying the casket from a discount store (such as Costco or other discount retailers) or even online (try FuneralDepot.com or Americancasket.com) instead of from the funeral home. They will ship the casket right away directly to the funeral home.

Compare homeowners' insurance quotes and companies. Insurance companies are dropping or turning away customers who have made (in their opinion) too many claims, live in areas susceptible to bad weather (such as Louisiana, Texas, and Florida), or have poor credit histories. If you're looking around for other options, check out www.quotesmith.com. If you're interested in how an insurance company ranks in terms of payment (and nonpayment) of claims, look at www.badfaithinsurance.org.

Carry homeowner's and auto insurance with the same company. You will often get a discount if you purchase your homeowner's and auto insurance from the same company.

Bite the bullet on car-insurance premiums. Pay your auto-insurance premiums on time and in total. Some states allow your insurance to be cancelled if your payment is even 1 day late, and most companies charge a fee for installment payments.

Buy insurance before you need it. If you are planning on purchasing life or disability insurance, get it when you don't need it. It will cost less, and you may not be able to purchase it later on if a problem develops with your health.

Consider this health-insurance option. COBRA (Consolidated Omnibus Budget Reconciliation Act of 1985) is a law mandating the availability of health insurance for up to 18 months after you leave your job—paid for by you, of course. The law applies to most employers with 20 or more workers. Under COBRA, you will pay no more than 102 percent of the employer's cost for your insurance. It's pricey, but this may be a better option than purchasing an individual policy. You can use it as a stopgap policy after you retire if you don't qualify for Medicare and are looking to purchase a health-insurance policy. Another option is the AARP Health Plan: In a number of states, a program called Medical Advantage covers people ages 50 to 64 and includes physician visits, medical tests, and surgery. If you don't qualify for Medicare yet and don't have your own insurance, it may be something to consider. Contact AARP at www.affordable-health-coverage.com or call at 888-687-2277. And don't forget to check out www.ehealthinsurance.com to compare plans.

Choose the best Medicare health plan and Medicare prescription drug coverage plan for you. Call the Medicare hotline (800-MEDICARE), or go to www.medicare.gov and click on "Compare Health Plans and

---

"What's the quickest way to double your money? Fold it in half."
—Will Rogers

Medigap Policies in Your Area" in the right hand column and on "Compare Medicare Prescription Drug Plans." You'll be able to narrow down your health-plan choices and choose the plans that are right for you.

Compare long-distance calling plans. Try these Web sites that compare calling plans and recommend what's best for you based on your particular circumstances: www.tollchaser.com, www.reallycheapld.com, or www.saveonphone.com. If you're interested in using your broadband Internet connection for long-distance calls, try www.skype.com.

Spend less than you make. Enough said!

Clip coupons. Get Internet codes to receive discounts/rewards at brick-and-mortar stores, as well as for online shopping. Try www.coolsavings.com. Individual retailers often have newsletters that contain promotions as well.

Get rid of your private mortgage insurance. Drop your private mortgage insurance if the amount borrowed is less than 80 percent of the appraised value of your home. Have an appraisal done if home prices have risen, or make additional payments on your mortgage to lower the balance.

Find a deal. Use these Web sites to compare prices and products in many categories: www.mysimon.com and www.pricegrabber.com. Or go to www.senior discounts.com, which lists "over 120,000 deals for folks over 50!"

Maximize your interest on savings bonds. Cash in savings bonds on the day that they mature (or as soon thereafter as possible). This will ensure you get the maximum interest. A bank can supply this date, or you can get it online at www.treasurydirect.gov (enter "Individual/Personal" section, and then click on "Find Out if Your Treasury Securities Have Matured").

Take advantage of veterans' benefits. If you are a veteran, you may qualify for lower prescription prices if you were honorably discharged, are enrolled in the VA Health Care System, and have the prescription filled at a VA pharmacy. You may also save on health care, receive a free burial plot and marker, and get a break on loans by VA-approved lenders. Go to www.va.gov/health_benefits, www.cem.va.gov, or ww.homeloans.va.gov, or call the VA at 877-222-8387.

Switch annuities. Some annuities perform better than others. If you find a better one than what you have, see if you can change.

Get more for your money. For a variety of other money-saving tips, see www.cheapskatemonthly.com or www.stretcher.com.

Donate money to charity. When making charitable donations, a good rule of thumb is that the organization should allot at least 65 percent of contributions directly to its programs and 35 percent or less to overhead. Looking for some guidance? The American Institute of Philanthropy is a watchdog organization that provides a list of its top charities: www.charitywatch.org. (Although this isn't a money-saving tip, it helps ensure that your money does the most good.)

When Connie N., a single woman, moved to Florida from the Washington, DC, area, here's how she established banking relationships in her new location. Although she expected to open an interest-bearing checking account, she discovered that this required a minimum balance of $2,000 to be maintained to avoid a monthly fee and the interest rate was only .1 percent per year (yes, only $2 per year on the $2,000 minimum balance). Instead, she opened a regular, free checking account and linked it to her savings account at Emigrant Bank (www.emigrantdirect.com), which is paying her more than 5 percent on her deposits. And making it even better, she can transfer her savings from Emigrant Bank back to her checking account whenever necessary by doing it electronically on the Internet.

WHAT CAN YOU DO NOW?

Time is your friend if you start planning early, but if you wait too long to start, it will turn on you and become your enemy. The longer time horizon you have, the more you can do to increase the likelihood of meeting your retirement goals.

Reaching retirement doesn't mean you stop planning. Continue to monitor your financial health throughout your retirement years, and use the help of a professional if necessary. For some specific tax issues affecting retirement that were not addressed in this chapter, see Chapter 10.

10

WHAT ARE THE TAX ISSUES AFFECTING RETIREMENT?

"A tax loophole is something that benefits the other guy. If it benefits you, it is tax reform."
—Russell B. Long, former US Senator

Even though we all pay a lot of taxes, the truth of the matter is that the total tax burden in the United States is far lower than in many other developed countries in the world. For example, a recent report of the Organization for Economic Cooperation and Development concluded that the combined income and social tax burden in the United States is only 19th among the 30 countries studied—and close to the bottom of the list when total taxes (income, social security, sales, and other taxes) were included. Never-

theless, taxes are still a very important consideration in our retirement planning.

Although retirees face most of the same tax issues as everybody else, certain issues are more likely to come up. Some of these issues include the state tax considerations involved in relocating, the possibility of obtaining a moving expense deduction if and when we move, the rules for determining the taxability of Social Security payments and retirement distributions and, even though none of us want to think about this, estate taxes. But not to worry! In this chapter we provide answers to your questions and, since no taxation discussion would be complete without some savvy tax-saving ideas, we'll add some end-of-year tax tips, as well.

WHERE YOU LIVE AFFECTS YOUR TAXES

Question: What do the following nine states have in common? Alaska, Florida, Nevada, New Hampshire, South Dakota, Tennessee, Texas, Washington, and Wyoming. Answer: They do not have a broad-based income tax. Is this important to know? Perhaps. Although you'd probably rather not think about them, taxes are a crucial part of your retirement planning. Many federal and state taxes, including income tax, property tax, sales tax, and estate tax, can be particularly relevant to retirees. In fact, taxes can be your largest expense; add them up to prove it to yourself!

For example, if you are planning to relocate and are considering only the absence of a state income tax without taking into account other taxes (such as sales, property, and estate taxes), you are making a mistake. Keep in mind that if a state does not have an income tax, it must be getting its revenue somewhere else. That is why the answer to the question above is "perhaps." There are other taxes to consider.

Look at Alaska, for instance. It has neither an income tax nor a sales tax. Sounds like a retirement haven from a tax standpoint, right? But when you consider that Alaska has one of the highest costs of living in the United States, and that more than 50 percent of municipalities in this state assess their own sales tax (which can reach 7 percent), it may not be the best choice for a person on a limited income. You may also find unanticipated taxes in the form of refuse-collection fees, mental-health levies, fees for cleaning up the environment, occupational privilege taxes, etc.

Of course, before examining tax issues, you should look at lifestyle issues. If the climate, medical facilities, cultural/social/recreational opportunities, overall cost of living, and other qualities you are looking for seem a good fit, then look at the tax implications. Let tax considerations help you choose among locations, but don't allow taxes to be the most important consideration in your decision.

"Death and taxes and childbirth. There's never a convenient time for any of them!"
—Margaret Mitchell, *Gone with the Wind*

So how to make sense of the tax issues? Obviously, when deciding where to live from a tax perspective, the entire tax package in the area you are contemplating must be considered. (We provide a state-by-state summary of individual income tax and sales tax rates at the end of this chapter.) Property taxes, including the availability of homestead and senior-citizen exemptions, can also be a significant factor in your total tax package, but they vary so much from location to location that it is almost impossible to provide a meaningful table to help you. In addition, although the property-tax rate is important, it is equally important to understand how properties are valued and assessed. For example, one jurisdiction may typically value real estate much lower than its fair market value, while another may be right at market. Comparing just the two tax rates will not necessarily lead you to a good conclusion as to which has the lower property tax because it ignores the valuation issue. Call the county assessor's office and find out what the current tax rate is per thousand dollars of assessed valuation, and at what percent of real fair market value you can expect a residence to be assessed for property-tax purposes. If that is too cumbersome for you, ask the real-estate agents you speak with how property taxes are determined in areas of interest to you, and talk to people who have recently relocated to or purchased homes in the area.

Beyond these taxes, though, other state-tax issues need to be addressed. States vary in what income they tax. Although the typical state does tax most forms of income, there are significant differences. For example, New Hampshire and Tennessee tax only interest and dividends. This can be the equivalent of no tax at all if your income is coming from pensions, withdrawals from your IRA, and Social Security. Another example is Pennsylvania, which does not tax pension and IRA distributions. If that is the source of most of your income in retirement, it could almost be the equivalent of living in a state with no income tax. In other words, when choosing a place to live and factoring in the tax cost, you have to consider your individual circumstances to see how a particular location's taxes will affect you. In spite of the many articles and books ranking retirement locations based on cost, it's difficult to give a definitive list of the best places (taxwise) for retirement.

Of course, federal tax issues may also play a signifi-

For summary information on state individual income-tax rules applicable to retirees, go to www.retirementliving.com and click on "Taxes by State."

cant role in planning for your retirement. Many people don't need to explore the tax consequences of moving because they know they are staying put! But what about such tax issues as withdrawing from your retirement accounts too soon or withdrawing too little, or too late? How can the taxation of Social Security benefits affect your retirement? Will you have an income tax on the profit from selling your residence, even if you're just moving down the street to a smaller (or larger) home? What are some general tax tips to ensure you're retaining as much income as possible? For the many people who retire from primary jobs but work at second careers, there could be tax implications as well. For example, if you decide to work in your new location, can you deduct your moving expenses even if the job is only temporary? Let's explore some of these tax issues.

STATE INCOME TAXES

Most states have an income tax. It's rare, however, for it to be as simple as a flat tax rate applied to all of your income. Generally, a state will start with the income on your federal tax return and then make adjustments to it in arriving at your state taxable income. In fact, of the 41 states that impose a broad-based income tax, 36 base it on your federal tax return to some extent. Common adjustments in going from federal to state taxable income are subtraction of your Social Security income that was taxed for federal purposes (the table on page 430 shows the 35 states that do not tax Social Security), of interest income from U.S. government bonds and notes (state income taxation on this type of interest is prohibited by the U.S. Constitution), and of certain pension income, and an add-back for any state income taxes deducted on your federal tax return.

Some states base their taxable income on a modified federal adjusted gross income (income less certain adjustments, such as those for IRA deductions), while others are based on a modified federal taxable income (adjusted gross income less itemized deductions for contributions, interest expense, state property taxes, etc.). This distinction can be important if you have large itemized deductions.

After determining taxable income, most states apply some type of a graduated tax rate to calculate the total tax. The table on page 430 shows the income-tax rates in each of the states with an income tax. It is important to note that most states have a range of income-tax rates, rather than just one. Thus, rather than taxing all income at, say, 7 percent, a state may tax the first $3,000 at 2 percent, the next $10,000 at 3 percent, the next $30,000 at 4 percent, and so on until it eventually gets to the tax rate of 7 percent on the amount of taxable income in excess of, say, $100,000. So in addition to looking at the maximum tax rate used, one must also consider the structure of the tax brackets used by a state in actually calculating the tax. Clearly, then, in order to arrive at any sound conclusions on a state's income-tax burden, it is not enough to look only at the tax rate. Rather, you need to estimate the sources of your income in retirement and then put pen to paper and estimate a particular state's income tax with reference to its definition of taxable income, its tax rates, and its tax brackets. The conclusions you reach based on an actual calculation may be significantly different than the conclusions you reach just by looking at the tax rates.

Tax Freedom Day

One way to try to figure out which state is least expensive in terms of taxes is by looking at "Tax Freedom Day," which is determined each year by the Tax Foundation (www.taxfoundation.org), a nonprofit, nonpartisan research and public-education organization. Tax Freedom Day, which was on April 26 in 2006, is the day on which the average American's federal, state, and local tax bill is fully paid from his or her year-to-date earnings. As the Frasier Institute, a think tank, puts it, Tax Freedom Day is "the day you stopped working for the government and started working for yourself." In other words, this is the day (on average) that an individual has made enough to pay Uncle Sam, plus state and local taxes, and is now beginning to make the money that he or she will actually be able to spend on other things. As taxes get higher, Tax Freedom Day falls later in the year, while a decrease in taxes causes Tax Freedom Day to come earlier. So the earlier Tax Freedom Day occurs, the sooner your tax obligation has been met!

What is interesting—and less publicized—is that the Tax Foundation calculates Tax Freedom Day by state, taking into account the incomes of residents of the state as well as their total tax burden, and also performs separate calculations for federal, state, and total taxes. On this basis, and looking only at the state tax burden for 2006, the states faring the worst (having a later Tax Freedom Day) are Maine, New York, Ohio, Minnesota, and Hawaii. Those with the lowest state tax burden

---

A chart published by the Tax Foundation shows that Tax Freedom Day progressed from January 22nd in 1900 all the way to March 31st in 1950. Growth since then has been at a much slower pace.

(having an earlier Tax Freedom Day) are Alaska, New Hampshire, Delaware, Tennessee, and Alabama.

Another Way of Looking at the "Tax Bite"

The calculation of Tax Freedom Day does not take into consideration any special incentives given to retirees, such as for retirement income or for real-estate taxes. Several years ago, Kiplinger, a leading provider of financial advice, looked at the state income tax burden of a hypothetical retired couple living on a combination of Social Security, pension income, and IRA distributions, as well as on interest and dividends. Assumptions were also made as to the value of their residence, which varied by state, and expenditures. On this basis, the highest-cost states from just an income-tax standpoint were Montana, West Virginia, Minnesota, Wisconsin, and Hawaii, while the lowest-cost states were seven of the nine states mentioned at the beginning of this chapter as having no broad-based income tax, plus seven others— Delaware, Illinois, Kentucky, Michigan, New York, Pennsylvania, and South Carolina. (Even though they have no broad-based income tax, Tennessee and Florida were relatively high in the rankings at numbers 19 and 20, respectively, due to Tennessee's tax on interest and dividends and Florida's tax on intangibles. We should note here that, as of January 1, 2007, Florida has repealed its tax on intangibles, which should improve its place in these rankings in the future).

Comparing the Tax Freedom Day study with the Kiplinger study, we see that Minnesota and Hawaii come out as a expensive states in both analyses, and Alaska shows itself on both studies to be a state with a good tax deal. Is this the final answer? Of course not. As you'll see with some other studies trying to determine the tax-friendliest states, results are always predicated on the assumptions used in the study.

Property and Sales Taxes

As noted earlier, income taxes are not the sole criteria by which the total state tax burden needs to be judged. Property and sales taxes can also be significant. In fact, since retirees can spend a disproportionate amount of their retirement incomes in purchasing residences, a state's property tax may be far more significant in determining the total tax burden than its income tax.

For the full 2007 report on Tax Freedom Day, go to www.taxfoundation.org and type "Tax Freedom Day" into the search bar.

A Tax Foundation ranking of the per capita state and local property tax collections for 2005 shows the lowest such taxes are in Alabama, Arkansas, New Mexico, Oklahoma, and Louisiana. The highest per capita property taxes were in New Jersey, Connecticut, New Hampshire, New York, and Rhode Island. These rankings would be heavily impacted by the higher property values in some states as compared to others.

Another Tax Foundation ranking summarizes the per capita sales-tax collections by state for 2005 and shows the highest sales taxes were in Hawaii, Washington, Florida, Wyoming, and Tennessee. The lowest per capita sales taxes were in Virginia, Colorado, Alabama, Oklahoma, and Vermont. It is interesting to note that four of the five states with the highest per capita sales-tax collections are states without a broad-based income tax.

One last study worth mentioning here is a summary put together by the Tax Policy Center of the state and local tax revenue as a percentage of personal income. This summary shows the lowest taxes are in Alabama, Tennessee, New Hampshire, South Dakota, and Colorado. The highest taxes were in New York, Wyoming, Maine, Hawaii, and Vermont.

So What Does All This Mean?

Let's face it. In the end, it should be clear that each state needs to raise revenue in order to meet its obligations. Some get revenue from unique sources such as oil reserves (Alaska) or gambling revenues (Nevada), but most states get the bulk of their revenues from the local taxpayers. The tax rates and the various exemptions, such as for retirement income, vary by state and by type of tax. So don't just assume you should move to a state without a broad-based income tax; you might find that the real-estate tax, sales tax, or some other tax is significantly higher there than in some other state that does have a income tax. Or maybe one of the states with an income tax does not tax the type of income you will be relying on in retirement—such as Social Security income, interest and dividend income, or distributions from a qualified profit-sharing or pension plan.

Taxes are important to consider when planning your retirement. The amount of tax you pay is significant in determining what you have left for all of your other expenses. It is, however, probably a mistake to pick a retirement location based solely on tax considerations; yet it is also a mistake to conclude anything with respect to the total tax burden in any state without actually looking at your own facts and the tax laws of the states you are considering and estimating what your tax burden will be. As with many things in life, it may be wise to seek help in this exercise. We suggest that you ask the advice of a certified public accountant (CPA), particularly a CPA specializing in individual taxation.

CHANGING YOUR STATE OF TAXATION

Assuming you have decided to move to a new location, one question will come up: How does a state determine who is subject to its taxes? Since sales and property taxes follow from the location of the sales transaction or the property being taxed, there's rarely an issue as to who is subject to them. Determining whether an individual is subject to a state's income tax can be more complex, however. Often a state will subject an individual to its income tax if that individual either resides in the state or is a domiciliary of the state. Most people are domiciled in the same state in which they reside, but this is not always the case. The term *resident* generally refers to someone living within a state more than a minimum amount of time during a tax year (for example, someone working on a long-term project in Ohio could be a resident of Ohio, even if it's not her domicile), while the term *domiciliary* generally refers to an individual who is domiciled within a state (that is, "where the heart and home are," regardless of where his current place of abode may be). A domicile is generally the place to which an individual intends to return after a temporary absence.

Each state has its own rules as to whose income it will tax. It is possible to be taxed in a state where you are domiciled, even though your actual place of abode is outside the state. Likewise, it is possible to be taxed in a state where your actual place of abode is, even though you are domiciled elsewhere. It is even possible to be taxed in two different states at the same time. When this happens, the taxpayer is generally able to claim a credit in one of the states for the income taxes paid in the other. The result is generally that taxes will be paid at the higher rate of the two states.

This becomes especially important when you have two (or more) places of abode, as do the Florida sunbirds who escape to the north for the less humid summers. Do they pay income tax to the northern state in which their summer residence is located or, as winter residents of Florida, do they escape state income taxes altogether? They could end up being taxed in their summer location, either because they are domiciled there, or possibly because they were physically present there for more than a specified number of days during the tax year.

Not surprisingly, since all the states have their own tax laws, there is no standard test for income taxability, although there are some broad concepts most states use. States generally impose an income tax on an individual who maintains a place of abode within the state and actually occupies it for more than a specified number of days during the year (commonly 183 days is used as a benchmark), regardless of whether that individual is also domiciled in that state.

When a state is determining taxability based on residence, it is often necessary to keep track of every day an individual is in that state in order to determine if the threshold of taxability has been met. For example, Lewis and Julie S. lived most of their married lives in Virginia. When they retired, they moved to a new residence in Palm Beach, Florida, which they viewed as their permanent home and domicile. They also kept their old home in Virginia, however, so that they could return to it during the spring and summer months to enjoy the (relatively) cooler weather and to be with their families. In 2006 they were in their Palm Beach home from January 1 through April 30, their Virginia home from May 1 through November 1, and then back in their Palm Beach home for the rest of the year. Unfortunately, even though they thought of themselves as tax-free residents of Florida, Virginia treats anyone who lives within the state for more than 183 days during the year as a resident, and it required Lewis and Julie to pay Virginia income tax on all of their income for the year. Had they reduced their 185 days in Virginia by just 2 days, they could have completely avoided the Virginia income tax.

States will often also tax an individual who is domiciled within the state, regardless of whether he or she actually has a residence within the state, and often regardless of whether the individual has even been in the state during the tax year. For example, many states will tax the income of a domiciliary who has converted her residence to rental property and moved to a foreign country for a 3-year assignment, after which she intends to return to the state. To add to the confusion, some states will tax the income of a domiciliary only who has also actually been within the state for more than a minimum number of days during the year, thus potentially not taxing the income of the expatriate described above.

It is generally relatively easy to determine if someone is subject to income taxes in a state due to physical residence in the state. It's often a matter of counting the number of days of physical residence in the state and comparing that to the state's definition of resident. Determining whether someone is taxable in a state as a domiciliary is not always so easy, however, particularly when the individual has more than one home. As you might expect, a common tactic of taxpayers is to claim domicile in a state that has no income tax, or one with a very low income tax, while residing for much of the year in a state that does impose an income tax. Over the years, a number of factors have been used by the courts in resolving the issue of domicile. Some of the more significant criteria are as follows.

* Voting registration
* Driver's license
* Automobile registration
* Bank/brokerage accounts
* Country club memberships
* Church memberships
* Location of safe-deposit boxes
* Address used on federal tax return
* Ownership of real estate

So again, what does all this mean?

It will often be clear in which state taxes must be paid. Property taxes follow the location of the property, and sales taxes follow the state where the sale is completed. Income taxes are usually paid in the state of residence, which is usually also the state of domicile. Income taxes, however, can get muddy, especially when more than one residence is involved. There is no simple answer that covers all the states. Taxpayers are well-advised to seek professional advice whenever they intend to own and occupy residences in multiple states in order to gain a complete understanding of each state's rules on who is subject to the requirement to file an income-tax return. Forewarned is forearmed—these rules can often be used to your advantage, but to do so you need to understand them (or find someone who does!).

true LIFE **George W. devoted his career to building a landscaping business into a very successful enterprise in his home state of Kentucky.**

As he neared retirement age, he decided to sell all of the stock in his business and move to Florida to devote his efforts to golf, travel, and other forms of relaxation. While meeting with his tax advisor, however, he learned that by moving to Florida first, establishing domicile and residency there, and then selling the stock, he would avoid having to pay Kentucky income tax on the sales profit. Clearly, he was now able to afford a much larger retirement home. This strategy should work when moving to any of the states that do not have an income tax. ⓣ�L

HOME SWEET HOME AND THE TAX CONSEQUENCES OF SELLING

For many of us, our homes are one of our most valuable assets—and have also been one of our most profitable investments. The housing market over the past 30 years has generally been spectacular, notwithstanding the housing slump that began in mid-2006. Under the old tax law, in effect through mid-1997, the gain from the sale of a principal residence could escape current taxation as long as the sellers reinvested the net proceeds (sale price less selling expenses, but not minus the mortgage) into a new principal residence. The gain not taxed was deferred and used to reduce the tax cost of the replacement residence. This would have the effect of increasing the gain when the replacement residence was eventually sold, but once again, this gain could be deferred into the next replacement residence, and so on for residence after residence. This rule worked fine for most home sellers; after all, the goal was usually to sell an existing residence and move into a larger or nicer, and usually more expensive, residence. But for retirees selling their principal residences and planning to downsize for their retirement years, this tax break usually left them with some tax to pay whenever the net proceeds from the sale of their old residences were not all reinvested in the new residences. In fact, since the gain from the sale of many earlier residences could have continued to be deferred and used to reduce the tax cost of replacement residences, a failure to reinvest some or all of the proceeds from the sale of the last residence at the time of retirement could have caused some or all of the deferred gains over a multitude of residences to finally become taxable.

Fortunately, in 1997 Congress changed this rule and replaced it with a kinder, gentler tax break, especially for retirees who wanted to downsize. Under the new rule now applicable to the sale of a principal residence, some or all of the gain on the sale is not taxable as long as the taxpayers owned and lived in the residence as their principal residence for at least 2 years during the 5-year period ending with the date of the sale. The amount of gain that is not taxable is limited to $250,000 for a single taxpayer (or a married taxpayer filing separately) and $500,000 for a married couple filing a joint tax return. Significantly, unlike under the old law, this gain is eliminated from taxable income and is not deferred to reduce the tax basis of any replacement residence. In fact, there is no requirement to even purchase a replacement principal residence, which is one of the reasons this change is so beneficial to retirees and others looking to downsize. This tax break is available to taxpayers without regard to age and can be claimed multiple times, but generally only once every 2 years.

It is important to remember that when calculating the amount of gain on the sale of a principal residence, any gain deferred due to the purchase of a new principal residence under the old law, as discussed above, must be used to reduce the cost of a replacement residence.

What Is Meant by "Principal Residence"?

For those taxpayers owning and using more than one residence, it is important to be able to determine which constitutes the principal residence. For this purpose, the principal residence is generally located in the state in which the taxpayers are domiciled, and it's the home in which the taxpayers live most of the time. A principal residence can be a house, townhouse, duplex, condominium, cooperative apartment, or mobile home, but it cannot be just a lot. In fact, although it is not all that common, a principal residence can even be a houseboat or yacht.

For example, Stephanie and Mike B. own a residence in which they reside in Washington, DC. They also own and occupy a house in Long Beach Island, New Jersey, and spend most of every summer at the shore and make occasional trips there during the off-season (for example, for Thanksgiving and New Year's Eve). Their Washington, DC, residence is their principal residence. In the event that Stephanie and Mike sold their Long Beach Island house and realized a profit on the sale, they would not be able to escape taxation on the profit since it is not their principal residence.

As outlined above, it is generally necessary to have both owned and occupied the residence as your principal residence for at least 2 full years out of the 5-year period ending on the date of the sale to avoid taxation of a gain. Thus, it is possible to move out of a principal residence and rent it out for almost 3 years prior to a sale and still eliminate the gain from taxable income, since the 2-year test looks at the entire prior 5-year period.

It is important to ensure that the requirement for 2 years of use as a principal residence in the 5-year period preceding the date of sale is met. Imagine the pain if the sellers could not get to settlement in time to qualify. For example, Beth and Jeff owned and occupied a home as their principal residence for 10 years prior to moving out and renting it on January 1, 2004, due to a bad housing market. They then managed to sell it, with settlement scheduled for December 31, 2006, just barely meeting the 2- out of 5-year requirement that would have entitled them to eliminate all of the gain on the sale, except for an amount equal to the depreciation deductions claimed against rental income. Beth and Jeff would, however, lose the entire tax break if settlement were delayed until January 2007. Why? Because not settling on the house until 2007 would mean that they hadn't used it as a principal residence for 2 full years out of the 5 years preceding the date of sale. As they say, timing is everything!

Although the applicable rule requires 2 years of both ownership and use, there are exceptions—isn't that always the case in taxation! In this case, however, the exceptions are intended to help (surprise, surprise). If the taxpayers need to sell their principal residence prior to qualifying under the 2-year test, they can still qualify for a reduced exclusion if the primary reason for not qualifying for both the ownership and use test is due to

(1) a change in the place of employment, (2) health reasons, or (3) unforeseen circumstances. In each of these cases, the maximum amount of the exclusion is reduced by a formula that compares the number of qualifying days (or months, at the taxpayer's election) of ownership and use prior to the date of sale to 730 days (or 24 months).

For example, if Christi and Garrett needed to sell their principal residence in Cincinnati after owning and living in it for only 1 year and move to Cleveland due to a change of jobs, the amount of the maximum exclusion would be reduced from $500,000 to $250,000 (or 50 percent of the maximum exclusion, since they lived in the residence for only 50 percent of the time required for the full amount)—still a pretty good deal, since few of us are fortunate enough to own a house for only 1 year and sell it for a profit of $250,000.

The health exception applies to your illness or injury or that of a close relative (such as a spouse, parent, grandparent, child, sibling, or mother-in-law). The third exception, unforeseen circumstances, covers a number of contingencies that could force a sale of a principal residence: divorce or legal separation, multiple births resulting from the same pregnancy (not likely to apply to most retirees!), unemployment, and death, including the death of a close relative. For example, in 2006, Janine sold her principal residence in New York City, which she had purchased in late 2005, in order to move to Virginia to live with her mother, who was unable to care for herself. Since the sale of Janine's residence was primarily so that she could move to Virginia to care for her mother, Janine was eligible to claim a partial exclusion of the gain on the sale of her New York residence.

Another special rule provides that taxpayers can exclude the gain from the sale of a principal residence only one time in each 2-year period. Once again, however, the exceptions that apply when the 2-year ownership and use tests are not met apply here as well. To read more about the tax rules applicable to the taxation of the gain from the sale of your home, go to www.irs.gov and type "Publication 523" into the search bar or call the IRS at 800-Tax-Form.

A couple owning a principal residence and a vacation residence could sell their principal residence and exclude a gain of up to $500,000 (assuming they had both owned and used it as their principal residence for at least 2 years) and then move into their vacation residence for 2 years and then sell that residence also and exclude the gain again, up to another $500,000.

What Are Some Other Home-Selling Issues?

In addition to the rule allowing taxpayers to avoid tax on some or all of the profit on the sale of their principal residences, there are several other tax considerations to take into account when selling your home.

❋ The deduction for property taxes in the year of sale is prorated between the buyer and seller based on the number of days in the real property-tax year that each owned the residence. Don't forget to check your settlement sheet for the tax charge (or credit) proration and include it on your income-tax return for the year of the sale.

❋ Any points you may have paid on a prior refinancing of your home that were not deductible previously (points on a refinancing are generally not deductible when paid) are deductible when the mortgage is paid off at closing.

❋ Taxes such as transfer taxes, stamp taxes, and other miscellaneous charges and taxes paid at settlement are not deductible, nor is the commission paid to the real-estate agent. All of these costs, however, are taken into account in determining your gain on the sale.

❋ Any gain that was not taxable to you on the sale of a previous residence under the old rules that allowed you to defer the gain and use it as a reduction of the tax cost of a replacement residence must be taken into account in determining the gain on the sale of your current residence. Thus, if you deferred a $200,000 gain in 1990 on the sale of your last principal residence and have an additional $250,000 gain on the sale of your current principal residence, your taxable gain on the current sale would be $450,000—still not a problem if you qualify for the entire $500,000 exclusion.

❋ When you are selling your residence and moving, it is usually a great time to consider contributing unneeded items to charity. Examples would be furniture you no longer need and household items that you no longer have room to store. Under a change in the tax law effective for 2006, such items must be in good used condition or better in order to be eligible for a tax deduction. If you con-

---

A recent reprint by CCH Incorporated of the U.S. Income Tax Law enacted on October 3, 1913, was 26 pages long. In its first year, CCH's Income Tax Service publication, which explained the new tax law, grew to around 400 pages. Today, the CCH Standard Federal Tax Reporter includes more than 55,000 pages!

tribute more than $5,000 in goods, you'll generally need a qualified appraiser and Form 8283, Section B, attached to your tax return. To obtain a copy of this form, go to www.irs.gov and type "Form 8283" into the search bar or call the IRS at 800-Tax-Form.

Can You Deduct the Costs of Moving to a New Location?

As a general rule, the expenses of moving to a new location will not be deductible unless the move is in connection with the start of a job in the new location. Thus, for people moving for the sake of their new job called "retirement," the moving expenses will rarely be deductible. Since the tax rules do not require that the job in the new location be forever, however, it is possible to gain a deduction for these expenses—if you are willing to meet the requirement that you work full time for at least a specified period of time after the move. Regardless of age, a retiree who works in the desired retirement location for the required 39 weeks or more prior to actual retirement (78 weeks if you are self-employed) can gain a deduction for the moving expenses while also having a great opportunity to settle into the new community prior to actual retirement. For example, shortly after Brian and Jill S. moved to Palm Coast, Florida, following his retirement from a 30-year teaching career in Saint Paul, Minnesota, Brian was able to obtain a full-time job working in the Palm Coast public library, where he put his love of books to good use and met many of his new neighbors. After he had completed 39 weeks of full-time employment, Brian and Jill's moving expenses were deductible, even though Bill then retired completely so he and Jill could begin their retirement dream of traveling to each of the seven continents.

So what are the requirements to be able to deduct moving expenses? Essentially, two major tests must be met. First, you must work full-time in the new location for at least 39 weeks during the first 12 months after the move (and it doesn't have to be in the same job) or, if self-employed, you must work full time for at least 78 weeks during the first 24 months. The second test, likely the easier of the two tests to meet, is that your new principal job location must be at least 50 miles farther from your old residence than your old principal job location. So if your commute to work each day used to be 10 miles each way, your new job would have to be at least 60 miles from your old residence to meet this test.

A special rule allows for the deduction of moving expenses for individuals who have been working abroad and who move in connection with their permanent retirement. Among other requirements, the expatriate must have both lived and worked outside the United States—so those of you living in Detroit and working in Windsor, Canada, will not qualify. For example, Mark and Rita Z. lived for 5 years in Costa Rica, where Mark worked for a large U.S. multinational corporation. Following this assignment, they moved to Sarasota, Florida, and retired. Since Mark both lived and worked outside the United States and moved in connection with his permanent retirement, their moving expenses were deductible, and they didn't need to satisfy the usual requirement to work for at least 39 weeks in the first year after a move.

Deductible moving expenses include the costs of packing, crating, and transporting your furniture and other household goods, plus the costs of your travel to the new location (airfare, several nights in hotels, etc.). Also included are the costs of connecting and disconnecting utilities and the costs of shipping your cars and pets.

If you are interested in reading more about the rules for deducting moving expenses, get a copy of IRS Publication 521 by going to www.irs.gov and typing "Publication 521" into the search bar or calling the IRS at 800-Tax-Form.

WILL UNCLE SAM REALLY TAX YOUR SOCIAL SECURITY BENEFITS?

As unbelievable as it might sound, your Social Security checks are very likely to be taxable, at least in part. IRS Publication 915 (go to www.irs.gov and type "Publication 915" into the search bar) explains the rules for determining whether your benefits are taxable and, if so, for determining the taxable portion. Worksheets to help you with the calculations and examples are also provided, perhaps explaining why the IRS needed to publish an entire booklet to explain all this. Our goal here is to give you a general idea of the rule for the taxation of Social Security benefits without making your head swim with all the complexities of the actual calculation.

In general, a comparison is made between a base amount and the total of one-half of your Social Security benefits plus 100 percent of the rest of your income, including your nontaxable income. For simplicity, let's call this second amount your benchmark income. If your base amount is equal to or more than your benchmark income, none of your Social Security benefits are taxable. If your benchmark income exceeds your base amount, however, up to 85 percent of your benefits will be taxed. So what are the base amounts that your benchmark income must not exceed in order to avoid being taxed on your Social Security benefits?

* $25,000 if you are single, a head of household, or a qualifying widow(er)

* $25,000 if you are married filing separately and lived apart from your spouse for the entire calendar year

✳ $32,000 if you are married filing jointly

✳ $0 if you are married filing separately and lived with your spouse at any time during the year

Once your benchmark amount exceeds the base amount, a portion of your Social Security benefits is taxable. Initially, up to 50 percent of your benefits will be taxed. If, however, your benchmark amount exceeds $44,000 on a joint return or $34,000 on a single return, you will be taxed on up to 85 percent of your benefits. As we are sure you realize, having a benchmark amount of $44,000 is not a very high litmus test. For example, assume John and Tess C. (both over 65 and filing a joint income-tax return) received $9,000 in Social Security benefits and also had a taxable pension of $20,000 and nontaxable interest income from their State of Delaware bonds of $4,000. Their benchmark income amounts to $28,500 (half of the $9,000 Social Security + all of the pension + all of the nontaxable interest income). Since their base amount of $32,000 is greater than their benchmark amount, none of their Social Security benefits are taxable.

Including nontaxable income in the determination of your benchmark income can create a situation where income such as municipal-bond income (which is generally not subject to federal income taxes) can cause your Social Security benefits to be partially taxable—effectively making your municipal-bond interest taxable! Retirees who are close to having a benchmark income in excess of the base amount should think carefully about the impact that buying municipal bonds might have on the taxability of their Social Security benefits.

Taxing Social Security benefits may seem outrageous, and in many cases it is. After all, you paid for these benefits by paying Social Security taxes for many years, and you paid these taxes using your after-tax earnings. Although it is true that many retirees will receive Social Security benefits greater than the total of the Social Security taxes they paid during their working years (thus, taxing these benefits is not all that unfair after all), it is also true that many of us will receive benefits far less than the taxes we paid and really have a loss, not income!

By using a base amount of $0 for people who are married but file separately, the IRS has prevented retirees from escaping some or all of the tax on the benefits of the spouse with the lower earnings by using married-filing-separately status.

There is a special lump-sum election available to those who may have received benefits in the current year that relate to a prior year—for example, those who disputed a ruling that they were not eligible for Social Security benefits and won, receiving a lump-sum payment covering both the current and prior years. Under this election, you may be able to figure the taxable portion of some of the benefits under a benchmark amount calculation using the prior year's/years' income.

WHEN SHOULD YOU TAKE DISTRIBUTIONS?

The question of when you should start taking distributions from your tax-deferred IRA, 401(k), or other qualified retirement plan (defined as a qualified employee plan, a qualified employee annuity plan, and a tax-sheltered annuity plan under Section 403[b]) involves several issues. The whole idea of a retirement plan is to have funds put away to cover living expenses in retirement. To prevent these funds from being dissipated before retirement there is, in general, a 10 percent penalty if you withdraw them before you are at least 59½ years old, in addition to the regular income tax on the withdrawal. As with most rules in taxation, there are a few exceptions to this penalty, such as those for early retirement, disability, and distributions made after the death of the plan participant.

Since retirement benefits are intended to be paid out during your lifetime, instead of held for distribution to your beneficiaries after your death, another penalty is imposed if you do not withdraw at least a minimum amount (prescribed under IRS tables) each year, starting on or before April 1 of the year after the year in which you turn 70½. The penalty for failure to withdraw the minimum amount from a traditional IRA could be as much as 50 percent on the amount that should have been, but was not, distributed. For this purpose, the minimum required distributions are determined under IRS prescribed tables, which are based on your life expectancy. IRA trustees, custodians, and issuers must provide information relating to required minimum distributions to IRA owners by January 31 each year. If you want to compute these figures yourself, IRS Publication 590 ("Individual Retirement Arrangements") explains how, and it includes these tables in its Appendix C. Go to www.irs.gov and type "Publication 590" into the search bar for forms and publications.

Since your assets within these retirement accounts

Other than distributions (withdrawals) from a Roth IRA and a portion of distributions from a retirement account into which you made after-tax contributions (both of which were discussed in Chapter 9), amounts that you receive from your tax-deferred retirement plans will generally be fully taxable as ordinary income, regardless of what you do with the amounts distributed.

are generating earnings (such as interest, dividends, and appreciation) on a tax-deferred basis, it is frequently best to hold off as long as possible before you start taking distributions. Of course, this assumes you have other sources of funds on which you can live. Examples of these other sources would be pensions, tax-free municipal bond interest income, previously taxed savings, lower-taxed dividend income, and long-term capital-gain income. You must also take into account our system of progressive tax rates, under which your earnings start off being tax-free and are then taxed at ever-increasing tax rates. You would generally not want to defer a distribution from a retirement account from a year in which it would have been taxed at 15 percent to a year in which it will be taxed at 25 percent—although it is possible that you could be ahead even in this case if the future year of taxation is far enough into the future. The benefit of continued compounded earnings on the untaxed assets still within your retirement accounts could eventually offset even this 10 percent difference.

So a quick and easy answer would be to defer these distributions as long as possible, but only if your tax rate is not expected to go up. If it is expected to increase, then you need to do your homework to determine whether to take distributions sooner, rather than later. It is important to keep in mind when making this decision

that you will be required to start making the required minimum distributions no later than the year following the year in which you turn 70½ years old.

WHAT ABOUT ESTATE TAXES?

Graduated federal estate taxes are imposed on the taxable estate of a decedent (which is determined by subtracting deductible liabilities and expenses from taxable assets at the time of death, less an exemption amount). In 2001, major changes were made in the federal estate tax rules. Under the federal changes, the maximum exemption amount for purposes of determining the taxable estate was set at $2 million, and the maximum estate tax rate was reduced to 45 percent for 2007. In 2009, the exemption amount will increase to $3.5 million, while the maximum tax rate stays at 45 percent. In the year 2010, the federal estate tax will be completely repealed, but only for 1 year (how weird can our lawmakers get?). Starting in 2011, the federal estate tax law in effect in 2001 will become the law again, with an exemption of $1 million and a maximum tax rate of 55 percent, assuming that Congress does not take any action to extend or permanently enact these changes for future years.

Since none of us can be assured of dying in 2010, we will still need to give consideration to the impact of federal estate taxes when doing our retirement planning. Due to the unlimited marital deduction available for bequests to a surviving spouse (who is a U.S. citizen)—in other words, you can leave everything to your husband/wife with no federal estate tax being imposed on your estate—and the significant estate tax exemption, it should be possible for most married individuals to avoid having a federal estate tax imposed on their estates when they die. Surviving spouses, however, will be in a more difficult position when they die (but, of course, that might not be the worst of their problems!) if the estate is larger than the exemption amount, unless they remarry and leave assets to their new spouse. This presents an opportunity to plan for taking maximum advantage of the exemption amount in the estate of the first spouse to die, often through the use of a trust, in order to reduce the estate tax on the second spouse's death. It would be wise to consult a qualified estate planner (generally a CPA, CFP, or attorney) to undertake an analysis of the federal estate tax rules, to be able to determine whether any federal estate tax planning is needed, and to reach valid conclusions on the effect of this tax on your estate plan. It goes without saying that it is critical you have a current and valid will executed, and that you should also have your estate planning and will reviewed any time you move to a different state.

Each state has its own rules on estate and inheritance taxes. These state "death taxes" are imposed on either the estate itself or on the amount of property transferring to a beneficiary, or both. Many states used to have a tax equal to the maximum credit on the federal estate tax return for state death taxes paid, thus effectively negating the impact of the state's death taxes. However, due to changes in the federal estate tax rules in 2005, there is no longer a credit for state death taxes, which resulted in these states collecting no estate taxes under their methodology. Recently, 20 states have imposed their own estate tax, separate from the operation of the federal tax. Some states impose a tax on the transfer of property after death—often with exemptions for certain transfers—and others do not have such a tax. Due to the diversity of these rules in the various states and the impact of the changes in the federal rules noted above on many of these state death taxes, it is impossible to generalize the impact of state taxes on an estate. These taxes should be part of the analysis that ought to be undertaken with the assistance of a qualified professional.

YEAR-END TAX PLANNING

Although tax planning should be an ongoing process throughout the year, it is often relegated to year-end, when many of us start giving some thought to what can be done to reduce the tax bill. It is also the time of year when we are all running out of time to accomplish whatever can be done for tax reduction. Since tax and financial planning for retirement involves making the best use of the assets you have, it seems that closing this chapter with some tax-planning tips is appropriate.

Consider paying your mortgage payment that's due on January 1 before the end of the year. This will accelerate your deduction for mortgage interest.

Think about taking out a home-equity loan to pay off credit-card and other personal debt, such as auto loans. The interest on a home equity loan of up to $100,000 is generally deductible, while the interest on a credit-card or other personal debt is not. Additionally, you can often get a better interest rate on a home-equity loan. The biggest risk in doing this is that you might end up paying off this debt over a longer period, which would be a terrible thing to do. Who wants to finance an automobile over 10 or 15 years? You need to be disciplined here, and be sure to continue to pay these loans off at the same pace (or faster) than when they were credit-card or personal debt.

Use appreciated securities that have been held for at least 1 year to make charitable contributions. Obviously, this would work best for larger contributions, and it allows you to forever avoid paying income tax on the appreciation while getting a tax deduction for the full value of the asset contributed. The charity can sell the security tax-free, so everybody ends up a winner. If you're planning on giving a donation, check out the charity through these Web sites and phone numbers: Better Business Bureau (www.give.org or 703-276-0100) and the American Institute of Philanthropy (www. charitywatch.org or 773-529-2300).

Never contribute a depreciated security to charity. If you do, you will get a tax deduction for the value of the security, but you will never get a deduction for the decline in value from when the security was purchased. Instead, sell the security, deduct the loss on the sale, and contribute the net proceeds of the sale to the charity.

See if you qualify for job-related deductions. In order to take a deduction for work-related expenses, you need expenditures that equal more than 2 percent of your adjusted gross income, since they fall into the category of

---

Of course, accelerating deductions such as charitable contributions, interest, and taxes into the current tax year or deferring current-year income such as a bonus to a future year might not make sense if you expect your tax rate to be higher next year.

miscellaneous deductions. Here are some examples of allowable deductions: mileage (48.5 cents per mile for 2007) for that portion of your noncommute drive that is work related; union dues and professional organization fees (generally, work-related organizations that you are required to join and professional organizations that you are required or choose to join); work-related magazines/journals/books; purchase of uniforms that are required for the job; the cost of training and continuing education related to your job. You can also deduct job-hunting costs under certain circumstances, even if you are currently employed. Your search must be for a job in your present occupation, it cannot be a search for a first job, and there can't be a significant time break between the end of your last job and your looking for a new one. So if you meet these criteria, you can deduct postage, stationery, résumé services, phone calls, transportation related to your job search, outplacement agency fees, etc.

Check whether you can take other miscellaneous deductions; as noted above these are deductible if they (in the aggregate) exceed 2 percent of your adjusted gross income. They include fees and other expenses paid for tax preparation, investment advice, and estate planning. So if H and R Block prepares your 2006 tax returns, you can include their fee as a miscellaneous deduction in the year that you pay it.

Schedule your medical expenses for maximum tax benefit. Medical expenses are only deductible if they exceed 7.5 percent of your adjusted gross income, so if you are getting close to that 7.5 percent threshold, consider bunching your expenses. For example, can you accelerate that next dentist appointment or time elective surgery to produce the best tax result? Or maybe you should put them both off until next year, when other medical expenses will help get you over the 7.5 percent amount.

If you are paying for college tuition for your children but don't qualify for the Hope Scholarship or the Lifetime Learning tax credits, consider having the student claim the credit instead. This will require that you forego claiming your child as an exemption, but it's possible doing so did not save you much anyway due to the

---

Be sure to save the required acknowledgement from the charity for any gift of $250 or more and receipts and cancelled checks for gifts under $250. If you contribute over $500 in property, attach Form 8283 to your tax return; if you donate over $5,000 in property, you'll need a qualified appraiser and Form 8283, Section B, attached to your tax return.

phaseout of the deduction for dependents of high-income taxpayers. If the child does not have a tax against which to claim the credit, consider gifts of appreciated securities that can then be sold, generating a tax against which the credit can be claimed and creating proceeds that can be used to pay the tuition, room, board, etc., you would otherwise have paid.

Accelerate charitable contributions by contributing assets to one of the mutual funds qualified as a charitable organization. You will be able to direct those funds to charities of your choice in future years. One such fund is the Fidelity Charitable Gift Fund. For more information, go to www.charitablegift.org.

Deduct the cost of using your automobile for charitable purposes, such as when you participate in fundraising activities on behalf of the United Way. The IRS allows this deduction to be computed using a standard rate of 14 cents per mile for 2007. It could increase in future years.

Consider a charitable remainder trust. Using this estate-planning tool, you make a donation in trust of appreciated property to a charitable organization. You receive an annuity for life, get to take a tax deduction for the value of your gift that is going to charity (after factoring in the value of your annuity), and also avoid capital gains taxes on your contribution. With the right strategy, you end up with more cash in your pocket because of the contribution—but, of course, your heirs will not inherit the property you donated.

Defer income. If you think your income will decrease the following year, placing you in a lower marginal tax bracket, ask employers to hold off year-end bonuses until the New Year. If you are self-employed, bill your customers late in the year so payment will be received in the following year. But be careful when deferring earnings into a future year in which you will be retired. You may end up with a higher total Social Security tax cost if you are over the limit on compensation subject to this tax in the year of deferral since it will likely be fully subject to the tax in the next year, due to your retirement.

Give away all your unwanted clothing and household articles that are in good condition. Many charities out there (Salvation Army, Amvets, St. Vincent de Paul, etc.) can make good use of such items, and you will get a tax deduction for their fair market value.

See if you can claim a credit for Federal Insurance Contribution Act (FICA) overpayments. For 2007, FICA is collected on 7.65 percent of your income, up to a maximum tax of $7,459 (it's collected on compensation income up to $97,500). This amount is indexed each year to a higher amount to reflect inflation. If you switched jobs and your total earnings during the year were in excess of the $97,500, you will likely have overpaid your FICA. If so, you can claim a credit for the overpayment on your income-tax return.

If your itemized deductions are barely more than the standard deduction, consider bunching them together every other year, so that you claim the standard deduction one year and itemize the next. The same idea works when your itemized deductions don't exceed the standard deduction, but would if you bunched them together every other year. This is only workable for deductions for which you have some control over the time of payment, such as charitable contributions, state estimated tax payments, and possibly property taxes, since the deductions would all have to be paid during the year in which you claim them.

Estimate your state tax liability and prepay it at the end of the tax year rather than when you file your state tax return in April. This gets the payment as a deduction on the federal return in the current year. But be careful to consider the potential applicability of the alternative minimum tax in connection with this strategy.

Don't include your prior year's state tax refund in your federal income if you did not itemize deductions on your federal tax return last year, even if you receive a form from your state government showing the amount of this refund to report on your federal tax return. Under the tax-benefit rule, such refunds are not taxable since you received no tax benefit from the payment of the taxes in the prior year. The tax-benefit rule could also apply if you were subject to the alternative minimum tax in the prior year, since state taxes are not deductible for this tax calculation.

If you have securities in your taxable investment accounts that have declined in value below their cost but which you want to hold onto because you expect them to increase in value in the future, and you also have an IRA account in which you hold securities, consider selling the loss securities in your taxable account and repurchasing them in your IRA. Obtain the necessary funds in your IRA by selling securities that you can repurchase in your taxable investment accounts. If you execute the trades on the Internet, the commissions for the two purchases and two sales should not be much more than

---

The rules governing eligibility of home-office deductions are almost a book unto themselves! Although these deductions can sometimes be claimed, important exclusions and exceptions apply, and you should definitely avail yourself of professional advice if you work at home. That being said, these deductions can be taken. For information, go to www.irs.gov (type "Publication 587" into the search bar).

ALTERNATIVE MINIMUM TAX

This tax was originally designed to ensure that wealthy taxpayers don't avoid income taxes by taking advantage of such tax preferences as the deferral of income from the exercise of incentive stock options and accelerated depreciation. It is expected to apply to millions of Americans due to the combination of the impact of inflation on taxable income and the narrowing of the difference between the 35 percent maximum tax rate for regular income-tax purposes and the 28 percent maximum tax rate for alternative minimum tax calculations. Since state income and property taxes are not deductible in determining your alternative minimum tax, taxpayers in high-tax states such as New York and California are particularly vulnerable to this tax. If the alternative minimum tax applies to you, your tax planning takes on an entirely different focus, whereby you could very well end up trying to defer tax deductions into future tax years and to accelerate income into the current tax year.

$80, while the deductible capital loss could be in the thousands of dollars.

Time your capital gains and losses on your tax return. If you have a net long-term capital gain, it is subject to a maximum tax rate of 15 percent. If you have a net capital loss, it is deductible (subject to a $3,000 limit per year) against your ordinary income and could save you up to 35 percent. Therefore, consider selling enough of your securities that have declined in value so that you end up with a net capital loss of at least $3,000. Or sell securities that have declined in value this year in order to get the $3,000 capital loss deduction and wait until next year to sell the securities that have increased in value to generate a net long-term capital gain and get the benefit of the 15 percent tax rate.

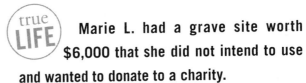 **Marie L. had a grave site worth $6,000 that she did not intend to use and wanted to donate to a charity.**

Since she did not itemize her deductions and would have gotten only minimal tax savings from the contribution, however, she gave the grave site to her daughter Kate, who did itemize her tax deductions. Kate then contributed the grave site to a charitable organization operating a children's hospital for its use for the burial of a child of an indigent family and claimed a substantial tax deduction for its value. There was no gift tax on the transfer of the grave site to Kate since it was worth less than the $12,000 annual exemption that applies to gifts. ⓛ

Ensure that you have maximized allowable contributions to your IRA or Roth IRA. Also, consider converting your IRA to a Roth IRA if your modified adjusted gross income (see discussion in Chapter 9) is under $100,000. In 2010 and later years, this $100,000 income limitation is repealed, and the tax cost of the conversion can be spread over 2 years, if desired.

Don't overlook the deduction for investment interest you may have paid. This is generally interest incurred on a loan where the proceeds of the loan were used for investment purposes, for example, interest on a margin securities account.

Consider changing the terms of your securities accounts at brokerage houses so that your securities cannot be used by the brokerage house for covering short sales of their customers (known as hypothetication). Such use generally is permitted on all accounts where margin purchases are allowed and can result in your receiving "payments in lieu of dividends" instead of dividends on your stock holdings, even though you never had a margin loan. Such payments do not qualify for the maximum 15 percent tax on dividend income and can be taxed at rates up to the highest marginal tax rates (currently 35 percent).

Consider setting up a Roth IRA for your kids. If you have children who have part-time jobs, think about establishing a Roth IRA for them. They are permitted to contribute to a Roth IRA the lesser of the amount of their earnings or $4,000 in 2007. This amount increases to $5,000 in 2008. By the time they are ready to move out, they may have a nice little down payment on their first home! A Roth IRA is preferable to a traditional IRA for this purpose since your children with part-time jobs should pay very low taxes or no taxes, so an IRA deduction will be of no benefit to them. On the other hand, the tax-free compounding within a Roth IRA for many, many future years will be invaluable to them.

Be careful when buying mutual funds in your taxable accounts close to year-end. Many funds declare dividends close to the end of their tax years and, if they do, you will have taxable income on the distribution even though you just bought the fund and probably have no real income. You do get to increase your tax cost for the amount of the reinvested dividends, but that will only reduce your future capital gain when you dispose of the shares. Why pay taxes sooner than you need to? Call the fund before you invest and find out the date on which the dividends will be payable.

Choose a tax professional wisely. If you need help doing your taxes, what are the options? More than half of

Americans seek help during tax time. Of course, your needs determine the level of expertise you'll require. Starting at the basic level, you could purchase computer software and do it yourself. Two popular programs include Intuit's TurboTax and H and R Block's TaxCut with purchase prices of $20 to $90, depending upon the sophistication of the software. Next, there are tax preparers such as H and R Block or Jackson Hewitt. These companies could be a cost-effective option if your return is not complex, as they often charge per form they fill out for you. An enrolled agent is the next step up the ladder. Enrolled agents specialize in taxes, are licensed by the federal government, and can represent you before the Internal Revenue Service. You can find enrolled agents listed under "Tax Preparation" in the Yellow Pages or call 800-424-4339 for a list of agents in your area. CPAs and tax lawyers top the list and would be the most expensive. If you're dealing with complex or major issues such as divorce, retirement, death, or buying or selling investment property, you may want to access this level of expertise. To locate a tax professional, contact the National Association of Tax Professionals (www.taxprofessionals.com or 800-558-3402) or the CPA Directory (www.cpadirectory.com or 800-CPA-Direct). Online searches can be by zip code.

If you're a married couple, weigh whether to file jointly or separately. Benefits of filing jointly include a lower tax-rate schedule and the option to claim certain deductions and credits that will be either eliminated or reduced if you file separately, such as tax credits for education or dependent-care costs. The benefit of filing separately is being able to use a lower adjusted gross income for purposes of determining the required reduction of certain itemized deductions. For example, if one of you has high health-care costs and a low income, the required reduction of medical expenses by 7.5 percent of adjusted gross income will have less impact. The same holds true for the miscellaneous deductions subject to a reduction of 2 percent of your adjusted gross income. What if you think your spouse is up to something sneaky in the tax returns? By insisting on filing separately, you may be on safer ground. Signing a joint return makes both you and your spouse liable for unpaid taxes. If your marriage is heading toward divorce, it may be wise to start disentangling yourself by filing separately. Finally, filing separately reduces the total tax in a number of states, but some of these states, such as Ohio, allow separate filing only if the federal return was filed separately.

"In spite of the cost of living, it's still popular."
—Kathleen Norris, American writer

2006 Tax Rates by State

State	Personal Income Tax Rate (%)	State and Local Sales Tax Range (%)	State Does NOT Tax Social Security Benefits	State	Personal Income Tax Rate (%)	State and Local Sales Tax Range (%)	State Does NOT Tax Social Security Benefits
Alabama	2–5	4–12	X				
Alaska	None	0–7	X	Nebraska	2.56–6.84	5.5–7	
Arizona	2.87–5.04	5.6–10.1	X	Nevada	None	6.5–7.75	X
Arkansas	1–7	6–11.5	X	New Hampshire	5—on dividends and interest only	None	X
California	1–9.3	6.25–8.75	X				
Colorado	4.63	2.9–9.9		New Jersey	1.4–8.97	7	X
Connecticut	3–5	6		New Mexico	1.7–5.3	5–7.813	
Delaware	2.2–5.95	None	X	New York	4–6.85	4–9	X
Florida	None	6–7.5	X	North Carolina	6–8.25	4.5–7.5	X
Georgia	1–6	4–7	X	North Dakota	2.1–5.54	5–7.5	
Hawaii	1.4–8.25	4	X	Ohio	.712–7.185	5.5–7.5	X
Idaho	1.6–7.8	6–9	X	Oklahoma	.5–6.25	4.5–10.5	X
Illinois	3	6.25–9.25	X	Oregon	5–9	None	X
Indiana	3.4	6	X	Pennsylvania	3.07	6–7	X
Iowa	.36–8.98	5–7		Rhode Island	25% of federal tax liability	7	
Kansas	3.5–6.45	5.3–8.3					
Kentucky	2–6	6	X	South Carolina	2.5–7	5–7	X
Louisiana	2–6	4–10.75	X	South Dakota	None	4–6	X
Maine	2–8.5	5	X	Tennessee	6% on dividends and interest	7–9.75	X
Maryland	2–4.75	5	X	Texas	None	6.25–8.25	X
Massachusetts	5.3	5	X	Utah	2.3–7	4.75–8	
Michigan	3.9	6	X	Vermont	3.6–9.5	6–7	
Minnesota	5.35–7.85	6.5–7.5		Virginia	2–5.75	4–5	X
Mississippi	3–5	7–7.25	X	Washington	None	6.5–8.9	X
Missouri	1.5–6	4.225–8.475		West Virginia	3–6.5	6	
Montana	1–6.9	None		Wisconsin	4.6–6.75	5–6	X (in 2008)
				Wyoming	None	4–6	X

APPENDIX 1: CHECKLISTS

SMART IDEAS CHECKLISTS

Exterior

❑ Low-maintenance exterior (vinyl, brick)

❑ Low-maintenance shrubs and plants

❑ Deck, patio, or balcony surfaces are no more than ½" below interior floor level if made of wood

Overall Floor Plan

❑ Main living on a single story, including full bath

❑ No steps between rooms/areas on the same level

❑ 5' × 5' clear/turn space in living area, kitchen, a bedroom, and a bathroom

Hallways

❑ Minimum of 36" wide, wider preferred

❑ Well lit

Entry

❑ Accessible path of travel to the home

❑ At least one no-step entry with an awning or other cover

❑ Sensor light at exterior no-step entry focusing on the front-door lock

❑ 32"-wide door

❑ Nonslip flooring in foyer

❑ Entry door sidelight or high/low peephole viewer; sidelight should provide both privacy and safety

❑ Doorbell in accessible location

❑ Surface to place packages on when opening door

Thresholds

❑ Flush preferable

❑ Exterior maximum of ½" beveled

❑ Interior maximum of ¼"

Interior Doors

❏ Minimum 32"-wide interior doorways

❏ Levered door hardware

Windows

❏ Plenty of windows for natural light

❏ Lowered windows or taller windows with lower sill height

❏ Low-maintenance exterior and interior finishes

❏ Easy-to-operate hardware

Garage or Carport

❏ Covered carports and boarding spaces

❏ Wider-than-average carports to accommodate lifts on vans

❏ Door heights may need to be 9' to accommodate some raised-roof vans

❏ 5' minimum access aisle between accessible van and car in garage

❏ If code requires floor to be several inches below entrance to house for fume protection, can slope entire floor from front to back to eliminate need for ramp or step

❏ Ramp to doorway if needed

❏ Handrail if steps

Faucets

❏ Lever or pedal-controlled handles

❏ Thermostatic or antiscald controls

❏ Pressure-balanced faucets

Kitchen and Laundry

Counters

❏ Wall support and provision for adjustable and/or varied-height counters and removable-base cabinets

❏ Upper-wall cabinetry—3" lower than conventional height

❏ Accented stripes on edge of countertops to provide visual orientation to the work space

❏ Counter space for dish drainer adjacent to or opposite all appliances

❏ Base cabinet with roll-out trays and lazy Susans

❏ Pull-down shelving

❏ Glass-front cabinet doors

❏ Open shelving for easy access to frequently used items

Appliances

❏ Easy-to-read controls

❏ Washing machine and dryer raised 12"–15" above floor

❏ Front-loading laundry machines

❏ Microwave oven at counter height or in wall

❏ Side-by-side refrigerator/freezer

❏ Side-swing or wall oven

❏ Raised dishwasher with push-button controls

❏ Electric cooktop with level burners for safety in transferring between the burners; front controls and downdraft feature to pull heat away from user; light to indicate when surface is hot

Miscellaneous

❏ 30" × 48" clear space at appliances or 60"-diameter clear space for turns

❏ Multilevel work areas to accommodate cooks of different heights

❏ Open under-counter seated work areas

❏ Placement of task lighting in appropriate work areas

❏ Loop handles for easy grip and pull

❏ Pull-out spray faucet; levered handles

❏ In multistory homes, laundry chute or laundry facilities in master bedroom

Bathroom

❏ Wall support and provision for adjustable and/or varied-height counters and removable base cabinets

❏ Contrasting color edge border for countertops

❏ At least one wheelchair-maneuverable bath on main level with 60" turning radius or acceptable T-turn space and 36" × 36" or 30" × 48" clear space

❏ Bracing in walls around tub, shower, shower seat, and toilet for installation of grab bars to support 250–300 pounds

❏ If stand-up shower is used in main bath, it is curbless and minimum of 36" wide

❏ Bathtub is lower for easier access

❏ Fold-down seat in the shower

❏ Adjustable/handheld showerheads, 6' hose

❏ Tub/shower controls offset from center

❏ Shower stall with built-in antibacterial protection

❏ Light in shower stall

❏ Toilet 2½" higher than standard toilet (17" to 19") or height-adjustable

❏ Design of the toilet paper holder allows rolls to be changed with one hand

❏ Wall-hung sink with knee space and panel to protect user from pipes

❏ Slip-resistant flooring in bathroom and shower

Stairways, Lifts, and Elevators

❏ Adequate handrails on both sides of stairway, 1¼" diameter

❏ Increased visibility of stairs through contrast strip on top and bottom stairs, color contrast between treads and risers on stairs, and use of lighting

❏ Multistory homes may provide either preframed shaft (i.e., stacked closets) for future elevator, or stairway width must be minimum of 4' to allow space for lift

❏ Residential elevator or lift

Ramps

❑ Slope no greater than 1" rise for each 12" in length; adequate handrails

❑ 5' landing provided at entrance

❑ 2" curbs for safety

Storage

❑ Adjustable closet rods and shelves

❑ Lighting in closets

❑ Easy-open doors that do not obstruct access

Electrical, Lighting, Safety, and Security

❑ Light switches by each entrance to halls and rooms

❑ Light receptacles with at least two bulbs in vital places (exits, bathroom)

❑ Light switches, thermostats, and other environmental controls placed in accessible locations no higher than 48" from floor

❑ Electrical outlets 15" o.c. from floor; may need to be closer than 12' apart

❑ Clear access space of 30" × 48" in front of switches and controls

❑ Rocker or touch light switches

❑ Audible and visual strobe-light system to indicate when the doorbell, telephone, or smoke or carbon monoxide detectors have been activated

❑ High-tech security/intercom system that can be monitored, along with the heating, air conditioning, and lighting, from any TV in the house

❑ Easy-to-see and -read thermostats

❑ Preprogrammed thermostats

❑ Flashing porch light or 911 switch

❑ Home direct wired to police, fire, and EMS (as option)

❑ Home wired for security

❑ Home wired for computers

Flooring

❑ Smooth, nonglare, slip-resistant surfaces, interior and exterior

❑ If carpeted, use low (<.50"-high pile) density, with firm pad

❑ Color/texture contrast to indicate change in surface levels

Heating, Ventilation, and Air Conditioning

❑ Heating, ventilation, and air conditioning system should be designed so filters are easily accessible

❑ Energy-efficient units

❑ Windows that can be opened for cross ventilation and fresh air

Energy-Efficient Features

❏ In-line framing with 2" × 6" studs spaced 24" on center

❏ Air-barrier installation and sealing of ductwork with mastic

❏ Reduced-size air-conditioning units with gas furnaces

❏ Mechanical fresh-air ventilation, installation of air returns in all bedrooms, and carbon-monoxide detectors

❏ Installation of energy-efficient windows with low-E glass

Reduced-Maintenance/Convenience Features

❏ Easy-to-clean surfaces

❏ Central vacuum

❏ Built-in pet-feeding system

❏ Built-in recycling system

❏ Video phones

❏ Intercom system

Other Ideas

❏ Separate apartment for rental income or future caregiver

❏ Flex room that can used as a nursery or playroom when the children are young and as a home office later; if combined with a full bath, room could also be used for an aging parent/aging in place

Source: ToolBase, a service of the National Association of Home Builders (NAHB) Research Center

MOVING PLANNER CHECKLIST

8 to 10 Weeks before Your Move

❏ Select an agent to perform your move and make arrangements for moving day. (Avoid peak periods for moving, if possible. The first few days and the last few days of the month are times when everyone wants to move.)

❏ Contact the chamber of commerce or visitor's bureau in your new community for information on your new city.

❏ Contact the IRS and/or your accountant for information on what moving expenses may be tax deductible.

❏ Remove unused items from your attic, basement, storage shed, etc.

❏ Start to use up things you can't move, such as frozen foods and cleaning supplies.

4 to 6 Weeks before Your Move

❏ Conduct an inventory. Decide what to move and what not to move.

❏ Make arrangements for your trip (hotel/airline reservations, driving route, etc.).

❏ Schedule a moving sale for items you won't move. Donate other items to charitable organizations (ask for a receipt for tax records).

❏ Arrange for packing. Your moving agent can make these arrangements and provide special packing cartons.

❏ Gather your personal records: medical, dental, school, birth, baptism, marriage, etc. Send transcripts of school records in advance to the new school.

❏ Close local department store and other local charge accounts.

❏ Arrange with employer to forward tax-withholding forms.

❏ Locate all motor-vehicle registration and licensing documents and check the auto-licensing requirements for your destination.

❏ Make arrangements to discontinue (current location) and commence (future location) the following services:
    ❏ Newspaper delivery
    ❏ Water-softener service
    ❏ Electricity (check for refund)
    ❏ Water service
    ❏ Gas service (check for refund)
    ❏ Fuel or oil delivery
    ❏ Garbage collection
    ❏ Lawn/pool service
    ❏ Other household services

❏ Mail change of address cards to:
    ❏ Post office
    ❏ Social Security office
    ❏ Insurance companies
    ❏ Credit-card companies
    ❏ Magazine publishers
    ❏ Friends and relatives
    ❏ Mail-order accounts

2 to 3 Weeks before Your Move

❏ Fill, transfer, and pack prescriptions for family and pets.

❏ Arrange for shipments of plants and pets. Get immunization records for pets.

❏ Safely dispose of or give away all flammables (paints, paint removers, etc.), as they will be impossible to move.

The Week before Your Move

❏ Defrost refrigerator and freezer, plus allow air-drying to prevent mildew. Arrange for disposal of frozen foods (sell, give away, or eat).

❏ Clean oven.

❏ Transfer/close checking and savings accounts.

❏ Drain fuel and oil from lawn mowers and other power equipment.

❏ Drain garden hoses.

❏ Pack items to be carried in car. Label "Do Not Move."

❏ Gather valuables from safe-deposit box, drawers, jewelry cases, and personal records. Pack safely to take with you.

❏ Send clothing, draperies, curtains, and rugs out for cleaning and leave in wrapping. Take down curtain rods, shelves, TV antenna, or satellite dish.

❏ Have car serviced for trip and have proof of insurance in car.

Moving Day

❏ Pack a box of the basics you'll need on move-in day (tools, paper products, all-purpose household cleaners, etc.). Be sure to have it loaded last so that it will be first off at your new home.

❏ Pack suitcases for trip.

❏ Remove all bed linens.

❏ Be available to check items on inventory sheet.

❏ Conduct a last-minute walk-through with your van operator. Make sure windows are closed and locked, closets empty, lights out, and doors locked.

Delivery Day

❏ Be available to check off items on the inventory as they are removed from the van.

❏ Be present during unloading so that you may direct the placement of your furniture in your new home.

❏ Check the condition of your belongings. If any items are damaged or missing, note this on the inventory list and report it to your destination agent so they can assist with the handling of details.

Source: North American Van Lines

RELOCATION CHECKLIST

If you're considering relocating to a foreign country, think about these issues first!

❏ What is required to obtain legal residency? Can I meet these requirements? What's the cost? How often does residency have to be renewed? What are the conditions of renewal, and what is the cost?

❏ What is required to visit, or while you are waiting for residency (visas, length of stay permitted, restrictions on residents on visa, or in tourist or temporary resident categories)?

❏ What is the political situation (dictatorship, democracy, monarchy, etc.)?

❏ How stable is the country (history of coups, potential for future unrest)?

❏ Weather (Do you like four seasons? Hot weather? Temperate all year? Snow?)

❏ Income taxes (Are you taxed on income brought into the country? Are you allowed to earn income in the country? If so, how is it taxed?)

❏ Other taxes (sales taxes, import duties, exit taxes, vehicle taxes, property taxes, etc.)

❏ How much will it cost you in fees, duties, and

taxes to bring into the country your personal possessions (cars, boats, appliances, electronic equipment, personal effects, artwork, etc.)?

❑ Rental property (rental rates, laws protecting tenants, lease laws, rental taxes)

❑ Purchase of property (property values, taxes, restrictions on foreign ownership, purchase taxes, legal and registration fees, laws about foreign property owners, history of government respect for these laws, expropriation laws, squatter's rights; if you're going to build, building regulations, quality of local construction companies, construction guarantees once finished, construction costs)

❑ Communications (Are there reliable phone and fax lines, cellular phones, connections to Internet and other computer communication services? Are there local newspapers, radio, or TV in a language you understand? Is there cable television or satellite TV available?)

❑ Transportation (How are the roads? Are flights available to places you wish to go? How are the bus, train, and ferry services? How costly is it to travel to and from your chosen country to frequent destinations, to bring in or visit family, business interests, etc.?)

❑ What time zone is your proposed country of residence in compared to areas with which you may want to be in frequent telephone communication, such as where there are family or business interests?

❑ Shopping (Would you have a choice of items that you wished to purchase to compare prices? In case of malfunction, are parts and service available locally for appliances, electronics, photographic equipment, computers, vehicles, furniture, fixtures, etc.? Is computer software support and repair service available?)

❑ Are the types of food to which you are accustomed readily available, both in restaurants and markets?

❑ If you have hobbies, are clubs, supplies, and assistance available?

❑ What cultural activities are available?

❑ What entertainment is available?

❑ What recreational facilities are available (golf courses, tennis, swimming pools, health clubs, recreation centers, other participatory sports)?

❑ Will your appliances, electronics, and electrical equipment work on the available power supply?

❑ If you like the beach, are good beaches available? Are they nude or topless? What is the water temperature?

❑ What is the situation with poisonous plants, insects, snakes, and dangerous animals?

❑ What is the violent crime rate? What about sneaky crime (theft, car, and house break-ins)? What support can be expected from the police department? How helpful are the police to local residents and foreign residents?

❑ How do the local residents treat foreign visitors and residents?

❑ What are the local investment opportunities? Is there any consumer or investment protection legislation for investors? What return can you expect on investments?

❑ Is the banking system safe and reliable? Can the banks transfer funds and convert foreign currency checks, drafts, and transfers? Are checking, savings, and other accounts you may need available to foreigners? Is there banking confidentiality? Are there exchange controls? Can money brought into the country be taken back out again?

❑ Are good lawyers, accountants, investment advisors, and other professionals available?

❑ How is the health-care system? Are there diseases that are dangerous to foreigners, and if so, does the local health-care system address the problem? What is the quality of hospitals, doctors, and dentists? What is the availability of specialists? How is the ambulance service? Is dentistry up to standards you are used to?

❑ How is sanitation? Can you drink the water? Do restaurants have good sanitation standards? Are pasteurized milk and dairy products available? Do meat, fish, and vegetable markets have satisfactory sanitary standards?

❑ How is the education system? If you have children, are good private schools available in the language in which you would like them educated? What is the school year?

❑ If you are interested in having domestic staff, what is the cost of cooks, housekeepers, gardeners, etc.?

❑ What legislation is there to protect foreign residents? What rights do foreign residents have in comparison to citizens? What is the government's past record in respecting the rights of foreign citizens?

❑ What natural dangers are there (hurricanes, tornadoes, typhoons, volcanoes, earthquakes, droughts, floods)?

❑ Where does the country stand environmentally? What are the environmental issues? What is the history in dealing with environmental concerns?

❑ Is there controlled growth and well-managed development?

❑ Can pets be brought to the country?

Reprinted with permission by the Association of Residents of Costa Rica

APPENDIX 2: FORMS AND WORKSHEETS

ARE YOU READY TO LAUNCH YOUR RETIREMENT?

For each question, choose the statement that best fits your thinking and frame of mind at the present time. More than one answer may seem appropriate, but you must pick only one.

1. How do you feel about giving up your job and career?
   a. My career is history. I'm ready to open a new chapter.
   b. I would enjoy meeting other retirees from my profession.
   c. I would like to stay up to date with trends and developments in my profession just to keep my hand in it.
   d. Once retired I'll be happy to mentor younger people in my profession.

2. How open are you to new adventures in your retirement?
   a. I'll probably do things I've done in the past, but now I'll have more time for them.
   b. I'm itching to try some things I never had time for during my career.
   c. I don't plan on changing my leisure activities that much.
   d. I earned my retirement so I'm going to have fun doing nothing.

3. What part will exercise play in your retirement?
   a. My outdoor activities will keep me in good shape.
   b. I'll keep my weight in check by walking.
   c. I plan to have a regular daily exercise program.
   d. I probably won't have a planned exercise program.

4. Do you plan to include weight training?
    a. Weight training may do me more harm than good.
    b. Weight and resistance training will be part of my exercise program.
    c. I'll get enough exercise through aerobic activities.
    d. Bodybuilding for seniors doesn't make sense to me.

5. How home-based will your retirement be?
    a. I'll spend a lot of time at home doing at least one of these activities—watching TV, talking on the phone, doing household chores, working on the computer, and reading.
    b. Chilling out at home is my idea of retirement.
    c. If I am home too much, I have to get out.
    d. I expect to spend a good deal of time carrying on activities outside the home.

6. How does your spouse's retirement coincide with your own?
    a. My spouse has already retired.
    b. My spouse does not plan to retire any time soon.
    c. My spouse and I plan to retire together (within an 18-month period).
    d. I don't have a spouse.

7. What is the status of your children?
    a. I still have children living at home.
    b. I have no children living at home.
    c. I have "boomerang kids" who may want to return home for a while.
    d. I have no children.

8. Are you at risk for depression?
    a. I have suffered bouts of depression in the past.
    b. My spouse has had some problems with depression.
    c. I have no history of depression.
    d. I get anxious now and then and down at times but not what you'd call clinical depression.

9. Are you a "hobby person"?
    a. I have no major hobbies, but I may find one during retirement.
    b. I have some hobbies to keep me busy.
    c. I don't really need any hobbies to enjoy retirement.
    d. There is at least one current hobby that I can devote more time to during retirement.

10. How active are you in community organizations?
    a. I'm not a joiner.
    b. I plan to become active in some organizations once I retire.
    c. I'm already active in several church/social/ civic organizations.

    d. I belong to some organizations, but I'm not very active.

11. Do you like volunteer work?

    a. I already do volunteer work when I find time.

    b. I have other activities that keep me busy and don't need volunteer work.

    c. I prefer to work for pay.

    d. I plan to volunteer some of my time during retirement.

12. What friends do you spend the most time with?

    a. I have close friends from work and outside of work.

    b. I make friends easily and my time with them varies widely.

    c. I spend as much as half of my social time with friends I know from work.

    d. I spend only a small part of my time socializing with work friends.

13. Do you have a good support network?

    a. I have at least five close friends that I see often.

    b. My social circle includes more than a dozen good friends.

    c. I enjoy my own company and am not really a social person.

    d. I have one or two friends I see regularly.

14. How will travel play a role in retirement?

    a. I enjoy travel more than my spouse does.

    b. I enjoy being close to home.

    c. I enjoy travel and look forward to many trips during retirement.

    d. My spouse enjoys travel more than I do.

15. How important is family time in retirement?

    a. I look forward to family visits during retirement.

    b. I plan to spend more time with family during retirement.

    c. Visits to family members won't play much of role in retirement.

    d. Visits to my spouse's family are too frequent or too long.

16. Do you and your spouse (or significant other) enjoy doing things together?

    a. We don't have the same interests.

    b. We have some interests in common.

    c. We like doing things together and separately.

    d. I don't have a spouse or significant other.

17. Will learning and studying play a role in retirement?

    a. They may play a role if I find something I like.

    b. I finished school a long time ago. Why go back to the classroom?

    c. My spouse or friends have encouraged me to take some courses.

    d. Taking courses on various subjects will make retirement more interesting.

18. How's your work/play ethic?
    a. I earned my rest so I don't plan to work at anything too hard.
    b. I'll throw myself into my retirement just as I did my work.
    c. The less work the less the stress in my retirement.
    d. I won't mind work as long as it's not too taxing.

19. Will you be acting your age during retirement?
    a. Now that I'm older I will be restricting some of my activities.
    b. I expect health problems will have some effect on my retirement.
    c. For the immediate future I expect only a few physical limitations.
    d. I don't feel my age. Mentally, I am decidedly younger.

20. Does the TV keep you company?
    a. On a typical day I have regular TV shows I watch.
    b. I watch TV but I prefer to be doing other things.
    c. On a typical day TV is my main source of entertainment.
    d. I watch TV fewer than 3 hours a day.

21. How easily will success come in retirement?
    a. I succeeded in my career and I'll be just as successful in retirement.
    b. I will have to change gears and think differently in retirement than I did during my career.
    c. Succeeding at retirement may take a little work.
    d. I'm not really sure.

22. Will you have enough money for retirement?
    a. Good financial planning will pave the way for my retirement success.
    b. I plan to work part-time to make sure ends meet.
    c. I'm not sure how financially prepared I am.
    d. It will be touch-and-go on the money, but I'll get by.

23. Will your native skills help you in retirement?
    a. I'm still at the top of my game.
    b. I'm not as mentally sharp as I was 20 years ago.
    c. Retirement means I won't have to push myself, so I'm not concerned about skills.
    d. Employers don't want an over-the-hill person like me for good-paying jobs.

24. How's your health?
    a. Good. No chronic diseases and the same for my spouse (if you have one).
    b. I'm okay, but my spouse has a serious health problem.
    c. I have some health issues, but my goal is to not let them slow me down.

d. My health is a problem and may seriously affect my retirement activities.

25. Are you prepared for retirement?
    a. I've been looking forward to it for a long time, so I'll be okay.
    b. Of course. I don't have to prepare for goofing off.
    c. I've planned a few things that should be fun.
    d. I've done a lot of planning and research on what I will do with my time.

Scoring

1. (a)4 (b)2 (c)1 (d)2
2. (a)3 (b)4 (c)1 (d)0
3. (a)3 (b)3 (c)4 (d)0
4. (a)0 (b)4 (c)3 (d)0
5. (a)1 (b)0 (c)3 (d)4
6. (a)4 (b)0 (c)4 (d)2
7. (a)0 (b)4 (c)2 (d)4
8. (a)0 (b)0 (c)4 (d)3
9. (a)2 (b)3 (c)1 (d)2

10. (a)0 (b)3 (c)4 (d)1
11. (a)4 (b)2 (c)2 (d)4
12. (a)3 (b)4 (c)1 (d)2
13. (a)3 (b)4 (c)0 (d)1
14. (a)1 (1b)0 (c)4 (d)1
15. (a)4 (b)4 (c)0 (d)1
16. (a)2 (b)0 (c)2 (d)4
17. (a)2 (b)0 (c)2 (d)4
18. (a)0 (b)4 (c)0 (d)1

19. (a)2 (b)1 (c)3 (d)4
20. (a)1 (b)3 (c)0 (d)4
21. (a)2 (b)4 (c)2 (d)2
22. (a)4 (b)3 (c)3 (d)2
23. (a)4 (b)3 (c)0 (d)0
24. (a)4 (b)0 (c)0 (d)1
25. (a)2 (b)0 (c)3 (d)4

Total Points:

Below 50—Abort your retirement mission immediately. Key systems are not functioning properly.

50 to 59—A launch hold is in effect. More preparation is recommended.

60 to 69—A launch is possible but prepare for a bumpy ride.

70 to 85—You're cleared for takeoff. A few system checks and repairs may be necessary during the flight.

Above 85—A-OK. All systems are a go.

Reprinted with permission of www.retirementrocket.com.

TIME ON YOUR HANDS

Will your retirement days be time-filled or time-empty?

To get an idea of how well you'll handle time once you're retired or how well you're presently doing in retirement, take this simple test. For a typical 1-week period, estimate in half-hour increments (.5, 1.0, 1.5, etc.) how much time you think you'll spend, or are spending, on the following activities:

Meal preparation _____

Housework, yard work, and maintenance _____

Gardening _____

Exercise (walking, jogging, swimming, aerobics, jazzercise, weight training, etc.) _____

Sporting activities (bicycling, golf, tennis, hiking, canoeing, squash, etc.) _____

Organizational activities (church or civic meetings, socials, religious services) _____

Volunteer work (church, civic, school or special causes) _____

Learning classes of any kind _____

Studying or prep for classes _____

Computer time (e-mail, Web surfing, IM, etc.) _____

Social events (lunch with friends, parties, get-togethers, plays, movies, concerts, entertaining at home, etc.) _____

Hobbies of any kind (not sport-related) _____

Plan/prep for a trip _____

Pet care (walks, grooming, vet visits, playing with pet, etc.) _____

Family visits _____

Reading _____

Shopping _____

Miscellaneous errands (non-shopping) _____

Part-time job _____

Total _____

If male, add 77 (for sleep, eating, and personal hygiene during 1 week)

If female, add 80.5 (for sleep, eating, and personal hygiene during 1 week)

Net total _____

Subtract this number from 168 (the number of hours in a week)

Total vacant hours per week _____

For an average day divide by 7 _____

Reprinted with permission of www.retirementrocket.com

SHOULD YOU STOP WORKING?

Examining the nonfinancial benefits of working can help you decide if you should continue to work at your present job, cut down on the hours you work, change jobs, or perhaps fulfill a passion—volunteer, start your own business, learn a new skill, etc.

Check yes or no for each of the following:

1. Working gives me a sense of accomplishment.
   Yes ❑   No ❑

2. I frequently socialize with my colleagues.
   Yes ❑   No ❑

3. I like my days to have structure.
   Yes ❑   No ❑

4. My feelings about myself are at least partly defined by my work.
   Yes ❑   No ❑

5. I get more satisfaction from work than leisure.
   Yes ❑   No ❑

6. I look forward to going to work.
   Yes ❑   No ❑

7. The pros of my job outweigh the cons.
   Yes ❑   No ❑

8. I can't think of many other things I'd rather be doing than going to work.
   Yes ❑   No ❑

9. There is a dream job I've always wanted to pursue.
   Yes ❑   No ❑

10. It's easier to continue working than to organize each day myself.
    Yes ❑   No ❑

How many times did you answer "Yes"? If at least half of your answers are in the affirmative, work provides significant psychological benefits that will need to be replaced by other activities if you stop working.

TO RELOCATE OR NOT TO RELOCATE: THAT IS THE QUESTION

Complete the following questionnaire to find out whether you could be a candidate for relocating. If you have a significant other, he or she should also complete this quiz.

1. Do you have a significant other?
   - a. Yes
   - b. No

2. How is your physical health?
   - a. Never felt better
   - b. More good days than bad
   - c. Physician on speed-dial

3. How is your financial health?
   - a. Rolling in dough
   - b. Enough (even though I would like more)
   - c. Thank heaven for Social Security!

4. Is the climate in your current location:
   - a. Something you'd love to flee
   - b. Tolerable
   - c. Ideal

5. To what extent does your children's location influence where you live?
   - a. Not an issue
   - b. Could play a role
   - c. Would be a priority in choosing a location

6. What is the level of social support in your current location?
   - a. Low/None
   - b. Medium
   - c. High

7. What is your level of involvement in your current community?
   - a. Low/None
   - b. Medium
   - c. High

8. When making a decision, you usually:
   - a. Carefully weigh alternatives
   - b. Do your homework, but also trust your instincts
   - c. Rely on your "gut" or intuition

9. What is your history of moving to new areas?
   - a. Story of my life
   - b. A few times
   - c. Born and raised in current area

10. Which of these most closely describes your attitude?
    - a. New relationships are the spice of life.
    - b. "Make new friends, but keep the old."
    - c. Old friends are the best friends.

11. Which of the following phrases most closely describes you?
    - a. Extroverted
    - b. Combination extroverted/introverted
    - c. Introverted

12. I am:
   a. Not responsible for aging parents
   b. Not fully responsible for aging parents
   c. Responsible for aging parents

13. I am:
   a. Not into babysitting or have no grandkids
   b. Someone who loves every minute with my grandkids, but . . .
   c. Crazy about my grandchildren—they are a high priority

14. I tend to:
   a. Enjoy travel to new locations
   b. Return to favorite spots
   c. Be a homebody

15. How do you feel about change?
   a. Ready and willing
   b. Generally accepting
   c. Dread it

16. Outside interests:
   a. Many and varied
   b. Some
   c. Hardly any

Scoring

Count your answers for each letter:

(a) _____

(b) _____

(c) _____

Give yourself 1 point for each (a), 2 points for each (b), and 3 points for each (c).

16 to 29 points: Start packing. You have the characteristics that make you a good candidate for relocation.

30 to 38 points: Think carefully about moving. You're on the fence.

39 to 47 points: Probably best to stay put! Your characteristics and feelings about your relationships and community could make relocating difficult.

COMPARE YOUR HOUSING COSTS

	Your Home per Year	New Home per Year
Mortgage/Rent Payments	_____	_____
Homeowner Dues	_____	_____
Property Taxes	_____	_____
Utilities		
Sewer/Water	_____	_____
Gas/Electric	_____	_____
Phone	_____	_____
Cable TV/Internet	_____	_____
Trash Service	_____	_____
Insurance		
Home	_____	_____
Car(s)	_____	_____
Memberships		
(Golf, swim, etc.)	_____	_____
Total	_____	_____

ADVANCE DIRECTIVE

Part A: Appointment of Health-Care Agent

(Optional form)

(Cross through this whole part of the form if you do not want to appoint a health-care agent to make health-care decisions for you. If you do want to appoint an agent, cross through any items in the form that you do not want to apply.)

1. I, _____, residing at _____

_____, appoint the following individual as my agent to make health-care decisions

for me: _____

(Full name, address, and telephone number of agent)

Optional: If this agent is unavailable or is unable or unwilling to act as my agent, then I appoint the following

person to act in this capacity: _____

(Full name, address, and telephone number of backup agent)

2. My agent has full power and authority to make health-care decisions for me, including the power to:

A. Request, receive, and review any information, oral or written, regarding my physical or mental health, including, but not limited to, medical and hospital records, and consent to disclosure of this information;

B. employ and discharge my health-care providers;

C. authorize my admission to or discharge from (including transfer to another facility) any hospital, hospice, nursing home, adult home, or other medical-care facility; and

D. consent to the provision, withholding, or withdrawal of health care, including, in appropriate circumstances, life-sustaining procedures.

3. The authority of my agent is subject to the following provisions and limitations:

_____

4. If I am pregnant, my agent shall follow these specific instructions:

_____

5. My agent's authority becomes operative (initial only the one option that applies):

_____ When my attending physician and a second physician determine that I am incapable of making an informed decision regarding my health care; or

_____ when this document is signed.

6. My agent is to make health-care decisions for me based on the health-care instructions I give in this document and in my wishes as otherwise known to my agent. If my wishes are unknown or unclear, my agent is to make health-care decisions for me in accordance with my best interest, to be determined by my agent after considering the benefits, burdens, and risks that might result from a given treatment or course of treatment, or from the withholding or withdrawal of a treatment or course of treatment.

7. My agent shall not be liable for the costs of care based solely on this authorization.

By signing below, I indicate that I am emotionally and mentally competent to make this appointment of a health-care agent and that I understand its purpose and effect.

_____   _____

(Date)   (Signature of declarant)

The declarant signed or acknowledged signing this appointment of a health-care agent in my presence and, based upon my personal observation, appears to be a competent individual.

(Witness) _____   (Witness) _____

_____   _____

(Signatures and addresses of two witnesses)

ADVANCE DIRECTIVE

Part B: Health-Care Instructions

(Optional form)

(Cross through this whole part of the form if you do not want to use it to give health-care instructions. If you do want to complete this portion of the form, initial those statements you want to be included in the document and cross through those statements that do not apply.)

If I am incapable of making an informed decision regarding my health care, I direct my health-care providers to follow my instructions as set forth below.

(Initial all those that apply.)

1. If my death from a terminal condition is imminent and even if life-sustaining procedures are used there is no reasonable expectation of my recovery:

_____ I direct that my life not be extended by life-sustaining procedures, including the administration of nutrition and hydration artificially.

_____ I direct that my life not be extended by life-sustaining procedures, except that if I am unable to take food by mouth, I wish to receive nutrition and hydration artificially.

2. If I am in a persistent vegetative state, that is, if I am not conscious and am not aware of my environment nor able to interact with others, and there is no reasonable expectation of my recovery:

_____ I direct that my life not be extended by life-sustaining procedures, including the administration of nutrition and hydration artificially.

_____ I direct that my life not be extended by life-sustaining procedures, except that if I am unable to take food by mouth, I wish to receive nutrition and hydration artificially.

3. If I have an end-stage condition, that is, a condition caused by injury, disease, or illness, as a result of which I have suffered severe and permanent deterioration indicated by incompetency and complete physical dependency and for which, to a reasonable degree of medical certainty, treatment of the irreversible condition would be medically ineffective:

_____ I direct that my life not be extended by life-sustaining procedures, including the administration of nutrition and hydration artificially.

_____ I direct that my life not be extended by life-sustaining procedures, except that if I am unable to take food and water by mouth, I wish to receive nutrition and hydration artificially.

4. _____ I direct that, no matter what my condition, medication to relieve pain and suffering not be given to me if the medication would shorten my remaining life.

5. _____ I direct that, no matter what my condition, I be given all available medical treatment in accordance with accepted health-care standards.

6. If I am pregnant, my decision concerning life-sustaining procedures shall be modified as follows:

_____

7. I direct (in the following space, indicate any other instructions regarding receipt or nonreceipt of any health care):

_____

By signing below, I indicate that I am emotionally and mentally competent to make this advance directive and that I understand the purpose and effect of this document.

_____   _____

(Date)   (Signature of declarant)

The declarant signed or acknowledged signing these health-care instructions in my presence and, based upon my personal observation, appears to be a competent individual.

(Witness) _____   (Witness) _____

_____   _____

_____   _____

(Signatures and addresses of two witnesses)

LIVING WILL

(Optional form)

If I am not able to make an informed decision regarding my health care, I direct my health-care providers to follow my instructions as set forth below. (Initial those statements you wish to be included in the document and cross through those statements that do not apply.)

A. If my death from a terminal condition is imminent and even if life-sustaining procedures are used there is no reasonable expectation of my recovery:

_____ I direct that my life not be extended by life-sustaining procedures, including the administration of nutrition and hydration artificially.

_____ I direct that my life not be extended by life-sustaining procedures, except that if I am unable to take food by mouth, I wish to receive nutrition and hydration artificially.

_____ I direct that, even in a terminal condition, I be given all available medical treatment in accordance with acceptable health-care standards.

B. If I am in a persistent vegetative state, that is, if I am not conscious and am not aware of my environment nor able to interact with others, and there is no reasonable expectation of my recovery:

_____ I direct that my life not be extended by life-sustaining procedures, including the administration of nutrition and hydration artificially.

_____ I direct that my life not be extended by life-sustaining procedures, except that if I am unable to take food by mouth, I wish to receive nutrition and hydration artificially.

_____ I direct that, even in a terminal condition, I be given all available medical treatment in accordance with acceptable health-care standards.

C. If I am pregnant, my decision concerning life-sustaining procedures shall be modified as follows:

_____

By signing below, I indicate that I am emotionally and mentally competent to make this living will and that I understand its purpose and effect.

_____   _____

(Date)   (Signature of declarant)

The declarant signed or acknowledged signing this Living Will in my presence and, based upon my personal observation, the declarant appears to be a competent individual.

(Witness) _____   (Witness) _____

_____   _____

_____   _____

(Signatures and addresses of two witnesses)

ORGAN-DONATION ADDENDUM

(If you want to be an organ donor, you can attach this page to your living will or advance directive. Sign it and have it witnessed.)

Upon my death, I wish to donate:

_____Any needed organs, tissues, or eyes.

_____ Only the following organs, tissues, or eyes: _____   _____

_____   _____   _____   _____

I authorize the use of my organs, tissues, or eyes:

_____ for transplantation; _____ for therapy; _____ for research;

_____ for medical education; _____ for any purpose authorized by law.

I understand that before any vital organ, tissue, or eye may be removed for transplantation, I must be pronounced dead. After death, I direct that all support measures be continued to maintain the viability for transplantation of my organs, tissues, and eyes until organ, tissue, and eye recovery has been completed.

I understand that my estate will not be charged for any costs associated with my decision to donate my organs, tissues, or eyes or the actual disposition of my organs, tissues, or eyes.

By signing below, I indicate that I am emotionally and mentally competent to make this organ donation addendum and that I understand the purpose and effect of this document.

_____   _____

(Date)   (Signature of declarant)

The declarant signed or acknowledged signing this organ donation addendum in my presence and based upon my personal observation appears to be a competent individual.

(Witness) _____   (Witness) _____

_____   _____

(Signatures and addresses of two witnesses)

Source: Office of the Attorney General, State of Maryland

HOW MUCH DO YOU NEED FOR RETIREMENT?

Current Monthly Expenses (Prior to Retirement)

Ongoing

Mortgage/rent	$_____
Car payments	$_____
Credit-card bills	$_____
Other loan repayments	$_____
Taxes (income, property, etc.)	$_____
Home insurance	$_____
Medical/dental insurance	$_____
Auto insurance	$_____
Other insurance (life, etc.)	$_____
Utilities	$_____
Cable	$_____
Telephone	$_____
Groceries	$_____
Clothing/laundry	$_____
Entertainment	$_____
Gas for autos	$_____
Subscriptions	$_____
Memberships	$_____
Saving for retirement	$_____
TOTAL	$_____
Multiply by 12 for annual expenses	$_____

Irregular expenses (calculate annual total):

Gifts	$_____
Education	$_____
Household maintenance	$_____
Auto maintenance	$_____
Medical/dental expenses	$_____
Travel/vacation	$_____
Donations	$_____
Other	$_____
TOTAL	$_____
TOTAL ANNUAL EXPENSES	$_____

(Keep in mind that sometimes there are large, one-time expenditures such as replacing a roof, renovating a kitchen, replacing a deck, buying a car, etc.)

Now, let's repeat this calculation, assuming you are retired (the "Saving for Retirement" line from above has been deleted). Predict what your expenses will be.

Retirement Monthly Expenses

Ongoing

Mortgage/rent	$_____
Car payments	$_____
Credit-card bills	$_____
Other loan repayments	$_____
Taxes (income, property, etc.)	$_____

Home insurance	$_____
Medical/dental insurance	$_____
Auto insurance	$_____
Other insurance (life, etc.)	$_____
Utilities	$_____
Telephone	$_____
Groceries	$_____
Clothing/laundry	$_____
Entertainment	$_____
Gas for autos	$_____
Subscriptions	$_____
Memberships	$_____
TOTAL	$_____

Multiply by 12 for
annual expenses $_____

Irregular expenses (calculate annual total):

Gifts	$_____
Education	$_____
Household maintenance	$_____
Auto maintenance	$_____
Medical/dental expenses	$_____
Travel/vacation	$_____
Donations	$_____
Other	$_____
TOTAL	$_____
TOTAL ANNUAL EXPENSES	$_____

Now, take a look at possible sources of income when you are retired.

Salary/wages/tips	$_____
Social Security*	$_____
Pensions**	$_____
IRA distributions	$_____
Investment income	$_____
Rental income	$_____
Partnership income	$_____
Alimony	$_____
Inheritance	$_____
Other	$_____
TOTAL INCOME	$_____

Multiply by 12 for
annual income $_____

*As mentioned in Chapter 9, the Social Security Administration mails a statement of projected benefits to people 25 and older not yet receiving benefits. You may also contact them at www.ssa.gov/mystatement or 800-772-1213 to request a copy. Be sure to read the fine print in order to understand the assumptions that have been made.

**Contact employer(s) for a description of the plan and the estimated benefits.

Subtract your total annual retirement expenses from your total annual retirement income. If there is nothing left over, or the answer is negative, you must increase your income or cut your expenses. How will you go about bridging this gap?

ESTATE-PLANNING REGISTER

(Or, your heirs are gonna love you for this!)

Copies given to: _____

_____

General Information

Name: _____

Social Security number: _____

Safe-deposit box number: _____

Location of key and box: _____

Safe location and combination: _____

Computer program or file and password: _____

Backed-up computer files: _____

Accountant name/phone number/address: _____

_____

Attorney name/phone number/address:

_____

Financial planner name/phone number/address:

_____

Insurance agent name/address/phone number:

_____

Stockbroker name/address/phone number:

_____

Employer address/phone number:

_____

Employer address/phone number:

_____

Other: _____

Personal Documents (Location)

Birth certificate: _____

Baptismal certificate: _____

Burial/cemetery information: _____

Marriage certificate: _____

Medical records: _____

Military records: _____

Social Security card: _____

Letters of last instructions: _____

Other: _____

Legal Documents (Location)

Original will: _____

Copies of will: _____

Trust agreements: _____

Living will: _____

Health-care proxy: _____

Durable power of attorney for finances: _____

Tax records: _____

Titles and Deeds (Location)

Car(s): _____

Home: _____

Other real estate: _____

Cemetery plot (or other arrangement): _____

Other: _____

Insurance Policies (Companies, Numbers, and Location)

Life: _____

Health: _____

Disability: _____

Long-term care: _____

MediGap: _____

Homeowner's: _____

Auto: _____

Other: _____

Financial Accounts

Annuities: _____

Savings account: _____

Account number: _____

Savings account: _____

Account number: _____

Checking account: _____

Account number: _____

Checking account: _____

Account number: _____

Checkbook: _____

IRA plans: _____

Account number: _____

Keogh plans: _____

Account number: _____

Brokerage firm: _____

Account number: _____

Contact/phone number: _____

Brokerage firm: _____

Account number: _____

Contact/phone number: _____

Mutual funds: _____

Account number: _____

Employee benefit information: _____

Business agreements: _____

Cash: _____

Credit Cards

Company: _____

Account number: _____

Company: _____

Account number: _____

Company: _____

Account number: _____

Loans

Car: _____

Real estate: _____

Additional obligations: _____

_____

Other: _____

RESOURCES

CHAPTER 1

Sources

AIG SunAmerica. Re-Visioning Retirement Survey. 2002.

Carter, Mary Anne, and Kelli Cook. 1995. "Adaptation to retirement: role changes and psychological resources." *The Career Development Quarterly* 44:67–82.

Firebaugh, Glen. 2005. "Relative increased happiness: Are Americans on a hedonic treadmill?" Paper presented at the American Sociological Centennial Annual Meeting.

Giles, Lynn et al, 2005. "Effect of social networks on 10-year survival in very old Australians." *Journal of Epidemiology and Community Health* 59:574–9.

Giltay, Erik et al, 2006. "Higher optimism levels associated with lower risk of cardiovascular death in elderly men." *Archives of Internal Medicine* 166:431-436.

Glass, Thomas, et al. 1999. "Population-based study of social and productive activities as predictors of survival among elderly Americans." *British Medical Journal* 319(8):478–83.

Holtzman, Elizabeth. University of Massachusetts. "Retirement: The Emotional Aspects." 4 April 2002. www.umass.edu/fsap/articles/retire.html.

Joens-Matre, R. R., and Ekkekakis, P. 2002. "Can short walks enhance affect in older adults?" *Journal of Sport & Exercise Psychology* 24: S75–76.

Lorraine Dorfman. 2002. "Stayers and leavers: professors in an era of no mandatory retirement." *Educational Gerontology* 28(1):15–33.

Lykken, David, and Auke Tellegen. 1996. "Happiness is a stochastic phenomenon." *Psychological Science* 7(3):188–89.

Michael, Yvonne, et al. 2001. "Living arrangements, social integration, and change in functional health status." *American Journal of Epidemiology* 153(1):123–31.

Moen, Phyllis, et al. 2001. "Couples' work/retirement transitions, gender, and marital quality." *Social Psychology Quarterly* 64(1):55–71.

Moen, Phyllis, William A. Erickson, Madhurima Agarwal, Vivian Fields, and Laurie Todd. *The Cornell Retirement and Well-Being Study: Final Report.* Ithaca, New York: Bronfenbrenner Life Course Center, Cornell University, 2000.

Ostir, Kenneth et al. 2004. "Onset of frailty in older adults and the protective role of positive affect." *Psychology and Aging.* 19(1).

Wilson, Sven E. 2002. "The health capital of families: an investigation of the inter-spousal correlation in health status." *Social Science and Medicine* 55:1157–1172.

Web Sites

www.aarp.com (formerly known as the American Association of Retired Persons)

www.demko.com (gerontologist David J. Demko's Age Venture News Service)

Recommended Reading

Retired with Husband by Mary Louise Floyd, Vanderwyk & Burnham, 2006

Learned Optimism: How to Change Your Mind and Your Life by Martin Seligman, PhD. Vintage, 2006

Authentic Happiness by Martin Seligman, PhD. Free Press, 2004

How to Retire Happy, Wild, and Free by Ernie Zelinski. Ten Speed Press, 2004

The Complete Guide to a Creative Retirement by Rob Kelly. TurnKey Press, 2003

Feeling Good by David D. Burns, MD. Avon, 1999

10 Essentials of Highly Healthy People by Walt Larimore, MD. Zondervan, 2003

The One Hundred Simple Secrets of Great Relationships by David Niven, PhD. Harper San Francisco, 2003

Don't Retire, REWIRE by Jeri Sedlar, Alpha, 2002

For Better or for Worse . . . But Not for Lunch by Sara Yogev, McGraw-Hill, 2001

What Do You Want to Do When You Grow Up? Starting the Next Chapter of Your Life by Dorothy Cantor and Andrea Thompson. Little, Brown & Company, 2002

What Happy People Know by Dan Baker, PhD, and Cameron Stauth. St. Martin's Griffin, 2004

CHAPTER 2

Web Sites

www.2young2retire.com (suggestions on reinventing retirement)

www.dontretirerewire.com (steps to a fulfilling retirement)

www.retiredbrains.com ("Helping Older Workers Find Jobs")

www.career-planning.com (its name describes it)

www.jobstar.org (click on career guides)

www.princetonreivew.com (click on "college," then "career quiz")

www.archives.gov/aad (explores records online at the National Archives database)

www.familytreeresearch.com (lots of links)

Recommended Reading

Bears' Guide to Earning Degrees by Distance Learning by John B. Bear, PhD, and Mariah P. Bear, MA. Ten Speed Press, 2003 (also publishes guides in specific areas such as education, computer, law, etc.)

How to Love Your Retirement: Advice from Hundreds of Retirees. Barbara Waxman, editor. Hundreds of Heads Books, 2006

How to Enjoy Your Retirement. 3rd edtion by Tricia Wagner. Vanderwyk & Burnham, 2006

Too Young to Retire: An Off-the-Road Map to the Rest of Your Life by Marika and Howard Stone. Plume, 2004

The Back Door Guide to Short-Term Job Adventures by Michael Landes. Ten Speed Press, 2005

The Complete Idiot's Guide to Genealogy, 2nd edition by Christine Rose. Alpha Books, 2006.

Family Tree magazine

CHAPTER 3

Web Sites

General

www.rollinghomes.com (tour Europe, United States, and Mexico by RV)

www.cdc.gov/travel (Centers for Disease Control and Prevention)

www.fodors.com (big name in travel)

www.frommers.com (another big name in travel)

www.generousadventures.com (on-line auction of trips; profits go to charity)

www.nudeplaces.com (if your birthday suit is your favorite outfit)

www.oanda.com (currency converter for 164 currencies)

www.roughguides.com (can read entire text online)

www.spafinder.com (almost 30 categories of spas to choose from)

www.who.int/en (World Health Organization)

www.transitionsabroad.com (work and travel abroad)

Budget Travel

www.budgettravelonline.com (Arthur Frommer's Budget Travel online)

Solo Travel

www.travelaloneandloveit.com (free newsletter; monthly solo travel tips)

Recommended Reading

Magazines

Condé Nast Traveler

National Geographic Traveler

Outside

Travel and Leisure

Travel 50 & Beyond

Arthur Frommer's Budget Travel

AARP magazine

General

1,000 Places to See Before You Die by Patricia Schultz. Workman Publishing Company, Inc., 2003

Encyclopedia of Haunted Places by Jeff Belanger. New Page Books, 2005

Budget Travel

Rick Steves' Europe Through the Back Door 2007 by Rick Steves. Avalon Travel Publishing, 2006 (also has other books in his travel series)

Unbelievably Good Deals and Great Adventures That You Absolutely Can't Get Unless You're Over 50, 2007–2008 by Joan Rattner Heilman. McGraw-Hill, 2006

Travel by Auto/RV/Motorcycle

Live Your Road Trip Dream: Travel for a Year for the Cost of Staying Home by Phil White and Carol White. RLI Press, 2004

2007 Trailer Life RV Parks, Campgrounds, and Services Directory by Trailer Life Enterprises. Trailer Life Books, 2006

Bed & Breakfasts and Country Inns, 18th edition, by Deborah Edwards Sakach. American Historic Inns, 2006

Great American Motorcycle Tours by Gary McKechnie. Avalon Travel Publishing, 2006

The Official Guide to American Historic Inns, 9th edition, by Deborah Edwards Sakach. American Historic Inns, 2004

Woodall's North American Campground Directory with CD, 2007, by Woodall Publications. Woodall Publications, 2007

Solo Travel

Traveling Solo: Advice and Ideas for More than 250 Great Vacations by Eleanor Berman. Globe Pequot, 2005

Traveling with Grandchildren

Traveling with Grandkids: A Complete and Fun-Filled Guide by Dean Hoch. Cedar Fort, 2006

Volunteer Vacations

Volunteer Vacations: Short-Term Adventures That Will Benefit You and Others by Bill McMillon, et al. Chicago Review Press, 2006

CHAPTER 4

Web Sites

www.designlinc.com (universal design)

www.homeexchange.com (swapping homes)

www.retirementliving.com (retirement communities and senior housing by state)

www.realestatejournal.com (extensive *Wall Street Journal* site)

Recommended Reading

Retire in Style by Warren Bland. Next Decade, 2005

Home Buying for Dummies by Eric Tyson and Ray Brown. Wiley, 2006

The Complete Idiot's Guide to Selling Your Own Home by Jeffrey Wuorio. Alpha, 2005

The For Sale by Owner Handbook by Piper Nichole. Career Press, 2005

Places Rated Almanac by David Savageau. Frommers, 2004

Where to Retire: America's Best and Most Affordable Places by John Howells. Globe Pequot Press, 2006

50 Fabulous Places to Retire in America by Arthur Griffith and

Mary Griffith (editors). Career Press, 2006

Boomerang Nation by Elina Furman. Fireside, 2005 (addressed to the boomerangers)

When Our Grown Kids Disappoint Us by Jane Adams. Free Press, 2003

Where to Retire magazine

CHAPTER 5

Web Sites

www.bestplaces.net (data about climate, cost of living, etc. to help determine your best place to relocate or work)

www.bestretirementspots.com (links and guides to help you pick the best spot for you)

www.livesouth.com (information on living in Alabama, Delaware, Florida, Georgia, North Carolina, South Carolina, Tennessee, Virginia, and West Virginia)

www.idealdestinations.com (search communities in states and in the Bahamas)

www.privatecommunities.com (investigate communities inside and outside the United States; also lists discovery tours)

www.seniorhousing.about.com (information on all aspects of mature living)

www.seniors-place.com (places to retire, shopping, and services)

Recommended Reading

Refer to the reading list for Chapter 4.

CHAPTER 6

Web Sites

www.rvclub.com, www.rv.net, and www.rvamerica.com (general RV sites) www.ashevillechamber.org or 828-258-6101 (Asheville Chamber of Commerce)

www.lvchamber.com or 702-735-1616 (Las Vegas Chamber of Commerce)

www.naples-florida.com or 239-262-6141 (Naples Chamber of Commerce)

www.sarasotafl.org or 800-522-9799 (Sarasota information center)

www.newrver.com/women.html

Recommended Reading

1001 Active Lifestyle Communities by Lisa LaCount. Authorhouse, 2006

50 Fabulous Gay-Friendly Places to Live by Gregory Kompes. Career Press, 2005

Complete Idiot's Guide to RVing by Brent Peterson. Alpha Books; 2006

The Essentials of Living Aboard a Boat by Mark Nicholas. Paradise Cay Publications, 2005

CHAPTER 7

Web Sites

General

www.escapeartist.com ("restart your life overseas," real estate)

www.internationalliving.com ("reinvent yourself overseas")

www.transitionsabroad.com (recommended books and general information on travel, living, and working abroad)

www.expatexchange.com (includes forums to "talk" to expats in other countries)

Costa Rica

www.visitcostarica.com (official site)

www.american-european.net (real estate in Costa Rica)

www.therealcostarica.com (site maintained by a former Chicago resident now living in Costa Rica)

Mexico

www.peoplesguide.com (information on traveling and living in Mexico)

www.mexperience.com (good source for travel, living, and business information)

www.mexretire.com (info on moving to Mexico)

www.mexliving.com (Mexican properties)

www.simplysanmiguel.com (if you're interested in San Miguel)

Panama

www.focuspanama.com (real estate, visitor information)

www.panamainfo.com (travel, real estate, info about retiring in Panama)

Recommended Reading

General

International Living magazine

Transitions Abroad magazine

Retiring Abroad by Ben West. Cadogan Guides, 2005

Costa Rica

Choose Costa Rica for Retirement, 8th edition, by John Howells. Globe Pequot Press, 2006

The New Golden Door to Retirement and Living in Costa Rica, 14th edition, by Christopher Howard. Costa Rica Books, 2005

Tico Times (English-language newspaper: 011-506-258-1558 or www.ticotimes.net)

Mexico

Gringos in Paradise by Barry Golson. Scribner, 2006

Choose Mexico for Retirement, 9th edition, by John Howells. Globe Pequot, 2005

Live Better South of the Border in Mexico: Practical Advice for Living and Working by Mike Nelson. Fulcrum Publishers, 2005

Panama

Moon Handbooks Panama. Avalon Travel Publishing, 2005

Choose Panama . . . the Perfect Retirement Haven by William Hutchings. Authorhouse, 2004

CHAPTER 8

Web Sites

General

www.cdc.gov (tons of information from the Centers for Disease Control and Prevention)

www.clinicaltrials.gov (contacts for joining clinical trials)

www.healthfinder.gov (links to federal government health information)

www.healthscout.com (check out media coverage of health-related topics)

www.mayoclinic.com (have information from this famous clinic at your fingertips)

www.medlineplus.gov (from NIH; updated daily)

Elder Care

www.ec-online.net (caring for the aged)

End-of-Life Issues

www.caringinfo.org (working "to improve care at the end of life")

Exercise and Health

www.firstpath.com (fitness and fat calculators, guide to equipment, nutrition information)

www.4woman.gov (about women's health by the Department of Health and Human Services)

www.traillink.com (locate old rail lines that have been converted to public trails)

Recommended Reading

Brain Fitness

The Memory Prescription by Gary Small, MD. Hyperion, 2004

Brainfit by Corinne Gediman. Rutledge Hill Press, 2005

Train Your Brain by Ryuta Kawashima. Kumon Publishing North America, 2005

Cosmetic Procedures

The Essential Cosmetic Surgery Companion by Robert Kotler. Ernest Mitchell Publishers, 2005

Elder Care

The Caregiver's Survival Handbook by Alexis Abramson. Perigee Trade, 2004

Emotional Health

The Joy Diet by Martha Beck. Crown, 2003

Spirituality

Celebrating the Rest of Your Life by David Yount. Augsburg Books, 2005

End-of-Life Issues

Chicken Soup for the Grieving Soul: Stories About Life, Death and Overcoming the Loss of a Loved One by Jack Canfield and Mark Hansen, editors. Health Communications, 2003

Good End by Michael Appleton. Hats Off Books, 2005

Exercise and Health

Health magazine

Men's Health magazine

Prevention magazine

Runner's World magazine

You: On a Diet by Michael Roizen. Free Press, 2006

You: The Owner's Manual by Michael Roizen. Collins, 2005

You: The Smart Patient by Michael Roizen. Free Press, 2006

The Volumetrics Eating Plan by Barbara Rolls. Morrow Cookbooks, 2005

Strength Training Over 50 by D. Cristine Caivano. Barron's Educational Series, 2005

The South Beach Diet by Arthur Agatston, MD. Rodale, 2003

CHAPTER 9

Web Sites

General Retirement Advice

www.fidelity.com

www.money.cnn.com

www.motleyfool.com

www.kiplinger.com

www.schwab.com

www.wiser.heinz.org (saving and investing for women)

Recommended Reading

The Total Money Makeover Workbook by Dave Ramsey. Neslon Impact, 2004

PricewaterhouseCoopers Guide to Tax and Financial Planning, 2007. Wiley, 2006

Start Late, Finish Rich by David Bach. Broadway, 2005

Personal Finance for Dummies by Eric Tyson. Wiley, 2006

The Retirement Savings Time Bomb . . . and How to Defuse It by Ed Slott. Viking Press, 2003

Health Care on Less than You Think by Fred Brock. Times Books, 2006

Dave Barry's Money Secrets by Dave Barry. Three Rivers Press, 2006 (hilarious satire of personal finance)

Women & Money by Suze Ormond, Spiegel & Grace, 2007 (finances for females)

Kiplinger's magazine

Money magazine

CHAPTER 10

Web Sites

www.deloitte.com (put "The Essential Tax & Wealth Planning Guide for 2007" into search bar)

www.bestplaces.net (cost of living calculator allows you to compare taxes between two cities)

www.irs.gov (source for Internal Revenue Service information)

www.retirementliving.com (Retirement Living Information Center has information on taxes for every state, as well as other resources concerning retirement)

Recommended Reading

J.K. Lasser's Your Income Tax 2007 by J.K. Lasser Institute. John Wiley & Sons, 2006

Plan Your Estate: Everything You Need to Know to Protect Your Loved Ones, 8th edition, by Denis Clifford and Cora Jordan. Nolo Press, 2006

Taxes 2007 for Dummies by Eric Tyson and David J. Silverman. For Dummies 2006

Helpful IRS Publications
(Find these at www.irs.ustreas.gov)

17 Your Federal Income Tax

502 Medical and Dental Expenses

529 Miscellaneous Deductions

521 Moving Expenses

523 Selling Your Home

524 Credit for the Elderly or the Disabled

INDEX

Boldface page references indicate maps, illustrations, and graphs.

Underscored page references indicate boxed text.